CRITICAL ACCLAIM
FOR *TRAVELERS' TALES*

"Like gourmet chefs sampling the produce in an overstocked French market, the editors of *Travelers' Tales* pick, sift, and prod their way through the weighty shelves of contemporary travel writing, rejecting the second rate and creaming off the very best. They have impeccable taste—a very welcome addition to the genre."
—William Dalrymple, author, *City of Djinns* and *In Xanadu*

"…A revolutionary new style of travel guidebook…"
—*New York Times News Service*

"The *Travelers' Tales* series should become required reading for anyone visiting a foreign country who wants to truly step off the tourist track and experience another culture, another place, first hand."
—Nancy Paradis, *St. Petersburg Times*

"I can't think of a better way to get comfortable with a destination than by delving into *Travelers' Tales*…before reading a guidebook, before seeing a travel agent. The series helps visitors refine their interests and readies them to communicate with the peoples they come in contact with…."
—Paul Glassman, Society of American Travel Writers

"*Travelers' Tales* delivers something most guidebooks only promise: a real sense of what a country is all about…"
—Steve Silk, *Hartford Courant*

"Like having been there, done it, seen it. If there's one thing traditional guidebooks lack, it's the really juicy travel information, the personal stories about back alleys and brief encounters. The *Travelers' Tales* series fills this gap with an approach that's all anecdotes, no directions."
—Jim Gullo, *Diversion*

"…The essays are lyrical, magical, and evocative: some of the images make you want to rinse your mouth out to clear the dust."
—Karen Troianello, *Yakima Herald-Republic*

"…*Travelers' Tales* is a valuable addition to any pre-departure reading list."
—Tony Wheeler, publisher, Lonely Planet Publications

T R A V E L E R S ' T A L E S

HONG KONG

INCLUDING MACAU
AND SOUTHERN CHINA

TRAVELERS' TALES

HONG KONG

INCLUDING MACAU AND SOUTHERN CHINA

⋆ ⋆ ⋆

Collected and Edited by

JAMES O'REILLY   LARRY HABEGGER

SEAN O'REILLY

TRAVELERS' TALES, INC.
SAN FRANCISCO, CALIFORNIA

Distributed by
O'REILLY AND ASSOCIATES, INC.
101 MORRIS STREET
SEBASTOPOL, CALIFORNIA 95472

Those who would take over the earth
And shape it to their will
Never, I notice, succeed.
The earth is like a vessel so sacred
That at the mere approach of the profane
It is marred
And when they reach out their fingers it is gone.

—LAO TZU

Table of Contents

Part Two
SOME THINGS TO DO

Part Three
GOING YOUR OWN WAY

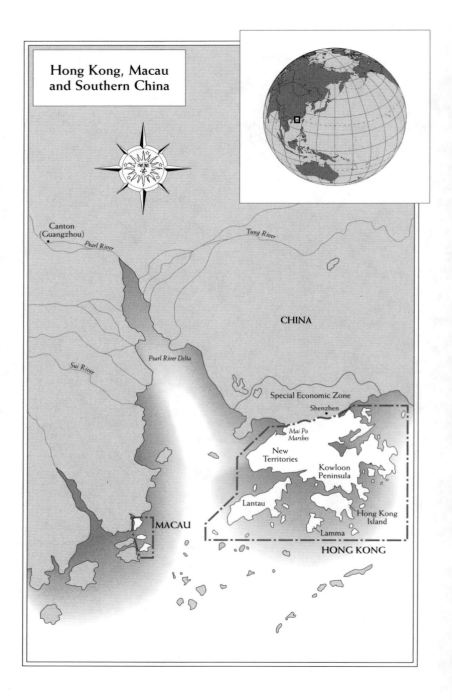

Hong Kong, Macau and Southern China

Preface

TRAVELERS' TALES

We are all outsiders when we travel. Whether we go abroad or roam about our own city or country, we often enter territory so unfamiliar that our frames of reference become inadequate. We need advice not just to avoid offense and danger, but to make our experiences richer, deeper, and more fun.

Traditionally, travel guides have answered the basic questions: what, when, where, how, and how much. A good guidebook is indispensable for all the practical matters that demand attention. More recently, many guidebooks have added bits of experiential insight to their standard fare, but something important is still missing: guidebooks don't really prepare *you*, the individual with feelings and fears, hopes and dreams, goals.

This kind of preparation is best achieved through travelers' tales, for we get our inner landmarks more from anecdote than information. Nothing can replace listening to the experience of others, to the war stories that come out after a few drinks, to the memories that linger and beguile. For millennia it's been this way: at watering holes and wayside inns, the experienced traveler tells those nearby what lies ahead on the ever-mysterious road. Stories stoke the imagination, inspire, frighten, and teach. In stories we see more clearly the urges that bring us to wander, whether it's hunger for change, adventure, self-knowledge, love, curiosity, sorrow, or even something as prosaic as a job assignment or two weeks off.

But travelers' accounts, while profuse, can be hard to track down. Many are simply doomed in a throwaway publishing world. And few of us have the time anyway to read more than one or two books, or the odd pearl found by chance in the Sunday travel section. Wanderers for years, we've often faced this issue. We've always told ourselves when we got home that we would prepare better for the next trip—read more, study more, talk to more people—but life always seems to interfere and we've rarely managed to do so to our satisfaction. That is one reason for this series. We needed a kind of experiential primer that guidebooks don't offer.

Another path that led us to *Travelers' Tales* has been seeing the enormous changes in travel and communication over the last two decades. It is no longer unusual to have ridden a pony across Mongolia, to have celebrated an auspicious birthday on Mt. Kilimanjaro, or honeymooned on the Loire. The one-world monoculture has risen with daunting swiftness, weaving a new cross-cultural rug: no longer is it surprising to encounter former headhunters watching *All-Star Wrestling* on their satellite feed, no longer is it shocking to find the last guy at the end of the earth wearing a Harvard t-shirt and asking if you know Michael Jordan. The global village exists in a rudimentary fashion, but it is real.

In 1980, Paul Fussell wrote in *Abroad: British Literary Traveling Between the Wars* a cranky but wonderful epitaph for travel as it was once known, in which he concluded that "we are all tourists now, and there is no escape." It has been projected by some analysts that by the year 2000, tourism will be the world's largest industry; others say it already is. In either case, this is a horrifying prospect—hordes of us hunting for places that have not been trod on by the rest of us!

Fussell's words have the painful ring of truth, but this is still our world, and it is worth seeing and will be worth seeing next year, or in 50 years, simply because it will always be worth meeting others who continue to see life in different terms than we do despite the best efforts of telecommunication and advertising talents. No amount of creeping homogeneity can quell the endless variation of humanity, and travel in the end is about people, not places. Places only provide different venues, as it were, for life, in which we are all pilgrims who need to talk to each other.

There are also many places around the world where intercultural friction and outright xenophobia are increasing. And the very fact that travel endangers cultures and pristine places more quickly than it used to calls for extraordinary care on the part of today's traveler, a keener sense of personal responsibility. The world is not our private zoo or theme park; we need to be better prepared before we go, so that we might become honored guests and not vilified intruders.

In *Travelers' Tales,* we collect useful and memorable anecdotes to produce the kind of sampler we've always wanted to read before setting out. These stories will show you some of the spectrum of experiences to be had or avoided in each country. The authors come from many walks of life: some are teachers, some are musicians, some are entrepreneurs, all are wanderers with a tale to tell. Their stories won't help you be an insider as so many travel books promise—but they will help you to deepen and enrich the experience that you will have as an outsider. Where we've excerpted books, we urge you to go out and read the full work, because no selection can ever do an author justice.

Each *Travelers' Tales* is organized into five simple parts. In the first, we've chosen stories that reflect the ephemeral yet pervasive essence of a country. Part II contains stories about places and activities that others have found worthwhile. In Part III, we've chosen stories by people who have made a special connection between their lives and interests and the people and places they visited. Part IV shows some of the struggles and challenges facing a region and its people, and Part V, "The Last Word," is just that, something of a grace note or harmonic to remind you of the book as a whole.

Our selection of stories in each *Travelers' Tales* is by no means comprehensive, but we are confident it will prime your pump, and make your use of regular guidebooks much more meaningful. *Travelers' Tales* are not meant to replace other guides, but to accompany them. No longer will you have to go to dozens of sources to map the personal side of your journey. You'll be able to reach for *Travelers' Tales*, and truly prepare yourself before you go.

JAMES O'REILLY AND LARRY HABEGGER
Series Editors

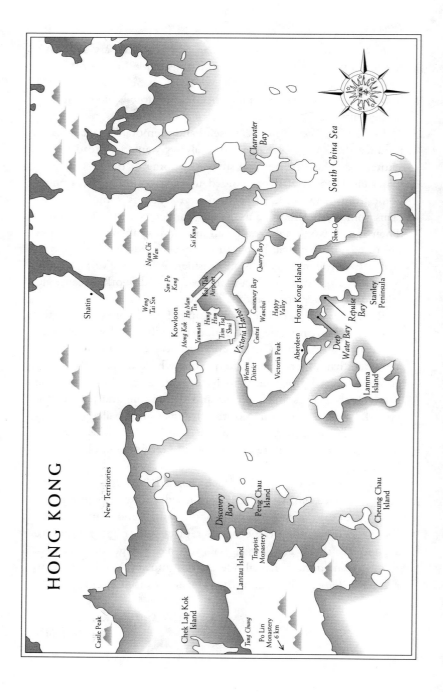

Hong Kong: An Introduction

Hong Kong is the crossroads of many worlds, many pasts, and many futures, and in it we might read our own fortunes as individuals and nations. Hong Kong is not only the most unique of world marketplaces, it is a city-state on the apex of history, as this remnant of the British Empire dissolves into the uncertain future of Chinese Communism, but the very certain future of control by the mighty commercial, political, and military engine that is China today.

How does one human being face change, let alone more than six million, and what is the price of that change? It is rare indeed that one has the chance to witness a transition between ideologies as vivid as the one faced by the people of Hong Kong. Will it be smooth, a kind of Berlin Wall-coming-down in reverse—or will it be the equivalent of a Berlin Wall going up, with its attendant horrors? No one knows, even those in Beijing implementing the plans.

This is of course what makes the Hong Kong story such a compelling one. Travel to Hong Kong represents a rare opportunity, and that is why we decided to publish a *Travelers' Tales Hong Kong* despite the uncertainty in this corner of the world. With China ascendant, all the world is involved in this seemingly local transition of power for good or for ill. This is also why you will find a number of stories in this book about southern China and Chinese culture in general, as one can no longer (as if one ever could!) separate Hong Kong from what is in essence the Motherland.

We should all hope, even against the odds, that the rulers in Beijing remember the wisdom of ancient China (which of course survived the purges of the Cultural Revolution), such as that found in the teachings of Lao Tzu.

In his introduction to *The Way of Life According to Lao Tzu*, translator Witter Bynner wrote in 1944:

> Herrymon Maurer in a postscript to *The Old Fellow*, his fictional portrait of Lao Tzu, notes how closely the use of life according to Lao Tzu relates to the principles of democracy. Maurer is right that democracy cannot be a successful general practice unless it is first a true individual conviction. Many of us in the West think ourselves believers in democracy if we can point to one of its fading flowers even while the root of it in our own lives is gone with worms. No one in history has shown better than Lao Tzu how to keep the root of democracy clean. Not only democracy but all of life, he points out, grows at one's own doorstep. Maurer says, "Lao Tzu is one of our chief weapons against tanks, artillery and bombs." I agree that no one has bettered the ancient advice: "Conduct your triumph as a funeral."

Will the leaders in Beijing heed such words? Recent years have seen a stunning transformation in the life and landscape of southern China as economic reforms have spurred growth on a scale comparable to the Industrial Revolution. But such reforms aside, the Chinese government has shown little inclination to listen to the voices of its people, preferring the time-honored practice of autocratic rule. In Hong Kong, British rule has been benign but not much more open to the common person until reforms pushed through by Governor Chris Patten. After more than 150 years, a form of democracy has taken root in Hong Kong. How much will be preserved, how much abandoned, when the Union Jack is just a fading memory? Such questions will only be answered with the passage of time, and the time to visit Hong Kong is now.

Hong Kong, world library of cultures and peoples and wisdom from both Asia and the West, is a petrie dish of enterprise and modes of humanity. It is London, New York, Beijing, and Tokyo, all rolled into one.

Hong Kong is the world's window onto tomorrow. Come lean on the sill, take a deep breath, and wonder.

PART ONE

ESSENCE

KEVIN RAFFERTY

⋆ ✱ ⋆

Approaching Planet
Hong Kong

Fasten your seatbelt.

FROM MORE THAN A HUNDRED MILES OUT IT IS VISIBLE, A SHINING,
beckoning jewel on a dark and distant shore. On some clear
summer nights you can see its lights from the air 200 miles away.
This is little short of amazing, a modern-day miracle of magic,
like seeing the lights of Liverpool or Paris from London, or seeing
Washington D.C. from New York. As the pilot takes the aircraft
lower and closer, attracted by the lights as a moth to the flame,
it becomes clear that it is a dark and inhospitable shore. The lights
come in highly concentrated patches. Between them are gloomy
stretches of water and high granite hills, steep and precarious
enough to defy all but the most ingenious and inventive of 20th-
century builders. Down, down...the aircraft roars as the captain
rumbles the flaps out and uses the spoilers to regulate the speed
and angle of descent. It's quite usual to jolt against wisps of cloud,
even in relatively clear skies, so that the whole experience is like
some badly coordinated dream: lights appear and are promptly
swallowed by dark cloud. Down, down, the aircraft goes and the
dream accelerates. Islands appear and just as quickly disappear; an

3

incongruous navy of boats comes into view, huge tankers and ocean liners, majestic mistresses of the ocean, down to small junks tossed about by every wave; skyscrapers seem perched impossibly on the edges of hillsides (or is it a Cubist painting?); then more clouds snatch away the sights before you can realize that they are real. Then suddenly the aircraft starts to make a steep starboard turn and the hills and skyscrapers and lights are marching in a rush to meet its outstretched wingtip. Is this the rude ending of a dream before waking, or is it a real-life emergency?

"No," says the captain, a senior Boeing 747 pilot, "this is quite normal." At every other sophisticated modern airport in the world the instrument landing system (ILS) leads the pilot to a safe landing, straight on to the runway. But here, things are so cramped that the ILS is guiding the pilot not to the runway but to a painting on a nearly-vertical hillside. This is hardly a masterpiece, just a huge square divided into big red and white checks, but it is a life-saver. When he sees the chequerboard from a minimum height of 675 feet, the pilot has to take his aircraft in a sharp 47.2° turn to starboard, and then he will be able to achieve the runway safely less than a minute later. So down the aircraft roars in one of the most exciting yet scary landings in the world. The kaleidoscopic dream is speeded up for an exhilarating final 45-55 seconds. On the starboard side skyscrapers seem to float up right out of the sea. One of them is topped by the neon advertising sign which consists of the word "CITIZEN" and then some Chinese characters, totalling 328 feet, or 100 feet longer than a jumbo jet, and made from three and a half miles of glass tubing. You hardly have a chance to read it. On the port side the view isn't quite so spectacular, mainly because the aircraft is still turning and the passenger there is peering over the hilltops at blocks of flats regimented like neat soldiers on a route-march across the country.

By the time the craft begins to straighten up, it seems to be doing a dance with death. A whole honeycomb city appears: washing on a line almost waiting to be picked up by the wingtip; a double-decker bus below so close it looks like the small prey of this hungry eagle: for a millisecond you have a grandstand view of a basketball game; traffic, buildings, people whiz past the window almost close enough to say hello. Then the aircraft lands. The thrills are not quite over. The pilot opens the throttle sharply in reverse, to avoid joining the ocean liners and small boats in the water. WELCOME TO HONG KONG (Heung Gong in the local Cantonese, or "Fragrant Harbour"—and immediately you notice the effluent stench of the Kai Tak nullah, an open drain alongside the runway). The crazy, jumbled-up images of the final minutes of the flight, the dazzling blur of lights, water, ships, islands, hills, buildings that seem to defy gravity, are only part of the mixture that is Hong Kong, one of the most international and probably the most exciting city in the world.

Kevin Rafferty is a British journalist who has worked in Asia for more than twenty years. He was in charge of the Financial Times' *Asian coverage and was also founding editor of the* Asia and Pacific Review.

✳

Hong Kong will always be a simple picture for me:

It is dawn in Aberdeen harbor, and I am sitting in the bow of a sampan— a Chinese water taxi—gliding through the murky green water of the South China Sea. High above me, the tops of a hundred modern apartment buildings are lost in a silent shroud of gray fog; lower, the weather-beaten brown hulls of ancient fishing junks nudge each other in the tide. The air is a combination of sea breeze and tropical humidity. The smell of the sea is laced with diesel fuel.

Slowly, the sky lightens. The neon billboards lining the harbor click off: Sony, Toshiba, then Canon. A rooster crows from aboard one of the junks and suddenly the entire harbor is alive with water traffic: sampans, junks, and scows cutting through the chop. An old fisherman brushes his teeth over the side of his boat; his sad-eyed mutt stares at us from the deck. The old woman steering the gray sampan smiles.

"You like Hong Kong?" she asks. Her mouth is a blaze of gold; she is squatting at the rear of the boat, one hand on the tiller, the other resting on a portable color television set. The money I've paid her for the water tour is tucked away under the heel of her sandal.

"Hong Kong is very…" I hesitate, groping for the right word, "…mysterious," I tell her finally, and she laughs.

"You can never really understand Hong Kong," she says, lighting a Marlboro in the warm trade wind. "You can only enjoy it."

Somehow, for as long as I can remember, I have always been fascinated by Hong Kong. It might be the way the words roll off the tongue: *Hong Kong*. The *sound* is exotic. On the other hand, it might be the impression formed by watching too many James Bond and Sidney Greenstreet movies: Fog. Intrigue. Danger.

—Bruce Feirstein, "Hong Kong: The Cultured Pearl," *Harper's Bazaar*

SIMON WINCHESTER

✶ ✶ ✶

A Perfect Pig

The contours of stone reveal the immensity of Chinese civilization.

A SMALL PIG, PERHAPS AN INCH LONG, FASHIONED FROM THE purest white, nearly translucent jade and manufactured in central China during the Sung dynasty, would probably make Mr. Chung Wah-Pui, one of Her Majesty's loyal British subjects in Hong Kong, the happiest man on earth.

Mr. Chung, who is a structural engineer and glad to admit that though not born to wealth he is now reasonably well-to-do, has been searching for such an animal for more than a decade. He says he must have inquired in the dark back rooms of every antiques shop between Kyoto and Kuala Lumpur; he has offered his bid at every auction room from Bombay to Boston; he has scoured the personal advertisements in every specialist publication in every language from Spanish to Serbo-Croat. But so far a blank.

No soothing white jade pig has come his way, no exquisite porcine carving in antique nephrite (which is what the best white jade is) to caress during long evenings in his collection room. The scores of thousands in folding money he has kept at hand for the purchase remain untouched, for the world of jade these days seems peculiarly and frustratingly pigless. After ten years, not a single beast has surfaced on the market—at least, not one both suitable and affordable. Mr. Chung, in consequence, is suffering acute symptoms of what he calls "a fearful disease."

An uncontrollable passion for jade is an affliction, and, as Mr. Chung would be the first to admit, he has a serious case. Nearly every night he comes home from the office to his pretty seaside flat on the peninsula of Chung Hom Kok—a rocky spur on the southern side of Hong Kong Island—and, after taking a light dinner *en famille*, goes to sit with an air of solemn reverence on a hard, straight-backed chair in his collection room. His back is to the window, so he is not distracted by the view of a sunset over the South China Sea or by the junks bobbing prettily on the waves. Nothing is permitted to divert him from his pleasure.

From dozens of silk-covered boxes, each closed with twin hasps of ivory and lined with black velvet, he removes his menagerie of precious animals made of jade found in north Chinese riverbeds and quarries. He takes out the catlike creature, who he believes was fashioned during the emperor Yung-cheng's time, in the early Ch'ing dynasty; he unveils a sleeping horse, colored gray "with black fissures and markings" and coiled around upon itself, nose resting on haunches "in the manner of the T'ang dynasty;" on his baize-covered table he places a pair of gray jade horses "not in combat but at play, suggestive of the Sung dynasty or later." There is a jade lapdog also from Sung times, though its age makes it impossible to divine who sat on the Heavenly Throne

> *Due to their rarity, pigs from the Sung (1100 A.D.) and (Tang 500 A.D.) Dynasties are the most highly sought after pieces. Unfortunately there are many symbolic carvings of pigs from the Han (200 A.D.) period; their commonality—despite their age—renders them far less desirable than the later Sung and Tang pieces.*
>
> —JO'R, LH, and SO'R

as it was being carved. He arranges the great green bullock, with a sleeping rider astride its back, that some unknown worker carved, painstakingly and lovingly, during middle Ch'ing times.

Animal after animal, some recognizable, some mythic, some figurative; here a chimera, there a rebus, here an ugly monster, there a lamb or a rabbit or another animal of gentle aspect: some are fairly large—the gray jade dog of the Sung dynasty is ten centimeters long; others are tiny, like the three-legged Ch'ing toad "with two small russet areas reserved to depict two pomegranates in the style of the Suzhou workshops"—it is just four centimeters long and weighs no more than a couple of ounces.

It takes Mr. Chung half an hour to remove all his choicest pieces from their elegant silk cases. Then they are arranged in rank upon rank on the blue baize, beneath the soft glow of the study lamp. Now he does what all passionate collectors do: he picks up each piece and feels it grow warm in his hand; he caresses it, strokes its flanks, explores its tiny crevices, smoothes its curves, runs his fingertips along its sharper angles, traces the delicate cuts and whorls and filigrees of musculature or hair or the facial expressions that the carver engineered so many hundreds of years ago. This he does with each piece for many minutes, until he is satisfied that he remembers every morsel of contour, every molecule of subtlety.

He may take a delicate brush of camel hair and remove the minuscule specks of dust that have lodged in the carving of one of the more complicated animals; he may gently buff the convex curves of one of the smoother pieces with a pad of golden lambswool. Or he may just line all his animals up, or otherwise arrange them in certain ways—by age, by species, by type, by supposed maker, by the Chinese region of their provenance, by the degree of perfection, by the order of his fondness for them, by cost, by value (the latter two categories being, in the world of jade, very different), by color—pure white, butter yellow, green, gray, or, choicest of all, the color of mutton fat.

Then, after perhaps an hour and a half, he will gently repack every piece in its snug velvet-and-silk lodging, put the boxes away in the collection-room cupboard, switch off the lamp, and turn the key in the lock. The animals will be there tomorrow night and, with good fortune, tomorrow and tomorrow.

It might be ungenerous to describe Mr. Chung's deep feeling for his jade as an ailment if the same sickness did not afflict scores of otherwise reasonable beings around the world. Over the centuries, hosts of great and good men have become enraptured with the stone. One of them was the great Confucius.

"Wise men," he wrote, "have seen in jade all the different virtues. It is soft, smooth, and shining, like kindness. It is hard, fine, and strong, like intelligence. Its edges seem sharp but do not cut, like justice. It hangs down to the ground, like humility. When struck, it gives a clear, ringing sound, like music. The strains in it, which are not hidden and add to its beauty, are like truthfulness. Its brightness is like heaven, while its firm substance, born of the mountains and the waters, is like the earth. *The Classic of Poetry* says, 'When I think of a wise man, he seems like jade.' That is why wise men love jade."

Chung Wah-Pui remembers very well the first piece of jade he acquired. His father, a carpenter, was a self-made man and moderately well off when Wah-Pui was growing up. After World War II, the family moved to a house in Wanchai, in those days a middle-class village, close to the markets and stalls that still sell all the marvelous oddities of the Orient. The stall that the twelve-year-old Wah-Pui liked to visit stood by the seaside, between the Luk Kwok Hotel and the Wanchai police station. (Both still stand, but the sea has been pushed a hundred yards back by land reclamation.)

"It was the New Year market in 1946. You could get New Year sweets, and I remember hot dogs, which had become popular after the war. There were all kinds of things to buy. One stall specialized in antiques. You could get a Ming vase there for two hundred Hong Kong dollars in those days—just nothing! I vividly remember picking up a

The Chinese have attributed magical properties to jade for many centuries; men and women wore jade on their person to prevent disease and accidents. It became a favourite medium of artistic expression, and the tinkling of jade discs on a string attached to one's clothing was esteemed as music of ineffable beauty. Jade was the supreme symbol of excellence and purity, as the Yu Hsi, or Jade Seal, was recognised, from the 2nd century B.C. onwards, as the symbol of Imperial power. Carved on the Seal were the words: "Mandate from Heaven—Long Life and Eternal Prosperity."

—Gene Gleason,
Tales of Hong Kong

piece of pure white jade that had been carved in the shape of a pear. I had no idea how old it was, whether it was worth anything. But it had a wonderful soft, friendly feeling about it. You knew it was hard stone, but it felt almost *alive*—the one quality of jade that all collectors revere more than anything else. So I bought it: five Hong Kong dollars—a few cents. I put it in my pocket and I kept it for years, transferring it from suit to suit. I loved it. And then I went off to London to study and gradually—though it grieves me to confess it—I forgot about it. I forgot all about jade in general and that particular piece. Goodness knows where it went."

It was another twenty years before that uncanny feeling that a carved stone can seem to be a living, breathing thing came back. Mr. Chung was by this time working near London, living with his beautiful Hokkienese wife, Fong Yu, in a suburb. He had by now acquired the credentials that will enable him and his family to leave Hong Kong before or after 1997, "should the balloon go up," though at the moment he says he feels "moderately optimistic" about the colony's impending fate.

"One of the engineers in the company, a Scotsman named McGuire, came up to me one day and said, 'Mr. Chung, you're Chinese, what do you know about jade?' And he tossed down a pair of white jade figures, animals of some kind, and we began to discuss them in engineering terms. How hard the stone was. How tricky they must have been to carve. How long it must have taken—they don't cut with knives, you know. It's all done with Carborundum paste, or a river sand that they say is made up of a mixture of quartz and almandine, garnets, and corundum. They polish for weeks on end. It can take a man a year to carve the tiniest figure. I got to know all about this just looking at McGuire's two pieces, and reading about how they were made. He could see I was fascinated, but he didn't want to sell them. They were worth a hundred pounds apiece—every penny I had. I wanted the pieces so very badly. And that, I suppose, is when it really started."

Then, back in Hong Kong, Mr. Chung met the legendary jade master James Watt, who came from New York on buying expeditions or to lecture, and who advised him that all jades, even inexpensive pieces, have the remarkable capacity to give real sensual pleasure to their owners.

"I began to buy, month after month. I would scour the shops, all over the East. I collected old pieces, discs, fish, pendants, medallions, tablets. I found tiger pendants of the late Shang times—1600 B.C. There were neolithic pieces, thousands of years older than that. And the jade still glowed and lived and felt warm and soft. I adored it. It cost the earth, but I was doing reasonably well and I could just about afford the indulgence. I was perfectly happy, collecting."

A salutary disaster ensued. In the mid-1970s he encountered one of the most knowledgeable Eastern jade scholars, Ip Yee, who looked carefully at the small but growing collection and, in a memorably dark moment that taught Mr. Chung what a high-risk occupation jade collecting can be, pronounced very nearly all of it fake. "It is so difficult to tell, with jade being so very durable, just what is old and what is new. It takes years of experience, months and months of handling and feeling and inspecting the pieces, before you can have any sense of certainty about what you have. The meeting with Dr. Ip was very chastening. It taught me to be careful. It taught me to get it right."

Jade comes from two different substances; nephrite, or soft jade, and jadeite, the so-called hard jade which is most often utilised in jewellery. Soft jade is about half as hard as a diamond; jadeite has 65 percent of the hardness of diamonds. Neither soft nor hard jade can be scratched with a sharp-pointed steel instrument—which is one method of establishing its genuineness.

—Gene Gleason,
Tales of Hong Kong

At this point, a Shanghai art dealer named S.H. Chan kindled his interest in very old jade, the archaic jade made before the Han dynasty began, around 206 B.C. He scrapped his old collection, selling most of the suspect pieces—for what they were worth, he insists, and no more—and began the long, painful quest for truly old pieces, mostly in the form of animals. He learned—from books, from the great museum collections in Taiwan, New York, and London, and from Dr.

Ip and his disciples—some of the deep subtleties of jade. He learned how to distinguish the delicate carving of old China from the cruder, more mechanical cutting of today. He learned the mysteries of jade's patina, the degree of polish and flawless convexity that no modern carver would be patient enough even to try to achieve. He studied for years before he was ready to risk his savings once again.

"I decided against large pieces, vases and bowls and statuary. I wanted small, rounded pieces that had a lot of detail and yet could fit into the palm of my hand. Animals were very popular throughout the Ming and Ch'ing dynasties and before, so I settled for them. I also collect a few bracelets and amulets and combs, but animals are my favorite. No live animals in the house. My only pets are jades!"

Now it is acknowledged that Mr. Chung's jades—the new collection that has emerged in the last twelve years—are exquisite. Alice Yuan Piccus, a recognized expert, calls it "a small but perfectly charming collection, where every single piece is a classic of its kind." A distinguished Scots lawyer, who prefers to be nameless, like many other Hong Kong jade collectors, says that Chung Wah-Pui's animals and archaic jades "are, each and every one, a joy to behold."

When the Min Chiu Society, a group of Hong Kong collectors dedicated to the idea of promoting a better understanding of Chinese art and culture, arranged a 1984 display of the finest jades in Hong Kong at the Museum of Art there, no fewer than 35 of the total of 300 jade objects on display were the property of Mr. W. P. Chung. "If the man can collect so well that in less than twenty years he contributes more than ten percent of the best exhibition that Hong Kong can put on, then he's certainly got a rare skill and a rare degree of foresight," remarked one of the Min Chiu elders. "There are collectors who have more pieces. There are richer men, too. But his choices have been, in virtually all cases, just spot-on."

Back in 1982, when they were last valued, some of his smaller pieces were worth $700 each. His gray T'ang horse was worth much more, at least $12,000, and its value now is double that.

Today his collection is worth well over $100,000. He reckons that some of the smaller pieces could fetch at least $1,200. But he is not insured. "What for? Mere cash could never replace what I have collected. You can't really translate the idea of jade into something so basic as money."

Mr. Chung is an amusing man with a wry sense of wonderment about why he—why anyone—collects at all. He has read with some misgivings about the fascinating psychology of those whose joy is to build a collection of whatever—butter yellow postage stamps, jade animals.

"I collect jade because I love it. I am convinced there is in my case no other reason. It is not money. I find real, profound joy in getting to know each piece in great detail—the style of the animal, the precise type of jade it is made from, the nature of the carving and polishing, the depth of the patina, all the tiny subtleties about a piece of jade that can give you the clues as to when and where it was made."

He holds up a chunk of uncut, transparent jade, weathered and pitted by years on a riverbed. He bought it in Urumchi, in northwest China, two years ago. "I just love to imagine one of the old court carvers, under Shun-Chih, maybe, or Kang-Hsi, looking at this piece, perhaps for weeks and months, and then deciding, 'I'll make a pig!' And he cuts it roughly, and then he cuts and carves and polishes, and it takes a year, ten hours a day, with water and powder and bamboo sticks and brushes and files, and then it is honed and

The pig is the Chinese meat, far outstripping other meats in importance. Indeed, the Chinese word for meat, yuk, *always means pork unless otherwise specified. Charles Lamb in his famous* Dissertation upon Roast Pig *credits the Chinese (albeit in ludicrous vein) with the discovery of the merits of roast pork. Certainly few Chinese would disagree with his heartfelt:*

Pig—let me speak his praise—is no less provocative of the appetite than he is satisfactory to the criticalness of the censorious palate. The strong man may batten on him, and the weakling refuseth not his mild juices…. He is all neighbours' fare.

—Dr. Hugh Baker, *Ancestral Images: A Hong Kong Album*

polished and carved again and polished again. And finally there it is, a pig, a lovely little pig, friendly, warm, translucent, soft but not soft, to be held and played with for hundreds of years. If he carved it during Shun-Chih's time, it would mean that for over three centuries people have been handling and fondling it. Jade isn't something you leave on a shelf. You have to *feel* it. You have to develop an intimate relationship with it. And to know that other men have had just the same intimacy, hundreds of years before you, with the very piece you hold in your hand—well, it gives you a sense of intimate connection with them, too."

It is perhaps hardly surprising that the animal that Chung Wah-Pui imagines his old carver to have made is a pig—the very pig for which he has been searching shops and galleries around the world. The reason for his singular obsession is simple enough, in a peculiarly Chinese way. He was born in Hong Kong in 1935, the Year of the Pig. To find the perfect white jade pig, then, would be to add a symmetry to his collection transcending mere beauty or worth or fame. "And as I collect these animals to bring me happiness," he says, "to achieve this most subtle of harmonies by finding the perfect pig—strange as it may sound to the Western mind—would bring me the greatest happiness of all."

Simon Winchester is a British journalist and author. He has written several books including Pacific Rising: The Emergence of a New World Culture, The Sun Never Sets: Travels to the Remaining Outposts of the British Empire, *and* Korea. *He also makes TV documentaries and interactive multimedia products.*

✳

On one of our first trips to Hong Kong, my wife and I wandered into an antiques store. We knew little about antique ceramics, and, anyway, we couldn't afford them. An old Chinese man watched silently as we admired some blue-and-white dragon plates. Eventually, he asked if we wanted to see some other pieces.

"Just looking," I said.

"Let me show you some of our things," he replied.

"We're really just looking," I said, putting up my basic defense against hard-sell artists. "Besides," I said, "we don't have any money."

"Doesn't matter," he said. "I will tell you about some of my pieces and you will learn about Chinese porcelains. Don't buy anything now. Next time you come to Hong Kong you will know more. Then you will buy something."

For the next hour, the man gave us a private showing of his favorite pieces, with all the love and affection of any avid collector. He taught us about the subtle differences in color and style that distinguish the work of one Chinese dynasty from the next. He showed us seemingly identical pieces thousands of dollars apart in price and explained the tiny nuances of perfection that made the differences.

"We really can't buy anything, you know," I said apologetically as we left.

"I know that," he said. Then he added, "But you will come back to my shop when you are rich and buy something then."

—Daniel Burstein, "Spree Market," *Travel Holiday*

FRANK VIVIANO

* * *

City of the Main Chance

The God of Prosperity has His headquarters in Southern China.

"I'LL PICK YOU UP IN TEN MINUTES," MR. CHAN SAID OVER THE phone. "Look for silver Mercedes."

When I passed that bit of information on to my companion, she laughed and pointed out our hotel window to Nathan Road. From the tip of the Kowloon Peninsula to the edge of the northern horizon it was a honking river of Mercedes, at least half of them silver. Spotting Chan Fook Cheung's steed in that high-stakes horse race would be about as easy as identifying a single Fiat in Rome.

Fortunately Chan found me, exactly ten minutes later, peering into the traffic from the corner of Nathan and Peking roads; bearded Italian Americans are less common in Hong Kong than the Mercedes Benz. A few minutes more and we were rocketing through the Cross-Harbour Tunnel toward Aberdeen, on the far side of Victoria Peak. It was a white-knuckle flight all the way, with Chan weaving through traffic bottlenecks with the casual finesse of a stock-car driver all alone on the final lap. His left arm rested on the seat behind his younger sister, Mrs. Yung, and his head turned toward me in the rear seat every time he felt the need to emphasize some point in conversation.

As usual in Hong Kong the talk was business and food, and the destination was a restaurant. Not just any restaurant. We were headed for the Jumbo: the largest floating dining room on earth. A culinary palace comparable to virtually nothing else in existence and part-owned, not incidentally, by Mr. Chan Fook Cheung, retired chief warden of Hong Kong Traffic Control, chairman of the Royal Hong Kong Police Old Comrades Association, right-hand man to Henry Fok the cement king, manager of the Far East Hydrofoil Service to Macao, and ex-director of the Hong Kong Soccer Football League.

"Actually, at least thirty different people own a piece of the Jumbo," he noted, screeching to a jaw-wrenching stop in front of the restaurant's parking jockey. "I'm a little guy, but everyone here still calls me Director Chan. It's a big joke with me and the waiters."

From the dock where we waited for a sampan to carry us out to dinner, the Jumbo resembled an Oriental Rose Bowl float built to the dimensions of a convention center. Up and down it rose and fell in Aberdeen Harbour, under a blaze of red-and-gold neon trim.

JUMBO, the skyscraper-sized marquee flashed across the water. JUMBO, JUMBO, JUMBO.

Everything about this restaurant was *sui generis* Hong Kong: its outsized dimensions, its garish self-congratulation and Byzantine multiple ownership scheme, its odds-be-dammed commercial tenacity. The Jumbo had gone up in flames twice in this decade, in kitchen fires that left nothing visible above the waterline except a charred hulk, which was promptly rebuilt and refloated a few months later.

Star Ferry

The Jumbo was also quintessential Hong Kong in the staggering cost of a meal—$120 for steamed fish, $100 for a single lobster, $250 for an especially high-quality shark's fin soup; unfathomably, the place still filled up in the afternoons with tables of grannies and their adolescent wards in the modified pajamas that are the everyday garb of the Cantonese working class. None of it added up. It was pure improbability. Pure Hong Kong.

Most of all, what made it Hong Kong was gamblers like Chan, who staked a crazy, improbable bet on some outside prospect, some long shot, and saw their luck come home. I never asked Mr. Chan what his bet was. In Hong Kong, that question is very seldom asked. Whatever it was, it didn't matter. The act itself—the risk—was what counted here. Hong Kong's lights celebrated the dreams of a city of six million gamblers. The city of the main chance.

Even an outsider felt it, the nervous excitement that translated into endless, purposeful motion. The motion of great crowds swarming each morning onto the Star ferries at the foot of Kowloon, disembarking Hong Kong side to mount elevated sidewalks that zigzagged into the office buildings and commercial hubs of Central. At Queen's Road the human flood merged with the stream of 1.5 million people carried daily by the Mass Transit Railway subway and another 4 million aboard buses from instant cites that had sprung up in the New Territories, cheek by jowl with the Chinese border.

Motion. Hong Kong seethed with motion, with raw ambition, with absurd fantasies. Anything could happen here. Anything was possible.

Nighttime Kowloon side, up Nathan Road beyond the tourist traps of Tsim Sha Tsui, the commercial guise of possibility was afire with neon, riotous colors stacked atop each other like some mad work of abstract expressionism, commerce expressed in its own spontaneous art form. Tom Lee's pianos announced themselves in a gargantuan yellow-and-blue blinking Steinway. Panasonic electronics commanded the 25-story face of an entire building in alternating bands of gold and red. Millie's

Department Store throbbed with a show-stopping peacock's tail formed of tens of thousands of individual lights.

Sometime after one o'clock, we wandered out into an evening gentler, more coaxing than any I could recall. The moon was so bright, and so bright the incandescence below, that the sky was the blue of faded denim. It felt like the last few minutes before daybreak, and I almost mistook the only diamond in the heavens for the morning star. Lulled by the sentimental muzziness of the faraway lights, buoyed by the sense of limitless possibility, I felt like wandering all night.

"It's a seductive city."

"It's a degenerate city."

—Pico Iyer, *Video Night in Kathmandu*

Under the peacock's tail, at Jordan Road, the human current poured off Nathan Road and into the back alleys of Yaumatei and Mongkok. This was old Kowloon, blocks of ragged concrete tenements where the newcomers and the not-yet-lucky lived, crammed together 543,000 to the square mile, 35 times the density of San Francisco. People slept in shifts in the airless rooms above these streets. They worked fourteen-hour days in textile sweatshops. And they gambled—everyone gambled; there were off-track betting shops on nearly every corner. In 1993, Hong Kong bet $8.5 billion (US) a year on the horses, $1,416 (US) for every man, woman, and child.

Before 6:00 p.m. the streets of Yaumatei and Mongkok served normal retail purposes and flowed with conventional automobile traffic. After six, in fifteen minutes flat, these streets became a bazaar, a thousand *dai pai dong*—market stands—materializing out of thin air, offering every conceivable product. Stir-fried clams and deep-fried pig's intestines were offered alongside Yves St. Laurent three-piece suits, actual and alleged. Souvenir coins from Nixon's visit to Beijing were pyramided next to radios and women's panties, cigarette lighters in pornographic shapes, pirated Rolling Stones cassettes, and hundreds of models of telephones (including one inexplicably equipped with a deodorizer). All of it was sold from commercial operations so compact that they frequently fitted on a two-foot-square folding television table.

But no one could persuade the *dai pai dong* vendors that they were wasting their time. They knew about the Director Chans, whose shops came in on the basis of a stake no bigger than the one they'd earn tonight, a few dollars well placed. And they knew about much bigger people who had started out like this. They knew about Li Kaishing, the land baron of central Hong Kong and quite possibly the richest man on earth, who launched his career peddling plastic flowers in Yaumatei. They knew about Henry Fok, the patron of Director Chan, whose small investment in a lime-rich Pearl Delta sandbar in the 1950s literally became the stuff by which the towers of Hong Kong were built in the 1960s and 1970s. They knew about all the people trading stocks and bonds on the other side of Victoria Harbour who first stepped onto the soil of Hong Kong dripping wet, after an all-night swim from China through the shark-infested waters of Mirs Bay. To a man, and woman, the *dai pai dong* vendors were believers, convinced they would one day be millionaires. They were dizzied by the sheer narcotic rush of Hong Kong. They weren't unlucky. They were the not-yet-lucky: *ting yat dai fook*—"big winner tomorrow."

The vendors remembered Chan Fook Cheung as a Yaumatei beat cop in the days when he too was *ting yat dai fook*. They recognized him when we walked down the street together: "Director Chan, sit down," they yelled from their tables. *"Nei sik joh mei ah?"*—"Have you had dinner yet?" He was a big man now. But jealousy wasn't remotely evident in their greetings. The

I tried my hand at karaoke for the first time late one night at the New World Harbor View. I was surprised at the passion and lack of embarrassment with which the locals sang. I was offered the microphone; they wanted the gweilo (foreign devil) to sing. I declined but later, fortified by smoke and drink, I belted out the Beatles' old standby, "Money Can't Buy Me Love." I received a hearty round of applause. It is amazing how digital sound can make even the most pedestrian singers sound good. Speaking of money, the Chinese respect it which is different than simply wanting it.

—Sean O'Reilly,
"City of a Million Dreams"

risks were still available for the taking. The nerve was still there. That's what mattered.

It was all a gamble, Hong Kong reckoned. The ground itself was unstable. Someone else held the deed.

When the British signed the colonial property away to China in the Beijing-London Pact of 1984, giving Hong Kong an ominous thirteen years to put its affairs in order or leave them behind, the bettors should have been scared off. That was the conventional wisdom in conventional Western business circles, in cautious places like New York and Frankfurt. But in Hong Kong the betting went on. They figured, Mr. Chan and everyone like him, that they even had the China angle covered.

They'd buy the place.

More improbable than ever. But that was the plan, if this kind of massive joint gamble could be called a plan. Mr. Chan did his part. He took some of his earnings from the Jumbo and put them into a seafood restaurant up in Shekou, just across Hau Hoi Bay from Hong Kong in China's Guangdong Province. Shekou had been one of the first foreign joint venture sites in the People's Republic, and Chan got in early. Then others followed, thousands of little investors and lots of the biggest: Li Kaishing, Henry Fok, Y. K. Pao the shipping magnate, textile barons, and food-processing magnates by the score.

Soon a critical mass of investment was achieved, a pattern established and documented. The big hitters had their photographs taken with party chief Hu Yaobang, Prime Minister Zhao Ziyang, and paramount leader Deng Xiaoping, the godfathers of the Special Economic Zones and the open door—the men whose reforms made the investments something more than a fool's bet, if something less than a sure winner.

The nest egg grew and grew; improbably, unbelievably, it grew. By the mid-1980s Hong Kong, with six million people, accounted for three times the combined total of all Japanese and American investments in China. In the Pearl Delta, the most highly developed part of the country, 90 percent of all foreign investment was in the hands of overseas Chinese, some from Taiwan or San Francisco or Singapore, but the vast majority from Hong Kong.

The money piled up and up, until it seemed there was nobody in Hong Kong who didn't own something in China. And to the astonishment of the cautious money in the West, it was China rather than Hong Kong that was radically transformed, even when the instrument of change was nothing more than a joint venture restaurant like Director Chan's.

I ate lunch at Chan's place across the border in Shekou on a muggy September Tuesday. Shameless, I dropped his name— *Director* Chan—with the hostess. She responded very professionally and discreetly nodded, so I knew there would be either a discount or a special plate delivered. It turned out to be both. Halfway into the meal, a smiling waiter led a parade of three kitchen helpers to the table, along with a cart atop which sat a small burner and a glass bowl of squirming live prawns. Also very professionally, the prawns were anesthetized in the best Shaoxing wine, then quickly poached: the celebrated "drunken shrimp." The discount, marked on the bill but never mentioned aloud, was 25 percent.

My lunch companion was an acquaintance of Chan's named Ho Kimun. He'd invited me to Shekou to see his own piece of the People's Republic, an electronics plant. The gamble here was considerable. Ho was betting he could train Chinese workers to make floppy disk drives that were good enough to be sold as components in IBM clones. If it worked out, the costs of production would be cut to less than a fifth of what he spent manufacturing the same disks in the New Territories, Hong Kong's suburban sprawl south of the Chinese border.

"Otherwise, I'll be marketing a lot of expensive scrap metal," he said.

The performance of the restaurant was a good sign. A few years before, even in Guangdong, mainland restaurants had almost all been in the mode of the Workers', Soldiers', or Peasants' halls favored by Chairman Mao, where clean plates were regarded as a counter-revolutionary frill and diners had to shove piles of discarded bones and scraps off the tables to make room for their meals. Now, in joint venture zones like Shekou, it was getting hard to tell that you were in the workers' paradise. The waiters and hostesses and maîtres d' were sent to Hong Kong for training. Hong Kong architects designed the restaurants. And almost always, the money was from Hong Kong and a Hong Kong cousin sat at the cash register, just to make sure.

By the mid-1980s, the good signs for Hong Kong's China gamblers were piling up as fast as the investments. A brand-new China ferry building was under construction in Kowloon, with computerized schedule boards to handle the mushrooming fleet of hydrofoils loaded with businessmen that already sped back and forth daily and sometimes hourly, from a temporary port terminal to Shekou, Zhongshan, Canton, Jiangmen, Guanghai, Zhuhai—the Pearl Delta funnels into which Hong Kong was pumping its insurance money. Every dollar brought another omen that the plan was solid: smoother handling of materials at the border (the smoothness increased in direct proportion to the customs officers' willingness to be bribed); workers who were better motivated (and better paid, under the table, where the state work unit salary scales were not a problem); and yes, better restaurants.

"You see, it's getting just like Hong Kong," Ho said, manipu-

The venturesome diaspora of some 55 million Overseas Chinese is emerging as far more than the main force behind the sizzling growth of the Pacific Rim economies—though that in itself is no small achievement. Spurred by a distinctive business culture that relies upon constant scanning for opportunities and an incomparable cooperative web, they are fast establishing themselves as nothing less than the world's most vigorous capitalists.... The Overseas Chinese are conservatively estimated to control some two trillion dollars in liquid assets. If these enterprising souls lived in one country, its gross national product would tally at least $500 billion— larger than the $410 billion GDP of mainland China. Now combine the People's Republic exports and imports with those of Hong Kong and Taiwan, and Greater China already accounts for a larger share of world trade than those arch-exporters, the Japanese.

—Louis Kraar, "The Overseas Chinese: Lessons From the World's Most Dynamic Capitalists," *Fortune*

lating a toothpick into a rear molar as we strolled through downtown Shekou on the way to his plant.

And although Tian Hongqiao wasn't who he was referring to,
Tian proved to be the best example I'd seen yet of the effect that
Hong Kong's plan was having on its real target, the mentality
of China.

Tian was from Beijing, and apart from his Liberation-era given
name, which meant "Red Flag," and that unmistakable northern
accent with its long drawn-out r's, he was like the new restaurants
on the mainland side of the border. You couldn't tell. Could have
been Hong Kong. Could have been Taipei.

He was waiting for us in Ho's office, a young man, probably no
more than twenty-five, in a nicely cut soft leather jacket and
pressed denims. But the clothes weren't the half of it; it was Tian's
manner that I really marveled at. There was none of the ramrod
straightness, the visible uneasiness this far from the capital, that
often made people from Beijing seem like hopeless prigs even
when they weren't. Tian put out his hand to shake mine when we
were introduced; he didn't wait for a cue. And he shook it seriously, returning the grip rather than doing his best to escape it, as
though a foreign palm might carry some disease. He didn't even
have the repressed cranelike stride you noticed in Beijing. It was
more of a jazzy lope, so replete with bravado that it made me think
of John Travolta in *Saturday Night Fever*.

Like everybody with a stake in China, Ho had set his plant up
to do import-export as well as manufacturing since he had to pay
for an export license anyway. That's what brought Tian down from
the north. He had a long, flat box under his arm: the goods. Tian
was a sales agent.

"Ho, my friend, this is going to make you rich. And you too,
my American friend, rich!"

Ho translated, although in fact Tian spoke an invented-on-the-
spot salesman's mélange of Mandarin and Cantonese, aimed at the
local market, that was surprisingly close to my own haphazard
jumbling of Chinese dialects. My presence didn't bother him at all,

especially since Ho had decided to tell him that I was an importer and not a reporter.

Tian yanked a black plastic gizmo out of the box. It was an electronic piano keyboard, a rip-off of the Yamaha instrument that was a big seller in the States. He set it on Ho's desk and stepped back, looking it up and down the way a Hollywood producer might ogle a starlet on the casting couch, and shook his head admiringly. Then he fumbled with the controls for a moment, and the unit obligingly played a sample piece that had been programmed into its memory. It was Stevie Wonder's "My Cherie Amour."

The device could be adjusted to mimic the sounds of string instruments, the brass section of an orchestra, or a baroque harmonium for those who preferred Bach to Motown. Tian demonstrated them all. It was a pity that the care that went into imitating the Yamaha original had slipped on the choice of a brand name. Someone had convinced the manufacturer up in Beijing to name it the Bony Keyboard, no doubt hoping it would be confused with Sony.

Ho passed on it, and Tian joined the two of us on a tour of the plant. The disk drive-makers were bent to their tasks just like their counterparts across the bay in Hong Kong, where the term "work ethic" was bandied about so often that it had become the most exhausted cliché in the colony. These young women—the workers were mostly women at Ho's plant, in their late teens and early twenties, who had been brought down to Shekou from villages in western Guangdong and neighboring Hunan Province—definitely had the work ethic. It was what happened when young people earned decent wages, and had the means to buy clothes and go to discos. They worked harder.

Ho took us to visit one of the dorms, where two embarrassed girls from the night shift sat on their beds in a room that measured about ten feet by sixteen. They'd decorated it with stuffed animals and frilly bedspreads that might have been found in a California teenager's bedroom.

So much was changing here, thanks to Hong Kong. I remembered the first time I'd visited the Pearl Delta, going into a bank at midday and finding the tellers all sound asleep, their heads resting on the counter. It felt like it must have been decades ago. It was only four years.

Things were moving very quickly indeed now, and the bets seemed safe. Except that there was sometimes the worry—both Ho and Tian expressed it, when we talked over a beer after the tour—the worry that the changes were coming too fast. It wasn't a dominant theme in conversation. They were businessmen and found it difficult to restrain their natural impulse to boosterism. The worry lay between the lines, alluded to in scattered observations that measured costs nobody had anticipated.

"We have to have a doctor on call for the girls all the time, you know," Ho said at one juncture.

I wondered if he was gingerly admitting that his plant had a problem with industrial accidents. But that wasn't it at all. The cost that had him worried, the evidence of too much change too fast, wasn't totted up in severed fingers or damaged eyes.

"We need the doctor," Ho said, "because so many girls have gotten pregnant since they came here."

Frank Viviano, author and lecturer, is a four-time nominee for the Pulitzer Prize and is the European correspondent for the San Francisco Chronicle.

✳

Hong Kong isn't usually regarded as a dynamic centre for the arts. Business, finance, and trade, yes, but who would imagine, a decade ago, that Hong Kong would have an equally booming market in plays, concerts, and wacky fringe festivals?

It had a slow start: it was only in the 1970s that a purpose-built Arts Centre was constructed and an international arts festival established, only in the 1980s, when Hong Kong's economy took off, that people had more time and money to devote to the arts. And more incentive: in 1983, the Sino-British talks on the future of Hong Kong created enormous debate and restlessness among local artists.

"They suddenly had to question who they were, where they belonged," explains Benny Chia, General Manager of the influential

Fringe Festival which was launched that same year. "There was an awakening of a certain self-worth."

The Fringe has provided a perfect focus for Hong Kong's emerging alternative arts scene. From 42 acts in its first year, it's grown to a 180-act event, featuring everything from Cantonese experimental theatre to a Chinese artist's sculpture made out of 6,000 teabags (don't laugh, it was later sold for a fortune).

Further significant developments have been the establishment of the Academy for Performing Arts, Hong Kong's first tertiary institute for teaching dance, drama, music, and technical arts, and a massive new Cultural Centre including a long-awaited Museum of Art. Regional arts centres and Cantonese-language theatre groups have proliferated, and dozens of talented potters, painters, and playwrights have emerged.

Artists here still face problems of funding, appreciation, and increasingly, political censorship. But at least that old tag, "cultural desert," has finally been banished.

—Julia Wilkinson, adapted from "The Arts in Hong Kong:
In the Limelight at Last," *Pacific Views*

JAN MORRIS

✳ ✳ ✳

Towards Fragrant Harbor

Looking back and looking ahead at the urban marvel.

EVERY NIGHT AT 10 P.M. A SHIP SETS SAIL FROM THE CHINESE PORT of Guangzhou, old Canton, and makes its way down the Pearl River estuary toward the South China Sea. If you ever take it, spend the night on deck. You will experience one of modern travel's supreme astonishments.

Most of your Chinese fellow passengers will stay below, and as the ship steams down-channel you will find yourself almost alone up there in the dark. There is hardly a sound to be heard, only the swish of the waves and the beat of the turbines, but all around you unexplained lights go swimming by, lights of sampans or of freighters, fishermen's lights, torch-beams out of nowhere, the 40-watt lights of the towns and villages that line the estuary.

It is like the hush in the theater after the overture. The dark grows darker, a few shadowy figures lean over the rail here and there, and you may feel, as you feel in the dress circle at another kind of show, a tremor of expectancy. Perhaps you will be tempted to go to your cabin and sleep, but if you are wise you will stick it out on deck until the first light dawns.

Have you nodded off despite yourself? Suddenly it strikes you that the engines have stopped, and the ship is lying motionless in a thick white mist. The water is quite still. The mist is of a swirling theatrical kind, like mists in music videos. You might be anywhere, or nowhere at all.

But then, like the rising of a theater's curtain, the fog begins to lift, rolling slowly upward from the sea, and you realize that you are at anchor off another port. First the ships show, hundreds of ships, ships of all sizes, ships of all shapes, cluttered about with lighters and apparently floating not on the water but in the mist itself. Then on each side of you buildings come into view, dense thickets of buildings, in concrete and steel and mirror-glass, with huge advertisements on them and aerials all over their roofs.

Up goes the mist, taller and taller those buildings rise, each higher than the one before, pressing upon one another, looking over one another's shoulders, immense clean buildings of white or gold or silver, up, up the city's heights until green mountainsides appear behind, and there are white villas everywhere, and snaking roads, and white domes alone on summits; and the rising sun, shining clean through the windows of an apartment block on a high ridge, suddenly seems to set the whole structure afire, blazing all white and red above the sea.

So, as to a fanfare, a futuristic metropolis reveals itself to you, like something from another age or sensibility, stacked around a harbor jammed stupendously with ships. You have reached the marvel of the China coast, Hong Kong—or, as the new Chinese orthography prefers, Xianggang.

It is proper to approach Hong Kong from the mainland, because although it is not exactly *in* China, it is decidedly *of* it.

Nearly 150 years ago the British, wanting a base from which to conduct their lucrative trade with China (largely in opium), forcibly extracted from the Manchu dynasty the sparsely populated 29-square-mile island of Hong Kong, near the mouth of the Pearl estuary. Over the subsequent 60 years they leased a slab of the adjacent mainland and a swarm of nearby islands, which they called the New Territories. It is this conglomerate, part peninsula, part archipelago, that remains to this day the British Crown Colony of Hong Kong, with a land area of some 411 square miles and a pop-

ulation of about six million. Its administrative headquarters is still
the island of Hong Kong itself, but its real fulcrum is that glorious
harbor, where the freighters lie in their armadas and the skyscrapers look down all glittering with profit.

We are seeing Hong Kong in its last days as a British possession.
More interesting still, we are seeing in it virtually the end of the
British Empire. Once this dominion ruled a quarter of the land-
mass of the earth, governed a quarter of its people and commanded
all its seas. Now its overseas possessions are reduced to a scattered
handful of islands and promontories, of which Hong Kong is infinitely the most important, its population being 35 times as great as
that of all the other dependencies put together. When the British
flag goes down over Hong Kong, it will go down in effect upon
four centuries of imperial history.

And it will go down, so to speak, with a bang. Hong Kong is an
astonishing epilogue to empire. One of the two largest container
ports in the world, it is also one of the half-dozen greatest financial and business centers, and an industrial power of marvelous
resource. It makes more movies than any other country except
India; it has more Rolls-Royces per head than any place else on
earth, and all in all it is one stupendous testament to the power of
capitalist enterprise.

So if you think Hong Kong looks exciting when it breaks
through the mists of dawn, wait until you see it in the brilliance of
noonday—from a high vantage point on the Peak, the central massif
of Hong Kong Island. From up there you can see almost the whole
territory; the island all around you, the mountainous mainland peninsula and, strewn through the surrounding blue-green seas, the
250-odd islands and rocks of the archipelago, humped or supine,
barebacked or built upon. It is a magnificent scene, all concentrated
upon the grand haven at its center, but scarcely soothing, because
almost everything seems to be in a state of irresistible motion.

Now, at the height of the working day, the harbor is crisscrossed
with the wakes of small craft, ferries, launches, hydrofoils, hovercraft, police boats, scavenger craft scooping up garbage, and dozens
of sampans and lighters, all threading a passage between the

freighters ranked at their moorings. On shore a multitudinous traffic clogs the highways on both sides of the harbor (Kowloon on the north shore, Hong Kong Island on the south), crawling along fly-overs, lining up to get into tunnels, squeezing aboard car ferries. Double-decker buses and old-fashioned streetcars sway through the hubbub, and a cable railway crawls up the precipitous Peak beside you. Jets seem to swoop between TV antennae to their runway, which protrudes dramatically into the harbor. The sidewalks below appear to be packed impenetrably with people. It is as though not 6 million but 500 million citizens live down there, all on the move, all working, all making money.

Time and again, above the rumble of the traffic and the whistle of the wind, a jackhammer sounds from somewhere far below.

Ninety-eight percent of the people of Hong Kong are Chinese, émigrés in person or by heredity from China proper. They range from multibillionaires to street sleepers. They live in mansions on the Peak, in floating colonies of sampans, in shantytowns and ancient villages, but most commonly in the huge government-built concrete tower blocks that sprout almost everywhere you look. Since most of Hong Kong is rough hill country, its urban communities are pressed hugger-mugger into the flat parts, and many of the poorer Chinese endure inconceivable congestion: parts of Kowloon are said to be the most crowded places in all human history, with some 264,000 souls to the square mile.

But however they live, the Chinese of Hong Kong bring to their circumstances all the staggering variety and energy of southern China. The moment they move into one of those tower blocks, so clinical, cold, and functional, the Chinese bring it magically to life with their fecundity; and the source of Hong Kong's legendary vigor is this vigor of the people themselves, peasant and industrialist, rich man and poor.

Wander through almost any part of Hong Kong—the harborside cities, the modernist New Towns that now dominate the mainland countryside, even the half-inhabited outer islands—and you will feel the presence of an ancient, tough, and infinitely complex culture. It expresses itself in a wayside shrine where old ladies in black are burning joss sticks beside a holy spring of animism, or in some rich and gaudy Taoist temple swarming with supplicants old and young, with soothsayers busy at their stalls and a veil of incense around the blackened altar gods. It is incarnate in a property magnate at the races, studying his race card with a calculator beside him while he awaits his bird's-nest soup and sea slug in his private box above the track. It shows itself in the old walled villages of the New Territories, symmetrical within their watchtowers, and in the wonderfully ostentatious floating restaurant at Aberdeen, where young brides are photographed dressed in the shimmering costumes of long ago, and where bright lights blaze across the water far into the night.

Nothing could be more quintessentially Chinese than a Hong Kong fishing boat putting to sea, all nets and bright buoy flags, its timbers blackened with pitch, oil, and age, its crew ranging from bent-back crones to babes in arms. The befurred Chinese ladies you sometimes see in the backs of white Mercedes are like the medieval courtesans of Beijing, and all the general pandemonium of Hong Kong street life—the deafening noise, the banners, the street stalls, the steaming bowls of noodles or crab soup, the caged birds, the electronic emporia, the smells of gasoline and duck-mess, the clatter of *mah-jongg* tiles, the laughter, the clanging radio music—all this, *mutatis mutandis*, is just as it must have been in China 500 years ago, and it forms the indestructible foundation of all that happens in Hong Kong.

What happens is largely the effect of empire. Hong Kong has remained British through all the convulsions of modern Chinese history, barring only four years' occupation by the Japanese during World War II. This has made it a stable conduit for the world's preoccupations with China. Though Hong Kong is now a great manufacturing center in its own right, its every activity is linked with China's condition, and in its time the Colony has been an entrance to China, an escape from China, a window into China and the one sure base from which the world can contemplate China in bad times and make its contracts with China in good.

Thus has arisen the cosmopolitan city-state that greets all its visitors so unforgettably, whether they fly dizzily into Kai Tak

Airport, in the very heart of the city, or sail as I did silently down from Guangzhou. Hong Kong's architecture is a loveless mix of conventional modernism and high-tech avant-garde, from a thousand indistinguishable square apartment blocks to the theatrical bank of Hong Kong headquarters, the most expensive office building ever, and the skyscraper that I. M. Pei designed for the Bank of China, the tallest building in Asia. Hong Kong's flavor is hard, rich, opportunist, hospitable and, like it or not, exhilarating.

> *Novelist Ernest Hemingway visited both Hong Kong and a war zone of the Sino-Japanese struggle in 1941 and got a good idea of the attitudes of British and Chinese towards each other. Hemingway, who had had plenty of rice wine, told a Chinese general what the British thought of the Chinese: "Johnny's alright and a very good fellow and all that. But he's absolutely hopeless on the offensive you know...we can't count on Johnny." The general asked who Johnny was. "John Chinaman," came the reply. "Very interesting," responded the general; "let me tell you a Chinese story. Do you know why the British staff officer wears a single glass [monocle] in his eye?" Hemingway said he didn't. "He wears a single glass in his eye so that he will not see more than he can understand."*
>
> —Kevin Rafferty, *City on the Rocks: Hong Kong's Uncertain Future*

Many of its leading characters are Chinese, but many are foreigners: Americans, Australians, Britons, Frenchmen, Germans, Indians, Japanese—mostly here just for a few years to make themselves richer. The whole ethos and paraphernalia of the capitalist system are here displayed, as in an exhibition: the eager young traders at their computer screens, the tycoons at their clubs, the incessant talk of merger and takeover, bankruptcy and insider trading, the stock prices on display in elevators and shop windows, the pages of financial news in the *Asian Wall Street Journal* and the *Far Eastern Economic Review.*

Hong Kong has had its economic ups and downs in recent years, as its future has been debated and negotiated, but at the moment it appears to be booming. The skyscrapers soar, the yuppies of all races celebrate, and every day brings news of some new incursion into the gigantic Chinese market—or, alternatively, some new investment by the People's Republic within China itself. I defy the soppiest liberal (me, for instance) to resist the no–holds–barred excitement of this ruthless trading place. Entering Hong Kong's financial and business center, on the island's waterfront, is like jumping into a metaphysical Jacuzzi.

The Chinese Communists have promised to give Hong Kong semiautonomous status after 1997, and to allow it to continue its capitalist way of life for another 50 years. Doubting either the Communists' good faith or their ability to keep their word, many Hong Kong Chinese have already left the Colony for Canada, Australia, or the United States, and many more are planning to follow them. Why not? Nobody can possibly know who will be running China a few years from now, how scrupulously it will honor its commitments, or how susceptible it will be to another crazy convulsion like the Cultural Revolution of the 1960s.

But for a short time longer the British Empire will be in command, and its last great challenge is how best to act in Hong Kong until 1997. On the whole it has been an honorable suzerain. It has kept the peace. It has given housing and sustenance to millions of refugees; it

The real question in Hong Kong is not what happens in 1997 but what will happen in 1998 and 1999. The SAR (Special Administrative Region) government would be foolish to show its hand too quickly. By the end of 1998 however, it will be clear what kind of place Hong Kong will be developing into. By then the police will have had time to take over the files. The new heads of civil service departments will have felt their way into their jobs and will have identified the likely sources of kick-backs. By 1998, the ousted democratic legislators will have been either deported or incarcerated. Some will have emigrated. The programme of public indoctrination will have begun, gently. There will be compulsory political study at universities and polytechnics. Secondary schools will be forced to introduce CCP (Chinese Communist Party) history into the curriculum. By 1998, broadcasting will be fully censored and the rest of the media will be practising self-censorship, which they already do to an increasing extent.

—Dr. George Adams, *Hong Kong Watching: The Essential Guide to Hong Kong People's Behaviour* has presided over a peaceful mingling of East and West; it has sponsored an impressive new middle class of educated, progressive and modern young Chinese. In one important way, though, it has failed to honor its own professed ideology: in the interests of stability and financial confidence, it has denied Hong Kong democracy. This able and literate city-state is still a Crown Colony of an archaic kind, whose government until recently was not in any way subject to the people's election or approval—a negation, it might be thought, of all that the British Empire has claimed to stand for in its last enlightened years.

Is it too late? That is the question the governor is pondering in his mansion on the hill, and it preoccupies his subjects too. To all the old excitements of money making and competition, to the stimulations of Hong Kong's fascinating history, magnificent cuisine, frenzied shopping and incomparable setting, there is now added a tumult of political activity. You can hardly escape it, in print or in conversation, in public debate or in private conviction.

It would be a gamble to turn Hong Kong into a true democracy so late in the day. But then Hong Kong itself is one great gamble, high-risk through and through, whose very presence gives its visitors just the same frisson that one gets from a dangerous adventure, a love affair on the edges of propriety: one of life's great astonishments.

Jan Morris has been wandering the world and writing about her experiences for more than 40 years. She is the author of numerous books and her essays on travel are among the classics of the genre. She lives in Wales, the only person in her postal code.

★

The origin of the name Hong Kong relates to the production of incense in the region. *Hong* means "fragrant," or "incense," and *kong* means "harbour." The romanisation is a rendering of the Tanka boat people's pronunciation.

Introduced from North Vietnam, the incense tree, *Aguilaria sinesis*, flourished in the soils around Hong Kong. The wood was collected from growers throughout the region, assembled at Tsim Sha Tsui and shipped in junks to Shek Pai Wan (Aberdeen) on Hong Kong Island, where it was loaded into large vessels sailing in and out of Canton.

Although it has now died out, the industry reached the height of its prosperity in the Ming Dynasty. Huge quantities of incense continue to be burnt at most festivals in the Chinese calendar. Incense from Hong Kong was used in cities as far away as Suzhou, hundreds of miles to the north.

Hong Kong is an alternative name for the bay, Shek Pai Wan, situated in Aberdeen Harbour. There was once a small village at the eastern end of the bay called Hong Kong Village and this village used to act as the sole export agent for a special variety of incense that was highly valued.

It is generally thought that the first British seamen who landed on the island at Aberdeen named it Hong Kong in error, perhaps on being told by the local boat people the name of what they considered to be the most important harbour.

—Sally Rodwell, *Historic Hong Kong: A Visitor's Guide*

ANGUS FOSTER

✦ ✦ ✦

My Hong Kong Neighborhood

Welcome to the daily grind on the South China Sea.

SUNDAY AFTERNOONS ARE THE WORST. THE CLACK, CLACK, CLACK of wooden tiles being slammed down on formica tables, then shuffled furiously, the sound rising in volume until it seems as if you are living in a cicada colony. The residents of Hing Hon Road in Sai Ying Pun, Hong Kong, are settling down to their weekly orgy of *mahjong*.

When I first moved into this flat the noise was deafening. Nine months later I am getting used to it, in much the same way, I suspect, as the local shopkeepers and inhabitants are getting used to my white face in what is still a very Chinese part of Hong Kong.

Sai Ying Pun is a small residential district on the western tip of Hong Kong island, of little interest to tourists or businessmen and far removed from the hustle of the shopping arcades of Central or Tsim Sha Tsui. It has a mixture of old colonial-style houses with graceful though crumbling façades, and newer, much taller buildings.

My flat is on the fourth floor of a twenty-storey apartment block. This being high-rise Hong Kong, where personal space is a reward only for the rich, I can see into the flats, and lives, of at least twelve Chinese families living twenty yards away across the road. They, too, can look in on me, although they now seem bored with their new *gweilo*, or Westerner.

The area is home for middle-class Chinese, perhaps working in banks or for the government, and manual labourers, often content with taking jobs as and when they are offered. Most of the shopkeepers own and live in their shops, selling curtains, building supplies, joss sticks, freshly-rolled noodles—anything.

In some ways it is still a traditional Chinese community with second—sometimes third—generation residents passing on their homes and businesses to their children—if they have not emigrated.

In spite of Hong Kong's image as a 24-hour city, Sai Ying Pun slumbers peacefully at night. By 6:30 a.m. the local market is opening and house- wives jostle to buy fresh veg- etables and milk for breakfast.

Mahjong tiles

Older people head for the "park," less than one acre in size, where they go through their morning exercises or practise *taijiquan*, a form of Chinese martial art. Workers queue for the endless stream of public buses and minibuses which head for the commercial and industrial centres of Hong Kong.

Children start school early and only housewives are left behind to go through the daily chores of washing, shopping, and prepar- ing for the evening meal, which is nearly always attended by the whole family. The routine is only broken by occasional hawkers peddling their wares. One, a wizened man with a high-pitched squeal of a voice, sells long bamboo poles which are suspended outside each flat window. The poles act as a mini washing line, transforming the road into a Chinese laundry each afternoon.

Cantonese culture remains strongly visible. On festivals and holidays women burn paper, symbolising money, on the street. The offerings are intended for ancestors and are accompanied by oranges, because the Chinese word for oranges sounds similar to the word for good fortune.

No one seems much bothered by the risks of lighting fires in the cramped streets, or by the swirls of ash and smouldering paper which threaten to land on every passer-by. After all, ancestors must never be slighted.

Chinese and Westerners keep to themselves. We exchange greetings in the lifts and chat about the weather in much the same way as neighbours in other countries. My few insights into local gossip come from Mr. Ma, who visits for tea and a chat some mornings.

Recently there was great excitement. Mr. Ma's friend, Mr. Cheng, like many older Chinese men, likes birds. He has several brightly coloured birds, which are proudly displayed each morning from his window in beautifully woven bamboo cages. But Mr. Cheng's girlfriend complained he was spending more time with his birds than visiting her. Did he love the birds more than her? she asked. In a huff, she threw one of the birds, complete with cage, to its death six floors below.

According to Mr. Ma, Mr. Cheng very nearly inflicted the same fate on his girlfriend, but only gave her a beating. It seems she was right about Mr. Cheng's affections. He has bought a new bird and stopped seeing the girl.

There is not much night life in Sai Ying Pun. The few restaurants nearby cater for labourers at lunch time and young couples and celebrating families in the evening. A take-away noodle shop does brisk business on Wednesday nights, as punters return from the betting shop where they have either won, or more likely lost, on the twice-weekly horse racing.

Otherwise, families are back home by 7 p.m. for the evening meal, followed by TV and early bed. The general calm is occasionally broken by a practising pianist, a passing police siren or the hum of a taxi bringing people home late from the buzzier parts of Hong Kong.

Angus Foster is a writer whose work has appeared in many publications.

★

Like New Yorkers, Hong Kongers seemed to pride themselves on their rudeness, their impatience with the slow or sentinental ("Am I being courteous?" said the badge worn with black irony by the conductor on the Peak tram who barked out orders and trampled on children as he kept the turnstiles spinning.) Like New York, above all, Hong Kong seemed to prize energy before imagination and movement more than thought.

—Pico Iyer, *Video Night in Kathmandu*

YVONNE MICHIE HORN

✦ ✦ ✦

A Leg up on Fate

Can the Gods reveal the future? Inquiring minds want to know.

NOISY, TEEMING, INCENSE-FILLED WONG TAI SIN IS HONG KONG'S largest and most popular temple, a one-stop supermarket of Taoism, Buddhism, Confucianism, folk-myth, magic, and supernatural practices. While most temples have a resident soothsayer, Wong Tai Sin has a fortune tellers' alley, a warren of 161 stalls, each with its own metal door that clangs down at closing time just like any other shopkeeper's.

Such commercialization of a place of worship is not at all bizarre to the pragmatic Chinese. The fortune tellers pay rent and attract droves of people who drop donations into the slotted box by the temple entrance and buy the paraphernalia of prayer from the temple keepers. Thus, shrines can be built and charitable works maintained.

Perhaps no Westerner can ever fully understand the religion of the ordinary Chinese—the pursuit of worldly success, the appeasement of the dead, and the seeking of hidden knowledge about the future. Ghosts and spirits must be kept happy lest they become restless and return to plague the living; the living must forge links with the dead and those yet unborn; numerous deities must be courted in order to avoid their displeasure. If misfortune occurs despite one's best efforts, answers and remedies are sought before the altar—and in the fortune telling stalls of Wong Tai Sin.

Few outsiders rummage about in this mystical, supernatural underside of Hong Kong. If one attempts to do so, it is essential to have a Chinese-speaking guide who is willing to talk openly. Mine was Perry Wong.

As the incense and cacophony of worship swirled about us, I was acutely aware, even with Perry by my side, that I was an interloper, a Caucasian voyeur in the midst of those intent on the ancient yet ongoing business of attracting good luck and averting disaster.

Adding to the babble at Wong Tai Sin was the incessant rattling of fortune sticks, one of the most popular methods of divination. Kneeling before the altar, a worshiper holds a round container filled with as many as 100 bamboo sticks and shakes it until just one works its way free and falls to the floor. A Chinese numeral is inked on each stick to correspond to a numbered fortune, called *chim*. Several soothsayers in the alley specialize in *chim* interpretations— and relay additional information from the temple's deities and spirits.

"Would you like to try?" asked Perry. To do so, I had to have several questions in mind—not just one, because the word "one" in Cantonese sounds much like that for "poison," and that would not do.

Since no real concern had brought me, I searched my mind for a pair of questions that would not appear frivolous to the temple's deities, spirits, or whatever might be listening. Finally I settled on inquiries about my future health and happiness.

But first the incense. I had to buy joss sticks, light three, and bow one time each to heaven, earth, and humanity.

That done, I collected a canister from the supply on the altar and found a few unpopulated inches in which to kneel. On my right, a man was fervently thrusting a fistful of incense toward the heavens; on my left a woman, tears rolling down her cheeks, touched her forehead to the ground before tossing *bui*, two pieces of wood, worn smooth by uncountable hands, that could be read "yes" or "no" according to their fall; two out of three would settle her fate.

Now I was shaking the canister, concentrating on my first question and fearful that more than a single stick or, heaven forbid,

nother strategy for predicting the future is called sing pei *or confirmation by Buddha's lips. Two carved pieces of wood, joined by a string or cord, are thrown in the air. When they land, if both "lips" land in the same position, with Buddha's mouth "closed," it means Buddha is saying "no." If one lands up and one down, his mouth is open and it means "yes." There seemed a 50-50 chance to this option, so I asked the lips all my questions. As the smooth pieces of wood moved against each other, it was like Buddha was whispering. Half the time I got yes, half the time, no. Once we knew what they were, we began to see* sing pei *everywhere: in temples, antique and gift shops, and booths on the street.*

—Judith Babcock Wylie, "The Whisper of Buddha's Lips"

the entire supply would tumble to the floor, a sure sign that I was not serious. At last one stick emerged from the pack, teetered at the edge of the canister, and fell—followed, as I zoomed in on my second question, by another.

Lam Ching Yee, the most popular reader of *chim* at Wong Tai Sin, was easy to find; hers was the stall flanked by a queue of occupied stools. An assistant recorded my *chim* number, asked my birth date, collected my money, and estimated that it would be an hour before we could be seen. We took a number from a dispenser, as if waiting our turn to buy bread at the bakery, and left to look for the stall of Chui Shu Kong, highly regarded among Wong Tai Sin's palm readers.

We found him—his queue of stools unoccupied at the moment—at stall 92. He looked to be in his mid-30s, with a neatly clipped mustache, crisp white shirt, burgundy tie tucked into navy vest. His gray suit jacket hung on a hook on the wall. His fee: HK$100, or about US$13.

I laid my hands palms up on his table and felt them begin to tremble as Perry translated Chui's reading of my character. The soothsayer accurately saw in my hands that I was a near-workaholic and that I tended to pinch pennies. He added that I negated the pinching with extravagant splurges. He noted my impatience with those less mentally or physically quick than myself. Yet he reported that I was a sociable creature who had many friends, that I loved to read (yet would rather be outdoors than in), that I played respectable games of golf and tennis. He told me about my siblings, my children, my parents, and, with Perry squirming to find euphemistic ways to phrase the information, precise details about my female organs.

"I have told you about yourself and your past so that you will believe me when I tell you about your future," he said. I would soon become seriously ill, and, unless I took precautionary steps, my life would not be long. Despite my protestations that I was always well and fit, a telltale vein at the base of my thumb told Chui a different story.

We left stall 92, me in stunned silence and Perry, who had learned more details about me than he'd bargained for in his role as guide and translator, acting inscrutably Chinese.

But this was Hong Kong, where positive fatalism is practiced. Here, no fate is written in stone. If one's fortune is good, there is nothing to fear. If it is bad, steps can be taken to change it. All I had to do now was find out what spirit I'd alienated and how I'd come to be out of tune with myself and my surrounding world.

"*Of course I go to the temples. It's fun actually, a part of the festivals. We all get together and go to Wong Tai Sin or to one in a village if we are in the New Territories. Just for luck really. Some people are really lucky. They win lotteries all the time. There are so many stories to tell. Everyone believes in luck. Even Westerners like you. We Chinese try to get the best deal from what's offered. You don't want to be limited to just the Buddha or worshipping the ancestors. That's too boring and you just don't know which one is right. I think the strict Buddhists must be crazy. I'm not really religious, not like the bible readers at work. Every Friday lunch time. Who wants to waste time doing that? Actually, Christians are very nice people. But they always want to make you think about their religion. Sin and all that. What does that mean? Sin. Am I sin? Sin. People do wrong all the time but how can you carry all that with you. Not only what you do, what you think as well! No one can be so cruel with themselves.*

—Dr. George Adams,
*Games Hong Kong People Play:
A Social Psychology of the
Hong Kong Chinese*

Perhaps my house was sited poorly, with bad *feng shui,* and I should have a geomancer come in to correct the placement of windows and doors.

Perhaps my *chi,* body energy, was in need of bolstering and I should embark on a program of acupuncture, *t'ai chi* exercises, or meditation.

Perhaps I should consult a *fu kay* practitioner, who would receive a medical prescription from the spirit world for me to have filled by an herbalist.

But right now I had the opportunity to tackle the problem in Western style—a second opinion—derived from the pair of questions I'd asked of the fortune sticks.

A glass door slid discreetly behind us, shutting out the hub-bub of Wong Tai Sin as we took our seats across the table from Lam Ching Yee. A middle-aged woman wearing a brown print dress with a lace collar, she was already at work on my two *chim,* selected by her assistant from an array of bright pink paper rectangles printed in red that hung on the wall. Each *chim,* written in archaic characters and style, told a story, almost a riddle, with obscure references to old Chinese legends.

Inexplicably relayed through a microphone, since we were seated but inches away, Lam Ching Yee dealt first with my future happiness. The fable she told—"Kwan Kung, the respectable and good, helped to send his two sisters-in-law to meet his brother safely"—appeared meaningless to me, but was unhesitatingly interpreted to mean that my future happiness depended on a consultation with two people before I took action.

Which two people? Before taking action on what? I would know, I was told.

On to my second question, which between the shaking of the canister and the reading of the *chim* had metamorphosed from cliché to concern. This time the text told of a farmer who discovered that his field was full of diamonds. Perry smiled as he relayed the interpretation: my years would be many, and each would sparkle with good health.

For a nonbeliever, I felt an inordinate rush of relief. Yet I also trusted the palm reader who had related so much that was accurate. A third opinion might tilt the scales one way or the other.

At stall 84, I sat across a small table from Richard L.H.Tsui, Life Member of the Society for the Study of Physiognomy, Hong Kong and London—so read his business card. For HK$200, I heard that my face revealed a person of intelligence, warmth, and beauty. I'd weathered rough spots in my life, but now I was like a fine horse running strong and free. I was surrounded by friends and family who loved and respected me; my financial future was secure; my career upward bound.

And, yes—why would I even question it?—of course I would have a long and healthful life.

Tsui's manner was that of a benign and wise grandfather. His face glowed in the reflection of my good fortune. I liked him immensely.

"What did you think?" I asked Perry once we were out of earshot of 84.

"I think," said Perry, "that he tells people what they want to hear."

That evening after dinner, Perry and I were wandering the Temple Street night market, Hong Kong's vast, clamorous, bazaar of improvised stalls dedicated to cut-price seconds, fake designer watches, and overruns. Midway, the market split into two sections with the walls of jackets and jewelry continuing on up Temple Street, while to the right, following the edge of a small park, something quite different was taking place.

In the street fronting the park, teams of child acrobats were bouncing and twisting in the glow of kerosene lamps.

Next door, amateur Chinese opera was under way, voices wailing to the chop and clash of wooden blocks and cymbals.

Farther along, a freelance dentist practiced his trade. His stoic patient was sitting on a tiny stool as the dentist prodded about in his mouth.

Next to him a bare-chested man flexed his muscles to demonstrate the effectiveness of the tonic he was selling, and down the block a letter writer was composing an epistle for a client.

Across the street, encircled by onlookers and seated at a fold-up table, was a man wearing round-rimmed glasses, his bald head shining in a pool of hissing gaslight. On the table was a small coop constructed of bamboo dowels and partitioned to house four matched white birds with bright red feet and beaks. Fanned in front of the birds were what appeared to be thick, brown playing cards. "Fortune teller," Perry whispered as we joined those gathered around. "I think this is one you should try."

I moved up on the queue of stools until I, too, was bathed in gaslight. The soothsayer's eyes widened quizzically as he looked up and into my Western face. Paying a reasonable HK$5 and abandoning my health concerns, I asked what my prospects for financial advancement might be in the coming year.

My question became an incantation to the birds. Then one was chosen for release, and the soothsayer pulled up several dowels at the front of the cage. With endearing efficiency, the bird hopped down the fan of cards until it stopped to tug one free of the pack with its beak. Task completed; it accepted a bite of birdseed from a matchbox and hopped directly back to its cage.

The soothsayer pulled what looked to be a Chinese version of a tarot card from its brown cover, took one look, and threw his head back in laughter, his

I did manage to find a snatch of romance in Hong Kong— at the Chinese opera. The Cloud of Eternal Sorrow was a ravishing pageant of water and air, through which was unrolled a water-color vision of turquoise valleys and misty waterfalls. Swains chased sylphs through a brushstroked never-never land. Shaven-headed chamberlains and goat-bearded sages strode through a plot as brocaded and magical as that of Turandot. Every speech was fleet and fragile as light snowfall. A valiant warrior marched onto the stage, and English-language subtitles flickered on the blue-velvet curtains framing the proscenium. "I am a hunter from Jade Mountain. My father's silver-maned horse is faster than the army's 3,000." Imprisoned, the lovely princess of his dreams could only weep beside her casement. "The palace is dark. The palace is lonely. The valleys are draped in a lilac shroud." The seasons drew on, and her pining grew more plaintive and more plangent. "The moon is so bright. These walls are so high. My heart is breaking." The curtain came down, and I went out into the night.

—Pico Iyer, *Video Night in Kathmandu*

stainless-steel teeth shining in the lamplight. According to the fortune translated by Perry, my prospects for wealth were nil because, speaking allegorically, I had abandoned my fruitful apple orchard in favor of chasing after jackrabbits. I laughed, too, albeit hollowly.

"Would you like a second opinion?" Perry asked, because right over there at another table bathed in gaslight was a diviner whose method involved the tucking of three old Chinese coins into a tortoise shell. I shook my head. The day had been long, and I'd poked about enough in a world where I did not belong.

Perhaps I'd do well to simply invest in a bag of fortune cookies. And keep a watchful eye on that telltale vein at the base of my thumb.

Yvonne Michie Horn is a travel writer whose work has appeared in newspapers and magazines in the U.S. and abroad. She lives in Santa Rosa, California.

✦

Amidst the incense and the chanting faithful at the Wong Tai Sin Temple, I took the divination sticks and shook them as I saw others shaking them. A stick with the number four written on it popped out. Four is the symbol for death. I suddenly had one of those experiences that are unbidden but wash over you. I felt that I was suddenly connected with some universal force that pressed a message upon me: "You face death." Upon later reflection, I realized that I must face death without fear, that it was something that I had been ignoring in my life. The realization had nothing to do with religion, but was more a balancing of yin and yang—and suddenly I was in balance.

—Sean O'Reilly, "City of a Million Dreams"

★ ★ ★

The Dragon-Lines

Even the forces of international finance
heed the advice of the feng shui *man.*

THE MAN I HAD ARRANGED TO MEET WAS STANDING BY ONE OF
the two bronze lions that snarl in the forecourt of the Hongkong
and Shanghai Bank. He wore a blue silk Nina Ricci tie, a gold
wristwatch with a crocodile strap, and an immaculate worsted
grey suit.

He handed me his card on which was written, in embossed
letters:

LUNG KING CHUEN
Geomancer
Searching and fixing of good location for the burial
of passed-away ancestors; surveying and arranging
of good position for settling down business and
lodging places, in which would gain prosperity and
luck in the very near future

The building has 47 storeys (including the helipad on the roof)
and stands on the site of the Bank's former Head Office—overlooking the Cenotaph, on the south side of Victoria Square. It is
the work of the English architect, Norman Foster, and is, by any
standards, an astonishing performance.

I heard the bank called, variously, "The shape of things to come;" "An act of faith in Hong Kong's future;" "Something out of *Star Wars;*" "A cathedral to money;" "A maintenance nightmare;" and "Suicides' leap."

This story was originally published in 1987, ancient history by Hong Kong standards, but it addresses issues that are timeless. The Hong Kong skyline has changed dramatically since then with the addition of several larger and equally innovative buildings, but the Hongkong and Shanghai Bank building remains a standout.

—JO'R, LH, and SO'R

Having exceeded its budget three times over, to the tune of $600 million U.S., the Hongkong and Shanghai Bank has also earned the distinction of being the most expensive office block ever built.

Architecturally, I felt it was less a "vision of the future" than a backward, not to say nostalgic, look at certain experiments of the '20s (when buildings were modelled on battleships, and Man himself was thought to be a perfectible machine): buildings such as the PROUNS of El Lissitzky; Vesnin's project for the offices of *Pravda*—the unrealized dreams of the Early Soviet Constructivists.

Mr. Lung, on the other hand, is a modest practitioner of the venerable Chinese art of geomancy, or *feng-shui*. At the start of the project, the Bank called him in to survey the site for malign or demonic presences, and to ensure that the design itself was propitious. Whichever architect was chosen, there was bound to be some anxiety; for the Hongkong and Shanghai Bank is the pivot on which Hong Kong itself stands or falls. With 1997 in sight, prosperity and luck must either come "in the very near future"—or not at all.

The afternoon was overcast and a sharp wind was blowing off the harbour. We rode the escalator to the first floor, and took shelter in the Cash Department. It was like entering a war-machine: the uniform grey, the absence of "art," the low hum of computerised activity. It was also cold. Had the building been put up in Soviet Russia there would at least have been a touch of red.

Behind a gleaming black counter sat the tellers—unscreened and unprotected, since, in the event of a bank-raid, a kind of portcullis slices sideways into action, and traps the raiders inside. A few potted palms were positioned here and there, apparently at random.

I sat down on a slab of black marble which, in less austere surroundings, might have been called a banquette. Mr. Lung was not a tall man. He stood.

Obviously, the surroundings were too austere for many of the Bank's personnel, and already—in the executive suites on high—they had unrolled the Persian carpets, and secretaries sat perched on reproduction Chippendale chairs.

"This," Mr. Lung began, in a proprietorial tone, "is one of the Top Ten Buildings of the World. Its construction is particularly ingenious."

"It is," I nodded, glancing up at the cylindrical pylons and the colossal X-shaped cross-braces that keep the structure rigid.

"So first," he continued, "I would like to emphasize its good points. As far as *feng-shui* is concerned, the situation is perfect. It is, in fact, the best situation in the whole of Hong Kong."

Feng-shui means "wind-and-water." From the most ancient times the Chinese have believed that the Earth is a mirror of the Heavens, and that both are living sentient beings shot through and through with currents of energy—some positive, some negative—like the messages that course through our own central nervous systems.

The positive currents—those carrying good *"chih,"* or "life force"—are known as "dragon-lines." They are thought to follow the flow of underground water, and the direction of magnetic fields beneath the Earth's surface.

The business of a geomancer is to make certain, with the help of a magnetic compass, that a building, a room, a grave, or a marriage-bed is aligned to one or other of the "dragon-lines" and shielded from dangerous cross-currents. Without clearance from a *feng-shui* expert, even the most "westernized" Chinese businessman is apt to get the jitters, to say nothing of his junior staff.

At a lunch I happened to tell an "old China hand," an Englishman, that the Bank had taken the advice of a geomancer.

"Yes," he replied. "It's the kind of thing they would believe in."

Yet we all feel that some houses are "happy" and others have a "nasty atmosphere." Only the Chinese have come up with cogent reasons why this should be so. Whoever presumes to mock *feng-shui* as a superstitious anachronism should recall its vital contribution to the making of the Chinese landscape, in which houses, temples, and cities were always sited in harmony with trees and hills and water.

Perhaps one can go a step further? Perhaps the *rootedness* of Chinese civilisation; the Chinese sense of belonging to the Earth; their capacity to live without friction in colossal numbers— have all, in the long run, resulted from their adherence to the principles of *feng-shui?*

"Now it so happens," Mr. Lung said, "that no less than five 'dragon-lines' run down from The Peak and converge on the Central Business District of Hong Kong."

We looked across the atrium of glass, towards the skyscrapers of the most expensive patch of real estate in the world.

Some of the lines, he went on—not by any means all—were punctuated here and there with "dragon-points" or "energy-centres," like the meridian-points known to acupuncturists: points at which a particularly potent source of *chih* was known to gush to the surface.

"And the site on which the bank stands," he added, "is one of them.

In rural parts of Hong Kong some old Chinese practices, long abandoned in China, continue. It is still possible for example to see traditional walled villages. In many of these, houses are packed closely together and all face in the same direction—towards what the Chinese traditionally always called south, whatever the compass said. The front of the house would be determined by the feng shui *but always known as the south or "red bird;" the left-hand side would be east or "green dragon;" the right, west or "right tiger;" and the rear, the north or "black warrior," sometimes "tortoise." Watch towers or walls would be built because of the serious fighting between villages. This continued long after the British extended their rule. Houses frequently had a wall in front of them and traditionally didn't have windows. Both devices were intended to deter evil spirits. Chinese believe that spirits cannot move except in straight lines. Sometimes the defensive measures were supported by strategically placed mirrors—evil spirits are supposedly ugly and afraid of seeing themselves.*

—Kevin Rafferty, *City on the Rocks: Hong Kong's Uncertain Future*

It is, in fact, the only 'dragon-point' on the entire length of the line."

Other lines, too, were known to have branches, like taproots, which tended to siphon off the flow of *chih,* and diminish its force.

"But this line," he said, "has no branches."

Yet another favourable point was the bank's uninterrupted view of the mountain. Had there been naked rocks or screes, they might have reflected bad *chih* into the building.

"But The Peak," he said solemnly, "is covered in trees."

Similarly, because the new building was set well back from the waterfront—and because the sun's course passed to landward—no malign glitter could rise up from the sea.

Mr. Lung liked the grey colour which, he felt, was soothing to the nerves. He also liked the fact that the building absorbed light, and did not reflect glare onto its neighbours.

I questioned him carefully on the subject of reflected glare, and discovered that glass-curtain-wall buildings which mirror one another—as they do in every American city, and now in Hong Kong—are, from a *feng-shui* point of view, disastrous.

"If you reflect bad *chih* onto your neighbours," Mr. Lung said, "you cannot prosper either."

He also approved of the two bronze lions that used to guard the entrance of the earlier building. During the War, he said, the Japanese had tried to melt them down: "But they were not successful."

I said there were similar lions in London, outside the Bank of England.

"They cannot be as good as these two," he answered sharply: so sharply, in fact, that I forgot to ask whether the lions had been put away in storage when Mrs. Thatcher made her first, ill-informed foray into Chinese politics—and gave the Hong Kong Stock Exchange its major nervous breakdown.

The result, of course, was the historic slap from Deng Xiaoping himself.

"So what about the bad points?" I asked Mr. Lung.

"I'm coming to them now," he said.

The Hong Kong waterfront was built on reclaimed land and there were stories…No. He could not confirm them but there were, nevertheless, stories...of sea-monsters and other local ghouls, who resented being dumped upon and might want to steal into the building.

This was why he had recommended that the escalator to the first floor—which was, after all, the main public entrance—should be so angled, obliquely, that it ran along a "dragon-line." The flow of positive *chih* would thus drive the demons back where they belonged.

Furthermore, since all good *chih* came from the landward, he had advised that the Board Room and Chief Executive offices should turn away from the sea: away, that is, from the view of Kowloon and the mountains of China; away from the cargo-ships, tugboats, ferries, drifters, coaling-barges, junks; away from the White Ensign, Red Ensign and that "other" red flag—and turn instead to face the "Earth Spirit" descending from The Peak.

The "historic slap" refers to Margaret Thatcher's refusal to acknowledge clear Chinese sovereignty over Hong Kong during discussions with Chinese leaders in 1982. The subsequent negative reaction of the mainland Chinese "caused" the stock market to go down. Essentially, China manipulated the market in such a way as to tell her "We can make this place go to hell in a hand basket and what can you do about it?" She played tough and so did the Chinese. She lost.

—JO'R, LH, and SO'R

The same, equally, applied to the underground Safe Deposit—which has the largest, circular, stainless-steel door ever made.

Finally, Mr. Lung said, he had to admit there were a number of danger zones in the structure—"killing-points" is what he called them—where, in order to counteract negative *chih,* it had been necessary to station living plants: a potted palm at the head of the escalator "in case of a fall;" more potted palms by the lift-shafts; yet more palms close to the pylons to nullify the colossal downward thrust of the building.

"Right," I said. "I'd like to ask you one thing. I believe that 'dragon-lines' never run straight, but are curved."

"True," he said.

"And isn't it also true that traditional Chinese buildings are almost always curved? The roofs are curved? The walls are curved?"

"Yes."

Chinese architecture—like Chinese art, Chinese language, and the Chinese character—abhors the rigid and rectilinear.

"Now, as a *feng-shui* man," I persisted, "how would you interpret this rigid, straight-up-and-down Western architecture? Would you say it had good or bad *chih?*"

He blanched a little, and said nothing.

"These cross-braces, for example? Good or bad? Would you consider putting plants underneath them?"

"No," he said, blandly. "Nobody sits there."

My question, I have to confess, was most unfair, for I had heard on the grapevine that the cross-braces were terribly bad *feng-shui.*

It was obvious I had overstepped the mark. At the mere mention of cross-braces, Mr. Lung moved onto the defensive. He back-pedalled. He smiled. He re-emphasized the good points, and glossed over the bad ones. He even left the impression that there were no bad ones.

At the foot of the escalator he shook my hand and said:

"I have done *feng-shui* for Rothschilds."

Bruce Chatwin was the author of several books including In Patagonia *and* The Songlines. *He worked for eight years at Sotheby's before abandoning his career to travel and write, and his stories were published widely in Britain and the United States. He died in 1989.*

✷

The magical force that flows through the environment is a kind of supernatural electricity called "mana" by anthropologists and is found in many cultures. In Chinese culture it is called *hey* (Cantonese) or *qi* (pronounced "chee" in Mandarin) and is found in positive and negative (yang and yin) states. The same *hey* or life force that flows through the body, according to acupuncture, flows through the earth in the form of a dragon's breath according to *feng shui.*

When the *hey* of the landscape is disturbed, it can also disturb the spirit world. In other words, although *feng shui* (a type of *hey* or *hey shui*) is magical, it is also linked to religion (as seen from a western anthropological viewpoint) in the sense that ghosts are thought to be affected by it. For example, when the villagers of Tai Pak on Lantau Island (west of Hong Kong) moved a stone religious statue from the bottom of a hill up nearer the top in 1970, people started seeing ghosts. These alleged apparitions were attributed to a loss of good *feng shui* which had been disturbed by the rearrangement of the statue in relationship to the hill.

Another connection between magic and folk religion lies in the importance of situating graves properly so that they will enjoy good *feng shui*. Not only one's ancestors but oneself can expect to benefit or suffer accordingly, just as with good or bad ancestor worship.

—Charles F. Emmons, "Hong Kong's *Feng Shui*: Popular Magic in a Modern Urban Setting," *Journal of Popular Culture*

* * *

Love Will Find a Way

A former British magistrate learns a lesson in subtlety.

THE COURT WAS RATHER MORE FULL THAN USUAL, MOST OF THE adult members of two families having come in. The two families were neighbours, living in a rather ramshackle, but fairly solid, row of wooden shop-houses in a congested part of industrial Tsuen Wan. Technically they were squatters, and the area was one of those we hoped eventually to see pulled down to make way for modern apartment blocks.

They were single-storey structures. In most of them, the shop section fronted the street; further in was the sleeping area, flimsily compartmented for various members of the family; after this came the kitchen and washing places, and a small rear yard, filled with the astonishing ragbag collections which Chinese of this type amass as some obscure part of their instinct for survival.

While this story does not apply directly to the mores of modern Hong Kong, the legendary love of indirection so common to Chinese negotiation and thinking is much in evidence here.

—JO'R, LH, and SO'R

The complainant family had a daughter, aged about eighteen and still unmarried, who was in the unfortunate position of expecting a baby; and her parents had come to demand that I order the twenty-year-old son of the neighbouring family to marry their daughter without delay, since, they alleged, he was the unborn baby's father.

The defendant family said that this allegation was preposterous nonsense, that their son had never had anything to do with the girl, and that they refused to be browbeaten in this disgraceful way, their son accused of immorality. There was no question of his marrying the girl, and there never had been. They scarcely knew their neighbours anyway, and their son had never even spoken to the girl.

The boy and the girl were present. Inhibited somewhat by their parents, who were doing most of the talking, they were both pleasant types. The boy worked in a factory; the girl worked at home making plastic handbags.

"Do you confirm what your father says, that you've never spoken to this girl?" I asked.

He confirmed it.

I turned to the girl's father.

"But you are suggesting that this is untrue," I said. "You are suggesting that your daughter has, in fact, spoken to this young man."

The girl's father was truculent. He didn't know whether his daughter had spoken to the boy or not. What he did know was that this was the young man who had interfered with his daughter.

"And are you saying, too, that you have never spoken to this young man?" I inquired of the girl.

She lowered her eyes, and would not reply.

"But you insist that he is the father of your baby?" I pursued.

She was silent for a long time. She had flushed, eyes always downcast.

"Yes," she whispered at last.

"Listen, young man," I said to the boy, "are you quite sure you're telling me the truth? Isn't there something else you *could* tell me, if your parents were not here—something you would prefer them not to know?"

Eyes downcast on his side too, his pale face gave no indication of a reaction. But my remarks produced a protest from his parents.

Their son had nothing to conceal, they insisted. They knew the position. The other family's allegation was totally without foundation.

"Are you sure," I went on, addressing the boy, "that you haven't met this girl somewhere outside?"

"No! Of course he hasn't!" shouted both his parents simultaneously.

"No," replied the boy, quietly and quite plainly.

It sounded like the truth.

I addressed myself to the girl's father.

"I must tell you frankly, I find it difficult to deal with this complaint of yours. What you are saying about this young man is a very grave accusation. You cannot expect me to believe it, or even listen to it, unless you can produce some facts to substantiate it."

"I have facts!" he retorted hotly.

"Well—?"

"In the shower!" he snapped out.

"I beg your pardon?" I inquired, vaguely wondering where there might be a shower in our office.

"Yes," he said. "In the shower! That's where!"

I cupped my chin in my hands.

"What shower? Where?"

"In my house!"

"Oh! I understand!" I exclaimed; then, finding that I didn't, added, "No, I'm afraid I don't understand. What do you really mean?"

"When she takes a *shower!*"

My acquaintance with Hong Kong and with things Chinese now extends over a quarter of a century and nothing has been a cause to me of more anxiety throughout that period than the fact that the Chinese and the European communities of Hong Kong, although in daily contact with each other, nevertheless move in different worlds, neither having any real comprehension of the mode of life or ways of thought of the other. This is a most regrettable misunderstanding which retards the social, moral, intellectual, and even the commercial and material progress of the colony.

—Governor Cecil Clementi (1936)

the wretched father shouted at me, almost overcome by my inability to understand.

"When she takes a shower," I repeated slowly. "Where *is* the shower?"

From my office one was always distantly aware of the bustle and noise in the other parts of the building; and at this moment I wondered why it was that I should have suddenly thought about this. Then it occurred to me. There were surprisingly few sounds from the rest of the building. There was, in fact—apart from the distant bustle of Kowloon—almost silence. There was, now I came to pay keener attention to the matter, more than silence. There was what is known behind the scenes in the London theater as a "deathly hush," which is a kind of indrawing of breath (accompanied by tiptoes and craned heads) so absolutely silent as to be painfully audible.

I did not have to be told. All work in the outer offices had stopped, while every member of the staff who considered himself sufficiently senior to do so had silently crept up the passage, where, just out of sight from the open door of my office, the lot of them had assembled, poised, listening to every word with bated breath.

"Where is the shower?" I repeated steadily, trying hard to control myself from yelling at the staff to go back to their work.

The shower, it appeared, was at the back of the house. With a projecting cover of some sort, it was external to the building, situated in the back yard, and modestly screened.

"You mean," I said, "that it is possible to pass from your back yard to your neighbour's?"

Certainly not! came the almost injured reply. There was a strong plank wall between the two yards, and it was impossible to pass.

"Then what do you mean? Where does the shower come into it?"

"He *saw* her!" the girl's father shouted at me desperately.

"I see. You mean, realizing she was having a shower, he managed to climb over the plank wall, and..." Modesty forbade the rest.

But the poor father only looked more desperate than ever.

"He *saw* her!" he repeated, with even greater emphasis.

This was becoming too much for the Special Magistrate.

"Look here, my dear man," I said reasoningly, "you are not, I hope, trying to tell me that if a young man chances to see a young girl having a shower, this causes the girl to make a baby. Or are you?"

From the youngsters there was silence. From the four parents there was a unanimous snort of disgust at finding they had journeyed all this way to be heard by a magistrate who asked such ridiculous questions.

"*He* doesn't understand," the father muttered contemptuously to my interpreter, using an off-hand word to describe me.

"No, he certainly doesn't!" I replied sharply, before the interpreter had time to translate. "If you have a genuine grievance against this family, or against this young man, why do you not tell me what it is?"

It seemed to me that their accusation against the boy was a cover, shielding the real cause of their animosity towards the other family. This real cause was evidently something quite different. But how to discover what it was?

There was silence.

"Well, I'm sorry," I said, "but if that is all you can produce to substantiate your statement I'm afraid my answer must be that this young man has no case to answer."

With triumphant looks and inaudible sniffs, the boy's parents turned their backs on the other parents, who remained silent, the girl's father staring at me with the helplessness an intelligent man evinces when trying to explain something to an ignoramus.

"Listen to me," I said to him, by this time almost in my own self-defence. "You have all more or less agreed that this young man has never spoken to your daughter. He may once have seen her taking her bath—perhaps you should make that plank wall higher. Your daughter must go out sometimes on her own. How do you know that she doesn't have some other boy friend, whom you know nothing about?"

They dismissed this out of hand. Their daughter did not go out on her own.

"Then, what you are telling me is that this young man, by having set eyes on your daughter when she was naked, has caused her to conceive a child."

All of them rustled about for a moment—Western magistrates, it seemed to them, had strange ideas—and then the girl's father muttered under his breath to the interpreter: "Can't he understand? At *night!*"

"At night?" I queried. "You mean, your daughter is in the habit of taking a shower at night?"

In the passage outside, there was a sudden renewed outburst of deathly hush. It evidenced the fact that the only person in the office who did *not* know what this case was about was the Special Magistrate, the game being to see how long it would take him to find out. They may even have been laying bets on it.

No, certainly not! came the reply to my query. The girl did *not* take a bath at night.

"Then what has night got to do with it?" I asked. "Where *are* you all usually at night? Sleeping, I presume."

Yes. They were sleeping.

"Well, where do you sleep?"

It appeared that the sleeping quarters in both houses were approximately adjacent, that both front and back doors were securely locked before everyone went to sleep, and that there was no possibility of anyone passing from one house to the other, or going outside, without waking someone up.

I had reached the end of this line of questioning, and it had

Traditional Chinese men and women don't touch each other in public. It's acceptable for women to show affection for each other and for men to be openly demonstrative toward other men—to hold hands on the street or even sit on each other's laps without any homosexual overtones—but cross-sexual physical contact is still uncommon. It's always hard for me as an exuberant American to remember not to give my male Chinese friends and buddies that quick hug or pat on the back when things are going well for us. Invariably, when I forget, the most well-meaning touch brings an instant stiffening.

—Paula McDonald, "South China Sea Journal"

led nowhere. But being for the moment at a loss to know what to ask them next, and being unwilling to show them I was lost, with wearied obstinacy I pursued the same line a little further, all the while thinking hard what really salient question to raise next.

"And where exactly do you sleep?" I asked the girl in a bored way. She slept in the same bed as her mother.

"And where do you sleep?" I inquired of the boy.

He slept alone.

It was meaningless to pursue the matter, but I went on listlessly. "Whereabouts do you have your bed?"

His bed was against the wall.

"Which wall?"

It was the wall of the other shop-house.

The deathly hush in the passage suddenly became so strident that it could have been called screaming deathly hush. It appeared I was on to something.

I addressed the girl's mother.

"And just where is your bed situated?"

Her bed too was against a wall—the wall of the other shop-house.

"And you say your daughter shares your bed with you?"

"Yes."

"Which—er"—it was difficult to know how to word it— "which of you sleeps on the room side of your bed?"

"I do," the mother replied.

"I see. So your daughter sleeps on the wall side?"

"Yes."

The wall was of wood, and perhaps a knotch had fallen out of it. Anyway, somewhere—and at just about the right place—there was a hole in it.

Not a very big hole. But just big enough.

This case occurred in my third year as a magistrate, when I should have known better than to have kept those six people in such prolonged embarrassment. I say all six were embarrassed, because, as the reader, who is by this time becoming accustomed to the happenings in a Chinese court, will already have realized, the boy's parents, despite the attitudes they struck were fully aware of what had happened. There was even a moment (when they swung themselves away from the other parents) when they thought that, with such an idiot of a magistrate, they were going to get away with it—because they did not really wish their son to marry, considering him to be too young.

Perhaps it was particularly hot and humid that morning—I can't remember—but anyway, I was extremely slow in the uptake, since I was not paying attention to the euphemisms being employed. In no language is euphemism used more than in Chinese, and on no subject are there more Chinese euphemisms than in anything pertaining to sex. Coarsenesses apart—and the Chinese language has its fair share of these—it would almost be true to say that sex, if it is ever mentioned at all in speech, can only be mentioned in euphemistic terms. The very word for sex—the secret thing—is a euphemism.

In what the girl's father was saying to me, the shower in the back yard had nothing to do with it. For "shower" read "naked," for "saw" read "touched," and it will be seen that the father was making a completely explicit statement: "When she was naked, he touched her in the night." He could not be more explicit without using unprintable words.

And there the six of them had sat, in acute embarrassment, because for some reason that morning I was too slow-witted to grasp it.

This is a story which, I think, gives an idea of the difficulties involved in understanding what goes on around one in a Chinese society. To appreciate how silly a foreigner can be in China, it is almost worth glancing at the dialogue of the case a second time, this time suffering with the two Chinese families, instead of struggling with the magistrate.

But to the reader who wishes to do this, let me first explain why they had come. What had happened was too shameful for the boy's parents to admit—the entire family would have lost face—and this had created a socially impossible situation, which the two families themselves could not resolve, and which could *never* be the basis of a marriage alliance. Once again, as with the case in which the magistrate outrivalled the wisdom of Solomon, authority was needed to put things right.

Very gently and kindly, the Special Magistrate inquired of the young couple whether they would like to start talking to each other—because it was true, they never had—and Mr. Lo, reading my meaning from my tone of voice, skillfully slipped my words into the perfect Chinese euphemism, behind which lay the implication, "Would you like to get married?"

Both smiled, and said they would; and the suggestion having come from so exalted a source, all question of shame was removed.

They all departed in a comparatively amiable state—I say comparatively, because none of the four parents had really yet recovered from the shock of discovering that they had produced offspring of quite such exceptional agility.

Austin Coates is the author of numerous books including Quick Tidings of Hong Kong, China Races, *and* City of Broken Promises. *This story was excerpted from* Myself a Mandarin.

★

"I have to remember that deep, deep down, behind all this that you see, I am more than anything else, Chinese. True, I may be a member of some splendid London clubs. I may smoke Cuban cigars. I may have had this big dinner party given for me. I may have been pretty well accepted.

"But I am, indubitably, a Chinese. My future is with China—just like the future of Hong Kong. It lies with China, whether the old colony cares to admit it or not. Hong Kong and its people need to know the West. But the citizens must not forget that they are a part, and their territory is a part, of one of the world's oldest continuing civilizations. I am too. And I am very proud to be so."

—David Tang, quoted by Simon Winchester,
"The Star of the West," *Town & Country*

* * *

The Food Doctor

The Western palate is indeed timid and limited—certainly when compared to that of the Chinese, who seem to eat everything that moves or grows.

THERE COMES A POINT WHERE NO MATTER HOW MUCH ONE LIKES eating, a line must be drawn. And I drew a line in the Yat Chau Health Restaurant, Hong Kong, when the menu offered me a choice of Double-Boiled Abalone and Ginseng with Chinese Caterpillar Fungus; Double-Boiled Turtle Glue with Wild Ginseng; or Fried Rabbit Slices with Lucid Ganoderma. This was after I had rejected an even more nightmarish selection, consisting of Double-Boiled Deer's Penis with Chicken, Double-Boiled Wild Duck with Deer's Penis and Gecko or—something of a chef d'oeuvre, this—Double-Boiled Black-Bone Chicken with Dried Oviduct Fat of Frog.

The whole uneasy episode began when I arrived at the restaurant and was ushered off to see the doctor. The Yat Chau is so serious about health food that it keeps a pair of white-coated practitioners (from the Chinese Traditional Medicine International Exchange Centre) at its entrance to give customers an examination before they choose what to eat. They inspect you to see if your yin and yang are in balance, as well as investigating any other complications, then they make a diagnosis. On the basis of this diagnosis, you order an appropriate medicinal meal and endeavor to restore yourself to physiological harmony. Thus, if you are tired, run-down and listless, you will need more yang, the active, male principle. This tends to be found in meat, fried and spicy foods and, oddly enough, in lychees: "One piece of lychee," I was told, "is like three sticks of fire." If, on the other hand, your blood pressure is high and you smoke or drink to excess, you will need to curb these yang tendencies with some yin—the passive, feminine principle. Fruit, vegetables, herbal tea, and beer (very yin, thanks to the hops) are all good in this respect.

I was seen by a bespectacled physician who put down his copy of the racing pages, felt my pulse and ordered me to stick my tongue out. He then peered at me dubiously for a minute, before arriving at his conclusions. These were translated to me as follows: I was enervated; I sweated too much; and I suffered from internal dampness. Evidently I was too yin and needed some strengthening yang food. Which is what led me to my impasse with the Caterpillar Fungus, Gecko and Deer's Penis. Indeed, however sweaty and feeble I might have been, I was beginning to wonder if my yin and yang were not better left unbalanced. Everywhere I turned, there seemed to be nothing but glue, abalone, penises, Gastroida tubers, and fungus.

You might imagine from this that the Yat Chau is some kind of fiendish Oriental den, hiding down a side-alley and accessible only to those who know the password. In reality, it is something of a paragon of swanky good taste and easily one of the cleaner and smarter restaurants that I visited during my time in Hong Kong. It stands in the bustling, tram-infested Des Voeux Road, next door to Hong Kong's financial district (in the shadow, indeed, of the Hong Kong and Shanghai Bank and the super-modern Bank of China), and its ground floor is taken up with gleaming mirrors, polished wood-work, and a handsome apothecary's shop, which is part of the whole Yat Chau field of operations.

The restaurant proper is upstairs and spreads over two floors. Here, all is warm apricot-coloured carpets, gilded handrails, ruched and swagged curtains, and mahogany panelling. The presentation of the tables is also visibly more upmarket than the average Hong Kong eaterie: the gilding extends over spoons and chopstick rests, the tablecloth is blindingly white and the tea is served in fist-sized glass goblets. The clientele mirror this opulence, consisting largely of shrewd-looking Chinese businessmen and intensely well made-up women. Conspicuous consumption of this kind of cuisine is, apparently, considered most stylish, along with French cognac and enormously large Mercedes. While I was there only the noise of a jack-hammer coming from the office next door (Hong Kong never stops build-

If you plan to explore Hong Kong, carry your own chopsticks. While most restaurants on Hong Kong's tourist routes provide forks, the tastiest and most interesting food is off the beaten path—on the street, up the hill, sold from sidewalk stands and noodle stalls. Most of these places use community chopsticks, simply stuck in a large glass of water to soak between customers.

—Paula McDonald,
"South China Sea Journal"

ing) disturbed the atmosphere of prosperous calm. Moreover, the Yat Chau is one of the few places outside mainland China where one can eat these traditional Chinese medicinal recipes. The owner, Mr. Chong Wing-King (also known as "The King of American Ginseng Pills"), has modelled it on the Herbal Restaurant at Yao-Hsien in the Chengdu province of central western China—a part of the world so hard to get at that it will almost certainly never offer any competition.

Given these exceptional circumstances, I felt I should try this once-in-a-lifetime experience. At last I hit upon something reasonably sane-looking: Spring Chicken with Sea Dragon and Sea Horse (a soup to "supplement the vital energy and replenish the vital essence; and to cure frequent urination and scrofula due to an accumulation of phlegm," as the menu informed me). I followed this up with Duck With Cloves ("To warm the spleen and stomach"), Fried Chicken Slices with Ginseng ("To strongly reinforce the vital energy and good for those suffering from general debility, fatigue, and amnesia") and Fried Rice With Wolfberry Fruits ("For the treatment of dizziness, vertigo, and weakness in the lower back and knees"). When the food arrived, however, I found that it was not so straightforward. For a start, I had made the mistake of imagining that the Sea Horse named as an ingredient in my soup would be some kind of vegetable or weed (as would the Sea Dragon). But as I stirred the contents of my bowl, what should I find, curled up, grey and very dead at the bottom, but a sea horse— and quite a large one at that. There was something about it which was both pathetic and revolting, and, despite the good it might have done my scrofula, at that point I had to quit the soup.

> *Nothing is allowed to go to waste in a Chinese kitchen, and no animal is forbidden. It is said that any creature that shows its back to heavens is acceptable to a Cantonese cook.*
>
> —JO'R, LH, and SO'R

The duck with cloves, on the other hand, was every bit as tasty as its name suggested. Until, that is, I dug into the unfamiliar, cold, transparent mass on which it lay. It looked like gelatine and was tough and faintly salty. I asked my interpreter what it could be, but for once she was lost for the right word. "Sea product," she ventured. "Jellyfish?" I suggested. "Ah yes! Jellyfish! That's right!" she cried and helped herself to some more, while I concentrated hard on the table cloth.

You have to remember that even at the Yat Chau, there is a vein of common sense running through the dishes, which would appeal to the most timid Western gastronome. Chinese culinary practice argues that moderation is important; that a balanced diet, bingeing neither on hot meats and spices, nor boiled vegetables and soft drinks, is the correct way; and it stresses the use of fresh ingredients, as well as the dried and processed variety with which the Chinese seem besotted. The problem is that the end product can be completely bizarre—whether you go to the extremes of the Yat Chau, or whether you try something a little simpler.

There are, for instance, fruit-juice stalls around Hong Kong offering health-improving restorative fruit drinks. These look all right on paper, but can taste revolting in practice. One such place offered me Carrot, Green Turnip, and Ginger Drink (good for cleansing the skin); Lettuce Flavor Cordial (for constipation, hair loss, and nervous disorders); and a mixture of Carrot, Cucumber, and Sprouts (good for vitality). None of these tasted anything less than unspeakable. The great thing at Yat Chau restaurant is to be nerveless enough to eat those ingredients which you can identify (sea horse, jellyfish, gecko) and incurious enough not to bother about those which the menu lists but are utterly unfamiliar (astraglus root, poria, Chuanxiong rhizome, and something called tremella). If you can manage this, then there is no question that a meal there does give you a lift.

By the time I had polished off the last piece of ginseng and drained my glass of tea, I felt ready for anything, my excessive yin comprehensively banished by my yang meal. Then again, I may be misinterpreting my own feelings. It is quite likely that what I was experiencing was not inner physical regeneration, but simple relief at not having to tackle the dried oviduct fat of frog.

Charles Jennings's work has appeared in a variety of publications.

✳

In the good old days, said the locals, one could usually buy such delicacies as monkeys but now the more exotic species have to be specially ordered. It is an animal rights activist's nightmare. A Hong Kong television station set out to film an exposé about the smuggling of rare animals from Guangdong to the banquet tables of the colony. The journalistic tables were rather abruptly turned when it was revealed that, once the Western reporter was out of sight, the Hong Kong Chinese television crew had themselves cooked and wolfed down the rare species they had just filmed.

—Teresa Poole, "Out of China," *The Independent*

ALISON DAKOTA GEE

* * *

On the Offensive

An Asian-American woman takes on the Chinese male chauvinist pig.

I CAME TO HONG KONG TO GET AWAY FROM CHINESE PEOPLE. IT might seem a tad illogical now, but at the time such reasoning made perfect sense. Aside from escaping my parents, I was also seeking refuge from an all-too-perfect life with an appallingly perfect American-born Chinese boyfriend. Of course, there was a plethora of other Chinese who were also getting under my skin, those PC ABCS—hopelessly earnest, politically correct members of the cultural tribe—who attempted to force bonding again and again over the same three issues: Amy Tan's *The Joy Luck Club*, Connie Chung, and the lack of decent Sichuan restaurants on L.A.'s west side.

I suspect my siblings had the same idea—my sister is now unearthing dinosaur bones in Scandinavia, my elder brother throwing ceramic pots in northern Mexico, and my younger brother arguing court cases for Elvis look-alikes in Nashville, Tennessee—except they made the slightly more intelligent choice of a destination *outside* Asia.

Still, I suppose I was not without my own brand of logic. My reasoning was that in coming to Hong Kong I would not be conspicuously Chinese to most of the population. In fact, to most people here, I would not be Chinese at all, but a strange breed of pod person who had appropriated one of their comrade's bodies. Fine with me. At least I wouldn't have to bond over Amy Tan with anyone any more.

None of us *needs* to bond over Amy Tan any more. Because in Hong Kong, we have myriad icons to bond over. There's television's out-to-lunch bunch of Nonie and Wu Man (otherwise known as David Wu), Jade, and Valerie. But more importantly, we can bond over presenter and columnist Gloria Wu—or *against* Wu as the present case seems to be. Her recent literary odyssey, "East is East and Pest is Pest: Travels and travails of the single girl in Asia," has been prompting cries of "NUKE GLORIA!" from bachelor flats lining Caine Road, from Tom Turk's near the free weights, and from Graffiti's party room on a Saturday night.

The outcry is coming from Asian men feeling betrayed by the fact that Wu has taken it upon her ABC self to expose every damning generalisation about Asian male culture to an island full of white men looking to justify their "I am the saviour from the West" mentality.

Wu laments that it's kinda tough being an Asian babe travelling alone through the patriarchal jungle that is Asia. After divulging that a Japanese man offered to buy her used panties "to smell," she goes on to dismiss all Korean men as "highly educated mamas' boys with big tempers," Chinese males as "men who slurp their soup so loudly people get up to dance," and Taiwanese men as getting their jollies from "peeking at a woman's underwear when her legs are uncrossed." As for men in Singapore, "no real men live in this country."

The six-page feature left men of Asian descent reeling many times over. Because alongside Wu's story (which I'll admit to having found amusing at moments), her Canadian counterpart Carol Hui attempted the

"But I am not sic leung." The expression caught my attention for some reason.

"What does the expression mean, Mr. Chan? If you don't mind my asking."

"It is Chinese for a dirty man. A colour wolf."

—Dr. George Adams, *The Great Hong Kong Sex Novel*

placatory offering: "One cheer for the Asian sexist." Hui concedes that if she "were a prostitute, she would much prefer the drunken Asian slob who passes out within two minutes to the conceited (Western) guilt-tripper who wants to share his most personal thoughts before proving his virility." Uh, are we losing our hearing or did we miss that advertised cheer?

"I'll tell you this much," said an inflamed Asian male acquaintance of mine, "I wouldn't buy either one of their panties."

I'm staying out of this one.

Revenge of the pod person was mine the other day—or so I thought. After standing on Robinson Road, frantically waving at blurred taxis for 25 minutes, an empty mobile finally pulled up and the autodoor popped open. I said a quick *m'goy* to the gods, settled into the seat and said in the best faux Cantonese I could muster: "*M'Goy, Jut Ye Chong, Nam Wah Jo Po.*" Quarry Bay, South China Morning Post, thank you very much.

"*Mut yeh?*" he cried, cupping his hand to his ear, which incidentally had an impressive collection of white and grey hairs jutting from it. I repeated myself, taking care to intonate and enunciate as best I could. "*Mut yeh?!!!*" he cried again, this time turning around to expose the throbbing veins in his head. He then started to scream in Cantonese, "If you are going to ride in my car then you better start speaking Chinese," to which I replied in English, "Look, you dying piece of wood, I'm not leaving your taxi just because you're having a bad ear-hair day. So you better start driving towards *Jut Ye Chong*"—I shouted that part in Cantonese—"and now."

It worked. He muttered under his breath and wheeled on to the highway. I was smugly sinking back into the seat when I noticed him glancing back in the mirror at me. At first, I thought he was just checking out the pod person in his back seat, but then I noticed his glances corresponded with a violent shaking of the taxi. We were accelerating on the freeway past Wan Chai at this point, when he glanced at me again. Only this time, his eyes were not filled with cultural disgust but with fear. The car began to shake violently and the next thing I knew, the dashboard charms were flying everywhere. The tissue box on the back shelf flew like a projectile through the car. And I was thrown onto the floor.

When I finally climbed back on to the seat, I realized the car had come to a halt in the middle of the freeway, which might have been due to the fact that its rear wheels had sheared off and rolled into the other lanes.

It seemed an elaborate scheme for the old coot to get up to, just to eject me from his car. But then again, should I expect anything less from a patriarchal Asian man? I should have offered to sell him my panties.

Alison Dakota Gee is a writer who divides her time between Hong Kong and Los Angeles. Her work has appeared in the Sunday Morning Post *and other publications.*

✳

Fired in the terrible crucible of Chinese social custom, the Chinese woman has in the past either crumbled into submission or, more often, melted without but hardened within. Docile, demure, modestly silent, and deferential as a guest accompanying her husband to the houses of others, she knew how to use every weapon she could lay hands on in order to remain mistress in her own home. If her husband was infatuated with her, she might sell her favors dearly for greater powers. If he was a fool, she would start keeping his accounts, then advise, then manage him. The best marriages are still run on the principle that the home of a Chinese is not his castle but his wife's fortress.

—Dennis Bloodworth, The Chinese Looking Glass

EDWARD A. GARGAN

✶ ✶ ✶

Shadow of the Manchus

Discrimination against women is eroding in the New Territories.

AWAY FROM THE MIRRORED CANYONS OF HONG KONG'S FINANCIAL district, across the Tai Lam hills that spill toward the Chinese border, women in broad-brimmed rattan hats tend fields of watercress rippling in the early spring breezes.

New houses in pastels of pink and peach edge the fields, circling and intruding along the paths that lace together Ma Tin village. Older brick houses with tiled, upswept roofs are giving way rapidly to the two- and three-story blocky, air-conditioned, antennaed homes that bespeak affluence and modernity.

But in Ma Tin, and in some 650 other villages sprinkled across the New Territories, the legacy that is slowly eroding is not one of British colonialism but of the Qing dynasty, the Manchu era that collapsed in 1911 but whose historic tendrils snake into the lives of 700,000 villagers.

"It is very common that women have no rights in the villages," Cheng Lai-sheung said in the local Cantonese dialect as she massaged a patient's ankle at her small acupuncture clinic. "You're not supposed to speak out because it's against filial piety and tradition. That's the way it's been since the Qing dynasty."

Indeed, even before. Law and custom from the Qing dynasty, a period of rule by Manchu invaders that endured from 1644 to

1911, derived in great measure from earlier Chinese dynasties. As the colony's British rulers continued to consolidate their control over Hong Kong Island and nearby territories in the mid- to late-1800s, Britain agreed that Qing law, and not British colonial law, would have force in the New Territories, a region that earlier in this century was little more than a scattering of farming villages.

Over the last few weeks, elections for village heads were held in the Territories, and in many villages women were not allowed to vote. In some, husbands voted for wives, and in others male relatives cast votes for widows, a tradition that has endured since the Qing dynasty.

But now this legacy is perhaps the last tangible remnant of China's dynastic history, after the British gradually introduced notions of Western liberal law in Hong Kong throughout this century. Last year, after a vigorous and not infrequently vicious debate, another Qing legacy was legislated out of existence: the practice of denying women in the New Territories inheritance rights.

A campaign for this change was largely provoked in 1991, when Ms. Cheng's parents died. Her brothers, who no longer lived in the village, decided to sell the family's home, although Ms. Cheng lived there and wanted to keep the house. But the brothers sold it anyway and the new owners occupied the first two floors. Ms. Cheng remained on the top floor. "I refused to budge," she said.

After two years of harassment intended to get her to leave, she began writing to the Government and legislators. "I wanted them to rescind the old law from the Qing dynasty saying women can't inherit anything," said Ms. Cheng, who is 43.

One legislator was Christine Loh Kung-wai, a former commodities trader for Salomon Brothers who in 1991 was appointed to the Hong Kong Legislative Council.

"Under Qing law," said Ms. Loh, who studied law before plunging into her twelve-year career as a trader, "even if your parents want to give you something after they died, they could not if you are a female."

So last year, Ms. Loh and her colleagues began the process of overriding Qing law with a new inheritance law, one identical to that in force in the rest of Hong Kong. Her effort stirred a wild-fire of protest from the male villagers, from the village heads and even from some members of the Legislature.

"Male villagers said I was destroying their culture," Ms. Loh said. "They said they were going to rape me, beat me."

The law was changed in the summer of 1994, but women like Ms. Cheng, who finally moved out of the house late that year, continued to press for changes that would extend equal protection in all facets of life, particularly in the village elections.

"Village elders don't do much," Ms. Cheng said.

Many village leaders are unhappy about the crumbling of tradition. Liu Kam-choi, the head of Sheung Shui Wai village, explained his view to a local reporter: "We welcome women to vote, but they are not interested. They trust us. It doesn't matter to them who wins."

Away from Ma Tin village, in Hong Kong's commercial district, Ms. Loh vowed that the law would be changed, that the last vestiges of Manchu domination, long since eradicated in China, would be erased from Hong Kong as well. Indeed even after China resumes sovereignty over Hong Kong, she said, laws made now will most likely be preserved and village elders should face that fact.

"There are still villages not prepared to give women the right to vote," she said. "One has no choice. We will change the law."

Edward A. Gargan holds several degrees in Chinese history from the University of Wisconsin. He has worked for The New York Times *in the United States, Africa, and China. He is a former Edward R. Murrow Fellow of the Council on Foreign Relations.*

★

But it was not, inside or outside the family, an egalitarian society. A Chinese proverb says: "Even your own ten fingers are uneven." The Chinese never entertained the manifestly absurd proposition that all men are equal, but only that they are born much the same. Otherwise they believe in the harmony of differences—not differences of inherited class but of rank and position, properly observed. "Heaven placed the people below, and gave them rulers and teachers," said Confucius—and heaven's object in doing so had been to destroy the concept of equality, for equality could only lead to anarchy and chaos. But if all men were not equal, they were still human. During centuries of neglect and oppression in which soldiers with long whips brutally lashed the streets clean of half-starved peasants before the four-man palanquin of this and that fastidious, overfed Mandarin, there has also grown up an on-parade-on-parade off-parade-off-parade tradition whereby the proprieties must be observed between those of different rank, but their private relationship may still be founded upon the vulgar proposition that no man has more than two testicles.

—Dennis Bloodworth, *The Chinese Looking Glass*

FRANK VIVIANO

✦ ✦ ✦

The Bones of Saint Francis

The remnants of a saint give rise to thoughts on the remnants
of Empire—and why Macao is so different from Hong Kong.

HE WOULD NEVER GO BACK TO LISBON. THAT WAS THE THING Mañuel Teixeira was insistent about, so insistent that his face would flush and redden in anger at the mere thought. In the 64 years since he had arrived in the Orient, a teenage novitiate awestruck with wonder, he had made the return trip just once, in time to see his mother again before she died. But no more. They couldn't make him leave Macao, and he would never do it voluntarily.

There was no phone number listed for the old seminary that opened onto a cobbled courtyard above the Praia Grande. The Church didn't provide much of a budget anymore, and a telephone must have seemed an unnecessary expense for a building that had just a single resident left in its labyrinth of peeling rooms. I'd hiked up the hillside stairway to São José half a dozen times before the housekeeper said yes, Father was in now, and he came gliding down the hall in his white cassock.

Teixeira gave me a start, that first time I met him in 1986. He was the very picture of Matteo Ricci, with the same waist-length gray beard and hawkish nose, the piercing eyes that look out from the great Jesuit missionary's 16th-century portraits. It was hard not to stare. Standing in the hallway of the seminary, with its creaky wooden floors and its shelves of books and letters documenting Rome's 500-year effort to convert China, he was the composite ghost of Ricci and Francis Xavier and the legions of others who had followed them east. To meet Mañuel Teixeira, the last Portuguese priest in the last (and first) European colony in China, was to commune with half a millennium of heroic but futile history on the very eve of its disappearance into dusty archives like the ones that lined his solitary retreat on the hill.

Francis Xavier, patron saint of Catholic foreign missions, was born in Spain in 1506 to noble parents. After teaching in Paris, he joined St. Ignatius Loyola and four other young men in founding the Jesuit order (Society of Jesus). He was ordained in Venice, went to India to preach and convert, and in 1549 sailed for Japan. A few years later, bound for China, he took ill and died in December, 1552.

—JO'R, LH, and SO'R

The Chinese, for the most part, had already forgotten that history, excised it from public memory. In Shanghai and Beijing and Hunan and Sichuan, where the missionaries had dug deep roots, the Christian legacy included dozens of institutions—churches and seminaries, colleges and orphanages, gymnasiums and hospitals. Without exception, their names had been changed and their commitments recast after the Communist Revolution. People over 65 could still dredge up the details, still tell you that the Number Three Elementary School down the road had been called Sacred Heart before 1949. But they were dying off.

That was Teixeira's vocation now: confronting mortality, battling the feebleness of memory. When I met him, the old priest had written more than a hundred books and pamphlets on that long, failed mission in the East. They were books of minute historical reconstruction, books that captured the China coast of the 16th and 17th centuries in exacting, detailed brush strokes.

He would die here, writing still. He was sure of that.

"They will never make me leave," he said again, speaking with a peculiar accent that added soft Portuguese vowels to the ends of

English nouns and rose and fell in a cadence borrowed from Cantonese.

"The Red Guards could not make me leave when the other priests went back to Europe in 1968 and 1969. They all tried, my son, even my superiors in Rome tried to convince me then that it was for the best..."

Thousands of Red Guards had stormed across the border into the colony during the Cultural Revolution, ending any lingering illusion that Lisbon could, or would, defend Macao if China wanted to take it over. The Church had ordered non-Chinese priests to leave afterward. Teixeira regarded the order as a betrayal of his mission and refused point-blank. He still spoke of it as a wound unhealed.

The two great Jesuit predecessors of Teixeira had never gone back to Europe either. Matteo Ricci, for whom Macao was but a preliminary staging ground in a lifelong effort to penetrate the inner sanctum of Chinese civilization, eventually succeeded in his task and became more Chinese than Italian, a valued official in the closed circle around the Ming emperor. There was little recollection of him on the streets off the Praia Grande, save for Teixeira's books and the occasional image of a curiously full-bearded Mandarin on some Chinese artifact in a back-alley antique shop.

A more substantial relic remained of Francis Xavier, who died on an island in the South China Sea just a few miles from the colony: a bone of his arm, the humerus to be precise. Ensconced in a chest, it sat in a small pastel church on the Macanese island of Colôane, next to the remains of a group of martyred 16th-century Japanese Catholics. The rest of Saint Francis was, in varying amounts, to be found in the Indian state of Goa, in Nagasaki, and in Rome, with alleged bone splinters and locks of hair scattered across the Spice Islands and in an ancient half-abandoned Portuguese village below Malacca where children still greeted visitors with *"bom dia"* 300 years after the Portuguese had technically surrendered their outpost on the Malay Peninsula.

Go back? Lost in his reveries on Ricci and Macao and China, sifting through the annals of all the places where Francis Xavier lay scattered, Mañuel Teixeira simply couldn't conceive of a life for himself, after so many years, in contemporary Europe.

"The world I was born to doesn't exist any longer, you see, and I don't know what I would do with myself in the one that replaced it."

Instead, surrounded by the annals of his faith, by its accumulated manuscripts and letters, the last occupant of the Seminary of São José spent his days reconstructing an even earlier world than the Lisbon of his birth.

Teixeira held court on the terrace of the Bela Vista Hotel. The manager, young Pinto-Marques, supplied him with glasses of chilled *vinho verde* and plates of olives or salt cod fritters. There wasn't a *taverna* in the colony that didn't see it as a religious duty to host the last resident of São José. But the old priest's heart was in the Bela Vista, which was the grand hotel of his youth and retained, in its advanced years, a cranky charm much like his own.

He was a boisterous conversationalist, ready to disagree with virtually any proposition, no matter how logical, just for the

Imagine the challenge of the 19th-century Christian missionaries to China and Hong Kong. Not only were the foreigners objects of suspicion but they were also confronted by a plethora of confused and conflicting ideas. In those early days, there was no motor transport, no refrigeration, no antibiotics. Disease was endemic, plague a seasonal occurrence. Bandits roamed and civil unrest flared at frequent intervals. The missionary and his colleagues were isolated with their little band of followers in whichever town or village they preached. If they fell sick, they were more than two months' sea voyage from their European homeland.

Today, prominent Christian monuments—cathedrals, churches, schools, and hospitals—stand witness to the success of brave priests of all denominations who withstood such perils to convert the locals to the faith.

—Hilary Binks, "For the Love of God," *Another Hong Kong: An Explorer's Guide*

sake of argument. People who wouldn't argue, who were unduly respectful, plainly disappointed and bored Mañual Teixeira. He also had a spot in his heart for pretty girls, and a way of putting them at ease with Old World courtesies in Cantonese or Portuguese or English or French, so that they were pleased rather than shocked when he leapt to his feet and embraced them with a warmth that sometimes exceeded decorum.

> *Macau's name comes from a legend involving Chinese goddess A-Ma, who, it was said, becalmed a raging sea to save a group of frightened sailors, taking them ashore at the ancient port of Hoi-Keang. Centuries later, when the Portuguese came to this peninsular port, they were told the village was known as A-Ma-Gao (Bay of A-Ma). The name evolved into Macau.*
>
> —Carolyn J. Yarbrough, "The Magic of Macau," *Tours & Resorts*

Down below, the great muddy bay separating the peninsula from Taipa Island was always aswarm with a cloud of dragon-sailed junks and sampans, pierced at fifteen-minute intervals by the sharp white spray of a Hong Kong jet foil cutting through the Pearl Estuary toward the casinos.

The Bela Vista was painted a relatively fresh pastel green, reflecting the Pinto-Marques family's latest—and as it proved, final—attempt at staving off their own departure into the musty oblivion of Macao's history. Three aging Chinese sisters owned the hotel then, and had for as long as anyone but Teixeira could remember. Draped in an intentional obscurity so unremitting that it gave them a certain air of mystery, they never came to the Bela Vista themselves, leaving its management to Pinto-Marques, the Macanese whose family had been its majordomos since the 1920s or maybe before.

"Even I cannot be certain when their tenure began," Teixeira admitted.

For his part, Pinto-Marques turned over the daily operational duties to a sullen elderly Chinese accountant, who invariably miscalculated the room bills and ran a small side business marketing Father Teixeira's more accessible monographs to tourists and reporters.

The best rooms were spread along the southeast side of the hotel and were equipped with small enclosed terraces that produced the sensation of being suspended in space over the weed-choked cliff, where an English sea captain had erected the rambling neoclassical structure as his private mansion in the early 19th century. It was the perfect place to write for anyone who preferred idiosyncrasy to strong air-conditioning, and I had developed a habit of taking up residence in the Bela Vista for a week or so whenever I was faced with knocking out a long magazine piece or newspaper series. There are a decade's worth of photos of me on these balconies, snapped roughly every two years, working at an Olivetti portable against a backdrop of the bay and a ridge line of jagged Guangdong hills.

But that's the past now. The Mandarin Group, a corporate hotel giant over in Hong Kong, bought the Bela Vista from the mysterious sisters in 1990 and renovated it, bringing it up to international standards. The Macanese, who had seen 500 years of modernization projects founder in their little backwater, were dubious.

The Macanese: they too didn't want to leave, for many of the same reasons as Father Teixeira, but intensified by their

> *He had been going to the Bela Vista for nigh on 30 years. He remembered the old days with fondness. "It was a really rundown, ramshackle old place," he started. "It was like Queen Victoria, an old queen o' the seas sittin' up there...an' they had that big, beautiful tree down in the courtyard, they used to put the band over here, an' dancing in the courtyard, coloured lights all around...."*
>
> He remembered the balls as wells (he had been to them all), especially the one before renovation when all the beautiful people had come over from Hong Kong and danced all night and scribbled their names on the walls to leave their mark. "Ay, they were grand times," he said wistfully. "But there'll be good times for other people again, won't there?" The nostalgia in his voice was tempered with marvel at the way a mere hotel could shed so many years at the flick of a designer's pen while its guests are rooted in their mortality.
> —Joel Forrester, "A Legend Lives On," *Mandarin Oriental*

five centuries of generating the very memories he was determined to preserve. In their tiny three-square-mile enclave on the periphery of the immense Middle Kingdom, their ancestors had literally given birth to the European dream of an East Asian empire. The dream was usurped by the Dutch and then the English and the French, who sailed east long after Macao was founded in 1557—usually with Portuguese pilots to guide them and Portuguese interpreters to translate for them—and soon brought to bear an industrial power that Portugal—which with a population of just over one million then ostensibly ruled half the known globe—could never muster.

But the Macanese were still here. The Dutch burghers were gone from their Batavia, now Jakarta; the French *colons* were no longer sipping *pastis* on the Rue Catinat in Saigon, now Dong Khoi, the Street of the People's Revolution in Ho Chi Minh City; and the British *tuans* had been ousted from their verandas in North Borneo, now the Malaysian state of Sabah. But Macao was still Macao.

That was the great difference, or rather, the fruit of a great difference symbolized by the Macanese themselves. They belonged in Asia, in ways that the Dutch, French, and British never did.

The Portuguese had always been too few in number to be rulers in any convincing sense, which left them only one resort, and they abandoned themselves to it. In Macao and Ambon and Flores, in Malacca and Ceylon and Brazil, in Timor and Mozambique and Angola, in the Cape Verdes and Goa, the Portuguese mixed. They married. They spawned. They became history's great enthusiastic miscegenators, going native with such alacrity that surnames like Silva and Nuñes and Perreira are nearly as common today in parts of the Orient as Chang and Lee and far, far more common than Smith or Vandeberg or Martinière.

To a degree that must have shocked the minions of Paris, London, and Amsterdam, their fellow imperialists from Lisbon abandoned their identity as Europeans to immerse themselves in new, synthetic cultures of astonishing richness and fertility. The *colons* and the planters of Malaya were Frenchmen and Britons, transposed through brute force to French imperial Indochina and the rubber plantations on the South China Sea. They were the legates of conquest. The Silvas and the Perreiras of Macao and Malacca, with their almond eyes, sharp Iberian noses, tawny complexions, and curly hair, represented something else—not so much conquest as conjunction. A wild, startling, and often quite beautiful mélange.

The marriage was sculpted into the faces on the Praia Grande. But it was also evident in food and religion, language and art. Indeed, almost everywhere you turned in East Asia, the synthesis spawned by Portugal had become inextricable from the idiom of popular life. The Cantonese called the incense they burned in Buddhist temples *joss*, a word borrowed directly from the Portuguese *deus,* for "gods."

The Japanese, who had no indigenous word for "thank you," adopted the Portuguese *obrigado*, rendering it as *arigato*. The Javanese and Malays picked up hundreds of Portuguese terms and made them their own: *armada* for "fleet," *roda* for "wheel," *tempo* for "time," *bola* for "ball."

The two-story, balconied shops that lined Asian main streets from the mouth of the Yangtze to the Indonesian Archipelago were of a recognizably Portuguese design. In the Straits Settlements of Penang, Malacca, and Singapore, Chinese merchants covered the façades of their houses with Portuguese flowered tiles and protected their roofs with red terra-cotta in the fashion of the Portuguese Algarve.

The Portuguese carried the chili pepper from Brazil to Thailand and Sichuan. They taught the Tamils to mix the chilies with vinegar and garlic in *vindaloo*, which is based on the Portuguese expression *vinho e alho*, "wine and garlic." They introduced deep-fat frying to Japan, where it took on a Portuguese name, *tempero*, used for a dish that now passes as the most characteristically Japanese item in Japanese cooking.

None of these phenomena, in its Asian setting, was Portuguese alone. They were all part of the conjunction, the marriage, that produced the Macanese and their far-flung cousins. They bespoke a sensibility, and a sensuality, that was a universe apart from what Paris and London and Amsterdam wrought in their empires. A sensibility that could be read in the stubborn will of Mañuel Teixeira, who refused, categorically, to live in Europe.

Mario Lim, a machine parts salesman, had tried. "In 1984 my wife and I put the kids into a Portuguese-language school, and she broke the news to her parents: we were leaving. Then I went on alone, to get things started. But fifteen months later I was in Macao again. My wife still hasn't set foot in Lisbon."

The problem wasn't money. In fact, the little garment factory he set up near the Portuguese capital showed promise very quickly.

"The wages, you know, are actually lower there than they are here. And they work hard, the Portuguese."

We shared a cabin on the overnight ferry from Canton, a flat-bottomed riverboat that floated slowly down the Pearl with the ebb tide and sidled into a wharf at the foot of Avenida Almeida Ribeiro as morning broke over the estuary.

There were four of us in the cabin, scofflaws to a man: I was a journalist traveling on a fraudulent tourist visa; Mario was returning from a trip to Hunan peddling German-made drill bits that were ostensibly banned by Chinese import restrictions. Our bunk mates were a Taiwanese toy manufacturer whose plant in Guangdong was technically prohibited by Taipei, and a cynical ceramics salesman from Shanghai whose night of drinking and unauthorized conversation with a Taiwanese and an American reporter were anathema in the eyes of Beijing.

But official eyes tended to blink in the heyday of China's business frenzy. It was an open secret in Asia that the biggest new factories in the communist People's Republic were financed by the enemy capitalists of Taiwan; that a reporter could get a tourist visa in three hours in Hong Kong or Macao instead of the six months required by the Chinese embassy in Washington for a press pass; that the published Chinese import restrictions were the best possible way of identifying the products that were actually being imported.

The cabin talk was politics. Not long ago the future of Macao had been penned into a contract between Lisbon and Beijing. December 20, 1999, the date when China would reassume control of the colony, loomed—like Karl Marx's proverbial specter—over every conversation. So it soon came out, as we talked, that Mario had once sold everything he owned and gone off to start a new life in Portugal, only to return after fifteen months.

The Shanghainese knew the vagaries of his own country all too well—how the blinking eyes of officialdom could suddenly become fixed, and with what devastating consequences. He scarcely dreamed of such an opportunity for escape, and couldn't imagine why anyone would pass it up.

"And now," he asked, incredulous, "do you feel you've made a mistake?"

It was the wrong question. Posed strictly in political terms, Mario admitted that he couldn't explain his return to Asia. It made no sense.

"I tried to live in Europe. It didn't work out."

He left it at that.

Mario Lim was not a Macanese Creole by blood, not in any genetically measurable way, even if there was some long-forgotten sailor from Oporto or the Azores among the ancestral gods whose shrine occupied the entrance hall of the concrete house on Taipa Island where he took me to meet his wife. Mario was Cantonese; at least 90 percent of the people in Macao were.

Statistically, Macao was as Chinese as Hong Kong. That fact and shared circumstantial details like a European colonial past and a Chinese contractual future—1999 here, 1997 there—made it convenient to lump the two places together. Guidebooks and magazine articles often presented Macao as a kind of down-market annex to Hong Kong.

But beyond the confines of its tacky casinos, its dog track, and a few international hotels on the waterfront, Macao wasn't Hong Kong, even writ small. And the Cantonese here were nothing like their cousins across the estuary. As much as the first Portuguese colonizers and their mixed-blood offspring, they had been altered, transformed by the temper of the place.

On Taipa, one of the two tiny offshore islands that made up Macao's rural hinterland (the other was Colôane, the last resting place of Francis Xavier's humerus) the differences were vivid. Along the village main street where the Lims lived, Chinese family life had blended almost imperceptibly into its Medi-

terranean equivalent. Shop houses and ancestral halls were jumbled
side by side with whitewashed cottages and churches.
At night everyone was in the street, Chinese and Portuguese
and Creole, their children's endless game of tag dodging through
a tangle of chairs and card tables brought out into the warm
evening air, where the sweet smell of Cantonese roast duck
was folded into the salty codfish steam rising from pots of
poached *bacalao.*

At Pinocchio's, the Macanese *taverna* at the end of the main
street, you knew who was from Hong Kong and who was from
Macao by the pace of the meal. The visitors gulped down their
chili prawns and grilled sardines, called for the bill, and headed
back to the casinos in half an hour. The Macao Chinese spent
entire languorous afternoons dawdling over one course, then
another, slipping into a doze that nobody cared to shake off as the
vinho verde took hold.

Across the big arched bridge that connected Taipa to the city,
urban Macao looked, from a distance, like the spin-off of Hong
Kong the travel literature alleged it to be. At night it was a row of
high rises flashing the same lurid neon welcome over the estuary
that was mirrored in Victoria Harbour. But even in the central
city, the differences between Macao and Hong Kong were far
more evident than the similarities. The high rises were a thin
façade of modern sheen behind which the Macao of Matteo Ricci
and Francis Xavier lived on in a tangle of dimly lit alleys and
courtyards that snoozed, like the Pinocchio's diners, in a haze of
wine and insouciance and the dusty clutter of the past. Hong
Kong, by contrast, had no history, no past, only a fealty to the
wrecking ball. You could hardly find a twenty-year-old building in
Hong Kong, much less a quiet 16th-century square or a ramshackle seminary inhabited by a single old eccentric.

Most of Macao's people were of the very same stock as the
Cantonese who made Hong Kong one of the world's most electric, most frantic, cities. But they were also of the same, unhurried
race that the Portuguese themselves had become as they drifted
through their long, sleepy Asian sojourn.

It was doubly ironic. In Hong Kong, where the British made it virtually impossible for all but the wealthiest to acquire British citizenship, there was a nonstop accounting of the merits of emigration and overseas investment. A Hong Kong business executive could reckon, to the dollar, how much profit might be extracted from a base of operations in the borderless Mecca of the European Union. In Macao they understood all that. They understood that a home in Portugal meant the freedom to climb, if one wanted, to the prosperous pinnacles of Germany or France. And the Portuguese, unlike the British, were obliging. Macao-born Chinese were welcome to apply for Portuguese citizenship and were generally granted it.

They had a thousand reasons to pick up stakes and move to Europe. But like the Macanese, like Father Mañuel Teixeira and Matteo Ricci before him, they seldom acted on them. For reasons no anthropologist and certainly no economist had ever calculated, they were different from their cousins across the estuary in Hong Kong and up the Pearl River in China, whatever the blood said.

The Macao Chinese just weren't suited to leaving. Mario Lim had tried. It didn't work out.

Frank Viviano also contributed "City of the Main Chance" in Part I. Both stories were excerpted from his book, Dispatches from the Pacific Century.

✷

And alone of the non-Communists who deal with the Communist Chinese, the Portuguese are able to get along with them. When they want to strike a bargain with the mainlanders they send couriers a few days ahead explaining what they will want to talk about. Thus the Chinese, suspicious of the intentions of all Westerners, have time to think out their own positions and do not feel that something is being sprung on them. When negotiations start, the Portuguese never put their cards bluntly on the table but let points gradually emerge, if possible not until the Chinese bring up a subject; they never allow their adversaries to lose face, helping them out of any position in which they would be trapped. This is essential to satisfactory bargaining with the face-conscious Chinese.

Similarly, the Portuguese never base an argument on principles but on bargains; when they must refuse Chinese terms, they never say the offer is unfair and that they will stand on their rights. This is a silly argument to Oriental minds; they believe disagreements must be negotiated to a mutually profitable conclusion. Instead the Portuguese say they cannot accept an offer because by so doing they would destroy themselves. This is an objection that the Chinese immediately understand; it involves no contradictory and incomprehensible collision of ethics but the simple fact of self-preservation. An American believes a test of his strength of character is his willingness to fight for his rights even if he loses by doing so; a Chinese believes: "A man who cannot put up with a small wrong ends up with disaster."

—Dwight Cooke, *There is No Asia*

DAVID YEADON

✦ ✦ ✦

Way Out Among the Islands

A long walk in the hills leads to questions with no answers.

SOMEWHERE DEEP IN DREAMS COMES THE ECHO OF BELLS AND THE rumble of gongs—long booms followed by the chitter of cymbals and then silence; I wake up suddenly; I can see branches swaying outside my window. I'm lying on a wooden board covered by straw matting and my back aches. It's very dark and hot, mosquitoes are doing kamikaze imitations and I can't remember where I am.

Po Lin Monastery

Slowly the real world returns. Right—I'm a guest at the Buddhist monastery of *Po Lin* (Precious Lotus) on Lantau Island, way out in the bay west of Hong Kong, and it's 4:00 a.m., time for the first service of the day.

I light my candle in the cell-like room, dress quickly, and creep downstairs to the courtyard. The air is cool. A breeze rolls down from the dark hills, rattling leaves, and bringing scents of early morning. The richly painted walls of the main temple, brilliant crimsons and golds, are illuminated by strings of tiny lights. Inside I can see the serene profile of a 25-foot high Buddha flickering in the glow of tiny candles, and down the ornate stairway I peer directly into a smaller temple lit by more candles. Fifteen black-robed monks chant in a low, slow monotone, like an endless mantra that seems to ease its way across the cobbled courtyard, over the pagodas on the high terraces above the temple compound, up the empty hills, and out into the starry blackness.

Hong Kong seems a galaxy away. Yet, a mere twenty sea gull-skimming miles to the east was one of the earth's most frenetic cities, the money machine of Southeast Asia, the "get-ahead-or-you're-dead, eat-'em-up-and-spit'em-out" nexus of our little blue planet. If I'd looked I would have seen the glow over the black hills, but I preferred to be just where I was, and so I didn't look.

I had left that frantic whirligig behind three days ago, bidding farewell to its six million scurrying residents, its 20,000 exotic restaurants, its neon strips, endless open-air street markets and food stalls, and its huddled sampans, jammed shanty-town fashion in the typhoon basins. I'd jumped aboard a ferryboat and waved good-bye to the organ-pipe jumble of chrome and glass towers and moved out into the mists of the bay, heading for a few days of walking on Lantau.

This sparsely populated place is the largest of all the 235 outlying islands (even larger than Hong Kong island itself) but more than half of its 155 square miles has been designated as protected areas, many with lovely secluded beaches, and all linked by sinewy networks of footpaths.

First stop was tiny Peng Chau Island. Here the air was cool, and I began strolling the narrow, winding alleys that smelled of brine and noodles and drying fishnets.

"Hey mister, you wan' sampan?"

My ramblings were cut short.

"Sampan here now. You take."

I had ordered a boat for the crossing to Lantau so—farewell Peng Chau. An old Chinese gentleman, very wrinkled and bent, scampered up to me, grabbed my knapsack and scampered back to the pier.

"Sampan go. Quick, quick."

He pushed me off the dock into a tiny wooden contraption bobbing around like a cracked eggshell and into the arms of an Oriental beauty wearing a broad rattan hat tied under her chin with a purple scarf. She smiled and lowered her eyes in that demure way Oriental women have of sending your heart pounding. Then she sat gracefully, adjusted her hat, snapped the engine into life with a quick tug on an old rope, and we were off, roaring across the choppy narrows. The engine sounded like a swarm of very angry killer bees.

I gazed across an ocean dotted

Lantau Island is well worth the visit, if only to see Hong Kong from the back of a junk raising itself out of the sea like a distant mirage. Lantau Island is heavily wooded and even though it is actually larger than Hong Kong Island, it is inhabited by a mere 6,000 souls.

The largest seated bronze Buddha in the world is there on the Mok Yue Hill at Ngong Ping. Devoted Buddhist monks tend to the relics of the Buddha which reside in a stunning gold and crystal tabernacle. The massive bell is struck by a wooden gong at precise, computer driven intervals. The long steps leading to the base of the Buddha were too tempting for me not to run up, after a day of butt-cramping bus riding and listening to the tour guide who was a former English cook working on a stand-up comic act. I believe I hold the world record for running up the steps (one minute and twenty-seven seconds).

—Sean O'Reilly, "City of a Million Dreams"

with small wooded islands as far as the eye could see. Directly ahead were the high hills of Lantau, burly green peaks rising layer on layer—a real walker's island; touches of Scottish highlands tinged with Irish emerald green, floating in a Mediterranean-blue ocean.

I had decided to begin my hike from the northeast coast at the Trappist Haven monastery, and within minutes of leaving Peng Chau my charming captain bounced us up on the shore below the church, perched on a bluff. I clambered out unsteadily. She handed me my gear, smiled that smile again, and vanished in a swirl of spray.

For a few moments I was alone; big blue butterflies arabesqued for me in the early-morning air. Then a small truck appeared, banging and clattering down a steep track, driven by Buddha himself. He emerged in rather grubby white robes and stood, plump and beaming at me with a face I had seen a hundred times before in pictures and statues, a face of utter contentment and knowingness. But, like the girl in the boat, he had business to do and started unloading milk churns from the back of the truck. I remembered that the Trappist monks rear dairy cows here and are the main suppliers of Hong Kong's top hotels. I also remembered that Trappists don't talk. So, after he offered me a seat by sign language, we rode in silence up the ridiculously steep hill to the monastery where he vanished (after one last all-enveloping grin) into a cow barn.

There was no one around so I strolled over a foot bridge across a deep ravine and into the simple church. A list of resident monks was posted near the door with only twelve names on it. From an adjoining list of eight daily services, starting with Vigils at 3:15 a.m. and ending with Compline at 8:00 p.m., it appeared they must be very busy people.

The views back over the bay and the islands were breathtaking but unfortunately I had little breath to give as I made the long climb up from the monastery, through shoulder-high elephant grass, to the first line of green ridges. The morning seemed to be taking pernicious delight in getting hotter by the second. A yellow snake sinewed into the bushes leaving its ominous imprint on the dust. A single sea gull hovered above me, dropped a little souvenir (it missed), and soared off in the spirals, pretending to be an eagle.

At the top of the fourth ridge the whole of Silvermine Bay (Mui Wo) opened up with its arc of white sand and wooden sampans bobbing near the shore. Kids frolicked in the shallows, and I had such a strong urge to join them that the two-mile descent seemed to go very quickly, at least, until the last section, when I got lost in a mini-jungle of thornbushes all wrapped in sticky spiders' webs with dozens of black spiders the size of campaign medals.

I finally emerged from the sweaty tangle, flung boots and pack on the sand, strode straight into the surf, and promptly disappeared. (The disappearing bit was unintentional—I had walked off the end of a hidden rock ledge.)

The serious leg of my hike began on the hills behind the bay. Local folklore claims that the same Chinese clan (once notorious pirates) has occupied a strange walled village on the north coast of the island for over a thousand years. That seemed a good enough reason for visiting the place.

Finding the correct route from Silvermine Bay was not easy. I made at least four separate starts on different paths before an old man on a mule put me right and I began the long climb up the valley past huddled villages of stones and timber houses. Gradually the country became wilder. Soon there were no houses or people; a cool wind blew down the hills, which now resembled the moors of Yorkshire in their bleakness.

After six long miles I crossed the high watershed and I was looking forward to a spell of easier downhill walking. I paused for water in a hamlet of poor stone houses and could see the trail wriggling hundreds of feet down the slopes to the ocean far beyond. And there in the far distance was the village—a sinister black-walled fortress with massive towers at each corner. A young man sauntered up, dragging a pink piglet on a string, and I pointed out where I was going. He scowled and shook his head.

"No good. Is trouble there. No good to go." I showed him the route on my map. The path was clearly marked. "No. No way to go. No road. People very sick there. You go back now."

Then something very odd happened. The sky ahead suddenly began to darken rapidly and long gray tentacles of cloud trailed across an oily black ocean. I could see sheets of rain obliterating the outer islands, moving toward the cliffs of Lantau and the strange walled village far below us.

"You go back. Now."

I don't usually put much faith in omens and suchlike but somehow I knew that the young man was right, so I thanked him and set off fast on the long trail back down to Silvermine Bay.

As I half ran I could sense the huge clouds crowding behind me, rumbling over the ridges, growing larger and darker. I turned and the hills were already gone in mists. I knew the rain was really coming, pushing the winds over the low grasses, bending the scrub bushes. I tried to run faster but my legs felt like cement blocks. The gale was shrieking now, tearing at my clothes; the first fat drops were here, hitting the trail like quail eggs. And then it was on me, sudden cold dousings of water falling in solid shafts, pounding my head, and making the trail into an instant streambed—pure and wonderful chaos; the land and the elements rolling together in a primeval tag match with me as solo spectator, right in the middle of it all....

I continued running downhill and arrived at a lonely house with stone walls, a tin roof, and a big blue door, which was half open. An old man was peering out, watching the downpour. He saw me, laughed, and beckoned me inside (an unexpected gesture— islanders seem to relish their own privacy). I almost tumbled down the two steps into a tiny dark room filled with pretty little girls who scampered around pushing bundles into corners and piling up cushions on the wooden floor. When all the scurrying ceased, the girls became very shy and an old woman, who sat almost invisible in the far corner of the room, sent them off to make tea in the rear of the house.

I could see a raised platform bed shrouded by a mosquito net and partially hidden by a bamboo screen. The main room was simply furnished with a chest of drawers, a statue of Buddha in a small house-shrine lit by tiny candles, two bamboo chairs, and a chipped wooden table by the door. Light came from a hurricane lamp, which sent flickering shadows across the unpainted walls.

I was served a small bowl of perfumed tea, followed by a much larger bowl of thick noodles in broth with chunks of bok choy cabbage and two sweet buns. The six little girls all sat in a circle on the floor. When I smiled, they giggled; when I ate their lips moved with mine. No one spoke.

Much later, when the storm had passed, I got up to leave. I looked in my backpack for gifts but all I could find was a small flashlight and a box of TicTacs, which they accepted with embarrassment, then grace. The old man came with me to the door and when I turned back to wave, all the girls waved back and giggled in unison. Their lovely smiles kept me company all the way down the long (and now very muddy) path to Silvermine Bay and the comforts of a beachfront hotel room.

Next day, everything was bright and blue again and I discovered one of the most unusual villages I have ever seen on my travels.

I took a local bus along the coast road, past lovely Cheung Sha sands, over the pass by Kwun Yam Shan Mountain, and down to a bay of ancient salt pans in a bowl of green hills. Tai O village is a jumble of tiny fishing shacks perched on stilts alongside a narrow inlet that neatly divides the community in half. Linking both sides is a tiny rope-drawn sampan, which always seems full of locals, wobbling around in upright positions, as the odd little craft is hauled across.

The day I arrived all the fishing boats were decked out in brilliant-colored banners and streamers in preparation for the great Tin Hau festival in May that celebrates the favors bestowed on the fishermen by the goddess of the sea. "Dragon boats," long thin racing craft ornately carved and powered by eight oarsmen, skimmed up and down the inlet to the beat of drums and gongs. The ferry made hasty crossings between the impromptu races, but then got tangled up with the prow of a large fishing boat that was making a clumsy docking with a large catch of flapping fish.

And fish is really what this zany little place is all about. Scattered everywhere around the hundreds of lopsided shacks are ornate little temples, door shrines, and painted posters pleading to the gods for bountiful harvests of fish, shrimp, abalone, squid, and even shark, whose dried fins and tails sell for enormous sums in tiny stores along the winding bazaar. I watched one bargaining session in progress with a group of casually dressed merchants sitting in wicker chairs around a dozen shark appendages. The price was already at $3,000 (U.S.) and climbing! Some fish here are so valued for medicinal purposes that a single average-size specimen can sell for over $800 (U.S.).

The whole village was redolent with drying shrimp (Tai O is famous for the quality of its shrimp paste), conch, tuna, and dozens of other denizens of the deep hanging like stalactites from store awnings. Combine this with the sight of thin golden sheets of drying tofu, drying seaweed strips, mounds of silvered whitebait, and enticing aromas from seafood restaurants offering just about every imaginable kind of shellfish and huge sea bass you pick yourself from crowded window tanks—and Tai O is one of those special places that lingers in the mind and on the palate for years.

But Buddha must have known of my need for sensory and gustatory relief. By evening I found myself on a wheezy old bus being carried up impossible grades high into the hills again to spend some time at the Po Lin Monastery.

If Qu Yuan had possessed anything resembling a sense of destiny in his pious soul when he cast himself into the Milo River, the virtuous minister of state would no doubt today be a thoroughly contented man. For more than 2,000 years after committing suicide in protest against the decadence of the imperial court, his memory is still revered by tens of millions of Chinese both at home and abroad in the ritual of the Dragon Boats.

Every year tens of thousands of believers, their numbers swelled by countless tourists, gather to witness the battle for supremacy in the waters of Asia's most spectacular harbour.

What used to be a purely domestic contest involving boats from the local fishing communities has grown into two separate and entirely different occasions. The best-known and most publicized is the International Dragon Boat Races, which normally take place on a weekend in early summer.

—Lulu Yu, *Discovery*

As soon as I entered the imposing stone gates, I found a tranquil haven of peace where I remained for what seemed like a modest eternity, among the temples, statues, and shrines. I intended to climb Fung Wong Shan Mountain with the monks to watch the sunrise; I planned to have long and convoluted philosophical discussions with the two bearded travelers who had drifted in, but somehow the tranquillity of the place seemed to remove all desire for diversion.

Well—until the following day at least when I met a lanky man with a vast frazzle of sun-bleached hair—while piling my plate with all kinds of unusual vegetarian delights in the communal dining room. He had come unexpectedly to this quiet place a few days previously and had decided to stay awhile.

"I don't know what it was. Just a feeling that I was in the right place—like somewhere I'd been coming to for a hell of a long time."

The elderly Buddhist monk didn't speak, but grinned and held out a bottle of San Miguel beer.

Five minutes later, still smiling, he brought peaches served in Bugs Bunny plastic cups.

The Po Lin Monastery is a happy place, and exuberantly commercial. Shops selling everything from bracelets to incense line the front driveway, and the refectory does a brisk business in vegetarian meals.

Visitors can stay overnight at the monastery, where they pay for the pleasure of sleeping on wood boards.

—Cheryl Blackerby, "Hong Kong's Pastoral Neighbor," *The Palm Beach Post*

Mike was not one of your religious dabblers—collectors of spiritual shards of knowledge, scrapbooking through the options of Zen, Buddhism, Hinduism, and a dozen or so other more esoteric "isms." I met them all the time on my travels and was often charmed at first by their newfound enthusiasms, their guru-gushings and patinas of centered calmness. Then I'd discover after long conversations that they were invariably as confused and anxious to nail down their spirits as most of us are, to define the edges of experience too precisely, to snigger at the unenlightened with the selfish smugness of eager disciples willing away their souls to the newest—or nearest—guru.

Mike was 43. A tall, tough Aussie adventurer, sinewed with life-on-the-road experiences, etched with a thousand traveler's travails and brimming with tales that made my toes curl with envy.

And Mike had the spirit of a child.

Behind the hooded eyelids and bushy beard and leathery face was a baby sparkle, a hardly repressed joy in everything and everybody around him.

Our night-long dialogue in the tiny bedroom cell we shared (the monks believe in spatial economy even though we were the only overnighters at the temple) was as exciting as any in my journeys and adventures. We talked like kids—ideas rushing out of wild minds; new concepts whirling around us like confetti; truths tumbling over more truths in great piles of half-digested wisdoms....

Looking back I see he helped me realize there are special moments when you acknowledge one of the givens of real travel— a desire to leave worldly distractions and allow the child inside to emerge again, open-eyed, open-mouthed, goo-gooing at the mysteries and magic of places unknown. A sudden shining of utter innocence; a rebirthing in the midst of strangeness; a rediscovery of recesses in the brain untouched, unexplored. The salve of spiritual serendipity.

The brain is so full of fun and wonder. Back in the "swinging 60s," rare (and invariably double-edged) dabblings with hallucinogens such as LSD, and other "consciousness-expanders" left me in awe of the mind's amazing resources. We all possess an Aladdin's cave of terrors and truths, memories and repositories of knowledge we never, never even suspected we possessed. Whole filing cabinets of the stuff, libraries; a Pandora's box of power and perception that most of us leave well enough alone.

Blasting through the barrage of "no entry" mind signs, you enter realms of untold riches, touching the infinities of the human spirit, discovering the links that tie us all together like tiny molecules in some enormous entity too vast to comprehend and yet—there! A dim recollection of prebirth embryo states? A reaching back to the knowingness of the newborn babe (Wordsworth's "streams of immortality"?). A desire to build again a new, surer foundation, to bring back the deepest perceptions to the blinkered grind of daily life?

But after all the excitement of such explorations, then come the dangers—the tolls of trespass. The fear of too much truth, too much new "reality," junking the petty patterns of half-lived lives. The alarming consequences of totally changed perceptions. A wish for safe pragmatism versus the bright lights of new being. The fear of losing what you have known and trusted for so long; the fear of never ever finding your way back to the comfortable confines of consistency and discipline and order and the "measured tread" of your previous life. The fear of a whole new spectrum of options, choices, and possibilities—of unleashing too much of the child again to romp and play and build anew with new blocks of knowingness. Ah—there's the rub! What if it was all wrong: What if the accumulated guilts, sorrows, pains and pangs, beliefs and faiths of the years have only been barriers—even comforting prisons—against the vast possibilities of humanity and the harmonies of a far larger whole?

As I walk the commercial docks in Kowloon late on a Sunday afternoon, reading the names displayed on hulls of all shapes and sizes, I am struck by the fact that no barriers—except the barriers of time and tempest—separate the waters below me from Shanghai or Singapore, Bombay or Bordeaux, New York or San Francisco. This notion brings with it a tremendous sense of freedom, enough to fuel my imagination with thoughts of distant lands and exotic cultures, of adventures I will never know, of the vast expanses of open sea over which jet travelers pass in an instant. Rationality melts away as I invent plots for stories Joseph Conrad might have written, about treachery and turmoil on remote South Sea islands, about Polynesian navigators traveling from island to island in outrigger canoes, and about European explorers spending years of their lives in oceans they did not know, sometimes meeting untimely deaths before they could sail back into familiar waters.

—Morris Dye, "Reflections on Victoria Harbor," *San Francisco Examiner*

Would you want to dabble further? Would you wish to continue the journey or rest in a safe haven? Would you prefer not to know all? I'm still trying to answer such questions.

David Yeadon has written and illustrated sixteen travel books, including
New York: The Best Places, Backroad Journeys of Southern Europe,
and most recently, Lost Worlds: Exploring the World's Remote Places.
*He lives with his wife Anne, in Mohegan Lake, New York. This story was
excerpted from* The Back of Beyond: Travels to the Wild Places of
the Earth.

★

According to one unconfirmed report, the fabulous Emperor Yao decided
that, as he was imperfect himself, he would abdicate the throne and offer
it personally to one of two Taoist hermits of exceptional virtue who, he
had been told, lived on the same high mountain. Advised that both old
gentlemen were fairly cross-grained but that the one who lived higher up
the hill was the more amenable of the two, he rode up to the cloud-
wrapped cottage of this sage and invited him to become emperor of China.

Without uttering a word, the disgusted recluse strode quickly to a
nearby mountain stream and began washing out his ears vigorously. Much
offended, Yao left at once and made his way to the simple dwelling of the
second hermit, which lay a short distance down the slope, only to find
him giving urgent orders to his one rustic servant. "Don't let the calves
drink from the stream," he was shouting. "The water has been poisoned
by Ch'ao Fu higher up the hill—he has been washing some filth he heard
out of his ears." Shortly afterward, the affronted Yao was persuaded to
return to his capital without repeating his obscene offer of the throne to
any other anchorite.

—Dennis Bloodworth, *The Chinese Looking Glass*

JOHN KRICH

* * *

Learning to Love Canton

Celebrating the "green China of abundance" in Canton.

THE REST OF CHINA TRIES ITS BEST TO HATE CANTON. WHILE IN Beijing, I notice there's little enthusiasm for the Chinese city that's always been "farthest from the emperor"—and also the most distanced from poverty. In ominous, and envious tones, the Northerners warn, "Those Southerners are too practical. Things are so clean and convenient in Guangzhou." That's the real name, which the British could never pronounce, for Canton. "There's nothing to see there. Just lots to eat." Since the rule in much of the People's Republic is the reverse, such pronouncements just make my final destination sound more and more mouth-watering.

I'm sure to relish a locale that matches my ambivalence: caught between West and East, neither comfortably socialist nor comfortably capitalist. Is Guangzhou China's great secret? Or is China Guangzhou's great shame? Arriving from elsewhere in the country, one is stunned by the foreign brand names plastered across massive billboards; the attractive storefronts surprisingly well stocked; the abundance of automobile traffic, including taxis run by the meter and with haste; and a police force that has abandoned foreboding khaki to dress like English bobbies. Disembarking at the train station after the three-hour express run from Hong Kong, one would be struck with equal force by the unrepentant drabness and overcrowding, the thousands of peasants in timeworn blue cotton frocks encamped on the sidewalks, the guards in olive army issue sulking uselessly everywhere, the dearth of goodies at the snack-shop counters, and an equal lack of beautification in the vistas beyond.

For the distance between Canton and Hong Kong—a city that might never have existed if the British could have had their way in Canton—is far greater than that of a mere ride up the Pearl River Delta. And while millions of tourists visit Hong Kong annually for a sterilized portion of what is essentially Cantonese culture, the true source of all the charm, color, and culinary distinction remains relatively undiscovered (and since the Tiananmen debacle, sadly boycotted for the sins of distant Beijing). And what about that mythic home, which immigrant hordes have carried with them and replicated all over the globe? Guangzhou is the place that gives definition to what passes, in most heathen eyes, for Chinese. That's obvious from the faces that peer out from doorway stoops or trading stalls. Squat and sage beyond their years, broad nosed and wispy eyebrowed, rounded as bowls and faintly gold colored, these are exact genetic blueprints for the multitudes of San Francisco's Grant Avenue and New York's Mott Street. The model for all the world's Chinatowns is Canton.

Familiarly guttural cadences punctuate a diaspora's back-alley wheeling and dealing. The Cantonese are like China's New

> *If it were not part of China, Guangdong province would be a decent-sized country with a population of 63 million. As an economic unit, it has two advantages over the rest of China, and is about to acquire a third. First, its people, the Cantonese, have traded with the outside world for centuries. In Hong Kong and the other outposts of the Chinese world, they are world-class businessmen. Secondly, Beijing's control over its southern provinces has always been haphazard.... Thirdly, in 1997 the remaining artificial barriers fall between Guangdong and one of the world's best natural harbours, which comes equipped with highly sophisticated trading and financial services: Hong Kong.*
>
> —Andrew Cowley, "Asia's Emerging Economies: Geography and Geometry," *The Economist*

Yorkers: their conversations sound like barely controlled arguments: they appear to speak far too urgently about far too little. But how many cities, after all, can claim to have promulgated so universal a language? *Bok choy* and *dim sum* aren't just Cantonese but American and Australian and Thai words. They're on the world menu.

I expect to find all the coarseness and commerce. What I haven't expected is the tropical lushness that lends Guangzhou untold greenery and a whiff of faded civility. Both are displayed on Shamian Island, once a trading entrepôt ceded to the British, now partially a ghetto for travelers on the cheap. The fruited promenades are studded with ramshackle European mansions utilized as schools and government offices. Strolling here, you feel quarantined from China—though Guangzhou's generous parks and miles of riverfront also offer a welcome respite from the ever-pressing *renmin*, Chinese for "amassed masses." At the tip of the island, commanding a great view of the big bend in the Pearl River, is the curved white slab of the White Swan Hotel. This is one of many ultradeluxe establishments throughout the city catering largely to interlopers attending the semiannual Canton Trade Fair and built, as one of my guidebooks rightfully notes, on a scale of ostentation made possible only by cheap socialist labor. Having no need for the White Swan's indoor waterfall and jade shops, nor for the room rates that double during the fair, I move across the street to the Pearl Inn. "The Poor Inn," the desk clerk seems to pronounce it. They don't have room service, but they do have Hong Kong TV, a rooftop disco, and prominently displayed photos of a health club, which doesn't exist.

I still have a decent view of the river embankment, where old men snooze away the afternoons on benches and disused English cannons alternate with municipal tennis courts that are the spiffiest in China. But cross the copper-green gangplanks and you're smack in the midst of Qingping. This is China's best known market, fanning off in various directions for blocks, with covered streets claimed by sacks of medicinal herbs, a hundred types of dried fungi, aquarium fish, and tropical birds. Qingping is infamous for the variety of exotica offered up as edible. Yes, Virginia, they really do eat fluffy kittens and puppies, snakes and tortoises, frisky forest monkeys, anteaters by the truckload, wise old hoot owls, freshly stunned baby deer with open starlet eyes still seeking a gentler fate. No place on earth offers more ammunition for your local Humane Society—or better proof of Woody Allen's contention that "nature is one huge restaurant." And one where no diner in his right mind waits to be seated. The leitmotif of Guangzhou is the decapitated carcass, all glazed and shiny; or the hanging rodent flank, tail included; or the pressed pig head complete with steamrollered eyeballs. In a town that once had a reputation for sinfulness, the most lascivious creatures in sight are the nude chickens that offer themselves rear end up in the restaurant windows. Don't ask which species might be getting a vivisection by cleaver. The answer might be the one I dreaded and got: "Woof! Woof!" In Canton, the only difference between the living and the dead is that one group has yet to be barbecued.

If there was a turning-point, it probably came in Zhaoqing, a pleasant city east of Canton famous for its Seven Star Crags. Away from the tourist sites, innocently dawdling through the food market, it was all too easy for the unwary to wander into the butchers' section.

And there they lay. Whole, but completely skinned, eyes bright, flat on their backs with their death-stiffened legs pointing straight to the ceiling. Except for one poor animal which had been sawn in half, and the back end sold. An ignominious end for man's best friend.

The scene was not to be forgotten. Never again would one feel confident about what exactly was in those Spring Rolls. Nor could one trust that Guangdong Hot Pot. It was obvious what had to be done. But, fellow-traveller, be warned: few will have experienced the true loneliness of the vegetarian in Canton.

—Teresa Poole, "Out of China," *The Independent*

As in all Chinese cities, country life has been replicated on a larger scale in Canton. Beijing has its *hutongs*—cramped, low-lying courtyards where much of traditional Chinese village existence carries on to within a hundred yards of the nation's lordly center, Tiananmen Square; and Canton has its *gai*. I have barely stepped off the curb of commerce when I'm plunged into a sheltered side-street world of old neighbors seated at low tables for the afternoon game of *mah-jongg*, bald babies being washed in plastic tubs, greens being chopped on stoops for the evening's soup, mischievous school kids racing home through a funhouse loop of narrow alleys, their elders pondering the newspaper or the mysteries of self-contentment. It's not for carved dragons, but for this, that people come to China, and should continue to come. You can take a turn down any alley around Qingping, in the ancient neighborhood of Liwan, and find yourself suddenly, intimately, in the midst of the most mundane aspects of Chinese life. And mundanity is what China does best: just being on the earth, with no frills, please.

The three-story balconies are overhung with potted plants; lines of laundry drying alongside strips of cured pork form colorful canopies. Cramming more humanity per square inch than today's urban planner would find feasible, the *gai* offer that marvelous mystery of expanding through their contraction. Before so many doorways, guarding the family better than the characteristic wooden bars, sits a distinguished, glaring grandmother—so weak and frail that everyone in the family is afraid of her!

Then, too, wherever you look closely in Guangzhou, you find some handmade workshop humming away. Behind the living rooms are looms and presses, metal stampers, all sorts of light industry. You get the feeling that while the Chinese invented paper, it's the Cantonese who invented the receipt.

Why trust those misguided guidebooks? China's oldest mosque turns out to be little more than a few Islamic scribbles carved on the wall: the library of writer Lu Xun is under reconstruction and is closed for two years; and the communal Orchid Park has no orchids in bloom. The only culture I find in the official Cultural Park is a bumper-car ride and an open-air billiards table. When I hop on a river ferry, imagining a ride downstream to some colorful market town, I get a quick shuttle to a nearby suburb known largely for a chemical factory.

Never mind. I still argue that Guangzhou offers three items largely unavailable in any other Chinese town, three criteria that could readily be used to determine the greatness of any city. First, there's the aforementioned availability of swift taxis. Second, there's an unlimited selection of discounted blue jeans, all cuts, all designers. And whereas the rest of China serves the people only at strictly designated hours, Canton's noshing and nibbling know no limit.

While it is nearly impossible to get a good meal in much of China, it is nearly impossible to have a bad meal in Canton. Among overseas connoisseurs, Cantonese cuisine may be considered somewhat bland: within China, Cantonese chefs are exported to bring other cities up to their level of cleanliness and creativity. Go for the goose or the greens: in any case, Cantonese cooking is far more than the absence of oiliness, the plenitude of sweet-and-sour. And Guangzhou is the world's noodle heaven—final proof, should anyone need it, that Italian pasta is indeed the longest-running culinary rip-off. For even the Italians don't have *chow mein* for breakfast. Or wheel out an endless selection of the dumplings and rolls called *dim sum*, served from lunch through tea and as dinner appetizers. The wontons are so freshly stuffed that any old street stall will do—though the dining rooms of the Shahe Hotel, on the city's eastern outskirts, are justly renowned for broad rice noodles made from a patented mix of rice flour and mountain water, then tossed in five sauces that range subtly from salty to spicy. The food tells the story that the streets tell: Guangzhou gives no quarter to the threadbare gray China of scarcity; Guangzhou celebrates the motherly green China of abundance.

The only mistake that I make in Canton is to leave Canton. On a quiet Sunday, I am lured out of town by the misguided description of the scenic Conghua hot-springs resort set in the verdant rice-bowl landscape of Guangdong Province. My first error is to purchase a ticket to the town of Conghua rather than the springs. For two and a half hours, I'm rocked and rattled on a springless, shaky Chinese bus. At one uphill point, the noise, vibration, and g-forces are so great that the peasants appear to cry out, "We're flying!" I wish I had landed on the moon rather than that hideous housing satellite of Conghua. Lugging my backpack down Main Street, I'm an easy mark for the taxi drivers who pretend to take me to the main hot-springs area but drop me instead near several sleepy, abandoned hotels where they will get a commission. I'm aware of the game, but it quickly gets too dark for me to explore further. Besides, all the electricity's gone out in the region. There don't seem to be any outdoor baths anywhere in these parts, and though the charming girl at the candlelit reception desk in my rural inn assures me that the tubs in the rooms are fed by springs, the water out of my taps never gets more than lukewarm.

In the morning, I hike through bamboo groves to the *real* Conghua, heralded by a hand-painted sign reading WELCOME TO THE BATHROOM! The provincial guesthouse here isn't much of an improvement, surrounded with trinket sellers, peasant hustlers, restaurants that haven't served more than tea in a decade. As I remind myself, this is still China. "Maybe hot springs hot," says the clerk, "maybe not!"

For a finale, there's nothing like an evening of snake and disco, an "only in Canton" itinerary. In fact, Guangzhou's Snake Restaurant turns out to be a four-floor affair that is as popular with the locals as with novelty-seeking "big noses." The menu is rather heavy on one ingredient, snake: Snake and Cat Mixed with Mun [sic] in Soup, Stir-Fried Giblets and Snake Slices with Greens, Stewed Three Different Snakes with Chicken Feet in Medicinal Herbs. For a little variety, there's always Stewed Fur Seals, Caracal with Mushroom, Rocky Turtle, Stewed Sucking [sic] Pigeon, as well as the ever-popular Stir-fried Ophicephalus Fish Ball with Vegetable and Stewed Frog. I hold my breath while a waitress with a vampirish look in her eyes brings me the nightly special. "Gallbladder," she announces impassively. At least this choice spares me the spectacle of watching my dinner get skinned alive. With deft skill, the combination handler/chef plucks one unlucky writher, seeks the requested organ, and does a bladderectomy with a kitchen knife, then returns the donor to his cage. At the table, the tiny dark-purple balloon is squeezed like a grape into a shot of rice wine, which cuts the bitterness of the bile. I don't want to down this all-purpose potion until the waitress mentions something about the beneficial effects on "man's problems." I dare not refuse such a souvenir.

After a week in Guangzhou's efficient tumult, I've nearly forgotten that I'm still in the heartland of the politburo. The Pearl Inn's disco might as well be named "People's Healthful Recreational Disco Facility Number Seventeen." The prices are outrageous, the service state-run slow, the ambiance pre-Lawrence Welk. Teams of waitresses hover close to make sure Iwepurchase the two-drink minimum. Both drinks are brought simultaneously—my second beer will be warm by the time I get to it—along with a single cellophane-wrapped rose. I sit through an hour's crooning into an echo chamber by two awful chanteuses, then get to join the dancers. Exactly at midnight, scandalously late for People's Republic time, all the houselights come on. The cadre of glum serving girls shoo everybody out, though they don't seem in any hurry to clear the tables. Returning to mine, I find my stale drinks but the rose, which I thought was my souvenir, has been removed for resale by the next evening's "work unit." And I left in a lovable state of confusion, wishing that I didn't have to depart this workaday Cina that comes without frills.

John Krich is the author of Music in Every Room, El Beisbol, Why Is This Country Dancing?, *and a novel about Fidel Castro entitled,* A Totally Free Man. *His work has appeared in many publications. He lives in San Francisco.*

★

Over there
Power adores Gold,
Over here,
Gold woos Power.
But what about the people?
The people
Have always been their gifts of betrothal.
—Gu Cheng, "The Two Realms of Love," *Xingxing*

PART TWO

SOME THINGS TO DO

✦ ✦ ✦

Paper Patterns

In which Hong Kong fits like a well-made suit.

THE STAR FERRY IS ONLY THREE MINUTES' WALK FROM THE Mandarin hotel in Hong Kong, and although I would probably never run for a commuter train in Connecticut, I am running now through a crowded ferry terminal to catch the next boat, running even faster than the scurrying Chinese, filled with an exhilaration I can't explain at my age. Is it pure joy at being back in a place I love? Or is it something else?

There is no real haste for me to cross the harbor at this moment—I'm going to be in Hong Kong for many days this time, praise be—but a pulse of memory urges me to run the length of the ferry pier as I did in the 1960s; to have the coins ready for the turnstile; to race against the light that will turn red and the bell that will clang to announce that the gate is swinging shut; to squeeze past the gateman in his blue sailor suit and step aboard just as the man on the pier throws off the mooring hawser with that same weary skill I remember so well. In short, to be as quick now as when I was 39.

But it isn't just a race against getting older that I run; the calendar sets its own relentless pace, after all, and it never loses the birthday game. I run a different race. It is to stay ahead of change.

If I'm quick enough, I say to myself, perhaps everything I love and remember will remain the same.

So today I run for the ferry.

It is often difficult for travelers to choose between the excitement of discovering new places and the bitter-sweet pleasures of going back to a favorite city, to memories and, yes, to changes. In a lifetime of travel the early years are the time for discovery. I will always remember my first astonished look at Hong Kong from the forward deck of the ferry. We were headed across the harbor from Kowloon to Victoria a quarter-century ago. A mass of tall white buildings was even then starting to creep up the green flanks of Hong Kong Island. I thought it the most exciting place I had ever seen.

Over the years I returned many times, and excitement turned to appreciation. Hong Kong and I matured together. Each time I came back, sometimes for only a few days, once for more than a month, I looked at my city as I look at my own face in a mirror. From year to year we didn't really change that much—did we?

Out of breath, I make the ferry. This one is *Celestial Star*. I wonder as I step onto the teak deck, How many times have I been on this same boat before? (And with whom as my companion?)

There are 235 outlying islands in Hong Kong waters, and just three of them—Lantau, Lamma, and Cheung Chau—have significant populations. These are the islands most accessible from Hong Kong—about an hour's ferry ride away from the Central business district. After a hectic day in the city, there's nothing more delightful than to sit on a ferry's open back deck with a can of beer in hand, and watch the urban frenzy recede into the haze as you sail into the sunset across the China Sea.

—Julia Wilkinson, "Winds of Change," Sojourn

I used to be able to name all the Star Ferries. It was a recitation, a trivia catechism: "*Morning Star, Night Star, Day Star, Celestial Star, Twinkling Star, Shining Star, Solar Star, Meridian Star, Northern Star....*" (Love empowers memory; you keep what your heart wants to keep.)

Once aboard the venerable vessel, the sounds are all as I remember them: the engine room bells, the slosh of the propellers, the creaking groan of the ferry's rub rail against the timbers of the pier, the chatter of Cantonese, the hiss of spume flung against the side curtains by the chop.

Seven minutes later, on the Kowloon side of the harbor, I allow myself to be surged off *Celestial Star* by hundreds of determined Chinese in a hurry; and I follow yet another impulse. Why not go see George Chen again? His shop is just nearby. People say he is still the best tailor in Hong Kong. He made suits for me long ago when he was less famous. One was a gray tropical with a fine red pinstripe; I always liked that one.

In the best tailoring tradition, George had made paper patterns according to my measurements. He assured me that if ever I wanted a new suit, I could send my order from Connecticut and my patterns-on-file would guarantee a perfect fit.

It made me feel special in those days to know that a famous Chinese tailor 12,000 miles from home had "my patterns;" that just by writing a letter to him I could have a custom-made suit with all those little extra pockets and buttons and a wonderful, colorful silk lining.

As things turned out, I never did that. When the '70s arrived, that old devil Change dealt me a blow and there were many things I needed more than tailored clothes. There had been a divorce, a return to a city apartment, an attempt at a new career. A dry cleaner had ruined the gray tropical, and I gradually lost track of George Chen.

Now, years later, he looks exactly as I remember him, which pleases me. His new, larger shop, its walls stacked to the ceiling with bolts of fabric, looks much like the old one: same curtained fitting rooms, mirrors, fluorescent lights, and clutter of pins on the carpet. Eric Ng and Johnny Ho, the two apprentices I remember, have grown up, but not grown old. They say they remember me, which is polite, but I doubt that.

"We never forget an old customer," George says. "Come look at the file, you'll see why." His thin tailor's fingers walk over a tightly packed drawer of index cards. "Here you are: Barnard, C., Darien, Connecticut. Then you move to East Seventy-fifth Street. But where you go after that? It says, 'Christmas card returned, no forwarding address.'"

"I don't remember those years, George," I answer, remembering them all too well, "but I survived, I'm here now. What else does that little intelligence file of yours say about me?" (What do I want it to say? Happily remarried and back living in Connecticut again?)

"It says, 'Paper patterns on file,'" George reads with a smile. "And," he adds, tapping at my midsection with the backs of his fingers, "your figure hasn't changed so much."

Suddenly I know I am going to have a suit made. That wasn't the thought that brought me here, but now it seems an imperative, a way to win a round against change. The paper patterns, symbols of constancy, have done it.

"You wouldn't happen to have a gray tropical fabric with a fine red pinstripe, would you?"

"We'll find one!" says George, his face lighting up and looking very pleased. Without even a signal from the boss, Johnny Ho starts pulling down big bolts of fabric.

At this moment, it doesn't seem to matter a damn how old I am. It is 1965 again. All the unwanted changes of a quarter-century are suddenly erased. Hong Kong, like an old friend, has put its arm around my shoulders again. All is not lost.

That's what paper patterns are for, after all.

Charles N. Barnard's work has been appearing in major U.S. magazines for 47 years and "he's still trying to get it right."

★

Some eight hundred years ago, according to an old Chinese legend, a Cantonese scholar, looking for a site for a grave for himself, found on the Chinese mainland close to the sea a stone bearing this prophecy in Chinese characters:

Across these waters, when 'tis dark, a million lights shall glow, and in their path, ten thousand ships go passing to and fro.

—Robert St. John, *Once Around Lightly: Travel Adventures in the Great Cities of the Far East from Teheran to Tokyo*

JAN MORRIS

✦ ✦ ✦

Perfect Pleasures

The simple things are the best.

OF ALL THE PROMENADES I KNOW, ONE MORE THAN ANY OTHER seems to me the Walk of Walks. It is the path that runs around Victoria Peak—"The Peak" for short—on the island of Hong Kong. Whenever I am in that demanding colony I do the Peak walk every morning before breakfast, and I come down to my corn-flakes in the city feeling not just the fitter for it, but the more serene too—as if, striding rhythmically as I do around the half-hour circuit of the hill, I have started the day with a commitment to the organic order of things.

The Peak itself is not generally considered a metaphor for natural propriety. It was developed, to-wards the end of the 19th century, as a hill station for the British colonists of Hong Kong, and for many years preserved a rigid racial segregation; only in the 1930s was the first Chinese allowed to build a house there, and he was not only half-European anyway,

*Before she arose
to the Peak
Matilda was timid and meek,
But now she offends
Her Bowen Road friends
With a smile that is cutting
and bleak.*

—1930s poem quoted by
Paul Gillingham in *At the Peak:
Hong Kong Between the Wars*

but enormously rich as well. The higher you lived, the grander you were, and the more absolutely you looked down, figuratively as well as physically, upon lesser residents below.

But snobby and racialist though the British Empire could be, it had a fine eye for landscape, and was particularly expert at pleasances. The path its engineers built around the Peak, through its bowers of jasmine and wild indigo, daphne, rhododendron, and shiny wax trees, is a classic example of the genre. Part of it is called Harlech Road, part of it Lugard Road, but it is really hardly more than a lane, and though here and there along it villas lie half-hidden in shrubberies, and cars are parked discreetly in lay-bys, for the most part it remains a secluded country walk of the subtropical imperial variety.

Sometimes I find the path all but obliterated by Hong Kong's notorious morning mists. Everything drips with damp then, and there seems to be nobody alive up there but me. More generally all is fresh and dewy in the early morning. Butterflies waver about my path, kites and long-tailed magpies swoop, and among the trees the racket of the cicadas falls torrent-like about me. As I progress, terrific vistas reveal themselves. Now I see the island-studded reaches of the south, away down the blue-gray China coast. Half a mile later, and there lie the vast fleets of merchantmen at their anchors in the outer anchorage, and a jet hydrofoil is streaming away towards the Pearl River estuary, and the hills of Kowloon stand in misty silhouette across the water. Finally, through a gap in the trees, I see the city itself precipitously far below, stirring tremendously in the morning. The early sun is catching the windows, the ferries are coming and going already, the traffic hurries to work across fly-over and highway. Seen from this high eyrie, in the cool of the early day, it seems to me like a city in someone else's imagination—like the city Satan showed Jesus, from the top of another mountain.

Even better than the prospects are the people, for soon after daybreak the Peak path is full of other exercisers, pilgrims of the morning easing themselves into the day. They are very varied. There are courteous Chinese gentlemen wearing Walkman headsets and carrying walking sticks, who smile and slightly bow. There are svelte European ladies exercising svelter dogs. There are groups of Chinese students, three or four abreast, chattering and laughing and waving to me as they pass. There are gentlemanly Britons who look like judges, and tall Americans who look like graduates of Harvard Business School.

Most numerous, most dedicated, most suitable, there are scores of Chinese men and women, mostly elderly, engaged in the slow and enigmatic system of exercise called *taijiquan*, the Grand Ultimate Fist. All along the path I see them as I pace by, sometimes alone and silent, sometimes shouting messages to one another across the stillness of a gully, and the stylized grace of their exertions, the measured shadowboxing, the expression of inner deliberation as they stretch their limbs or twist their hands, haunts me always with the power of the Chinese mystery.

I approach a tiny park where a group of energetic seniors are practicing tai chi *under the flame-orange bloom of a locust tree. One man stabs the air with a plastic sword, pulls it close to his body, then lunges in the opposite direction.*

Spears of sunlight slice through the trees. The cicadas are at a fever pitch again. Little do they know that their love beacon could signal their demise. Two days ago I saw The Cicada Catcher, an elderly man who snares cicadas and turns them into soup. He says the concoction helps to improve a person's eyesight.

—Jon Resnick, "Bowen's World"

An influential Chinese device, as influential in Hong Kong as it was in the China of the Manchus, is the philosophical system called *feng-shui*, literally "wind and water"—the ancient art of balance and placement. It decrees how all man's constructions, his buildings in life, his graves in death, should be situated in the context of nature itself.

The British empire-builders, when they laid out Harlech and Lugard roads, were certainly not deliberately honoring the concept of *feng-shui*, which they would doubtless have dismissed as heathen superstition, but their route around Victoria Peak seems magically to obey it anyway. The path never disturbs the character of the hillside. It never seems to jar. It follows the 1,300-foot contour line courteously, as though not to disturb the spirits of the place, and its vistas north, south, east, and west are like views allegorically opening upon life itself. The butterflies are perfectly at home along its course. Beside it the trees seem to grow affectionately.

No wonder those devotees of the Grand Ultimate Fist go to the Peak to practice their stately gyrations; and no wonder that I find my morning exercise up there more than just a physical refreshment, but a tonic for all the senses. Only a fool would run around such a belvedere; it is just made for that happy reconciliation of mind and body, rest and labor, the walk before breakfast.

Jan Morris also contributed "Towards Fragrant Harbor" in Part I and "Archipelago" in Part II.

★

I found *tai chi chuan* an admirable form of exercise, particularly when I sat down on a park bench to watch others perform it. It requires very little space and has a picturesque terminology. "Carry Tiger to Mountain" is a fairly easy squat-and-rise motion. "Fair Lady Works Shuttles" is a bit more complex, with considerable foot-shifting and hand-turning. "Needle at Sea Bottom" involves some simulated motions of retrieving it, and "High Pat on Horse" is about what you would anticipate. "Golden Cock Stands on One Leg" could throw you off-balance if you are not careful, while "Snake Creeps Down" will show you what a snake's backbone has to go through while travelling about the countryside. "Step Back and Repulse Monkey" may prove useful if you are ever set upon by an organ-grinder's financial assistant.

The eight basic positions or stances are supposedly derived from the Eight Trigrams of the *I Ching* or *Book of Changes,* but if these philosophic and mystical elements are lost on you it is none the less possible to profit from the exercises. They are graceful in execution, resembling a slow tempo dance, and no one in Hong Kong laughs at the earnest exercisers in the parks. Their undemanding pace makes the exercises suitable for both sexes and all ages. I find it hard to imagine anyone suffering a heart attack while practising *tai chi chuan* and this alone gives it an advantage over weekend tennis.

—Gene Gleason, *Tales of Hong Kong*

NURY VITTACHI

* * *

Loving the Alien

Encounters with robots and wild monkeys.

PICTURE A LANDSCAPE OF GIANT, MULTICOLORED LEGO BRICKS, piled up in irregular constructions on a flat surface. It is dusk, and you are walking among these blocks, some clusters of which are as tall as four-storey buildings.

Suddenly you hear a sound. From between two clusters proceeds a long-legged beast which looks as if it has trundled straight out of a Star Wars film: it is nine or ten metres high, with four unbending metal legs, and it has that half-machine, half-animal look of a "transformer" toy. There are two wheels on the end of each leg. Each of the legs is connected to a grid at the top, but the creature curiously seems to lack a trunk or head.

With an unearthly hum, it propels its angular limbs through the clear passage in the alien landscape, and then disappears behind a further wall of giant building blocks. Behind you, another of the long-legged trundlers wheels itself into your vision. This one pauses thoughtfully at a seven-metre high pile of giant rainbow Lego bricks, as if considering whether to graze upon it. You notice that the creature, which is bright red, has a small glass box suspended from the grid, and this contains a human figure: Is it a rider, a driver or the creature's lunch?

Strange thoughts crowd your mind when you are in the hi-tech landscape of the world's busiest container terminal either at night or early in the morning. But it is hardly surprising: the Kwai Chung area of Hong Kong is probably one of the most surrealistic parts of the territory.

In many ways, Kwai Chung and other industrial new towns comprise the true Hong Kong, the real power source of the bright lights: they are a unique and baffling mix of unbelievably productive industry, mind-boggling jam-packed urban sprawl, world-beating import-export facilities and a constant buzz of activity. But there's one other thing about Kwai Chung. Tourists don't go there. Even foreigners who have lived in Hong Kong for years have rarely visited it. The only foreigner the locals ever see is the occasional Western businessman (usually identified as a newcomer by the fact that he is wearing a heavy suit, and sweating), puffing along the street to arrange the shipment of a million boxes of personal computers to—to where? It might be anywhere, from Addis Ababa to Zaire.

About 65 percent of Hong Kong's industrial work force is employed in apparel, textiles, electronics, plastics, and watch and clock manufacture. Together, these categories account for 61.5 percent of Hong Kong's domestic exports. But with between 60 and 70 percent of the colony's manufacturing capacity expected to move to China by 1997, the portion of the manufacturing sector that is not simply fading away is shifting from labor-intensive to capital-intensive pursuits.

—Edward G. Hinkelman,
Hong Kong Business: The
Portable Encyclopedia for Doing
Business with Hong Kong

If you like to take striking photographs, and are truly intrepid, take your finest lenses along to the container terminals at Kwai Chung. Ideally, you should phone first to get permission from the companies running the terminals (the one I described above was Modern Terminals Ltd. (MTL), but similar operations are run by Hongkong International Terminals Ltd. (HIT), Sea-Land Services Inc. and a number of other firms).

People with iron nerves and plausible faces have been known to just march in past the guards and stroll around, but on the whole this is not recommended: if one of the metal beasties drops a giant Lego block—actually, a seven-metre-long metal container—on your head, no-one will take the blame or pay compensation.

To get there, you take the MTR from the heart of Hong Kong Island or Kowloon to Kwai Fong Station. Exit the station and stroll around the town; you can already see the giant piles of boxes on every spare space. The inland area—really a cluster of little towns, most of which are made up of old and new high-rise blocks, with factories and industrial estates in between—is generally considered spectacularly unattractive, although sociology students, town planners and, one would hope, the odd "Hong Kong explorer" find it fascinating.

Ask a passer-by for Container Port Road; walk straight down it for fifteen minutes and you will reach the container terminals. This appears to be the one part of Hong Kong where taxis are not the dominant form of road life. As you approach the terminals, 90 percent of the vehicles are articulated lorries.

What the government has set out to do is to lay down the basic infrastructure and provide conditions in which business can flourish. From the start, the government took the view that it wasn't the business of civil servants to try to be involved in business. For a time immediately after the war the government was involved in directing exports and imports and actively controlling large chunks of the economy. Eric Himsworth, in charge of trade immediately after the Second World War, said it was a conscious decision for the government to get out of business as quickly as possible and leave it to private enterprise.

—Kevin Rafferty, City on the Rocks: Hong Kong's Uncertain Future

For the less intrepid, or the nonphotographers among us, the area still offers fascinating sights. One of the most interesting is the smugglers' route from the sea up into the hills that overlook the region.

To try this route, the best bet is to do it backwards: take the MTR to Sham Shui Po, then get a taxi to the Kowloon Reservoirs.

There's a trail marked on the left side of the main road, which at the beginning is wide enough for vehicles, but eventually

narrows to a pedestrians-only track. It is on the way to Tai Lam
Country Park. The trail from the Kowloon Reservoirs partly
overlaps with the MacLehose Trail, a famous ramblers' route set up
by a previous governor. Head down the path to the Shing Mun
(Jubilee) Reservoir.

Look out in this area for families of wild monkeys. You are
bound to see them in the trees, or even on the path. They are often
not in the least frightened of human beings, and can be quite
threatening—keep small children at a distance.

At one point in the woods, you will reach a stage where parents
turn to their children and ask them to listen to the dragon's breathing. The legend, of course, is that Kowloon is built on the backs of
eight dragons (Kowloon means "nine dragons"—the ninth was a
human emperor). There is an unmistakable low, periodic rumbling,
like the breathing of a large animal. Don't tell the children, but it
is actually the sound of a water-pumping plant tucked away in a
valley in the woods.

At one point, you will see the openings of several small tunnels,
with the names of British railway stations attached to them:
Charing Cross, King's Cross and so on. These are a network of tunnels cut into the ground by British soldiers during the last war, in
a bid to protect Hong Kong from the invading Japanese. The idea
was similar to that of the "rat holes" used during the Vietnam War.
The Japanese, incidently, penetrated the system in two days.

Follow the signs to Smugglers' Ridge, and you'll reach a fairly
steep path, which winds and climbs over a rather mountainous
piece of terrain, and eventually you'll break onto the other side.
Below you is Kwai Chung—a stark, practical mass of huge high-
rise estates and industrial buildings.

In the distance, you can see Tsing Yi island, now connected to
the mainland by a road bridge. Tsing Yi, it is interesting to speculate, is a miniature of what Hong Kong must have been in the past:
a largely barren rock, with a growing cluster of buildings spreading out from the centre of the bay.

Keep walking and you'll eventually come down the hillside,
where you can easily get to Tuen Mun, one of the main townships

in the Kwai Chung area. There you can put your feet up in a local teashop—and take a taxi or the MTR home.

Nury Vittachi, one of Asia's better-known humorists, has written a number of best sellers. His book Travellers' Tales *(which is not affiliated with this* Travelers' Tales *series) is a pan-Asian collection based on his column of the same name which is printed weekly in the* Far Eastern Economic Review. *He also writes a daily column in the* South China Morning Post *called "Spice Trader."*

★

Travelling by taxi is always boring, a dead spot in the bustle of urban life. However, taking a taxi can be very different if one is lucky enough to catch a ride with cabby Frankie Ng Hing Lam. Frankie's cab is unique in having many photographs posted inside, and this arouses the interest of many passengers. Most of the photos are of Frankie with film stars—he has had his photo taken with about 800 local and international stars in the past five years—because Frankie himself is a part-time actor.

As Frankie himself put it, "There is always a gap between taxi drivers and passengers. The photos which I took with the pop stars serve well as a common topic for both sides to talk about. This makes the mood warmer and more relaxing throughout the journey."

He also keeps two bags of photos in the cab for passengers who want to see more. "Some passengers find it so interesting that they are not willing to get out," said Frankie happily with his eyes sparkling.

People may wonder why Frankie still drives a cab rather than devoting all his time to acting. "I will never be a full-time actor because I could never be one of the main characters. Moreover, I have to support my family, and the income of a temporary actor is not enough, and it is unstable. I just hope that I can keep on with my present life."

As he approaches 50 years of age, Frankie has an established philosophy: wish for nothing, demand nothing. "I never thought of becoming anything great. I would be glad if I could achieve something. If I cannot, I won't mind," Frankie said.

—Jessica Shum, "A Taxi Driver Tells About His Other Career"

BURLEY PACKWOOD

✦ ✦ ✦

Dim Sum Et Cetera

A walk through the streets reveals the many moods of Hong Kong.

JET LAG JARRED US AWAKE. IT SEEMED WE HAD SLEPT THE NIGHT away, yet it was only nine o'clock and we were fully charged. We were on the street in fifteen minutes, victims of curiosity. Darkness enhanced Hong Kong's mystique, but we entered the neon-lighted streets refreshed with firm determination to resist the lure of Hong Kong bargains. We didn't need cameras, watches, or jewelry. Gift shopping could come later. Betsi clasped my hand in a firm pact. No matter the temptation, we would buy nothing during our evening stroll.

Chinese characters exploded in colorful arches across streets. Exotic signs glowed like skyrockets, and the delirious hum of evening shoppers created a strange dizziness as we plunged through traffic. The kaleidoscopic effect tilted our judgment. "We're only looking," Betsi said to bolster our determination. The tide of Chinese citizens flowed with the traffic lights. Thunderous foreign chatter filled the streets, for Cantonese is the chief language of Hong Kong, and is said to be the only language that cannot be spoken in a whisper. But neither night nor lights nor language defeated us that evening. Our ruin came from an unexpected source.

The lady needed help. She was old, tiny, and hunched in the

shoulders. She grunted loudly at the far end of her overloaded cart. An uncooperative four-wheel dolly, the type seen on docks transporting heavy loads, roosted against the curb, and like a stubborn mule, refused to advance. Glancing backward, the woman's almond-shaped eyes opened in distress, and she bent nearly double leveraging against the cart. Her stubby fingers pressed on the box with every ounce of her strength. Low desperate moans escaped and her feet slipped in the moist gutter. She glanced backward again.

"Why doesn't someone help that poor old woman?" Betsi cried, and rushed toward the desperate lady. "Do you want help?"

"*Hai, hai,*" (yes, yes) she replied not looking up, then slipped her finger under a loose sandal, scooted her foot into it and pushed with all her might. The cart did not budge.

"Help me," Betsi said, moving to the overloaded dolly. We managed to raise the cart an inch and the lady grunted it over the curb. I coaxed the rear wheels forward and pressed the heavy load into sidewalk traffic. The tiny crone straightaway assumed command.

She waved wildly to remain at our stations and push. She guided her cargo through intense foot traffic by running to the front and shouting at the world to move aside. The night was damp and hot and within fifty feet the cart disappeared into a pocket of darkness and banged against a collection of garbage cans. The old lady leaned into the refuse and panted. We fell against the cart breathing deeply. We had obviously escaped from something.

"Police?" I turned to Betsi. "Now what have you got us into?" Thoughts of cocaine, a parcel of heroin, or even (God forbid) a dead body stashed inside the overloaded cart, set my heart palpitating. A cruel and persistent pain invaded my hips.

"Shsss!" the woman cautioned. She raised a squinted eye above the load, pressed a finger over her lips and uttered the dreaded word: "Police!"

I fingered a soggy passport inside my secret damp pocket. How could we explain our presence? No one, among thousands of onlookers, had offered to help. Why had we? What if the police seized our passports? What if we spent the night in jail? A lifetime in a

Chinese prison? Why had we stopped to help the old hag in the first place? Feelings of guilt and fear exploded in my chest and I broke into a prodigious sweat...and blamed Betsi.

The old woman straightened and cracked a cunning smile with a twist of the devil in it. In semi-darkness her face beamed smugness. She shuffled around the cart, straightened its contents, and squinted toward the street. After a minute she motioned us to help steer the cart again. Pinioned against fragrant garbage, I welcomed her suggestion.

The woman quick-stepped into the street to double-check for police. She was incredibly short and bounced up and down a few times as though on a pogo stick. During her absence Betsi ran her hands into the cart's contents.

"T-shirts!" she said. Disappointment struck her ego. She had expected at least one dead body. "There are hundreds...no thousands of t-shirts. I don't feel a corpse or cache of dope." While Betsi ransacked the cart the old lady bounded back.

Betsi's search made the grandmother happy. "Good, good," she cried plucking a handful of merchandise from the cart. She flung shirts into the air so that we could inspect them.

Ralph Lauren's proud Polo emblem stared from every shirt. I rapidly calculated retail prices. It had to be hot! Stolen! Illegal! We had stumbled onto a bootlegging operation and Betsi, who had never received so much as a parking ticket, was up to her elbows in contraband merchandise. The thrill of discovery dulled her sense of danger.

The old woman beamed at Betsi's enthusiasm. She waved an armload of shirts under my nose, and said, "You my children. Here. You help. For you...." She forced three shirts into my hands and stated her price.

It was a steal! A few U.S. dollars for an authentic illegal Ralph Lauren Polo shirt! Bought in Hong Kong in the dead of night. Stolen from a pirate's mother? A tremor of delight surged through me and my hips refused to ache. I felt like a pirate boarding a captive vessel. I sought to control my embezzling passion and turned to Betsi. Her reaction astonished me. Wide-eyed and eager, she pawed through the cart like a feline sniffing catnip.

Our Chinese ally inched under our arms. "I'm your mother," she said. "Take plenty."

"We'd better follow mother's advice," Betsi said, and started thrusting shirts into my arms.

I didn't argue. The colors were brilliant, the patterns exquisite, and the price: cheap, cheap, cheap! We quickly selected ten large shirts when a fleck of inspiration struck. What about presents? Mr. Lauren would solve our birthday gifts, Christmas gifts and what-can-you-buy-for incidentals. At mother's prices we could afford to be generous. Betsi selected a blue and red stripe for the postman and a startling mauve color for the dependable Mexican newsboy. I picked a blue check shirt for a man I hadn't spoken to in ten years. How lucky we were. We tallied everything, then added four for good measure. During the search I discovered two patterns not included earlier, and Betsi picked out three for herself. Ecstasy claimed us, and we congratulated each other with sharp shoulder smacks and smug grins. We had defeated Hong Kong without sweating.

But the total number astounded us. Forty-eight genuine illegal Polo by Ralph Lauren shirts balanced on the bin's edge and we hesitated briefly. After a second, Betsi said, "What the hell. Let's do it. Our shopping is fin-

The Beijing Rule of Shopping is the Asian version of our Moscow Rule of Shopping; it had nothing to do with shopping in Beijing, but does come with a twist.

Now: *The average shopper, in pursuit of the ideal bargain, does not buy an item he wants on first seeing it, not being convinced that he won't find it elsewhere for less money. This is human nature. A shopper wants to see everything available, then return for the purchase of choice. This is a normal thought process, especially in Hong Kong, where every merchant seems to have exactly the same merchandise. If you live in Beijing, however, you know that you must buy something the minute you see it, because if you hesitate it will be gone. Hence the name of our international law. If you live in Hong Kong, you know the guys from Beijing can come over the hills anytime soon and take it all away. So you buy it when you can.*

—Suzy Gershman and
Judith Evans Thomas,
Born To Shop: Hong Kong

ished. Now we can enjoy the rest of the trip." She tossed in two more shirts to make an even fifty.

Betsi counted out her Hong Kong dollars. It did seem like a lot for t-shirts, but our Hong Kong shopping was completed in a single hour, and we forked over the cash with pleasure. The smiling lady scraped and bowed to her sandals. "You my children. You plenty good boy," she beamed, and hugged my belly.

Overwhelmed with our new mother and 50 fluttering shirts, we staggered away. The shirts seemed alive, ready to fly, and we clutched them tightly. The spectacular bargain raised our rapturous spirits and we skipped like children back to the hotel, eight blocks away.

The desk clerk noted our entrance with an attitude of quiet disdain. "Good evening," he said. "I see you have been shopping." It was not an amazing deduction since the shirts had loosened in our arms and threatened to escape. We had barely reached the YMCA without serious losses because late breezes had blown several shirts over Betsi's head and she peered at the clerk like a curious child peeking through a multi-colored knot-hole.

The shirts threatened to explode across the desk if we barely loosened our grip. "Room 216," I said with slim dignity.

The clerk nodded and raising his head, smiled arrogantly. He placed the oversized key between my fingers. "It is my painful duty to suggest that you may have been, as you Americans say, taken." He spoke as if he was saving a mouthful of snot in his throat.

I began to loathe him with great precision. "How?"

"You believe those sports togs to be genuine?" His smile curled into a delicate sneer.

"Well," I said defensively, thinking of pirates and copyrights and my Chinese mother. "They may be copies."

"Not even good copies," he said with satisfaction. The police have been trying to close that operation for months."

"They look good. What's wrong?"

He appraised me as if speaking to a small child or a witless old man. "Everything is wrong. They're usually missized. A medium size may be small and a small size may be large, but that isn't the worst." We waited for his catastrophic descriptions. Betsi had loosened her hold on the bulging bundle and they draped on the counter, ready to spring like a Jack-in-the-box. He paused dramatically and spread his large hands. He had dirty fingernails. "They will shrink and fade with each washing. And the emblem is fake. It probably isn't even sewn on." He flicked his long soiled fingernail under a Polo emblem and it fluttered away, then another and another. Seven times his accusing nail slipped under the racing polo player, and each prancing horse joined its mates like a discarded stack of cards. The clerk shrugged his shoulders. "You see," he said triumphantly. "All fakes. Cheap fakes." Then he added, "Greed makes Hong Kong look bad."

We retreated to the comfort of the elevator and faced nose to nose. Betsi snickered first. "Your mother took us good. Her own son."

"I thought she was your mother," I said when the elevator stopped at the second level.

"Not mine. She looked like your side of the family."

Without further discussion we pressed the elevator down, marched past the triumphant clerk and hurried through the door, t-shirts fluttering. In the corner shop we purchased a giant backpack, stashed every garment inside its bulging pockets and dashed into diminishing night traffic to find our mother.

We heard her half a block down the street touting her shirts. She seemed smaller than we remembered. Wisps of hair fluttered in the night wind, her hands exposing the emblems of pirated Ralph Lauren wares. The bin's contents were surprisingly low. Customers stopped, inspected, and bought. We pressed closely and I screamed, "You sold us bad shirts. We want our money back."

She looked at a drifting night cloud and began speaking Cantonese.

"We want our money back," I said firmly, and removed the backpack.

The little woman ignored us, but from the corner of her mouth said, "Go away, Joe!"

"Return our money. You cheated us." Betsi pulled a dozen shirts from the top pocket of the backpack and waved them in her mother's face.

"Who are you? I no see you before," she muttered and shoved a Polo emblem toward a passerby. "Beautiful shirts. Plenty cheap."

"Don't buy," I warned. "They're fakes. No good." The man bought, and mother smiled.

"Go away. You bad man," mother snarled.

I edged closer. "Look here. You sold us phony Polo shirts thirty minutes ago and we don't want them. They're no good. Return our money."

The dwarf Chinese squinted at Betsi and said, "I never see you before."

"We helped you escape the police," Betsi cried pulling another batch of fake Polos from the pack. "You sold these shirts to us under false pretenses. We're your children! Don't you remember?"

"I never see you before," the woman said innocently. She hoisted her skirt above her ankles, turned, and pivoted her cart into the thinning crowd.

Onfucianism expresses a huge dissatisfaction with the concept of government by law. For the law always falls one step behind manners and morals; the most charming things men do are always those that rise above legal obligations. "Guide the people with administrative measures and regulate them by the threat of punishments, and the people will try to keep out of jail, but will have no sense of honor. Guide them by morals and regulate them by good manners, and they will have a sense of honor and respect.... In presiding over law-suits I am probably as good as anybody. The point is that there should be no law-suits at all"

—Lin Yutang,
Between Tears and Laughter

"Good-bye, mother. May the devil crawl in your fart sack tonight and give you crabs," I shouted, and swung the overloaded pack to my shoulders.

We stood friendless in the crowd. "I'm tired," I said. "My hips hate me. Let's go home."

The load seemed heavier walking back. We had barely dodged a collision with a trotting fabric merchant when Betsi spotted the DAIRY FARM EXPRESS ICE CREAM PARLOR.

The brilliantly lit room boasted six small crowded tables and an ice cream menu nearly surpassing the choices of NEW GOOD COMPANION FAST FOOD SHOP. Ice cream burgers, banana boats, and a dozen exotic flavors teased us. Half a hundred teenagers bubbled inside, laughing and screaming Chinese happiness.

"What'll you have?" Betsi asked.

"Surprise me." I leaned against the door and prayed for an empty table. God listened, and a couple arose leaving two empty seats. I sank into the chair. Two quiet love-struck Chinese children (they couldn't be more than ten: so small) sat on opposing seats. They alternately fed each other from a common cup with tiny long-handled plastic spoons. He swept a drop of cream onto the spoon and anointed her tongue, all the time embracing her with hot brown eyes. She swallowed slowly, her long lashes flickered gentle love bulletins. Then her hand dipped toward the cup and re-trieved a spicule of cream and delicately brought it to his lips. His tongue made an "o" and she inserted the gift with a corkscrew motion. They sighed deeply, their free hands twisting ever tighter.

"Quiet," I raised my hand in warning as Betsi returned with two overloaded cones.

Betsi smiled at the lovesick couple. "I remember those days," she said, and handed me a dripping lemon–dash cone. She dropped to her chair and sucked the edges of her mango cream, carefully avoiding the entwined legs under the table.

"That's love Chinese style," I whispered.

"It's the same the world around." Betsi smiled affectionately at the couple.

A second wind came over us as we licked remnants of our cones. Without moving their heads two pairs of almond eyes fol-lowed us. Betsi helped with the pack and we glanced at the love-birds.

"Good-bye," Betsi said, and there was a hint of moisture in her eyes. "All the best."

The girl's lashes flickered. "Hello," she answered.

"Good-bye children," I added. "Good luck."

"Hello," she repeated and opened her lips for another sip of soft ice cream. A whiff of the child's subtle perfume crossed the table.

Lighthearted giddiness struck both of us and the pack seemed lighter. I wanted to kick my heels knowing I would fall in a heap.

But I felt young again! Like a crusader who has glimpsed the Holy Grail. Inspired! Yes, that was it, I was young again! Heads high against the evening breeze we hurried home to the YMCA.

We swept through the lobby, daring the desk clerk to admonish our greedy stupidity, but he no longer defended his fortress. A young Indian girl, sari clad with lavender eyes, had replaced him. "Good evening and welcome to Hong Kong," she said with a slight bow, touching her palms. "I hope it meets your expectations."

Betsi's eyes moistened, "It's overwhelming."

She smiled warmly and placed key 216 into my palm. "That's a normal reaction. It's your first day isn't it? Wait until tomorrow."

The next morning we went in search of breakfast and found a tiny Cantonese restaurant named A VERY PLEASANT PLACE TO EAT in an alley off Nathan Road. The place was immaculate. The floor had been mopped only minutes ago. Stainless silverware gleamed and red carnations dressed each small table. An ornate hanging, nearly covering one wall, declared: DEEP REASONING AND HEAVY MANNERS.

A button-nosed, bright-eyed child (why did they all seem so young?) materialized with a single-sheet menu. Her yellow gingham skirt smelled of strong soap and black shining braids dropped to her hips. There was an honest welcome in her voice. "You Americans?" We nodded. "I bring coffee."

"No, not coffee. Tea. Plain hot tea. No cream. No sugar. Only plain hot tea. Understand?"

"Understand. What more you want? Hot cakes, beef steak, French toast? I make all. You think. I bring," she sang, and padded quickly into the rear kitchen.

A man, pale, wrinkled and doubled with arthritis, shuffled from the cubbyhole kitchen and painfully hobbled toward us. He swung a large, ill-shaped mystery parcel draped in white muslin in one hand and, approaching us, sucked in a loud painful breath.

"Good morning," Betsi called, in a mood to be friendly with anyone. The man leaned heavily against our table.

"Mmmmm," he muttered, turning vaguely away. His sandals pointed toward the door, but his nose faced us. Blind eyes, enor-

mously distorted through cataract glasses, stared without understanding. "Mmmmmmmmm." He licked his lips through toothless
gums, "Mmmmm." Then he launched into Cantonese, turning at
odd angles, trying to locate us at
his elbow.

The shining waitress returned
with a steaming teapot and cups.
"Is good," she said, pointing to
the tea, her voice pitched to a
sublime musical level. "Is daffodil
tea." She filled two porcelain
thimbles.

While we sniffed the delicate
brew Betsi inquired, "Is this man
your father?"

A volcanic giggle burst from
the waitress. Her fingers latticed
across her face and she bowed
toward the gentlemen. "Oh no,
mistress. He, how you say, grandfather's father," and she bowed in
his direction.

"He is rather old," Betsi ventured, recognizing the impossi-
bility of totaling the number of
corrugated wrinkles in his ancient face.

"Old, old," the child admitted,
"He no hear, no see, he no smell."

"What's under the cloth?"

The girl refilled our cups.

Even when you've mastered Cantonese though, it's no good. People just don't believe you. A friend of mine has been learning and speaking Cantonese for 28 years. He began learning it in the police and he has all kinds of qualifications in the language. He even appears on TV from time to time on the Chinese channels as a sort of alibi gwailo. Everyone seems to be able to follow him. But this taxi driver doesn't want to understand him. "It's like that sometimes," my friend says. "They see your face and they just can't believe you're speaking their language. It's a kind of racism really, not believing a foreigner can speak your language even though he's doing it. But you learn to live with it."

My friend is an exception of course. Most foreigners who have lived in Hong Kong for many years hardly know how to count to ten in Cantonese.

—Dr. George Adams, *Hong Kong Watching: The Essential Guide To Hong Kong People's Behaviour*

"Birds," she said. "Grandfather's birds." Then rapidly, if incoher-
ently, she told us her great grandfather owned fourteen birds and
took one of them outside each morning searching for bugs.

"What kind of bugs?"

"Jumping bugs," the child replied. To augment her answer she began leaping between tables and flapping her folded arms as though flying on crippled wings. Short, erratic hops, accompanied by a remarkable imitation cricket chirp, quickly carried her around the room.

"Of course. Jumping bugs," Betsi agreed, then in her lowest tone whispered, "What are jumping bugs?" I shrugged. Entomology never had categorized that family of insects.

"Where can your grandfather's bird find jumping bugs in all this traffic?"

Her eyes sprang wide at our simplicity. "He no find, he buy."

She pantomimed a bird eating jumping bugs and to our astonishment tore aside the white shroud, displaying a magnificent bamboo cage with a lovely, fluorescent yellow bird sitting on its perch gazing at Betsi. In response to light the bird leaped to the cage wall, threw back its head and trilled high C a few times. The girl shouted into her great grandfather's ear in Cantonese. He could not straighten, but lifted his shoulders a bit, and twisted in our direction, "Mmmmmm,MMMMM,mmmmm,mm,mmmmmmmm-mmm," he said.

"Grandfather glad you like the bird but it hungry and he must find food," the girl said. She covered the cage and the nightingale's song ended in mid-aria. "Much noise and strange happenings make Trilby sad," she explained. "He no can see when he covered. When he no see, he no sing." The old man shuffled through the door carrying Trilby into daylight and Nathan Road traffic. Our child waitress (her name was Tso) turned to us. "What you want?"

"One order of French toast for my wife and a small rare breakfast steak for me...and more tea please." The tea had been an unexpected wonder.

"French toast and beef steak," she echoed. "I bring."

Our eyes roved the room. There was not much to see and we poured tea. "I wish grandpa would return with his jumping bugs," Betsi said.

"He'll never get back alive," I predicted. "A 140-year-old deaf-blind cripple won't get a hundred yards in that jungle, much less return."

"A Snickers bar says he'll make it."

"You're on," I said. Tso made noises in the kitchen and strange odors drifted from the kitchen. In remarkably short time she bustled to us with a steaming tray, her face beaming. Two-foot chopsticks dipped into the tray and dropped freshly steamed dumplings on our plates.

"I ordered steak. My wife wants French toast." Thinking of saving face for both of us I said gently, "What's this?"

The magic-wand chopsticks touched our dumplings. "Is good," Tso stated firmly. "Eat!"

"I ordered a little breakfast steak...rare."

"Don't make a scene," Betsi reminded me. "You're the one who wanted to come to Hong Kong." She sniffed the hot moist dumpling and nibbled at its edge. Her eyes widened. "God, this is good! Shrimp, mushrooms, ginger, and something else." She ate rapidly to the middle of the bun. Tso waited patiently, her face widening into a broad smile. "Is good?" she asked.

"Is good," Betsi told her. "Now the French toast."

Tso vanished into the tiny kitchen, her black braids flying.

"I think you just finished your French toast," I said wiping my chin with an inadequate paper napkin. "But it is good. Damned good. Now for my Chinese breakfast steak."

We were on our way to dim sum, a morning ritual for thousands of working Hong Kong Chinese. But Chester swung open the glass door to a huge room packed with people at oval tables, hunched over their morning newspapers, sipping tea and poking at miniature egg custards and shrimp balls.

The clatter of plates clashed with high-pitched conversation as Chinese women, pushing carts loaded with food, called out the names of the delicacies in covered wooden boxes. We nudged our way around the tables to the far end of the room as Chester signaled to a waiter he has known since his father began bringing him here as a small boy. The waiter led us to three seats at a table filled with men reading newspapers.

"People come here for the papers and the tea," Chester said, slicing an egg custard in two with his chopsticks. "The food is not so important. Read some papers, drink some tea, and relax before the rushing starts. That's what it's all about."

—Carol Pucci, "Day by Day in Hong Kong," *Seattle Times*

We glimpsed Tso's rabbit-like movements in the kitchen. Her brief arm flurries were concentrated around a well-blackened wok under a yellow flame. Cinnamon and lime odors floated from the dingy hole and curled to the table. "That's China," I told Betsi inhaling a gingery-pepper smell, and visualizing Tso in a bikini, "Pure China."

Betsi giggled. "Tso's a good looking Chinese babe. Makes no difference if they're pure or impure. You like 'em all. Remember?"

She was so right. Age had never curtailed my libido.

Tso suddenly popped from the kitchen carrying an assortment of deep-fried dumplings. Betsi arose from her chair and waited. She snatched one of the delicacies from the tray and smacked her lips. "Spiced meat balls and orange peel slivers. No, it's kumquat flavor." She finished the dumpling with a flourish. "That's the best breakfast steak you'll ever eat," she said, nibbling another dumpling.

Her eyes roved to the door. "You owe me a Snickers bar," she said quietly, "but I don't need it now."

Great-grandfather groped through the door and set the cage on a window ledge. He slowly unveiled the cage as if raising a theater curtain. The bird instantly sang, yet slowed its aria when the old gentleman extracted a small container from his pocket. We could not identify its contents, but a number of moving parts tumbled inside the fist-sized box.

"Grasshoppers!" Betsi finally gasped.

Pleasant memories of blooming balsamroot fields, clogged with leaping grasshoppers, flooded Betsi's mind. It was an easy source for fish bait. Long ago we had fed a million or so insects to rainbow trout on the Stillwater River, but never considered them bird food. The canary thought otherwise and hopped to the cage wall waiting for its *dim sum*. Great-grandfather picked an insect from the box and jerkily plugged the smallish kicking hopper between his lips, then locked the remaining insects tightly inside the container. The old man took the insect from his lips and amazingly, considering his arthritis and blindness, impaled it to a steel fish-hook device that was fastened to the cage. The bird hopped directly to the hook and nipped a chunk of raw steak from the grasshopper's belly.

"Trilby's no vegetarian," Betsi said.

The grasshopper ignored the weeping hole in its thorax, and calmly fluttered long antennae at Betsi who, surprisingly, waved back. The songbird, satisfied with the appetizer, hopped to his perch and sang while the old man searched for the kitchen.

Then began a series of events that we sorted for months, delighting in every reexamined memory. Several more hungry customers wandered into the small room. Tso returned with steamed dumplings and sweet-spiced Chinese sausages and her great-grandfather reappeared groping his way through the increasing crowd. His crippled hands toted two more large covered bird cages. He finally trembled them to the window ledge. When he uncovered the cages birdsong filled the room. Italian tenors never contributed more excitement to an improvised performance. A VERY PLEASANT PLACE TO EAT exploded with magical wonderment.

Screeching, trilling birds vied with hungry sing-songing Cantonese patrons; kitchen kettles banged and cinnamon–clove perfume filled the room. Tso's clanging wok battered against the two-burner butane stove competing with the cacophony

If you are vegetarian, or like us, simply don't like much meat, be wary of those Chinese banquets in Hong Kong. Usually ten to fourteen courses long, 90 percent of which are dedicated to meat, seafood, and poultry. Courses are served one at a time, so you don't have the option of selecting what you like and leaving the rest. You also don't have the option of picking at the vegetables on the side of your plate because when you are served the sea cucumber (a.k.a. sea slug) for instance, all you get on your plate is a chunk of sea cucumber. So if you are not too fond of the course, it soon becomes apparent to all the other people at the table, who often wish to see their foreign guests enjoy local cuisine. There are vegetables and rice to be found at their banquets, but, being considered lowly fare and not worthy of guests, they bring up the rear, a couple of hours after the first course is served. So, all you have to do is avoid the first ten courses inconspicuously, and satisfy your hunger at the end of the meal when everyone else is pretty much finished. Good luck.

—James and Firouzeh Attwood,
"Hong Kong Diary"

of Chinese animated conversation. We felt jettisoned into the vortex of an Oriental gypsy carnival.

"Shall we leave?" I shouted above the din.

"I don't think we can get out," she said. "Anyway, here comes Tso with more vittles." We fed each other miniature translucent dumplings stuffed with chopped shrimp and bamboo shoots. Then she brought a platter of crisp bite-sized, blood-red spareribs and we gnawed at the bones as though we were starving. The tea-pot emptied again.

Impossibly, more diners arrived, completely blocking the door. Great-grandfather limped through the throng exchanging greetings with everyone. Cigarette smoke, ginger, garlic, and cilantro odors choked the room as Tso, arms high, pressed sideways between the tables, hefting steaming trays.

No matter how packed the room, more diners pressed in. No one left. Canaries trilled in our ears, occasionally pausing in mid-song to nibble an impaled grasshopper. One insect's belly was completely chewed away yet its head continued functioning, its eyes appraising the happy customers. The eviscerated insect's antennae waved languidly, almost tickling the canary, its legs stretched as though aerobically exercising.

Throughout the hubbub, grandfather fed every bird. Overflowing hungry Chinese pressed around us. Others, more sociable, brought miniature three-legged stools and squeezed between our chairs. Many stood. A black Labrador, who appeared as much at home as anyone, pranced into the bedlam, almost sitting in Betsi's lap, and scratched vigorously. Tables came together forming a communal food counter. We laughed. New Chinese friends chopsticked gingered pork dumplings at us. More clumsily, but with immense enthusiasm, we returned ham-scallioned meatballs at them until Betsi said, "I can't eat another bite." At that moment, Tso placed a stacked bowl of lychee nuts on the table. "Sorry," Betsi confessed, spearing a lychee. "I just found a little more room."

A man sprang to the table top and limbered his arms, grasping his leg and stretching it above his head. No one noticed. Then he exercised around an imaginary tree trunk as though chasing himself in slow motion. His fingers traced long arcs in the room, his body extending angularly across the table. The amazing *tai chi* devotee continued while Tso returned with the check. We handed her 50 Hong Kong dollars. She made change and blew a kiss. We returned the courtesy and pushed outdoors.

"How much?" Betsi asked.

"Less than six U.S. dollars."

"We'll go back, and bring grasshoppers next time." Betsi nodded happily. "Yeah," she meditated. "I'll do it. I've never brought a bucket of grasshoppers as a hostess gift."

A wreath of contentment covered her face and I prayed for a continuous supply of VERY PLEASANT PLACES TO EAT.

Dr. Burley Packwood is a retired dentist and World War II veteran who grew up along the Yellowstone River in Billings, Montana. He is the author of Quail In My Bed *and* Bird Turd Peppers and Other Delights, *from which this story was excerpted. He is currently working on a novel based on West Indian life.*

★

Foods play a prominent role in Hong Kong superstitions, from eating noodles on birthdays (long strands symbolize longevity), using *fat choy* (sea moss) as a prosperity-propitious ingredient in dishes, or using peach pits as amulets for babies. The meal as medicine is also a topic whose lore could fill volumes, whether it is drinking snake blood or taking chrysanthemum petal tea. If a malady exists, there is a dish or a drink to remedy it.

—James O'Reilly, "Long Life in Every Alley"

DONALD W. GEORGE

* * *

Time and Again

The author sees Hong Kong anew—this time with his children.

WE LANDED AROUND 10:30 AT NIGHT, PICKED UP OUR BABY
stroller and bags, and waded through huge swinging doors into
the disorienting chaos of the arrivals area at Kai Tak airport—
clamorous with Cantonese and packed with people straining to see
someone, but no one for us.

Then we emerged into the sleek black calm of the hotel lim-
ousine area, where a smiling man in a blue suit and a smart cap was
indeed waiting for us, holding a sign that said The Omni Hong
Kong Hotel. He ushered us into a Mercedes, then embarked on a
twisting-and-turning, stopping-and-starting, amusement-park ride
through the neon-bright night. When we reached the hotel, with
Jeremy asleep in Kuniko's arms and Jenny in mine, we exited, eyes
blinking, into an opulence of marble and chandeliers; bellmen
scurried around us to carry bags, open doors and help us down
stairs, and we drifted, as only people who have been on an airplane
for fourteen hours can drift, into our room.

Now the rest of the family is asleep, and I stand at our window
and look out at the glittering constellation of nighttime Hong
Kong, pulsating with promise. That old wave of excitement sweeps
over me—what exotic possibilities await out there?—but I look at

my sleeping family and sigh: not for me. Not this time. Welcome to Hong Kong. And good night.

In the morning I set out with Jeremy and Jenny in search of breakfast and discovered a McDonald's—ah, the globe-girdling Golden Arches—around the corner from the hotel.

We were sitting in the happily, messily crowded down-stairs chomping on our Egg McMuffins and potato fritters when I noticed a trio of women at a nearby table smiling our way.

I returned their smile and one said, "You have very nice children. You want *amah*?"

I knew vaguely that *amah* is the local word for housekeeper, or maid—a multipurpose household helper who does every-thing from scrubbing floors to cooking to babysitting. Stupidly, I assumed they knew we were from the United States and were making a little joke.

"Oh, yes, of course!" I replied. "I would love to have an *amah*."

"I start right now!" the same woman said.

They do like this joke, don't they, I thought to myself. But then something in the woman's eye and tone caught me—she was seri-ous. And I surmised that she was one of the many Filipina women I had read about, who come to Hong Kong desperately in search of employment. Suddenly the whole situation tilted.

"I'm sorry, but we're from the United States. We *live* in the United States. We're just visiting."

"Ah." Her smile collapsed—then ascended again. "Anyway, you have nice children! Maybe you take me back with you?"

Welcome to Hong Kong. I was here a decade ago, and some things haven't changed: the streets teem now as then with people rushing somewhere, and signs in Chinese characters jut crazily from the buildings, demarcating the sky. But all in all, it seems a funda-mentally different city. I didn't much like Hong Kong ten years ago. It seemed too crowded, too noisy, too dirty, too obsessed with profit. I called it "the city without a soul."

But now, after a day of wandering, it seems magical rather than mercenary. No doubt this difference reflects changes in me as much as changes in Hong Kong, but whatever the reason, I find something admirable and amazing in the energy that shoots through the streets and the purposefulness of the people who crush around us—always being careful to sidestep our stroller—as we waddle along.

Hong Kong. Lightning flashes above Kowloon. The glow of a monstrous Motorola sign reflects off the harbor, capturing the squat ferry like moonlight, and it's beautiful, a symbol of Hong Kong, this quintessential capitalist haven, where the glowing lights of commerce can substitute for moonlight and we can look with awe and say, yes, it's beautiful. Gazing out over the water, to the mass of highrises and the huge commercial signs, you can feel the energy of a place open for business, but one where that very concept feels romantic.

*—Larry Habegger,
"New Days in Hong Kong"*

Most impressive of all is the astonishing harbor. From whatever vantage and at whatever hour, it surges with life and energy—boats of all sizes, speeds, shapes, and intents: fishing boats, ferries, container ships, pleasure craft, tugboats, destroyers (U.S.); a sea of amazing variety and vitality. And I am moved by the poetry of the skyline and the Peak—a mercantile poetry, if you will, the skyscrapers all gleaming steel and reflecting glass and audacious gold: the ultimate talismans/symbols of prosperity.

Today was devoted to family sightseeing, and it was wonderful. An extremely convivial young woman from the astonishingly efficient Hong Kong Tourist Association spent the entire day shepherding us around. We began with a ride on the green and white Star Ferry from Kowloon to Hong Kong, the ride probably every travel article ever written about Hong Kong has called—with considerable justification—one of the world's great travel bargains.

Our ride began on a misty gray morning, a chill wind coming off the bay. We bundled into the ferry's enclosed passenger area, and watched Hong Kong come to life as the vessel plowed into the waves. Around us, water traffic of infinite variety plied the gray waters—tiny fishing boats with inverted U-shaped roof covers, sleek sightseeing ships, long, low-slung boats and short, tubby boats. Beyond this ceaseless flow, gleaming skyscrapers rose toward the clouds, wave upon wave of concrete and glass, some long and sleek and others short and stubby as the ships. Beyond the skyscrapers, green hills lined with expensive houses and apartments rose into clouds, their peaks utterly obscured.

From the ferry terminal— and after a long pause for Jenny to stare at grizzled old men casting fishing lines into the oil-slicked water—we drove to Aberdeen and were treated to another side of Hong Kong's watery life, threading by sampan through the floating community there. This allowed awkward but endearing glimpses of intimate family life—babies bawling and mothers cradling, kids playing cards, women washing vegetables and stringing up laundry. As fishing craft chugged around us and boat-repairers clambered over damaged hulls, it also reinforced the realization that part of Hong Kong still lives on and by the sea.

You don't see it on the beaches, nor do you really notice it in busy Victoria Harbor, but when you hike into the hills or drive to scenic overlooks Hong Kong's bathtub ring is hard to miss. I first saw it on Lamma Island after strolling along a beautiful beach, then again looking down on the breathtaking sight of Clearwater Bay in Sai Kung: a white line of flotsam ran along the rocky coastlines as far as the eye could see. It was almost all styrofoam—take-out containers from fast-food restaurants and chunks of cheap coolers—deposited by the tides after being dumped from boats or tossed carelessly into the harbor. I was amazed the beaches were kept so clean.

—Larry Habegger,
"New Days in Hong Kong"

In the grand tourist tradition, we ate a delicious *dim sum* lunch—course after course of shrimp and scallops and other seafoods with ingeniously prepared vegetables—at the Blue Ocean Restaurant overlooking the harbor.

Then we drove on to Stanley Village, on the opposite side of the island from the skyscrapers and Star Ferries, to discover an entirely different aspect of Hong Kong life. Part of Stanley Village is a market selling everything you find elsewhere in Hong Kong, but in two crammed blocks of bargain shops: jewelry, clothes, camping supplies, produce. Another part is a street of mostly charming restaurants with no-frills names—Stanley French Restaurant, Stanley Japanese Restaurant, Stanley Oriental Restaurant, etc.— plus two pubs with dart boards, TV sets tuned to tennis and soccer matches and, at least today, brew-quaffers in shorts and rugby shirts spilling exuberantly onto the sidewalk.

The area serves a large European population as well as the tourists who bus or taxi in every day, and while Jeremy and Jenny played on the beach, I tried to imagine what it would be like to live here. Earlier in the day I had been reading in the *Far Eastern Economic Review* about elections in South Korea and new art movements in Thailand, legal problems in Malaysia and reforms in China—the kind of news U.S. publications barely touch—and reliving the old exhilaration of residing in a foreign country: how every day is a vibrant lesson, every preconception endlessly challenged; how overlooked areas become illuminated and day-to-day life around the globe becomes a vivid complexity.

As I pondered this in Stanley Village, two blond children in school uniforms strolled down the street carrying textbooks. I looked at Jenny and Jeremy and realized that my options had been infinitely simpler when I packed my bachelor bags for a two-year stay in Japan a decade and a half before.

Well after dinner, I finally find time to turn to today's *South China Morning Post*, only to find this latest variation on the theme:

"Files kept on activists, says official."

"Beijing admits it is gathering information on alleged anti-communist activists in Hongkong.... However, the Public Security Minister, Mr. Tao Siju, denied a report in a London newspaper that hundreds of Hongkong residents were blacklisted for persecution after takeover...."

"According to Mr. Tao, the Chinese Government abided by a strict 'standard' in their assessment of people who are the targets of intelligence."

"'We follow a political criterion. And it is whether [the person being evaluated] loves the country and loves Hongkong,' he said."

Somehow I don't think this is going to reassure a lot of people.

I sit in the sixth-floor restaurant at the Omni Hong Kong sipping English breakfast tea and watching the harbor scene outside. As always, boats endlessly ply the tarpaulin-like surface of the harbor, and beyond it, Victoria Peak slumbers like a folk-tale dragon in a bewitchment of mist and mystery.

Actually, I know the Peak exists: I ventured up there a few nights ago to attend a reception at the gracious house of the American consul general. All we could see of Hong Kong through the wide living room windows was foggy, far-off lights—Jenny said, "It's like living in a dream!" and one official chuckled and whispered to me, "She doesn't know how right she is"—but the bus ride up gave a good sense of the expansively handsome and hideously expensive dwellings on the way, and of the markedly—and perhaps I should say disproportionately—Western expat populace that lives there.

Cellular phones are the inescapable symbol of contemporary Hong Kong. In the bar in my hotel's lobby, four dark-suited businessmen sit down and ceremoniously set their telephones on the table. On the Star Ferry a passenger opens his briefcase, takes out his phone and conducts business as we roll toward the skyscrapers on the Hong Kong side. Every day I am brushed by businessmen walking rapidly down the street and talking rapidly into their phones. And yesterday as I breakfasted at the Regent Hotel, the man at the table next to me buttered toast, scanned the *Asian Wall Street Journal* and ordered catering arrangements for a weekend party of twelve at his home all at the same time.

In a wonderfully compact way, these mobile phones symbolize the masterful manipulation of—and some might say addiction to—technology in Hong Kong, and also the almost desperate sense of urgency, the feeling that you have to be on top of things every minute here or you may lose out to the other guy.

These phones seem to take on the aura of power objects à la Carlos Castaneda; they are more than communication links—they vividly embody the city's ongoing adrenalin rush, the ever-present sense of living on the edge.

As with most places, I begin this last day in Hong Kong not wanting to leave, feeling that I have barely scratched the surface of an intriguing and impenetrable culture.

How can I take home the energy I felt last night walking along the side streets near my hotel? There was a market lit by bare bulbs with a fantastic variety of fruits: durian, mango, papaya, mangosteen, orange, strawberries, apples.

Durian

Portable stalls sold skewered squid and dough balls dipped in honey. Pastry shops showed creamy sweets, and restaurants served up a mind-numbing variety of treats. Clothing stores and jewelry stores with hand-lettered signs touting "Sale! Sale!" were crowded with customers. Neon signs blazed everywhere over the sidewalk throngs.

And how can I preserve the passion that has taken root in my children here? When we take the Star Ferry, Jeremy almost climbs out the windows straining to take in all the waterborne life. And Jenny has been delighted by the never-ending variety of shops and streetside sights; fortune-tellers, snakes in store windows, ageless old men practicing *tai chi* in pocket-size parks.

Yesterday was a special success: Jenny was enchanted by the Sheung Yiu Folk Museum, an evocative restoration of a 19th-century Hakka village complete with kilns, kitchens, and everyday furniture and implements; and both Jenny and Jeremy loved the Ocean Park entertainment complex, especially the dancing dolphins and wave-making whales in the ocean theater and the bowl-balancing, plate-spinning, body-contorting exploits of the acrobats in the Empress Theatre, part of the altogether terrific Middle Kingdom area that traces Chinese history from 2205 B.C. to A.D. 1911.

I enjoyed these, too, especially the Middle Kingdom's exhibit of everyday Tang Dynasty village life, with flour-doll making, wood-block printing, fortune-telling and the like, and the re-creation of the Qing Dynasty emperor's extravagant summer palace. But the greatest thrill of all for me was our journey through the New Territories to the Chinese border. We passed by a succession of residential areas—a rumble-tumble hodgepodge of dingy shops and shrilling signs, dreary apartment buildings with laundry hung outside, and people waiting in interminable lines. Then, after perhaps 45 minutes, cultivated fields began to appear, and groves of trees; soon we were passing farms and isolated roadside shops, rice paddies and green hills—wide-open scenes.

Finally we turned up a hilly street, and parked in a pine-bordered lot, then followed a short train past desultory souvenir sellers to Lok Ma Chau, the prime spot where, in the old days before China was open to visitors, travelers would go to peer at the forbidden fields and hills. Something of that thrill remained in the air, and although fog painted the scene with a *sumi-e* brush, I could still make out the Shenzhen River that demarcates the territories, watery rice paddies and the checkpoint for entrance to China, where a dozen trucks waited.

I stood and looked for a long time, and Hong Kong's complicated role as a pawn in imperial power struggles—a place of refuge, riches and ruin, dream and despair—came back to me, and the *frisson* of 1997 shivered through me. Then bird song threaded through my thoughts, and the scent of wet pine. After all the crowds and chaos of the preceding days, I sighed at the peace and freedom of this poignant spot. And peering into the misty vastness of China, I wondered: What will become of this savvy, tenacious, unexpectedly compelling capitalist outpost? Will it even be here a generation later when Jenny and Jeremy return, perhaps with children of their own?

The birds sang, the pines perfumed the air. And I thought that even as I gazed into China, a world away on Hong Kong's other side, stocks were being sold and fortunes were being told, deals were being closed and clothes were being sewn, noodles were being slurped in slapdash stalls and in lavish restaurants, exquisite abalone was being served to men who were talking urgently into cellular phones.

I looked at my children, surprised by sudden tears in my eyes, and answered with sentimental certainty: Hong Kong will survive.

For eight years, Donald W. George was the award-winning travel editor of the San Francisco Examiner. *His career as a peripatetic writer started in Paris, where he lived and worked and fell in love (several times) the summer between his junior and senior years at Princeton. He is the editor of* Travelers' Tales Japan.

★

As I sit digesting a fine meal from the Café Deco atop Victoria Peak, my gaze lingers over the slender towers of Hong Kong which forest the city in the vertical images of a city from another planet. I think of the incoming Communist bureaucrats and the Hong Kongers fighting over various protocols for the transfer of power. Both sides would do well to recall the words of Hsun-tzu:

> There was a man of Ch'u fording the Yangtse whose sword fell from the boat into the water. At once he cut a notch on the boat and announced "This is where my sword fell from." The boat stopped and from where he had made the notch they went into the water to seek it. The boat had traveled on but the sword had not; wasn't he deluded to seek the sword like that? Governing one's state with the old standards is just the same. The time has shifted but the standard has not; how can you expect to govern with these?

Later, gazing at the sun setting on the South China Sea, the humidity holding me close, I am stunned by the beauty of the place, the splendor of its economics, and the ambition of its people. The sun tells me that a million dreams remain in the many colored towers around me, and my heart tells me that here a world is waiting to be born.

—Sean O'Reilly, "City of a Million Dreams"

JULIA WILKINSON

* * *

Land of Pearls

The old ways of life are getting harder to find.

NOT SO MANY YEARS AGO, A TRIP TO THE FAR NORTHEAST corner of Hong Kong territory from my island home in the south-west would have been a major excursion. After the one-hour ferry to Hong Kong island, there would be a bus trip to Hunghom station, followed by a slow ride on the funky old train that pottered north to the border. I'd be lucky if I got to the New Territories' market town of Tai Po by midday, let alone to the remote mountain areas lying to the northeast.

Things have changed: the electrified Mass Transit and Kowloon Canton Railways can rush you to Tai Po within 40 minutes of leaving Hong Kong island's Central district. But there's still a sense of adventure in exploring the lands far beyond Tai Po, where no public transport goes. North of Plover Cove, south of Starling Inlet (named not after resident birds, but survey ships of the 1840s) lie some of the least-trodden hills of Hong Kong, where wild boar still roam and leopards once lingered.

This is the land of the Hakka people, more recent arrivals than the Punti Cantonese-speakers. Old Hakka villages, many now abandoned, cling to cultivated coastal strips. Rough stone paths, established centuries ago, weave across grasslands, climb the fern-

153

clad hills, and drop into bays where no boats pass. The peaks of China lie close to the north, and to the east are the wild isles of Crooked Harbour and Double Haven. Not even Lantau, my neighboring giant of an island, can provide such variety, such a feeling of remoteness.

There were two places in particular I'd never managed to reach, and always yearned to see: Lai Chi Wo, and So Lo Pun. For all I knew, both could be in ruins, abandoned long ago, and overgrown by weeds. Or they could be flourishing market towns, with hundreds of busy Hakkas tending their crops, playing their *mahjong*, trading with the outlying islanders. I had to find out.

The villages lie on the coast facing Crooked Harbour. The only way to reach them is to walk. So I began at Wu Kau Tang, the nearest village accessible from Tai Po. This plateau north of Plover Cove Reservoir is a pugnacious little place. The residents of its half-dozen hamlets have always been fierce, harbouring anti-Japanese guerrillas during the war, and communist sympathies ever since.

I wouldn't be surprised if their ancestors were soldiers of the Sung Dynasty. Many were stationed near here to guard a lucrative traffic of pearls that travelled from Double Haven along a fort-lined Pearl Road westwards to Tuen Mun, and thence by ship to Canton.

Pearls were first found in the "Tai Po Sea" over a thousand years ago, and by 900 A.D. the monarchs of China were sending teams of divers to harvest the gems. Legends quickly spread about the rulers' obsession: one had an underground "pearl nullah," another decorated all the pillars and beams of his palace with pearls. Exploitation of the pearl beds was so thorough that when four Japanese pearling companies tried to reestablish the industry in Tolo Harbour in the 1960s, they found it was in vain.

Even if Wu Kau Tang wasn't exactly on the road to riches then, it certainly is now. Standing beside the crumbling ruins of old houses are dozens of fancy two-storey villas—"sterling houses" built with money villagers have sent back from Chinese restaurants all over England. Prominent 1967 and 1969 dates on the houses show when the trend began.

The ancestral hall is glistening with gaudy tiles and brilliant new colors. "It was only built three years ago," said a black-scarved old Hakka woman proudly when I peered in to have a look. But she showed little inclination to chat some more, and turned to sweep up firecracker papers lying in piles like autumn leaves. Firecrackers are, of course, illegal in Hong Kong. But who cares out here? As the old Chinese saying goes, "The mountain is high, and the king far away."

From Wu Kau Tang there were two routes I could take to Lai Chi Wo: the "direct" mountain one to the north, or the longer, gentler trail in the foothills, circling the 416-metre peak of Tiu Tang Lung to reach Lai Chi Wo from the south. I chose the softer option.

Nearly all the land round here is in the Plover Cove Country Park, and trails are well-marked, well-worn. But off the public path, the wilderness begins at once—dense groves of trees, eroded mountaintops, and hills of "iron-fern," the ubiquitous Hong Kong bracken. In the skies above, black kites are constantly gliding.

Until 1669, most people in Hong Kong area and the Pearl River estuary had been Cantonese speaking. After 1669, however, the depleted Cantonese clams who returned after the military campaigns against Koxinga were unable to bring back into cultivation all the lands they had previously controlled. The Imperial Government, anxious not to lose the taxes from these lands, urged the old families to sell off land to new settlers. These were mostly Hakka speakers from the northeast. Between 1669 and the mid-18th century hundreds of Hakka groups moved into the area, taking up the more marginal lands in the mountains, particularly in the east. It was a mixed society, of old Cantonese clans in the fertile west, newer Hakka families in the less fertile east, plus a few groups of Tanka and Hoklo boat people, that characterized the area when the British first appeared on the scene.

—Elfed Vaughan Roberts, Sum Ngai Ling, and Peter Bradshaw, *Historical Dictionary of Hong Kong & Macau*

The first abandoned hamlet soon appeared: Ha Miu Tin, once the home of 80 Hakkas, is now nothing more than a debris of fallen roofs, smashed doors and broken bowls and teapots. Much has been left behind, perhaps to appease the kitchen god. But the chests of clothes and rickety chairs, the chopsticks and bottles of cooking oil provide an atmosphere of unnerving desolation.

I moved on quickly to Sam A Chung, now a popular campsite on former paddy fields, a few minutes' walk from the sea. But around the corner was the prettiest spot yet, Sam A Wan. This protected cove faces the enchanting blue bay of Double Haven and is backed by wooded slopes. What a place to live!

I spot a row of old houses set inland from the sea, tucked into its own private hillock, and surrounded by silence. A large horse-shoe grave is in the place of honour on top of the hill, looking straight out to sea, so that "the melody of nature can refresh the departed spirit." What a place to die.

Nearby is the village of Sam A Tsuen. It looked perfect for exploring: a traditional New Territories village, with its terraced houses built in tight units to make the most of the best *feng-shui*, a nice little protective grove behind, and a stream in front. No one seemed to be around, though one of the front row houses had "Store" marked in English on its door.

I was just about to step off the path when two huge dogs came rushing for me, ferociously barking, teeth bared. Guard dogs are another New Territories tradition. It's not unknown for them to attack to the death. I picked up a stone and walked away as quickly as I could, the dogs snapping at my heels until they'd chased me off their territory.

A hillfire was my next encounter: a bamboo grove was crackling wildly, and flames were spreading quickly. What to do? Did anyone know this fire had started? A few steps on, and a man stood in the path, looking calmly at the fire.

"That fire dangerous?" I asked.

"Uh-huh," said the man, and kept on staring. "OK."

I was glad to reach Siu Tan after all this. Gentle, peaceful Siu Tan, with woods full of singing bulbuls and pipits, and a large expanse of water in three huge fish ponds reaching to the sea.

Pond fish farming began as a Chinese village custom more than 2,000 years ago, serving not only as a source of food, but also as a defense system and as a means of enhancing *feng-shui*. It became an industry in the New Territories this century, and now you can see ponds everywhere.

The ones at Siu Tan were still active, with work huts scattered all around. But this was no time to investigate further, for my goal was coming closer. The path turned sharply round the coast, and there, set back from the sea, almost hidden by trees, was Lai Chi Wo. Low lines of old, grey-tiled houses, backed by wooded foothills, a defensive wall in front, two gates, and a large temple on its outskirts. It was larger than any settlement I had yet passed, and it looked magnificent.

As the path weaved slowly across dry grasslands, through groves of twisting banyans and across the temple forecourt, I felt as if I were approaching a medieval city. But no one stood at the gate in the wall to greet me, no dogs came rushing forward with bared teeth. I entered the city alone, in silence.

It was obvious people still lived here: the rice-drying ground before the spirit-deflecting wall was full of piles of firewood; there were geese and chickens in cages; and a dog—I cringed—running away with its tail between its legs!

I began to walk up the central alley between the terraces, and soon startled two black-scarved old women sitting by their door. "Morning! *Jo sun!*" I said.

"*Jo sun!*" came a cackling reply.

"Are there many people living here?" I asked one of the women in Cantonese, as she plucked away at a ragged chicken. But she replied in a dialect I didn't understand. And only another cackling *"Jo sun!"* sounded from the doorway. The old women laughed and beckoned me closer. There, in a cage, was a black mynah bird.

"It only knows '*jo sun*,'" said the chicken-plucker's companion. "And we only know Hakka."

I smiled, and turned away. The lanes of the city were empty; nearly every house was shuttered, a light bulb glowing above the door, a spirit mirror in the window. Only 30 years ago, as many as 445 Hakkas lived in Lai Chi Wo, all belonging to the Tsang clan. Now where were they? In Manchester and Leeds, Glasgow and London?

"Hello!"

From round the corner of a house peered a little girl. But giggling, she ran away, down an alley, up a lane, away to the furthest corner of the village. Then I saw a man, middle-aged, well-dressed, unloading soft drinks from a trolley to a front-row house. He nodded curtly, said nothing. The Country Park path goes past this village—in one gate, out the other. There's probably some business to be had from selling drinks at weekends. But how do they make their living?

> *How many overseas Chinese who have lived and prospered in foreign lands all their adult lives say that when the time comes for them to leave this earth, they pray for enough warning to return to the mainland to live out their last days and be buried in the city, town or village where they drew their first breath? How many others toil at ironing boards, restaurant sinks or sewing machines not for themselves but for family members across the seas whom they know only by name? How many eminent Chinese, having won fame and fortune in the West, prefer to contribute their services and treasure not to the countries that nurtured their talents but to China, where their talents, had they remained, would never have flourished?*
>
> —Bette Bao Lord,
> *Legacies: A Chinese Mosaic*

"Money?" laughed the old woman. "We have no money!" And she went on plucking the bloody-necked fowl. "Everyone's gone. Some come back at New Year. Others never."

So I wandered alone past the terraced houses, listening to the hollow chime of a clock from some locked house, and the sound of singing birds from woods beyond. Occasionally, I glimpsed the man walking aimlessly, up and down, up and down, tracing the grid of alleys.

The imposing Hok Shan Temple outside seemed well looked-after, with an altar of plastic flowers before its red-faced, black-whiskered god. But there was no caretaker there, shuffling bamboo *chim*, or sweeping up the firecracker papers.

I walked out to the lovely bay, where a few small boats were hovering. *Kai-dos* still call here from the border town of Shautaukok, the only connection with the outside world. Once, it must have been a busy route, calling at other coastal villages like So Lo Pun, just north of Lai Chi Wo. But what would I find at So Lo Pun today?

I searched for the path. This obviously isn't a route that's often taken. All the signs from the jetty point the other way: and the path, when I found it, was overgrown and tangled. Invisible wild cows breathed heavily from dense thickets; only white grave chambers stood out clearly in the distance.

The old stone track climbed steeply up a fir and fern-clad hill, hugging the deep indents of the coastline. At the tip, the view was staggering: spread out below lay the extraordinary Crooked Harbour, with its crazy collection of islands (once land-based mountains), and the peaks of China in the distance. Several of these islands are still inhabited—particularly Kat O Chau, the largest and most crooked island of them all. Even little Robinson "Ap Chau" island hosts a small community (including, so it's said, a fanatical religious sect).

My gaze turned inland, seeking So Lo Pun. But all I could see were empty fish ponds. Down in the valley, across a muddy marsh-land, I found the village in ruins. Creaking bamboo groves sur-rounded a dark and narrow path that led past smashed doorways, all tangled up in ivy. In one house, large black and white pho-tographs of ancestors still hung on the wall. In another, ashes of fires showed where squatters had camped. On the thresholds of many houses stood, inexplicably, a single earthenware pot.

This was no place to linger. I clambered back up the hill, back down to Lai Chi Wo. How many years before this village, too, would be abandoned? I paused at the side gate. And as I turned to walk into the hills, I glimpsed, from the corner of my eye, the shadow of the little girl running away.

Julia Wilkinson is an English freelance travel writer who set off for Australia sixteen years ago and happily got stuck en route in Hong Kong. She has traveled extensively throughout Southeast Asia writing for many publications as well as contributing to several guidebooks. For the last ten years she and her husband have divided their time between Hong Kong's Cheung Chau Island and a cottage in the Wiltshire countryside.

★

"My name is Chan," said the elderly man. He thrust a camera my way and asked me to take his photo, chatting all the while, giving me his life story in what seemed like 25 words or less. "I live in Cleveland now. I'm American," he said proudly. "But I was born right here, in this village."

Behind him were the whitewashed walls of Sam Tung Uk, one of about a dozen walled villages that survive in Hong Kong's vast hinterland, the New Territories. They were founded by ancient Chinese clans who migrated to this region from points further north, people fleeing war and famine and pestilence. The migrants found peace and relative prosperity in the isolated valleys behind the Kowloon Hills, places like Sam Tung Uk, where the Chan family settled in 1786—just five years after the end of the American Revolution and a time when most of China was lost amid the chaos and decadence of the Manchu Dynasty.

"It wasn't like this when I was a boy," said Mr. Chan. He gazed up at the modern apartment blocks that surrounded his village. "This was all countryside. Our fields went down to the edge of the bay." Mr. Chan shook back and forth, as if to say: How times have changed.

—Joseph R. Yogerst, "The Land Beyond: Hong Kong's New Territories"

DAVID E. SCOTT

* * *

A Bottle a Day Keeps the Chinese Doctor Away

Wine or snake oil—you be the judge.

"YOU KNOW THAT SMELL THAT HANGS AROUND AFTER A HOUSE fire? Well, that's what this wine tastes like," Betty said, gingerly taking another tiny sip.

"I think with the right kind of food it could be quite pleasant," Eric said, rolling some of the Tzepao Sanpien Jiu around his mouth.

"It's like LePage's glue," was Wendy's contribution.

My palate sided with Betty's. The dark, oily wine smelled like slivovich but its bouquet was decidedly that of burned paint.

There were eight people at this informal wine tasting in my Hong Kong hotel suite, but only four were taking the exercise seriously and we were not to be hurried. Not when we were sampling a wine which cost about four dollars for a twenty-ounce bottle and which promised to cure: "untimely senility, kidney trouble, neurasthenia, sores in waists and backs, overburdens of the brain, anaemia, dizziness, poor memory, involuntary perspiration, insomnia, pale faces, and poor appetite."

It was one of six bottles I had bought in a Kowloon department store. Eric, a Hong Kong-based Canadian friend, had told me

161

about the Chinese wines. "Just look at the claims they make," he suggested. "They promise to cure everything from headaches to bunions." Betty, a friend visiting Hong Kong from Honolulu, was another willing volunteer as was my long-suffering wife, Wendy. She'll try almost anything—at least once.

We moved on to the Zhenzhu Hungchien wine which was the color of muddy varnish. It should be noted this was a serious tasting. Each wine was introduced to a fresh glass and tasters had glasses of bottled water to rinse their mouths. (The hotel's room service had been perplexed by my order for 48 wine glasses, 8 water glasses and several liters of bottled water.)

The molasses-colored China Nutritious Liquor at eight dollars a bottle made the wildest claims: "enables the blood in good circulation, has special effect towards the diseases as sexual impotence, pre-age weakness, pains in loin and vertebra, faint in kidney and spleen, no birth, etc. It can refresh your spirit, increase blood supply, reblacken the hair, restore high complexion so you will be constantly healthy, and can prolong your life to the maximus."

"It's just like that cough medicine they took off the market in the States because it had too much codeine in it," said Betty.

Eric, whose palate had weathered many years in Hong Kong, was more charitable. "Pleasant," he said. "It grows on you." But he didn't drink nearly enough for it to even start blackening his light brown hair.

The Cordyceps Tonic Wine from Shanghai had been distilled from "the rare, valuable Chinese drug *cordyceps sinensis* in combination with high quality wine of sorghum." Frequent drinking of it, the label said, "has a marked nutrient effect on senility and general debility during convalescence."

The vintners apparently concentrated all their skills on medicinal properties, leaving bouquet and taste to chance. "Like white lightning overlaid with dandelion bitter," Betty ventured.

It was perhaps presumptuous of us to expect the Boat Brand Special Tiger Bone Tincture to fondly recall a vintage Bordeaux or Medoc. Manufactured by the National Changsha Pharmaceutical Works, some of its many ingredients include: "tiger bone, 5.6

percent; *Rhizoma ligustici wallichii*, 5.6 percent and *Fructus chaenomelts lagenariae*, 11 percent." It was described as "mellow, a roborant and anti-rheumatic of remarkable potency."

"It has a woody taste…but not the burned-down house taste," proclaimed Betty, now at ease with oenological terms. "It's the worst yet."

"It has hundred-year-old-egg smell," Eric said, "but it tastes like varnish."

"Yech!" contributed Wendy, heading for the bathroom.

The most interesting wine was saved for last. This was the Chartreuse-colored Snake Bile Wine. It tasted just as one might have imagined snake bile would taste…and snake bile, for the benefit of those with unsophisticated palates, tastes uncommonly like rubbing alcohol.

Wendy, after carefully scrutinizing the fine print on all the labels, noted that the six wines I had selected claimed to cure or improve every spiritual malady known to man, and every bodily organ she had ever heard about. Except the liver.

*N*o animal has been graced with a greater aura of power and majesty than the tiger. Ironically it is this prodigious mantle of respect which is leading it down the path to extinction. Tiger Bone Wine is just one of many products which people believe to be an elixir of life. To ingest the tiger is to gain its vigor! Tiger bone medicines and tonics are believed to cure impotence, rheumatism and ulcers, to calm fright, prolong life, and protect against evil spirits. In the 1980s, a factory in Taiwan, an island which has never had an indigenous tiger, was using 2,000 kg of tiger bones a year to bottle 100,000 bottles of Tiger Bone Wine. [This represents 100-200 tigers.] The devastating slaughter of the Siberian and South Asian tiger has all but precluded their survival, and has created such a scarcity that the great tiger reserves of India and Nepal have become, in effect, shopping malls to satisfy a market based on ancient Chinese customs. With no proven medicinal value whatsoever, the strong belief in the efficacy of tiger bone medicine may soon lead to the disappearance, forever, of this magnificent animal from the forests of Asia.*

—Brian K. Weirum, "Tiger Bones"

David E. Scott is the author of five travel guidebooks to Ontario, has been published in most major North American magazines, newspapers, and travel guidebooks and was travel editor of The London (Ontario) Free Press *for fifteen years. He has wandered through 97 countries and lived in half a dozen of them. He has owned three weekly newspapers in Ontario and a bar-restaurant-discotheque in the European Co-Principality of Andorra.*

★

The Chinese have always been great herbalists, and in the 16th century they produced a *materia medica* that listed 2,000 drugs and some 8,000 prescriptions which included iodine, kaolin, and ephedrine, a form of inoculation for smallpox, and a treatment for syphilis. By the mid-19th century they had published a *Research into the Names and Virtues of Plants* that ran to 60 volumes and contained 2,000 accurate drawings.

—Dennis Bloodworth, *The Chinese Looking Glass*

* * *

Shop! In the Name of Love

Even the most diehard anti-shopper can be seduced in Hong Kong.

AH, HONG KONG, WILL I EVER BE THE SAME? PROBABLY NOT. NOR will anyone else who sets foot on the world's most beautiful filthy streets. The bargains are theirs for the carting away. The savings are there to be spent, again and again.

Who cares if I pay a *gweilo* tax—that tidy bit of profit made on the fact that I am a foreigner? Who cares if some of the fabulous is fake? Does anyone mind that I came here with a tooth-brush and I am leaving with a lifestyle? Excuse me if I huff and puff. My heart is beating faster; my palms are beginning to itch. When confronted with the deals and steals that make Hong Kong all that it is, I tend to be greedy. I am the ultimate of compulsive shopoholics—I just want more. Sometimes I have to take savings of 100 or 300 percent, even with the *gweilo* tax. Sometimes I just have to cope.

And cope you will when you hit the streets of Hong Kong, of Tsimshatsui and the factory neighborhoods of Kwun Tong and Lai Chi Kok. On the second day you will realize what a fool you were on the first day; the third day you will have learned enough to know how green you were when you began, and how green you would remain if you stayed in Asia forever. It is the beginning of wisdom, Hong Kong style. Confucius says: the smart shoppers keep on shopping.

She who can walk through a mile of blinking neon lights, surrounded by millions of dollars' worth of golden trinkets, watches, angora sweaters, seed pearls, and video cameras, and can still hold her head up, will remain victorious. All others will fall prey to Hong Kong Overdose: a feeling of confusion that leads to headache, a gnawing fear that just down the street lies another bargain, rumbling in the pit of the stomach that soon leads to an aversion to crowds, to clothes with little alligators and to anything cooked in a wok.

Shopping in Hong Kong can be heaven or hell. Some will run on adrenaline, as they snatch the goodies and paper the shop counters with their Hong Kong dollars. Others will retreat to the Regent Hotel to stare blankly at the sampans in the harbor while they start to stutter in their stupor. Ordinary men will do extraordinary things in Hong Kong. Women who have lots of credit cards will do even more extraordinary things.

Shopping in Hong Kong is a serious sport. Indeed, Hong Kong has immortalized the art of shopping till you drop. Some may train for years for Wimbledon or the Boston Marathon; I've trained for a lifetime to conquer Hong Kong.

I never go to Hong Kong without a list of what I want to buy—how many suits to be made for my husband; how many pairs of shoes to be copied and of what color and leather; how many pairs of glasses to choose; how many Donna Karan bodysuits to have duplicated; how many cheap gifts that look expensive.

There is method to my madness. I keep a notebook in my purse, listing those stoops I wish to conquer. I have the U.S. prices listed per item, each on a separate page. I spend the flight time from Los Angeles to Tokyo in second-stage preparations, studying guidebooks, fashion magazines, and free handouts. I sleep from Tokyo to Hong Kong, sealing in my new-found knowledge and steeling myself for the excesses to come. An athlete must be well rested.

As I wait for my suitcases, I remember with glee that the international luggage allowance is two pieces—weight no longer matters. My suitcases are the largest ones made, and they are empty save for the nylon tote bags—also empty—that are stuffed inside them. Before the bags arrive I practice the litany of my creed. I repeat the basics over and over again.

Home in on the winners. Suze, I tell myself: the best high-end bargains are on first-quality merchandise in top-of-the-line stores where the goods are made locally. Thou shalt forget about jewelry. Suze, China and porcelain savings can be worth the cost of shipping. Avoid European designer ready-to-wear, cameras, electronics, computers (hard and soft ware), pearls (except seed) and antiques without provenance. Spend money to save; forget the junk that's bulky or heavy.

Give each piece you buy the evil eye and check for the spelling of the brand name (Kolak is not Kodak; Rollax is not Rolex), the thickness of the watch, the weight of the jewelry (gold is heavy), the hand of the fabric (if it bites—forget it), the clarity of the silk screen.

Meet your tailor on your first

The translucent plastic bag, besides being the representative national fish and flag of Hong Kong, appears to have been invented to only partially conceal its contents and thus satisfy the eternal curiosity of Hong Kong people for other people's shopping. Hong Kong people peer through bags in the street and on public transport with an impertinence not usually ascribable to Chinese people as a whole. Mainland people are of course great gapers but what is not usually remarked upon by foreign observers is their mastery of the surreptitious gaze. Hong Kong people are intensely curious about the contents of wallets, handbags, drawers, briefcases and, one must add, trousers and brassieres, and their gazes are often far from surreptitious.

—Dr. George Adams, *Games Hong Kong People Play: A Social Psychology of the Hong Kong Chinese*

day in town in order to have at least three fittings for custom work; warm up by working the clean stores, the fancy factory outlets and the Hong Kong side. Take the 40-minute bus ride to Stanley Market on the morning of the second day, then graduate to Kowloon—but just in small doses. On the third day, be strong enough (and smart enough) for more of Tsimshatsui, or take a

$\mathcal{H}$ong Kong is king of the business suit, and as in Shanghai and Singapore, you can quickly get exactly what you need in cut, quality, fabric, color, and weight within a few days. You are, however, warned to avoid the 24-hour custom-made suit.

—Edward G. Hinkelman,
*Hong Kong Business: The
Portable Encyclopedia for Doing
Business with Hong Kong*

more adventurous trip to Kwun Tong or Lai Chi Kok. Visit Sham Shui Po and its crazy electronics center only when you're fresh, never when you're tired. Keep your cash in a money belt, wear comfortable shoes and a small handbag strapped across your body, and you might want to carry a backpack.

Never regret a price paid, and never forget. Leave town with a smile, and consider that Douglas MacArthur was just a few islands off. It was Hong Kong to which he meant to return.

Suzy Gershman is one of shopping's royalty and former editor at a number of major publications. She writes regularly for Travel & Leisure *and her series is used by the Harvard business school to help form new capitalists. She lives in Connecticut with her husband and son.*

★

A petite, and well-dressed Chinese woman picked up a linen embroidered tablecloth in a bustling store on Kowloon's Granville Road, and gestured to the shopkeeper asking a price. After a long preamble describing the fineness of the work, and the hundreds of hours spent on it by needle-workers in Suzhou, he confided it would cost about $6,000 (HK).

There followed much sucking of teeth, accompanied by gestures of disbelief, and many minutes of commentary about how many shops sell such tablecloths, and how cheaply they are made in China.

In the minutes that followed, the mysterious rituals of haggling unfolded. Voices were never raised. There was much smiling and laughing. There were many restatements of honourability, good faith, and being a good customer. Promises were made about bringing more business to the shop by getting friends to come. There were inquiries about a better price if she bought two. Emphasis was placed on the fact she could pay in cash.

It all took half an hour. Both seemed happy as a deal was sealed and the cloth gift-wrapped—though the shopkeeper made occasional protests of how much money he was losing. When she emerged, she had in fact paid $1,250 (HK).

Haggling in Hong Kong has been refined to an art form in which most western shoppers are timorous amateurs. While certain shops stick to fixed prices, haggling is taken for granted in most of them, and most western shoppers miss out on the sport that for many Hong Kongers appears to be the principle point of any purchase: it is the travelling, rather than the arriving, that makes it all worthwhile.

—David Dodwell, "Hong Kong: A Paradise for Hagglers,"
The Financial Times

GARRY MARCHANT

✳ ✳ ✳

Hiking Hong Kong

How to get lost less than one block from home.

THE LIGHT WAS FADING RAPIDLY, AND WE WERE LOST IN THE jungle without a torch. Banshee shrieks and screeches echoed from the dark trees that pressed in from all sides, and night creatures rustled in the undergrowth. Vines hung across the path like menacing, multilimbed reptiles, thorns scratched at our arms and legs, and insects buzzed around our heads. It was now so dark, we could barely make out the white stones on the path ahead. With no moonlight to guide us, we faced the prospect of a long, eerie night huddled together in the darkness. Then, carrying through the still air, we heard voices ahead.

Half an hour later, we were sitting in a little Korean restaurant in the former fishing village of Aberdeen on the south side of Hong Kong, with thin slices of marinated beef sizzling on a gas burner before us. Hiking in Hong Kong, one of the world's most densely populated cities, is forever an exercise in contrasts and surprises.

For here, more than anywhere else in Asia, raw wilderness encroaches on a dynamic, modern city, and is easily accessible to the casual explorer. On this particular afternoon, hiking the mountainous southern slopes of Hong Kong Island, we were never more than a few hundred metres above high-rise apartment blocks, yet still managed to lose ourselves in the forest.

Hiking the territory's hills offers an easy escape from the raucous, teeming city of six million souls, providing both adventure and relaxation; a much sought-after sense of space and sufficient solitude to satisfy a cloistered monk. Passing the start of most trails, you can often walk for hours without seeing another human being.

I took up hiking quite by chance, when my lady friend and I found ourselves atop Victoria Peak one sunny August Sunday during our first summer in Hong Kong. Spying a path head-

Many people think of Hong Kong only as a city bursting at the seams. The territory of Hong Kong is actually 70 percent countryside with twenty-one parks and seventeen reservoirs; it includes Hong Kong Island, the Kowloon peninsula, the New Territories and 235 other islands. You can walk for hours in some of these places without seeing a soul.

—JO'R, LH, and SO'R

ing down the hill, we decided to follow it. Soon, it seemed, we were walking where no man (aside from those who cut the original path) had ever trod. After a long, steep, and exceedingly hot descent, we arrived, exhausted, but exhilarated, in the island's Western District. Enjoying our first restorative chilled pint, we learned from the radio that the day was the hottest in Hong Kong for 100 years.

In time, weekend hiking—this high-pressure city's most convenient no-frills stress reducer—was to become a hard-and-fast habit. The trails are easily reached by ferry, train, or bus (many are a mere taxi or Peak Tram ride from the city's Central District), and unlike windsurfing or golf, hiking requires no special equipment. A pair of ordinary training shoes will take you almost anywhere worth going in Hong Kong. Grab one of the excellent Countryside Series maps from the Government Publications Centre in the Central Post Office, or from any good book store, and you are almost set.

For warm-weather hiking, a small cotton towel is useful to wipe the sweat from your brow, and to dip in streams for cooling off. A small, cheap rucksack will carry energy-boosting snacks of oranges, chocolate bars or peanuts, and a plastic bottle of water. (Marchant's hiking tip No 1: Leave the bottle half full in the freezer the night before; top it up just before setting out, and you'll have a cool drink the rest of the day.)

Hong Kong hiking can be as easy as a short stroll around the paved path of Victoria Peak, or as strenuous as a long, steep trek up the rival slopes of Sunset, Lantau, or Tai Mo Shan. And if you are properly prepared, it's safe. Years of hiking here have taught me two basic rules: it gets dark at night and if there is no line on the map indicating a path, and no path in sight, there is probably no path. Elementary map-reading skills help for those leaving the main routes. The day we were lost above Aberdeen, I made a basic navigational error, turning left where the map said right.

Geography accounts for the abundance of wilderness abutting this over-crowded city. The mountains are too steep for even Hong Kong developers to build on, but not too difficult to climb. Passengers peering from the portholes as they arrive in Hong Kong by air will see a sight that jars with the standard image of the city. This is a dramatically rugged setting, with vast and unexpected space, bare mountains and unpopulated islands. About three quarters of Hong Kong's 1,000 square kilometres is rural, including 40 percent which is designated as country park. And hiking trails cross all this empty land.

Some are little more than ancient stone paths connecting pre-colonial villages, others dirt trails leading to traditional hillside graves. Many are access roads to parks or reservoirs, or concrete drainage culverts that circle the bulging mountains like stays in a girdle.

In this rugged land, it pays to stick to these well-defined paths. On Lantau Island, an ill-fated attempted shortcut across a river valley led us to a steep slope where the underbrush had recently been burnt away. We finally struggled out, and walked into prim Discovery Bay covered with charcoal like a pair of chimney sweeps.

Once, we left the main road to Shek O village to follow a path leading down the valley towards the jumble of roofs below. The "path" disappeared in tangled overgrowth near the valley bottom, but we could tell by the yelping puppies ahead that we were close to our destination. Struggling on, we became ensnared in undergrowth near a stream bed, stumbled across a traditional Chinese grave site scattered with pieces of ancestral burial pottery, and finally, clothes ripped, emerged into a vegetable patch. The "puppies" were a pack of baying farmyard hounds, growling and snapping at our heels as we rushed for a gate, slamming it shut just in time.

Despite such minor misadventures, happy images linger from my hikes: sea eagles and kites swirling lazily in the sky; cattle grazing on hillsides, and farmers tending vegetable fields; a family burning incense at a hillside temple; lying back in the tall grass on Lantau Island, watching giant 747s, gracefully descending towards Kai Tak Airport; dozing to the soothing sound of wind through grass, and the ripple of a nearby stream.

Trudging these hills, I'm always struck by the territory's varied geography. The famous description of Hong Kong as a "barren rock" was accurate in its time. By the 1840s, farmers had cleared native oak forests so that Hong Kong Island was grassy hills, much like Lantau Island today. Throughout the late 19th and early 20th century, the former Botanical and Forestry Department planted hundreds of thousands of native and exotic trees in water catchment areas to prevent soil erosion, effectively covering this "barren rock" with a green blanket of pines, gum trees, and bamboo.

During a short outing on Hong Kong Island a hiker may encounter dense rainforest with vines, ferns and thick trees, stretches of high grasslands, bare ridges topped with wind-sculptured scrub, and bare rock hillsides. More rugged Lantau has wide vistas of open, grassy hills, where waterfalls plunge down sheer cliffs, deep valleys with stands of bamboo, flowering trees, and mangrove, rocky promontories and sandy beaches.

Hikers may also discover something of Hong Kong's history through chance encounters with abandoned villages, ancient monasteries, old Chinese forts or concrete bunkers from a more recent conflict, all long since reclaimed by the spreading jungle.

One of the eeriest sights I've seen came after a long, steep hike up Lantau's Sunset Peak when the midday, midsummer sun forced us to cool off in a stream. Near the top, the skyscrapers of far-off Hong Kong were clearly visible, but as we approached the peak, patchy fog set in. Then, between jagged snatches of mist, appeared an abandoned police post and several strange, box-shaped stone bungalows perched on the bare ridge. It would have been the perfect setting for a Sino-Gothic horror movie.

I learned later that these were old holiday homes once owned by missionary societies and various clubs. One romantic story has it that escaped British prisoners of war hid out there during World War II, but this seems unlikely, unless they were herbivores content to graze on the long grass for the three years of Japanese occupation.

Another time in the hills further west, past the giant yellow Flying Dragon sculpture perched on a large rock, we happened on a vision of Old China. Loong Tsai Ng Yuen is a private villa with zigzag bridges crossing a large lotus pond where giant golden carp swim among the lily pads, traditional pavilions, overgrown gardens, moon gates, and crumbling old pagodas. The only person in sight was an old man sitting by the entrance, selling drinks cooled in a rippling stream.

Once, leaving Lantau's Po Lin Monastery, crowded with weekenders who had come to view the giant Buddha statue, we headed down the path towards Tung Chung village. Other hikers walked only as far as the Tei Tung Tsai Monastery where monks and nuns in ancient attire tended their gardens. We continued alone along the wooded path to the coast. Halfway down, we happened on another, deserted monastery, its solid buildings locked up like an off-season holiday cottage. Weeds, flowering bushes, grasses, and scented orange trees grew wild in the yard. We picked some mandarins and relaxed in the midday silence, looking out across the water towards Kowloon. Hiking is exercise for the soul as well as the body.

Beginners can easily take up hiking by following one of three well-marked trails. These are broken up into stages which can be reached by public transport. The 50-kilometre Hong Kong Trail on

Hong Kong Island runs from Victoria Peak to the village of Shek O at the southeast end of the island. The more difficult 70-kilometre Lantau Trail circles that island along high ridges and the scenic northern coast. The newest, and most difficult, the 100-kilometre MacLehose Trail links eight parks as it crosses the New Territories from the eastern sea, over the highest mountain in Hong Kong, Tai Mo Shan (957 metres) ending in Tuen Muen.

I was once shanghaied into leading a walk for a half-dozen hikers, all of different physical abilities and degrees of enthusiasm. Our party included a delicate English rose in white shorts and knee socks, fresh off the plane from London, a wisp of a Chinese girl elegantly outfitted in designer sportswear, and several city dwellers, like myself more accustomed to bar crawls than hill walks.

I chose a route on Lantau, from Silvermine Bay to Discovery Bay. It seemed simple enough, except for one small, green valley in the middle with no path through it. No problem, I thought. It was only about a centimetre on the map. When we reached the edge of the valley, we could see the other side, and the main path, just a few hundred metres away. We could either cut through the bush for a few minutes, or take a long detour high up over the mountain. There seemed to be no contest, and so we plunged into the shrubbery. A half-hour later we were entangled in the thick underbrush down the hill, with no visible path forward or back.

"Follow the stream down," said one of the city dwellers, recalling lessons learned from early boy-scout manuals. "It's bound to lead to the river, and the beach." The rocky stream bed did lead down—to a sheer rock face that led in turn to an ankle-deep swamp amid near impenetrable undergrowth.

We lived to tell the tale, and several gruelling hours later, mud splattered and bleeding from scratches and insect bites, we reached Discovery Bay. Exhausted but grateful to be out of the woods, we agreed it was an "adventure" (at least in the sense a friend defines it, as what happens when something goes wrong). There the neophyte hikers conceived the third essential rule of Hong Kong hiking (after "don't hike after dark," and "keep to the map trails"): never follow a certain writer into the woods.

Garry Marchant started his career as a copy boy and reporter for the Winnipeg Tribune *but later quit his job to roam around the world. He worked for small weeklies for awhile, then hitchhiked to Rio de Janeiro where he became editor of the* Brazil Herald. *Later, he spent several years working as a reporter for the* South China Morning Post *and as an editor for the* Far Eastern Economic Review. *He currently resides in Hong Kong.*

★

Visit Lantau Island's northern coastline and you'll be greeted with an astonishing sight off-shore: a massive new plot of land, six kilometres long and three-and-a half wide. Once there was a simple little island here called Chek Lap Kok. Now it's been flattened and expanded to make the site for Hong Kong's new multi-billion dollar airport, expected to be operational in 1998.

The infrastructural links between the airport and downtown Hong Kong are as staggering as the engineering challenge of the airport site itself. Under construction are the world's longest road-rail suspension bridge, 34 kilometres of expressways, a mass transit rail-link and a third cross-harbour tunnel. Where once there was a sleepy little fishing village called Tung Chung, opposite Chek Lap Kok, will eventually be a new town for 150,000 people.

The political background to the airport's development has been just as dramatic. The method of financing the project and the choice of consortiums for the valuable construction contracts (worth US$3.8 billion) has caused political turmoil for years, with well-publicised bickering between China, Britain, and Hong Kong which frequently stalled work.

Creating more waves have been the environmentalists, insisting the government save precious mangroves, tiny frogs, sacred hilltops, and endangered dolphins. Local fishermen have complained about the muddied seas and demanded compensation. And aviation experts have voiced concerns about the number of new airports in the area. All this money, effort, and hullabaloo for an airport that some critics say won't even be needed post-1997 and others claim will soon be incapable of handling the growing volume of passenger traffic.

—Julia Wilkinson, "Hong Kong Notes"

✦ ✦ ✦

Tao of the Racetrack

A would-be punter gets the jitters.

I'M NOT A GAMBLER. I KNOW NOTHING ABOUT HORSES. BUT I WAS drawn irresistibly to the track in Hong Kong. I'd heard the amazing numbers about gambling on the horses here, more money being bet on one race than in a week's racing in the U.K., or more in a season than in all the tracks in the U.S. combined. Something about this seduced me, and I had to go see for myself.

The horses weren't running that day at Happy Valley so I took the MTR from Central to Shatin in the New Territories, reflecting on the last time I'd been to a horse race. It was 1979, in another land heavily influenced by the British: India. I was idling away the autumn in the hill station of Darjeeling, where the ponies ran every Saturday at a track high on a ridge. Everyone in town went to the track that day, sitting high up the hillside for the best views, and I followed. For less than a dollar you could place your bets, and I joined in, picking ponies at random, losers all.

> *There is an old Chinese expression that says, "With money, a dragon; without money, a worm."*
>
> —JO'R, LH, and SO'R

They didn't have a starting gate then, so to begin the races the

ponies lined up facing away from the starting line. They trotted in
the wrong direction, then turned on a signal and raced for the
start. In the next-to-last race my pony forgot to turn around with
the rest of the pack and ran four or five strides in the wrong direction while the rest were off and running. After finding his way
my horse made a gallant effort, passing most of the field in the
two-lap race but finishing just out of the running.

In the last race I had a chance to make up my day's losses. My
horse came out fast, led through the first lap but was lagging in the
home stretch. Still, as I leapt and shouted he hung on to win by a
nose. Elated, I went to collect my winnings, but the clerk just
handed me back my ticket and said it was no good. I looked, and to
my astonishment discovered I'd been given a ticket for the wrong
horse. Two names sounded similar and the man who had accepted
my bet had misunderstood. I'd won, but I'd lost again.

I arrived at Shatin in the middle of the day's events. The place was
huge, with a capacity of more than 50,000, nudged against brilliant
green hills. It was packed and buzzing, but no one was sitting up
the hillsides here. Out on the track nothing much was happening
other than half a dozen women walking slowly down the track,
tamping clumps of turf down with wooden blocks on the ends of
poles. The green track would have made the finest gardener proud.
Beyond, a huge electronic screen flashed results of earlier races.

People were poring over race forms. I climbed to get a better
view and squeezed in with the crowd, being welcomed with smiles
and a laugh by those around me. In time a race was about to start.

The race began near the eventual finish line and the chatter rose
a notch as the horses took off. When the horses went into the first
turn and almost out of sight I realized that everyone was watching
the race on the electronic screen, what looked to be about the
biggest TV ever built. There we were, thousands of us, together,
adrenaline rising, not watching the race at all, but watching TV.

It was hard to take my eyes off the screen, harder still to know
what part of the track the horses were on because they kept running
across the screen. I lost all sense of the race's continuity until I
pulled myself away and looked up the track where the horses

would appear in the home stretch. And there they were, a tiny band flying across the grass, growing larger by the second. For a moment it was glorious—beautiful, silent movement that should have been thunderous as the field of horses raced our way, accompanied by the rising roar of the crowd—and then they rushed past the finish line and the jockeys rose out of their saddles and the horses began to slow.

I had no idea who had won or lost, but the energy was high. Results flashed up on the screen and the noise of the crowd fell to a low hum. And in a little while, out came the line of women with their wooden mallets to put the turf back in shape again.

Before the next race I wandered into the betting area to see where all this gambling happened. I saw a man punching numbers into a hand-held computer and asked if he was figuring the odds, but he said he was placing his bets for the next five races.

I was perplexed.

"I can place my bets here," he indicated the computer, "or I can place them over there," he said, gesturing toward what looked like an ATM.

"So it's like gambling with a bank account?"

He nodded. "If I win, it goes in my account. If I lose, it comes out."

All you need to bet on the horses in this high-tech town is an account and a bank card. No tickets, no exchange of currency or coin, just plug in and smile at your winnings. How efficient; how frightening.

Would my bank card work? I wondered. I walked slowly to the ATM. I pulled out my wallet and

It isn't even necessary for would-be bettors to come to the track. Deep in the bowels of the large stand at Shatin, 1,810 clerks with earphones sit at TV terminals accepting bets by phone. Above the screams, stickers proclaim, "Good Service is the Policy of Our Jockey Club" and "Be Polite, Be Gentle to the Customer." Manager David Lam told me it is the biggest such facility in the world; 620,000 people have accounts into which they have put a deposit. They call in with their code number and place their bets.

—Ross Terrill, "Traveling in Style: Irrational Hong Kong," *Los Angeles Times* fingered my card. I reached out, then saw my reflection in the screen.

I'm not a gambler, I thought. I know nothing about horses. And even with electronic efficiency I'd probably still get the wrong horse. So I went back outside with the crowd to enjoy the fresh air, the gleaming green track and surrounding hills, to watch TV.

Larry Habegger is co-editor of the Travelers' Tales *series. He is also co-author of "World Travel Watch," a monthly syndicated column that appears in newspapers throughout the United States.*

★

While Hong Kong has prospered under free-wheeling capitalism, its racing has flourished under the auspices of a central racing body that controls all aspects of the sport. The Hong Kong Jockey Club, founded in 1884 and given the prefix "Royal" in 1960, has become one of the most powerful organizations in the colony, many of its 15,000 full members among Hong Kong's business and political elite. The non-profit Royal Hong Kong Jockey Club, sometimes likened to a benevolent dictatorship, orchestrates everything from the scheduling of meets and the amount of prize money to the awarding of licenses to owners, trainers, and jockeys.

"The system we have here wouldn't work in any other part of the world," said the chief executive of the club, Major General Guy Watkins. The Jockey Club even limits the number of horses—three—an owner may have. "We are trying to make sure racing is not dominated by a few rich men who are running twenty or thirty horses each," Watkins said.

—Jacqueline Duke, "Hong Kong's New Heights," *The Blood-Horse*

STANLEY KARNOW

* * *

Hong Kong's Stanley

Good feng shui *lasts and lasts.*

I'VE ALWAYS DOUBTED THE ADAGE THAT YOU CAN'T GO HOME again. It's a matter of perspective: you're bound to be disappointed, perhaps even depressed, unless you accept the reality that nothing remains the same.

Guided by that notion, I recently went back to Stanley, a village sandwiched between two bays, on a narrow promontory pointing like a crooked finger into the China Sea from the southern coast of Hong Kong Island. I lived there for nearly a decade during the 1960s when I was a reporter in Asia, and, returning after an absence of nearly twenty years, I savored the bitter-sweet taste of its change and continuity.

Like Hong Kong itself, Stanley has been a crucible of West and East, where a few Americans and Europeans with a penchant for local flavor have preferred to reside among Chinese rather than segregate themselves in enclaves. Thus it belies Kipling's thesis that never the twain will meet.

My wife and I originally stumbled onto the tiny hamlet, then chiefly occupied by fisherfolk, while hunting for a house. We had ventured into the open market, situated in the square, where fishermen attired in black cotton pajamas and broad basket hats were proclaiming their catch of the day in singsong Cantonese. Peasants in similar garb presided over bins of fresh fruit and vegetables, which they had carried in on swaying shoulder poles from plots nearby.

Main Street, actually an alley, comprised a handful of small shops, among them a grocery, a tailor, and a barbershop. Eclipsed by lacquered ducks and joints of pork dangling from hooks, a butcher wielding his cleaver with the skill of a surgeon carved up meat and poultry, carefully saving such esoteric delicacies as gizzards, hearts, and lungs. A sweating cook in a filthy apron, his wok engulfed in the blaze of a roaring stove, served bowls of pan-fried noodles and steaming rice to customers seated on stools at outdoor tables.

At the tip of the peninsula stood Stanley Fort, whose rotating regiments, replete with bagpipes, symbolized the last British bastion in the Orient. The Union Jack flew over a minuscule police station, and Chinese constables—the surrogates of Britain's imperial presence—patrolled the village in starched khaki shorts, nominally maintaining the peace in a place, I later learned, where the only disorders were intermittent squabbles between neighbors.

The little port then was packed with sampans, and out at sea we saw high-sterned junks cruising lazily among faraway islands, their battened sails silhouetted like the wings of giant moths against the misty horizon. The vista could have been a classic Chinese painting, and we instantly fell in love with the spot.

I might add that its name, my own, also appealed to my ego. In actuality, Stanley was so christened to honor an English peer who, as secretary of state for the colonies, oversaw the war between the British and the Chinese, which resulted in the takeover of Hong Kong in 1842. The Chinese called the place Chek Chue, which for some obscure reason signifies "crimson pillar." The name has also been linked to the term for "pirates' lair," memorializing buccaneers like the fabled Cheung Po Tsai, who reputedly sallied forth from Chek Chue to prey on ships and settlements in the region. Periodic expeditions to retrieve his treasure, said to be concealed in a grotto in the vicinity, have proved to be futile.

We found a dream house tucked into a quiet lane at the edge of *Tai Tam Wan*, or "big bay." The view of the water framed against a background of verdant slopes was breathtakingly beautiful. Stone steps curled down between boulders to a private cove. A gnarled flame tree shaded the garden, which was blooming with pots of plants and flowers.

The rent was right, and the owner, an amiable Chinese dentist who chose to be near his office in town, was versed in ancient wisdom. As we sipped a ritual cup of tea after signing the lease, he confided to us, "You are very lucky. The *feng shui* is perfect."

Baffled by his cryptic remark, I hastened to bone up on *feng shui*, literally "wind and water," a concept that has pervaded Chinese thinking for centuries. It stems from an ancient folk belief that the universe is dominated by the opposite cosmic forces of yang and yin, active and passive, male and female, hot and cold, light and dark. Kept in equilibrium, the two yield a harmonious environment.

Our house, as the landlord suggested, fit the idea admirably. Its perch over the bay presaged a fortunate balance of wind and water. The elevation was healthy, and the windows faced the dawn, a portent of renewed life. Several other features were favorable: a

Zhang Baozi (Cheung Po-tsai in Cantonese) was the son of a fisherman in Guangdong Province who, at the age of fifteen, was carried off by the pirate king, Cheng Yat, to live the life of an outlaw.

In 1808 Cheung Yat's ship foundered in a storm near Indonesia and he was drowned. His wife assumed command of his fleet and she fell in love with the young Cheung Po-tsai. Cheung swiftly rose to power, and he was given command of a division of the robber fleet. He soon made a name for himself as a man of integrity, treating his followers fairly and refraining from exploitation of the villagers from whom he bought provisions.

Cheung's fleet numbered more than 270 ships and 30,000 men. He is said to have built Man Mo Temple in Hollywood Road and a fort half way up Mount Gough, between May Road and Kotewall Road, while the Tin Hau temples at Ma Wan, Cheung Chau and Chek Chue (Stanley) were apparently used as outposts.

—Sally Rodwell, *Historic Hong Kong: A Visitor's Guide*

clump of bamboo on the lawn augured stability, and a turning staircase would discourage evil spirits, which travel in straight lines.

On the advice of a Chinese friend, we installed wind chimes, which also deter demons. The address, 29, though not ideal, would have been worse had it contained a 4, or *shih*, the Chinese homonym for death.

All this may sound like incomprehensible mumbo jumbo, but I did feel an indefinable harmony in the atmosphere. It gave me the energy to work around the clock. Or, sipping a sundowner on the veranda as dusk dimmed the hills in the distance, I would gaze at the fishing boats, their kerosene lanterns flickering like the reflection of fireflies on the water below. My wife, children, and even our *amah*, a jewel of a woman despite her bossiness, shared my sense of tranquillity. Natural or supernatural, the years in Stanley were radiant.

The village has flourished during the decades since, as I gathered on my journey back, and it occurred to me that its auspicious *feng shui* may account for much of the prosperity—just as, I would submit, a magical quality partly propels the extraordinary dynamism that has made Hong Kong one of Asia's economic miracles.

But a few reservations nagged at me as I observed that vitality during the drive to Stanley one morning not long ago. The landscape was almost unrecognizable. A freeway has supplanted stretches of the scenic road that once snaked around the hills. Bulldozers have leveled nearly every inch of terrain, even precipitous cliffsides, to erect skyscraper apartment buildings—and more are being constructed. Giant towers blight Repulse Bay, formerly the site of a splendid British colonial hotel dating back to the 1920s. Aberdeen, whose harbor had pulsated with junks and sampans, is now a canyon of factories. Stanley, when I finally arrived there, was a massive traffic clog.

More tourists, most of them lusting for bargains, visit Hong Kong than any other place in the Far East. Every day and especially on weekends, thousands converge with typhoon velocity on Stanley, where Main Street, the sleepy alley of yore, has become a hub of frenetic consumerism. Struggling through the throngs, I discerned a cacophony of languages, from English, German, Chinese, to the unadulterated American of a quartet of sailors from a U.S. aircraft carrier. Shops and stalls sell nearly everything, and the jostling crowds seem determined to buy it all—silk ties and scarves, robes, jackets, shirts, blouses, suits and frocks, perfumes, suitcases, tennis rackets, golf clubs, jogging shoes, and such gimcrackery as bogus antique snuff bottles and counterfeit ivory statues.

As touted, the merchandise is cheap. The overwhelming majority of it is made in China, where increasing numbers of Hong Kong companies manufacture goods to take advantage of low labor costs. I didn't encounter stylish logos, since true Hermès, Gucci, Ralph Lauren, and Louis Vuitton articles are only available at downtown Hong Kong outlets—at Paris, New York, and Palm Beach prices.

The Aberdeen boat people are the Tankas. These are refugees from Fukian Province in China who came to Hong Kong but were not allowed to come on land. Instead they could harbor off Hong Kong Island in Aberdeen. At times up to 40,000 of them lived their entire lives on boats, most never knowing what it is like to walk on land. They were ethnically different from anyone else in Hong Kong. They had their own religions, holidays, and rituals. Now with times becoming more enlightened Hong Kong authorities are going to get rid of the sampans and try to assimilate the boat people.

—Mark R. Leeper,
"Southeast Asia"

Instead I found brands apparently contrived to convey an impression of chic, like purportedly designer dresses bearing such unfamiliar labels as Louis Philippe and Lefevre.

Targeting either the myopic or the illiterate, one hawker was flogging Rolon watches. My wife, who has tracked down deals around the world, gave the bazaar a mediocre C.

"Seoul and Beijing are better," she sniffed.

Predictably, the old market had vanished except for a couple of vegetable stands and a sweaty cook, perhaps the son or nephew of the one I recalled, frying noodles over an outdoor stove. I searched in vain for fishermen, but was informed that most are either retired or dead, and their children had spurned the vocation as unprofitable. Besides, nobody wants fish from the surrounding polluted waters.

But if its quaint past has faded, Stanley has acquired a trendy, offbeat personality. Young entrepreneurs, artists, and freelance journalists inhabit Main Street flats, whose rents are moderate compared to those of the skyscraper apartments occupied by corporate representatives with fat perquisites. Consistent with its new yuppie character, the village has a disco.

In contrast to my era, when dining out required a trip to town, there are four or five creditable eating places. In an unadorned Chinese restaurant, a lunch of chicken with bamboo shoots and a shrimp omelet costs six dollars. The fancier Oriental is eclectic Asian, with a menu that includes Chinese, Thai, Vietnamese, Indonesian, and Indian dishes, and a pastel view of Stanley Bay that, apart from a few sampans, reminded me of the Mediterranean. At Lord Stanley's Bistro, an English-type pub, you can snack on fish and chips to the din of a jukebox.

The upscale restaurants belong to a group of partners, among them Rory Nicholas, a portly Oxford graduate who has made the village his home since 1974. As we chatted over a beer late one afternoon, he described Stanley as Hong Kong in microcosm. "Both took off in the late 1970s, when the colony's economy soared, business boomed, and property values skyrocketed. It's cooled off a bit lately, but there's no cause to worry."

Many villagers have done astonishingly well, as I discovered one morning, when to my surprise I ran into our old *fah wang*, or gardener, who had also sold us vegetables. A dwarfish figure with spectacles and a leathery face, he must have been close to 80, yet he looked remarkably spry. He greeted me with a grin and said proudly, "I'm still working."

But I was told by a local gossip that he had amassed "millions" from shrewd real estate investments—probably a gross exaggeration but, on the other hand, maybe true. For years, while doubling as a vegetable peddler, he had an arrangement with the cooks who customarily bought the food for their employers. He would pad the bills and give them a modest kickback, which they usually shared with the other servants. Known as the "squeeze," the system has been practiced in China from time immemorial, and like everyone else we tolerated it rather than disrupt tradition.

A decade ago the British colonial government injected a dose of democracy into Hong Kong by creating partially elected district boards. The most active member of the local board, Chan Yan Yue, is a bouncy man of 47 who strides briskly through Stanley, a beeper his emblem of authority. Born in the village, he attended a church school there, adopted the alternate name of Lawrence, and learned to speak fluent if tonal English.

His father had sold kerosene and bottled gas, chiefly to fishermen. After his parents emigrated to Canada in 1984, Lawrence took over the business. It faltered as commercial fishing declined, and he opened a toy and gift store on Main Street, which he runs in tandem with his civic duties. Though no such title exists, he is widely looked on as mayor.

The district's biggest problem, he says, is traffic, along with the smugglers who land boatloads of illegal Chinese immigrants in the inlets around Stanley and ship contraband like electrical appliances to China.

Lawrence's own headache is dealing with the 4,000 squatters who have lived for years at Ma Hang, or "Horse Stream," an area that lies beyond Stanley. Their houses are scheduled to be razed soon, and they will be moved to a government apartment project being built nearby, and Lawrence has had to listen to their concerns. One morning he invited me to accompany him on a visit to the community.

The redevelopment of Ma Hang Village, Stanley, is underway. Phase One has been completed and many villagers have been moved to their new quarters. This is typical in Hong Kong, which for many years has had one of the world's largest public housing programs.

—JO'R, LH, and SO'R

We climbed a path between clusters of bamboo, which I had frequently trod before, but the place had changed. Now, I noticed, there were no pigs and chickens, and the rice wine distillery, which had emitted an awful stench, was shut down—in both cases, Lawrence pointed out, on the grounds that they caused pollution.

The ramshackle wooden huts I remembered were also gone, replaced by sturdy cement or brick houses amid neat little gardens. Their doors were decorated with the icons of guardian gods with fierce expressions or bright red posters in Chinese ideographs that announced, "The Sun Shines on Our Prosperous Home" or "Health and Good Fortune." I could hear the click-clak of *mah-jongg* tiles coming from one house.

Not all the squatters were poor, Lawrence explained. "Some made money from selling property in the village. Or they own shops that they lease to merchants. Naturally they are reluctant to transfer to the apartments, where they'll have to pay rent. Here they live free."

Most are elderly folk whose children, attracted by good jobs elsewhere, have moved away. Lawrence's task that day was to assure them that all would be well. It was not easy.

We called on Koon Wai Fong, a shriveled crone in her 70s. Her house, one room with a tiny toilet attached, was furnished with bunk bed, refrigerator, television set, hot plate, ceiling fan, and a portrait of Buddha on the wall.

Unmarried, she had been a cook for a local family. She was cheerful but still fretful, even after Lawrence promised her that the apartment would be an improvement. "I'll miss my garden," she lamented.

Though resigned to their fate, other squatters voiced similar worries, and I wondered whether demolishing the settlement made sense. But this was Hong Kong, where nothing is allowed to stand in the way of progress.

Strolling back to the village, I paused at one relic that is bound to remain intact—the temple to Tin Hau, the patron goddess of seafarers, which was constructed in 1765. Legend has it that Tin Hau was a maiden who lived in the coastal city of Foochow during the 13th century and miraculously rescued fishermen from typhoons.

Stone lions crouch like sentinels at the entrance, and inside, mythical warriors with scowling faces protect her statue, enshrined in a niche on an altar. She is a functioning deity, as evidenced by offerings of fresh fruit on the altar and the thick odor of incense pervading the air. In the past I had seen the faithful burning joss sticks and kowtowing to her image, or shaking a box of numbered sticks that tell fortunes. Worshipers flock to her annual birthday festival on the 23rd day of the third moon, which is celebrated with dances, songs, and boat races. But this time the only person in the temple was an old woman sweeping the floor.

Still in quest of history, I trudged up Tung Tau Wan Road, our street, to the British military cemetery, which contains nearly 700 graves. They mark the deaths of only about one-quarter of the British, Canadian, Indian troops, and Hong Kong volunteers who died while resisting the Japanese attack against the colony in December 1941 or in captivity later.

Children were playing among the graves, which are separated by race—Westerners in one part, Asians in another. Some tombstones date back to World War I, like one inscribed "Coolie San A Kim," for a member of the Chinese Labour Corps killed in France on December 22, 1914. Those were the days when the sun never set on the British Empire.

On my walk back I stopped to peek into our old house. I was let in by a Filipino maid who told me that it is now occupied by a British executive and his family. Drastically modernized since our time, it had a spacious kitchen, gleaming bathrooms, and central air-conditioning. The *feng shui*, I am happy to report, is undisturbed.

Stanley Karnow, acclaimed journalist and author, studied at Harvard University and at the Sorbonne, University of Paris. He is the author of several books including Southeast Asia, Vietnam: The War Nobody Won, Vietnam: A History *and* In Our Image: America's Empire in the Philippines.

＊

It was Good Friday, my first full day in Hong Kong. Ten of us were launching an expedition from there the following day to catch and catalog reptiles on the Outer Islands and in mainland China's rainforest, but somebody figured why waste a perfectly good day in the city. So we took a taxi to the jungle—straight up the hill past the slums, past the housing projects with their confetti streamers of drying clothes, past the last joggers and the furthest limits of the civilized city. We paid the driver and just walked into the topknot of rainforest left up there, wearing our backpacks and hauling gear.

Later, on the floor of the forest clearing, we had a feast of herring sandwiches and mangoes with sweet crackers and then started working our way back downhill, wading waist-deep in the root-beer water of Hong Kong's highest drainage ditches, searching for things that go slink in the night.

Far below us, cruise ships spit out and sucked back thousands of shoppers each hour, the Star Ferry putted back and forth, and the tram took sightseers almost as high as our view. There were tourists, economists, bankers, honeymooners, businessmen below. We were the snake catchers above.

That's how different Hong Kong is.

—Paula McDonald, "South China Sea Journal"

JAN MORRIS

✶ ✶ ✶

Archipelago

Go to the islands for a taste of old China.

HONG KONG INHABITS SEVERAL WORLDS. IT IS PART OF THE immense and incalculable Chinese world. It is a glittering outstation in the world of high finance. It is a prodigy of the Orient and a late anachronism of Empire. But it is also the center of a world that is all its own, consisting of 235 tightly grouped and variously fascinating offshore islands.

The chief of them is, of course the island of Hong Kong itself, Asia's Manhattan, one of the most celebrated and astonishing of all the islands of the earth. But when in 1898, the British leased from the Chinese a slab of mainland to act as a *cordon sanitaire* for their island colony, they acquired at the same time the whole adjacent archipelago spilling through some 400 square miles of the South China Sea. Most of its islands are infinitesimal; one, Lantau, is bigger than Hong Kong itself. Some had immemorial histories, some were known only as pirate hideouts, and others had never been inhabited at all.

From the top of Victoria Peak, the crowning summit of Hong Kong island, where the financiers and the mandarins of government look down from their villas upon the splendid city-state below—from up there you may see the archipelago spread in the

sea around you. Especially in the evening it is a wonderfully suggestive sight. Humped or supine in the setting sun, the islands seem
to lie bewitched along the dim blue coast of China; and as the skyscrapers burst into blazing neon at the foot of the hill, and the riding lights twinkle from the hundreds of ships at their moorings in
the harbor, sometimes it seems that those ethereal places out at sea,
so silent against the blush of the evening, are not really there at all.

But they are, and one of the more seductive distractions of eastern travel is to go a-sailing through the particular small world of
the Hong Kong archipelago.

Swoosh! With an arrogant rumble of engines and a plume of
spray the hydrofoil leaves the pier, on the waterfront of Hong Kong's
financial district, in a wide, wide sweep for the islands of the west.
Every kind of vessel plies between the islands of Hong Kong. A
fleet of sensible ferries plods regular as clockwork between the main
ports of the archipelago. An armada of homely sampans links the
lesser islands, chugging up shallow creeks, calling at out-of-the-
way settlements, with mother at the helm as likely as not, father
down in the greasy engine room and small children contentedly
pottering, in the Chinese way, in and out of the wheelhouse.

There are sundry launches too, and small shambled craft called
walla-wallas, and posh motorized junks flying the flags of the great
merchant houses, which take the rich, both Chinese and Europeans,
sybaritically toward distant pleasure-places. And through them all
from time to time, weaving a passage among the massed ranks of
merchant men, one of those thundering hydrofoils launches itself
spectacularly toward the outer islands.

The island waterways, then, are in a constant state of motion,
edging toward congestion. You are never traveling alone—always,
wherever you are sailing, a distant sampan is traveling in the same
direction, a tug is towing a sluggish string of barges, a customs
launch is watching, pacing you, or a group of country boats, piled
high with nets, crates, dogs, pigs in conical wire baskets and com-
placent old ladies in wide straw hats, is racing you to the harbor.

Yet when you disembark you may discover among the islands,
just as that prospect from the Peak suggested, places of magical

serenity. Of course development threatens all of them—nowhere in Hong Kong can be immune to progress and profit. Even so, most of the islands are uninhabited, mere protrusions of shingle, sand and coarse grass unvisited from one year to the next except by picnicking weekend sailors. On others only a few fisher-families live huggermugger in their huts. Even on the bigger, well-frequented islands, a few short miles from the Peak and the sky-scrapers, there remain unexpected expanses of open country—the nearest thing to pristine countryside left within the ferociously crowded limits of Hong Kong.

On the island of Lamma, for instance, half an hour in a sampan from Hong Kong island, there are wide tracts of green moorland, wind-swept and tangy above the sea. It is true that in the northwest the chimneys of a power station grimly protrude above the skyline, but there are only two small villages on the island, there are no cars, all is still and quiet, and the hill tracks that alone connect Yung Shue Wan at one end with Sok Kwu Wan at the other wind their way through landscapes almost Scottish in their exhilarating emptiness.

Better still is Lantau. This is the largest of all the islands, some 15 miles from end to end—twice as big as Hong Kong itself, but with perhaps one sixtieth of its population. Holiday villages and retreats for the bourgeoisie are sprouting on the coast of Lantau, but inland you may find yourself in proper mountain country, wild feeling even now, with few roads, fewer villages and a grand sensa-tion of space and liberty (though as it happens several of Hong Kong's penal institutions are ironically sited here). There is pony-trekking on Lantau. There is fine hill walking—well over the 3,000-foot mark. And in the wet, when these highlands are shrouded in damp white mist and the foliage shines with warm moisture and the boggy ground squelches beneath your feet, a proper sense of wilderness informs the place, and makes you feel you are a thousand miles from the nearest computer printout or the latest financial index, somewhere altogether indeterminate among the China Seas.

Over some of the islands an evocative air of antiquity impends. Nobody knows for sure who first lived in this archipelago, or what forgotten tribes-people carved the patterns to be seen here and there on rock faces and cavern walls. But even the recorded history of the islands is long enough, and often you may be reminded that long, long before the British reached these parts, a great civilization held sway here and quite another stately empire flew its flags.

Ceaselessly, all through the day, an elderly ferry, manually propelled, crosses and recrosses the saltwater creek at Tai O, on the western coast of Lantau. No cars enter the village, which straddles the waterway, so that life revolves around the navigations of that humble craft, backward and forward, backward and forward down the centuries, setting the pace of everything and dominating the style.

In this as in much else, Tai O is the very picture of a traditional Chinese settlement. Except perhaps in remoter parts of Taiwan, there are probably no other villages anywhere so redolent of the immemorial Chinese past. Tai O lives entirely from the sea, and its society is pungently amphibious—fishing boats moored in apparently inextricable confusion along that creek, houses projecting on wobbly stilts over the water, strong fishy smells wherever you go. In the morning the village streets are loud with the doings of open-air markets, in the afternoon they echo to the clack of *maj-jongg* counters from shady living rooms; everywhere joss sticks burn in small domestic shrines, and arthritic figures disappear into the recesses of wayside temples.

There's yet another surprise for the truly curious. On the land fronting Joss House Bay has been found the oldest inscription in the entire territory, this from an 11th-century VIP talking about cultivation.

On the same inscription, it speaks of two sailors who were saved from a storm at Tung Lung Island across the bay (then called Nam Fat Tong—Southern Buddha House). In honour of being saved, they built a temple on the island.

The ruins of that temple have never been found. But Tung Lung is small enough that the amateur archaeologist could well stumble across a mound, and that mound could reveal the oldest artefacts yet found in Hong Kong—an added fillip to an already-fascinating journey.

—Harry Rolnick, "Fortress Hong Kong," *Another Hong Kong: An Explorer's Guide*

It is like China in a novel, China in somebody's memoirs; and in many another part of the archipelago, too, you may feel that here, and perhaps here alone, a tremendous culture is tenuously defying the passing of time and ideology. Scattered through the islands are settlements of fishing people, Tankas and Hoklos from southern China, with their intricately fretted and tangled sampans, their jumbled houses, their sweet, simple shrines to Tin Hau, goddess of the sea; and occasionally you may see gliding past a headland a genuine engineless sailing junk from China itself, its patched, thin sails ribbed like the skin of some ancient bird and its helmsman lolling at the tiller precisely as his forebears must have lolled through these seas for a couple of thousand years.

Though many a young person leaves the islands for more exciting opportunities elsewhere, still the traditional communities of the archipelago are full of gusto, and nothing is more fun than to sail to one of the remoter islands on a bright fall day, say, in search of Sunday lunch. Wherever there is a settlement in these waters— on *Kat O Chau*, Crooked Island,

The ferryman seemed anxious as I stepped onto the pier at Tap Mun, one of the remotest of Hong Kong's 235 outlying islands. "Last ferry at five, don't forget!" he called. Unconcerned, I waved and smiled. But as I turned to walk towards the village, I passed a sign with rust-eaten lettering that echoed the ferryman's warning: "Picnickers are advised not to visit the outlying islands unless they have checked in advance that a reliable means of return is available."

Not many visitors make it to Tap Mun. The island, which is officially known as Tap Mun Chau and whose name means "breaking the mouth of the harbor," lies in the far northeast corner of Hong Kong territory, at the entrance to the vast Tolo Harbor. There's only one direct ferry each day from the mainland. But once you've set foot on Tap Mun, it's easy and rather pleasant to imagine being stranded for awhile, and hard to believe that Hong Kong's manic city life is a mere two hours away.

—Julia Wilkinson, "A Sense of Something Sacred"

which is only a mile or two from the China coast, on Tap Mun in Mirs Bay, where the deep-water fishermen live, on the inaccessible Sokos or the Po Toi islands in the south—wherever there is life there is almost sure to be a restaurant. To sit out there at a gimcrack table on the waterfront, shaded by tarpaulins, watching the activities of boat people and eating mussels and stewed eel, or clams with ginger, is to share in one of the most fundamental of all Chinese pleasures, pursued in absolutely the same way, without benefit of microwave, deep freeze or for that matter dishwasher, as it was in the days of the Celestial Emperors.

And the Emperors are present too, if only in memorial, for distributed through the islands are the forts, watchtowers, and customhouses of their lost authority. One of the best-preserved is the fortress of Tung Chung on Lantau. There the Imperial Chinese Government maintained a naval base, and its formidable stone walls stand in the lee of a wooded ridge, looking over marshy flatlands to the sea. Once this stronghold, as an offshore outpost of the Middle Kingdom, specialized in accepting homage from tributary nations; now it has been taken over by a local school, and when I was there recently, poking about its courtyard and inspecting the old guns that still line its ramparts, the schoolroom burst into sudden song.

The words of the song were Cantonese, and beyond me, but the tune, though sung in a mournfully approximate kind of singsong, seemed vaguely familiar; and as I left the fortress to catch my ferry at the harbor I found myself singing, more or less in harmony with the exotic rendition that pursued me through the gate:

Just remember the Red River Valley,
and the cowboy who loved you so true.

Even more evocative of past time, past values, are the holy places of the archipelago, which are myriad. There are Taoist temples and family shrines wherever you go, some unobtrusive in village streets, like shops, some lonely on promontories where fishermen pause to pray for luck on their way to sea.

The island of Cheung Chau is by no means among the most otherworldly of the islands. Thickly populated, easily accessible, it is popular as a weekend resort for Europeans living in Hong Kong. Nevertheless its one great moment of the year is essentially a spiritual occasion—the event known to foreigners as the Bun Festival, which is centered upon the temple of the sea god Pak Tai. Then for three days the island becomes a place of pilgrimage, as hundreds of boats swarm in with devotees, sightseers, or mere merrymakers from all over Hong Kong and beyond. Amazingly recondite processions move through the cramped village streets, and beside the temple three gigantic towers of buns are erected, said to be for the pacifying of hungry ghosts but eventually, on the last day of the celebration, eaten one and all by mortals.

For the rest of the year the temple of Pak Tai dozes in a kind of timeless haze, oblivious to change. It is everything you expect a Chinese temple to be. The interior is dark, but flickering with candles. It is incense-fragrant, image-littered. At tables beside the door elderly caretakers sit, sometimes caressing the temple cat, sometimes eating rice from metal bowls, and now and then villagers wander in, in the casual Chinese way, to light a joss stick or say a prayer. And though in fact the building is little more than 200 years old, it feels utterly beyond calendar, as though the very same caretakers have been stroking the very same cat more or less forever.

Holy places of another kind survive among the rough hills of Lantau, for it has always been an island of monasteries. One of them, the Buddhist shrine of Po Lin, is very famous, very rich, very spectacular, and is visited by thousands of tourists on day trips from Hong Kong—it has a splendidly showy modern temple, all golds and crimsons, in the best Hong Kong style, the largest image of the Buddha ever made.

Other Buddhist monasteries are less ostentatious. They are hidden away among the moorlands, to be reached only by arduous footpaths, or they meditate the years away on hillside terraces—a shrine, a cluster of houses, an eating room, a garden from whose purlieus, when the wind is right, you may hear the haunting rise and fall of sacred chants and the jingle of prayer bells.

And on the island's eastern shore, high on a ridge above the sea, there stands a Christian holy place, the Trappist monastery of Our Lady of Joy. You can reach it only by walking over the hills behind, or by taking a sampan from the nearby island of Peng Chau;

whichever way you go, once you enter its presence you will feel yourself almost eerily encapsulated. A church crowns the little settlement, with living quarters around it and fishponds and pleasant gardens, and it is inhabited by a handful of Chinese monks, ejected from the mainland years ago, and an English abbot, all of them living in perpetual silence.

Far in the distance you may see the white concrete towers of Hong Kong. The spectacle thrills me always, for if there really is a spell over these islands, as it seemed from the Peak, it is the spell of that astonishing city itself. As the skyline of Manhattan is to Queens and Brooklyn, Hong Kong is to the archipelago, and sailing back to the city from Lantau or Cheung Chau is a never-failing wonder. It may sadden you at first, as the green calm shapes of the islands slip behind your stern, to feel that you are returning from fantasy to reality, from almost imaginary places to a place unquestionably, unforgivingly true.

But then, as that terrific mass of shipping closes all around your boat, as the skyscrapers rise higher and higher against the hills, as the roar of the city traffic reaches you over the water, mingled with the thumping of steam hammers, the shriek of sirens or the shattering blast of a passing hydrofoil, it will dawn upon you that sometimes, in worlds of travel as in realms of literature, fact is more extraordinary than fiction.

Jan Morris also contributed "Towards Fragrant Harbor" in Part I and "Perfect Pleasures" in Part II.

★

At 4:00 p.m. yesterday we took a village bus into the high hills of Lantau Island, then hiked up to Po Lin, the Buddhist monastery to spend the night. Goal: to try to photograph a rare singing toad in its natural habitat—while it was singing. Ha! The damn thing turned out to be a quarter-inch long, mostly invisible, and its natural habitat happened to be the slimiest, slipperiest swamp in the South China Sea. We spent until midnight crouched in thigh-high green water trying to set up camera equipment without scaring the shy little sucker back into his burrow. Big Jim was the designated cameraman, with Little George valiantly trying to hold him upright in the slime and not let him fall with the camera. Naturally, the night became an endless litany of toad praise: "God damn! Son of a bitch!" We got our photo, finally, and the mosquitoes got us.

It was midnight when we rolled into bed at the monastery—or rather rolled into rope contraptions minus mattresses, with pillows filled with barley. We were too tired to care. And, still covered with mud, we rolled out again at 4:00 a.m. to catch a different litany—the Buddhist prayer ceremony at the temple up a ways further into the cloud forest. There we were, pre-dawn, three mucky science-types with wild, unkempt hair, hunched in the back row trying to look inconspicuous in a room full of shaved female heads.

An elderly nun with fingers made of steel clamps made me kneel on a rock-hard pillow for almost an hour. I thought my knees would never unlock and work again. Then they made us march around and around the temple with them. The drums were earsplitting—huge booming bass beats accompanied by gongs that seemed to pierce your brain. I could never be a Buddhist. I can't even handle an alarm clock.

—Paula McDonald, "South China Sea Journal"

MICHAEL CARUSO

✦ ✦ ✦

Our Feathered Friends

Whether they are watched in the wild, cooked in a pot, or caged as pets,
birds are a fascinating element of Hong Kong life.

THE FIRST THING I SAW AS I FLEW INTO HONG KONG'S International Airport, even before the neon riot of Central and the spanking green-and-white ferryboats of Kowloon, was a single jet-black cormorant that glided near the plane's wingtip, a one-bird welcoming committee. How amazing, I thought, that most travelers reach a foreign city by air, and never give flight a second thought once they're safely on the tarmac. As my taxi plunged into the cacophony of Hong Kong, one of the most densely populated cities on earth, threading through the crowds and incessantly honking cars, I longed to recapture the silent tranquillity of that cormorant. Wanting to retreat from the city's all-out assault, I decided to spend a day with the birds of Hong Kong.

Surprisingly, I didn't have far to go. A ten-minute ride on the city's speedy Mass Transit Railway left me at Mong Kok station in Kowloon. I walked west on Jordan Road and turned left onto Hong Lok Street. There, sandwiched between Nathan Road and Shanghai Street—two of the grandest shopping boulevards—is a back-alley bird market, an unexpected sliver of old-world Hong Kong. Sheltered beneath sea-green corrugated-plastic awnings is an ornithological Babel, stall after stall of white-eyed mynahs, green parrots and yellow-bellied wren warblers. Wizened old vendors hawk intricately carved bamboo cages, tiny blue-and-white porcelain water bowls, yellow seeds in bins filled to the brim, squirming worms sold by the spoonful and big green crickets packaged in cellophane wrappers like living prom corsages.

The squawking *souk* of Hong Lok is no refuge, but it was the first place I found in the city where pedestrians mosey along, insulated from speeding cars. The bird market is an odd social club, in which gray-haired old women and young boys with bamboo cages on their shoulders stop for unhurried conversations, comparing the merits of red-whiskered bulbuls and green white-eyes, the most prized of all pet birds. The beady-eyed market denizens are captured by the thousands in great nets throughout the countryside, as they have been for hundreds of years. Pet birds have always been a mark of wealth in China—the bigger the bird and the more ornate the cage, the greater the sign of good fortune.

If the birds nabbed here aren't stroked and pampered, they're roasted and garnished. So many menus devote space to the innumerable ways birds, usually pigeon, can be served. "You haven't been to Hong Kong until you've had baked pigeon with lemon sauce," a friend said before my trip. "Just be sure to watch out for the head."

I kept this in mind as I took a taxi to one of the best pigeon eateries, the Hotel and Restaurant Lung Wah in the small New Territories fishing village of Shaten. Standard procedure, I soon learned, is to drop off the unsuspecting visitor on one side of a busy freeway—even though Lung Wah is on the other side.

How did the chicken cross the road? By a nearby overpass. Gamely, I made my way along a zigzag path up to the restaurant past terraces of clacking *mah-jongg* tables—and a small aviary. Perhaps this is no different from a seafood restaurant with a huge lobster tank, but it didn't help my appetite to hear lunch cooing hello.

At the top of the path was a pinwheel of color: red-checked tablecloths shaded by yellow, blue, and orange umbrellas. Inside the glass-walled family-style restaurant, the tone was more subdued. This is a place for serious pigeon eating. The round linen-covered tables seat no fewer than six people, and at midday they're often crowded with parties of twelve.

An elderly waiter came over to fill my cup with tea and then decided to relinquish one of his precious plastic menus. Most diners knew in advance how they would like their bird done. I was a novice, so I had to scroll down the list, which included soy pigeon, baked pigeon, pigeon with lemon sauce, pigeon with spring onion in black-bean sauce, saté pigeon, baked pigeon giblet with salt, stir-fried minced pigeon, even pigeon's egg with fresh mushrooms. Try as I might, I couldn't stop thinking about a phrase I'd picked up in New York: "A pigeon is a rat with wings."

I watched apprehensively as an old woman shuffled out of the kitchen and served the next table a sizzling platter of what looked like a giant barbecued nest—a half-dozen whole brown roasted pigeons with heads and beaks intact. The delighted diners dove in, grabbing their favorite pieces as if they were dealing with a bucket of Kentucky Fried Chicken. Knives, forks, and chopsticks sat by their plates, unused.

I ordered baked pigeon with lemon sauce and, just to be on the safe side, a hot pot of yellow noodles and mushrooms. All dishes come with a vertical identification tag poking out of the sauce, so if you read Chinese, you're in luck. But I had no problem telling the difference. The pigeon meat was all dusky; no wonder it's precious—there's precious little of it. I repeated the mantra that has gotten me through dozens of strange dishes in foreign lands: "It tastes just like chicken."

Once they've eaten their fill, the heartiest diners complete their culinary adventure with a tour of the kitchen, where 5,000 pigeons pass through daily and as many as 10,000 on busy festival days. On request, waiter Wah Chung will lead you outside the dining hall and behind the patio, past a Buddhist altar enclosed in chicken wire, to an open-air shed staffed by a gaggle of men in white uniforms. The grisly operation moves with assembly-line precision. Two men open a cage full of birds and neatly slit their throats, one by one. They are dumped, wings still beating, into a wide shallow vat of boiling water, which a second team stirs with three-foot-long paddles. The pigeons are denuded and carried to the next room, where a 30-foot-long black stove studded with clay cooking rings awaits. Pigeon doesn't get much fresher—20 minutes from coop to plate.

Fortified by lunch (the hot pot was delicious), I sought out a friendlier feathered place. Less than an hour's drive farther north into the New Territories, at the crook of an inlet called Deep Bay, lies Mai Po, a rich preserve of mudflats, fishponds, and mangrove marshes close to busy Tsimshatsui. The 740 acres, managed by the World Wide Fund for Nature, are an increasingly important stopover for thousands of migratory birds that fly from China to Australia and back.

I arrived in late afternoon, the best time for birdwatching if you don't do it around sunrise (really the best time). It's also advisable to go on a weekend, when the World Wide Fund for Nature runs three-hour guided tours. Equipped with a pair of binoculars I'd rented at the visitor center and a handy tracking card that had color pictures of Mai Po's 30 resident birds and 250 migratory species, I set off, hoping to spy an Asiatic dowitcher, a Dalmatian pelican, or one of the few hundred black-faced spoonbills left in the world.

Within minutes, I seemed to be a million miles from nowhere. The shady dirt path, lined with fluttering horsetails, fat elephant-ears, and Chinese banyans, cut between placid ponds that lure shorebirds during spring migration and water-fowl in winter. Off the paths, boardwalks lead deep into the marshes.

Eleven wooden blinds are strategically positioned throughout the preserve for up-close observation. While perched high in a three-story green one that overlooked some ponds and a stand of mangroves, I listened to a nearby nest of bird-watchers buzz at the sighting of a pied kingfisher, the official bird of Hong Kong (locals joke that it was chosen because it's black and white and, therefore, cheaper to reproduce in pictures). But all I saw was mud and reed grass. Then, above the cheeps of far-off tree sparrows, someone whispered "three o'clock," and all binoculars swung to the right to catch a red-throated pipit.

Now that I'd caught the heat of the hunt, I was no longer content to gaze at moorhens and gray herons poking in the mud at the water's edge. I scanned the sky for imperial eagles, little-ringed plovers, falcated teals, and long-toed stints. I finally settled on a common buzzard, which looked uncommonly graceful as it came wheeling out of the blue.

"Birds mark a part of the world just the way people or architecture do," a bespectacled man sitting nearby said. He turned out to be Fred Baumgarten, a National Audubon Society staffer who was leading birders on a trip run by Classical Cruises, an ecotourism company. "Southeast Asia is one of the greatest crossroads of birds in the world, but the species here are among the most endangered," he added. I couldn't help but remember my lunch.

According to my guide, Wyan Go, the number of migratory birds that stop at Mai Po has increased steadily every year—from 17,000 in 1979 to 50,000 in 1983—because other habitats in China have been destroyed. From certain places in the preserve, you can see the booming city of Shenzhen, just over the border in China, which seems to be inching closer by the minute.

At Mai Po, the extraordinary often passes unnoticed by the untrained eye. I walked past an island of mangroves without giving it a second glance until Wyan Go pointed out the scores of blackcrown night herons hiding in the branches, visible only because of their cinnamon chest markings, which can be mistaken for leaves or fruit. And I barely noticed a white-barked tree that looked like a dead birch, with a pair of cormorants perched near the top.

"That's actually a casuarina," Wyan Go said. "We call it the Christmas tree because of its color."

"Why is it white?" I asked.

"Bird droppings."

No matter. The tree looked beautiful against the darkening sky.

It was time to race back to the beating heart of Central for a late dinner and maybe a throbbing nightclub afterward. But I lingered a last moment, not wanting to leave. In the distance, a flock of pond herons sailed across the silvery water in black silhouette, and I imagined myself with them in a moment of soaring freedom, a flight of fancy in the dying light of Hong Kong.

Michael Caruso is a bird lover despite his meal of pigeon.

✳

You could hardly call Hong Kong an eco-friendly place. For decades, the land-hungry territory has encroached on precious wildlife areas to build its offices, housing estates, deluxe apartments, and even golf courses. It has reclaimed harbours and seas for yet more development and seized unspoilt valleys for power stations and refuse dumps. Take a trip on the Star Ferry across the harbour and you'll witness one of the filthiest stretches of water in the territory. Every summer, popular beaches are officially closed to swimmers, not because of sharks (though that's another hazard), but because of unacceptable levels of pollution. Largely thanks to dredging and dumping work related to the new airport at Chek Lap Kok, the seas to the west of Hong Kong are murkier and dirtier than ever, and the number of endangered Chinese white dolphins (there used to be hundreds in this area) has plummeted to as few as 80.

It's not all bad news, however. After years of prevarication, the Hong Kong government has finally listed Deep Bay, including its bird haven, the Mai Po Marshes Nature Preserve, under the Ramsar Convention on Wetlands of International Importance. It has earmarked two coral-rich sites—Hoi Ha Wan and Double Haven—as marine parks. Another, Cape D'Aguilar, will become a marine reserve. And in response to growing concern over the white dolphins, it has promised a 1,000-hectare dolphin sanctuary (although few dolphin-lovers believe this will guarantee protection).

—Julia Wilkinson, "Hong Kong Notes"

PART THREE

GOING YOUR OWN WAY

JUDITH BABCOCK WYLIE

* * *

Heavenly Wardrobe

Put it on for eternity.

I HAD PRETTY MUCH RUN THROUGH THE OPTIONS OF FORTUNE telling for the living but I was interested in one more thing: influencing the afterlife. I'd always wanted to see the paper offerings that Chinese burn at services for the dead to insure that certain possessions of the good life are taken with them into heaven. Some Chinese even have the real thing burned. A college student I'd met on my last trip to Hong Kong told me her grandfather had exacted a promise that his beloved fur coat would be burned at his funeral.

Most people settle for paper effigies, whether of things they own or would like to own. A friend patiently led me to the neighborhood where the paper offerings shops were located, on Queen's Road West. I expected something ethereal, but these stores looked as practical inside as a Midwestern dry cleaners. In one an older man and his daughter sat on stools eating noodles from cups, regarding us without speaking. We peered at shelves full of boxes of six gold foil watches each, fat wads of fake money, written on the Bank of Hell, and then looked up at the ceiling where three-foot long paper mâché servants dangled. The shop seemed empty, but Betty explained that most families special-ordered items for the deceased—cars, furniture, airplanes—so there was not a lot of stock to see. We did see one shocking pink villa, like a junior high student's diorama, complete with Mercedes Benz in the driveway, servants, mistresses, and tiny trays of food.

I bought some watches and money, but decided I could never get one of the yard-long servants into my luggage. As we left, we paused under the overhang just outside the shop. Hanging from the beams were gaily wrapped packages with ribbons and dragon stickers. I asked Betty what they were.

"Clothes for the next life."

The packages looked about the size of a good wool sweater wrapped as a Christmas present. The bundles came in two colors, red or green. One for women, the other for men. I asked what the clothes looked like, but Betty didn't know. "We never open them. It isn't done. We just burn them at the funeral still wrapped," she said, her serious eyes steady.

"But suppose it's just shredded paper? How do you know?"

"We don't," she said quietly. "I guess it could be. We just don't open them."

I ducked back in the shop and bought a package of the women's variety.

The heat and humidity kept the city under its grip that entire week. We distracted ourselves by eating too much of too many delicious things: fried prawn balls in chili sauce, sticky rice balls with black sesame in sweet wine sauce, pigeon, abalone, sea cucumber, and drunken chicken. In between we shopped, buying hand-worked pillows, beaded handbags, leather slippers, jade children's amulets, and silk bomber jackets. Normally, I try not to eat too much or buy too much while traveling, but in Hong Kong all bets are off.

The next time I remember being really cool again was just after stepping into the plane bound for home. I mopped my brow with the icy cloth offered by the stewardess, sank into the seat and went to sleep.

At home, I tossed the package of clothes for the hereafter on the bedroom bureau. No matter how many times my eye rested on it in the weeks that followed, I didn't open it. I have always had a horror of being disappointed, in both small and large matters. I was curious about the clothes, but not curious enough to face there being only a wad of shredded paper, like a mass of convoluted cookie fortunes.

The days were getting shorter and slightly cooler on the farm where I live when late one night, near midnight, the phone rang in the bedroom.

It was my friend Pat's sister, calling from another city, where Pat was in the hospital. "You'd better come now, right away, if you want to see her one more time and say good-bye," Karen said quickly.

To yield is to be preserved whole,
To be bent is to become straight,
To be hollow is to be filled,
To be tattered is to be renewed.

—Lao Tzu

I hung up and sat on the bed, my mind racing. While I'd known she was failing, I hadn't realized Pat was that close to the end. While I'd been in Hong Kong she was still traveling for work, at a meeting in Chicago. I called the airline and started tossing things in my suitcase for an early morning flight. At the last minute my eye was caught by the light from the bedside lamp shining on the package from Hong Kong. I threw it in.

When I got there, Pat was still aware, and although very thin, her eyes were still their incredible electric blue and her cheerful, energetic self shone out even in this condition. She knew time was running out and she wanted to get everything done.

Surprising us all, she did not die that day, or the next, but lived for almost two more weeks. Every night in her hospital room, her friends and family, with Pat's direction, arranged for entertainment of some kind. One night everyone shared photos of vacations we had taken together. Another evening a music professor came and played classical guitar selections so Pat could choose the music she wanted at her memorial service. Her grandchildren came and shared drawings from school. A sonogram of the grandson she would never meet was tacked to the bulletin board.

One evening I brought out the bright green package from Hong Kong, (for Chinese, green is the color of eternity) and asked

Pat if she would like to open it and take the clothes into the here-after. "Oh great, sure!" She smiled her good broad smile, ready for anything and still positive about any new idea.

At 7:30 p.m. we all gathered around her bed as she pulled the red ribbons from the soft package. "Did you like Hong Kong?" she asked, still hungry for new information. I started to tell her about the way it looks silver and green, with sleek metallic buildings backed by the lush undulating hills of the New Territories; about the shops selling snake and "1,000-year-old eggs;" about the sweet-sour smell that is Hong Kong, made up of delicious street food cooking, gas fumes, fish, and expensive perfume.

But just then the package fell open, revealing the most beauti-ful heavy paper evening pajamas, with delicate embossed gold leaves. Frogs made the closures. As Pat picked them up, delighted, a paper undershirt, a flowered fan, and a paper cape also fell out. In the center, revealed last, were a pair of three-dimensional black Chinese slippers, of paper mâché.

The group around the bed sighed its wonder in unison, as we lay the outfit out on Pat, who looked down and smoothed them out on herself carefully, just as she had always done with real clothes, meticulous as ever.

"Gee, they're beautiful, I'll be the best dressed one there," she said, with her old, true laugh.

I thought then about how unpredictable life is. About Mr. Tsui, the Hong Kong fortune teller who said not to worry, to take everything step by step, and not to be selfish. Maybe life is not pre-dictable, but maybe it is manageable, with good friends, the right advice, and a little luck.

Judith Babcock Wylie is a travel correspondent and organic farmer who lives on an apple farm in the Santa Cruz mountains of California. She is associate editor of Romantic Traveling, *and co-author of* The Spa Book, *and* The Romance Emporium. *She teaches travel writing at New York University, University of California, Berkeley, and UCSC. She is the editor of* Travelers' Tales Love & Romance.

After our Hong Kong business passed through a stockmarket crash unscathed, the Chinese director in charge of trading, whom I trusted completely, told me that we ought to have a proper ceremony to give thanks for safe deliverance. This turned out to involve bringing in a whole roast pig into the office, plastic sheeting having been laid on the floor to catch the dripping fat. Each member of staff in turn clapped hands to attract the attention of the spirits, bowed to the shining red face of the pig, and planted a burning joss stick in front of its snout. Then we devoured the greasy pork with our bare hands. Some of the expatriates refused to participate in this pungent ritual, finding it altogether too pagan and sinister.

But I was glad to bow to the inscrutable beast; like much else about life and business in Asia, the forces at work were a mystery to me, but I needed all the help I could get. It is a region of powerful spirits....

—Martin Vander Weyer, "Full of Eastern Menace," *The Spectator*

JOHN WILLIAM FISHER WITH
YVONNE MICHIE HORN

* * *

A Return Home

Discovering a father's past uncovers old Hong Kong.

My father was with me as we skimmed through darkness over the China Sea in an aircraft's silver cocoon. Pa, ashes and bits of bone now, was tucked into my pockets in a half-dozen little black film canisters. We were on our way to Hong Kong.

A kaleidoscope of memories whirled through my brain—me as a six-year-old perched on the high wall that surrounded our house in Kowloon while I shouted a phrase in Chinese at passing coolies. The taunt, whatever it meant, would send them into a frenzy of leaps as they tried to knock me off the wall with their shoulder poles. But skinny-legged kids are always fast.

I thought of the evening General Wong came to the house just as my parents were on their way out. He must have been a lonely man for he offered to stay with me. We passed the time exploring the mechanical intricacies of our grandfather clock. There we were when they returned, a guilty looking kid and an equally guilty looking general sitting on the floor surrounded by springs and tiny screws. That was the same General Wong that Pa secreted out of Canton.

But now, just like that, we were in a whirlpool of neon descending toward Kai Tak's runways through Victoria Harbour's gaudy reflections. The non-stop flight from San Francisco had taken but thirteen hours. Mind-boggling. When we left Hong Kong on October 21, 1938 aboard the *President Coolidge* our trans-ocean voyage took 28 days. Ours was the last ship out before the Japanese launched their attack on the Crown Colony less than two months later. I'd lived there for my first eight years. Fifty-three years later—"We're back, Pa."

Kai Tak had the look of a flying club 53 years ago. We went there often, for Pa's business was airplanes. He'd left his job as chief test pilot of Arrow Aircraft Corp in Lincoln, Nebraska as the Great Depression deepened in the United States with an intriguing offer from Wallace Harper Co., Ltd., Hong Kong's Ford dealer. They would sell planes to Chinese warlords.

Pa brought seven Arrow Sports from the states, unassembled, in boxes. A "demo" would stay in Hong Kong. He took the remaining six by ship to Haiphong, transferring to a narrow-gauge railway that would take him to Yunnanfu, a three day trip since the train only ran by day.

Pa assembled and tested the Sports, putt-putting them through their paces over the strange, mist-drifted monoliths of Yunnanfu. He was prepared to be on his way when warlord General Lung Ngan announced that his departure would be delayed until his "air cadets" learned to fly. It took three months, but when he returned there was money to be put in the bank and Far Eastern Aviation Company was on its way.

I'd intended to scatter a canister of Pa at Kai Tak when we arrived. My father, a man who never lived in the past, would have marveled over the flying field's metamorphosis into one of the busiest international airports in the world, but I could not find a patch of earth or grass and it did not seem appropriate to sprinkle my father about on cement.

I'd already left some of Pa in Buenos Aires, in the rose bushes under the flags flying in the breeze in front of the Plaza Hotel where he liked to stay, and in Rio, in the surf in front of our still-standing apartment house on Leme Beach. After leaving Hong Kong, he had worked for Lockheed and we lived here and there in the far reaches of the world.

But it was Hong Kong where my father was at his most daring-do, his exotic exploits kept alive by his retelling of tales. We talked of returning for a visit one day, but the years scurried past and then it was too late.

I love it when people tell me I haven't changed. Well, I have and I expected no less of Hong Kong. Nevertheless, more than a half-century later, I was certain I would know my way about.

Teeming, jam-packed, skyscraper punctuated, neon-glitzed, shopping mall exploited—Hong Kong was exactly as I thought it would be. Yet, just as I am still the skinny-legged youngster that once was, albeit my waistline widened and hair departed, I recognized Hong Kong and felt at home. Gleefully I noted landmarks—the mountains edging Kowloon; Signal Hill where the tower—now, of all things, a historic building!—gave warning of the severity of typhoons; the Peninsula Hotel where my mother worked in the dress shop until the airplane business took off; Victoria Peak; Central's classic government buildings; the green and white Star ferries fearlessly plowing a path across Victoria Harbour pushing aside junks and dories, battleships and barges.

In my suitcase I'd packed clues to the past, black and white photographs faded sepia and picturing the debonair man with the pencil mustache that was my father and the woman with marcelled hair, my mother. There was one of my parents lounging with friends on the wooden steps of our matchshed at the beach, everyone wearing scratchy looking woolen swimming suits. Background detail might help me find the matchshed's location.

There was a photo of Dum Jai, my *amah*, holding my hand as we watched a funeral procession march by our house on Prince Edward Road. Surely the hill across from where we lived, really a gigantic rock, would be there even if the house no longer was.

I caught double-decked bus #1 at its stop near the side entrance of the Peninsula Hotel and rode the length of Nathan Road that in a mere twinkling of a half-century had turned itself into a blaring avenue of electronic gadgets, luggage, jewelry, discount fashions, cameras, and Chinese fast food. I jumped off at Prince Edward Road, near where Wallace Harper & Co. Ltd., had the first modern automobile showroom and repair garage in the colony, and began looking for number 292.

I walked past apartment buildings that now lined the wide street, some with underground parking garages, well-tended gardens, and code-operated iron gates. Tucked between them here and there were multi-storied, walled houses, carbon copies of the one in which we had lived. I walked faster, could it be that our house was still there?

Number 292—a derelict apartment complex settled into a debris-sprouted weed patch. I checked the return address written in my father's hand on a yellowed envelope, 292. And yes, across the street, sandwiched and dwarfed by high-rise buildings, was the rock. I opened a canister and left a bit of Pa near the driveway. It began to rain. At least Prince Edward Road was still there. Perhaps that was enough.

My mental kaleidoscope began again. Dum Jai, gentle Dum Jai. "Little Master," she'd whisper me awake in the early morning and we'd go to the market so that I'd not run about the house in her absence and disturb my parents' sleep.

To my generation the idea of domestic service seems to belong to another world, so I sought the advice of my mother-in-law who was for some years an Army wife in Singapore. She spoke volumes of her experience with amahs, but warned me they are no respecters of the feminist cause.

She recalled finding one amah standing patiently for some time over my husband, then six years old. Asked what she was doing, the amah replied: "I am waiting to see how son number one would like his egg: boiled, poached, scrambled, or fried." His sister, meanwhile, had to take what she got.

"What really irritated me was the way the cook served sardines. She always meticulously boned my husband's sardine but left mine untouched."

—Angela Palmer, "The Snake that Lost Its Bite," *The Daily Telegraph*

Dum Jai, along with her parents—Ah Fong, her father, was our cook; Cui Jai, her mother, took care of the house—had quarters in the basement where, wonder of wonders, they rested their heads at night on "pillows" of porcelain. There, Dum Jai allowed me bowl after bowl of rice before dinner and feigned ignorance about why

I pushed my plate away in the dining room. She bathed me, spoiled me, and tied my shoes for me long after I was old enough to do so. My father, returning again from weeks away, would demand that I be taken in hand and learn to tie my own shoes and for God's sake stop talking that awful pidgin English. To this day, Little Master could still dine happily on rice and prefers slip-on loafers because he "no likee" tie his shoes.

I telephoned Phyllis, Wallace Harper's daughter, my constant playmate of some 50-plus years gone by. Phyllis and I planned to marry one day, except that "the Portuguese" already lived next door and it was unthinkable that we'd live farther away. Phyllis, married to another, continues to live in Hong Kong.

We met for dinner at the Hong Kong Club, that venerable sanctum sanctorum bastion of Crown Colony expatriates.

Phyllis brought with her more pictures and, yes, she did remember where the matchshed was, at the 11.5-mile marker on Castle Peak Road. No, she had no access to Harper Motors' records; the business, which continues to light up the sky on Aberdeen Bay, was sold long ago. But she did have with her an issue of the Hong Kong Automobile Association's magazine that featured an article of reminiscence written by her father shortly before his death in 1977.

In it he relayed one of my father's exploits. Pa had been summoned to Canton, ostensibly to see General Wong Kwong Yui about buying more planes. Once there, however, he learned that the general feared imprisonment because of his loyalty to Chiang Kai Shek. He wanted to be flown immediately and secretly to Hong Kong. Via a trusted emissary, Pa got a note to Harper.

In the predawn hours, my father, flying one of the planes the Canton Air Force had earlier bought from Far East Aviation, snatched the general from the end of the runway, pulled him into the plane by the seat of his pants, and headed for Fanling golf course. Harper, dressed in golfing attire and bringing extra outfits for my father and the general, was waiting in a car parked at the edge of an agreed-upon fairway. Off they drove, three gentlemen ready for an early round of golf. "There was a great to-do in the newspapers," wrote Harper, "about a Canton Air Force plane found abandoned at Fanling."

Morning found me at the Bureau of Records in Central.

It was not that I disbelieved Pa and Harper's account, but time has a way of allowing embroidery to grow on stories. I barely acknowledged it to myself, but I needed to measure my father against outside verification.

The Bureau of Records was in the process of putting its collection of newspapers on microfilm. It would be slow going since I did not know the date of the Fanling escapade, but I was welcome to look through the originals of the *South China Times.*

For three days I buried myself in the Bureau of Records, stepping into a time machine as I read of seemingly isolated happenings, hidden stepping stones, that I knew would lead inexorably to a world disaster. An account of two Japanese fighters following a China Airlines plane and forcing it down 20 minutes out of Hong Kong—that must have been the plane Pa took me to see, returned by barge to the end of Kai Tak's runway. I read of the sinking of the U.S. navy ship, the *Panay*, in December 1937. Japan claimed it a mistake. The terrorizing of passenger trains into Canton. Didn't they know? Couldn't they tell what lay ahead? Watch out, Hong Kong. Watch out, world.

Other items caught my eye, distracting me from my purpose. I read of the opening of Walt Disney's *Snow White* "at a theatre near you," which in my case was where I had seen it at the Alhambra on Nathan Road. I read timetables of the comings and goings of steam ships and was amazed to find that Fanling tee times, which frequently included my father's name, were dutifully printed as news.

I emerged one day to hire a taxi to take me to Castle Peak Road. At the 11.5-mile marker, I asked the driver to wait while I made my way down a stairway beside a small apartment house. There was the familiar curve of sand and across the way Ma Wan Island, toward which I'd headed more than once in my kayak. Studying my photographs I discarded one location and another. There, that had to be where the matchshed had stood. Satisfied, I took off my shoes, rolled up my pants, uncapped a canister and let Pa go for one last swim in the South China Sea.

The day before I was to leave, I gave up on my newspaper search. Time had run out. Written verification or not I had to get to Fanling.

When Pa had put down on the fairway, Fanling was far in the country, a place where a tigress hung about the eighth green and cobras and pythons were not unknown hazards. Now housing estates punctuated the skyline. Then there was but one course, now three. It would have to be the one called The Old where he had landed.

I walked The Old until I came to a fairway edged by a road. Close enough. I opened my last canister and in my heart of hearts I knew that my father had no need to embroider on his past. As he had lived it, it was extraordinary enough. Good-bye, Pa.

John William "Bill" Fisher inherited his father's love of flying, albeit in the less exotic skies of northern California. Travel writer Yvonne Michie Horn is his wife. She also contributed "A Leg up on Fate" in Part I.

★

A hanging scroll in a swirl of colors, lacking line
An algebraic formula, simple but unsolvable
A one-string lute, strumming a rosary of raindrops from the eaves
A pair of oars that never reach the opposite shore

Silently waiting, like a swelling bud
Distantly gazing, like the setting sun
Somewhere, perhaps, a vast ocean lurks
But only two tears trickle out

O in the vistas of the heart
in the depths of the soul.
—Shu Ting, "Longing," *Wenhui Monthly*

JASON GOODWIN

* * *

Professor Tea

How can one live without drinking tea?

HONG KONG SPRINGS FOREVER FROM THE DRAWING BOARD, LIKE
some rubberoid cartoon optimist. Young California's first order
from the new city of Hong Kong was for "slop clothes and wooden
houses (shipped in frame)." Little has changed, really; when the
bathrooms for Foster's Hong Kong Bank were winched into position, the soap was found already Scotch-taped to the trays.

In Hong Kong the inanimate do business along with the quick.
Each ramp on a concrete flight of steps proclaims the merit of a
product; dustbins call your attention to the Hong Kong Bank;
an enormous Marlboro cowboy hangs tough on the flank of a
high-rise—you come close, he shyly disintegrates into a swirl of
meaningless squiggles but recomposes himself, as moody as ever,
as you walk away. At night, across the city, house-high neon
takes his place: SONY, PHILIPS, HITACHI. We love you! they cry. We
want you! Look at us! Even in the hotel room you are not invi-
olate, for at night repellent colors do soft corporate battle across
the ceiling.

Hong Kong has a non-Hong Kong Chinese population of
about 300,000 residents, a town the size of Cheltenham or
Dubuque. While I was there, the papers announced that the British

were no longer the largest foreign community, overtaken at last by the Americans.

Its dinner parties could have been used by a quiz master: What is the smallest number required to make up five parties of eight people in such a way that half the people at any party are previous acquaintances, but not the same people on consecutive nights? I met very few Chinese this way. On my birthday I went to hear a Requiem, and was surprised to recognize three people in the chorus.

One morning I woke to a dreary English voice on a phone-in programme complaining about the amount of flyposting in the city. "There are about a dozen in Pedder Street, two in Queen's Road, one in Elgin Road, no, I'm sorry, two I think, yes...." I dozed off. When I reawoke, he was still there, climbing the Peak road by road, irritably pointing out posters from memory. Or perhaps he was phoning from his car. He was allowed to stumble halfway across Hong Kong, pointing out things he didn't like, before the radio announcer said: "Yes, I think you've got a great point there, and if anybody's got something to say on the subject of illegal fly-posting, bill-sticking, or indeed anything at all for that matter..."

Almost every evening I found myself sharing a dinner-table with Jeremy, an amateur wine buff, salting away a fortune from supplying veneer to clients around the Far East. He spent much of his time on the phone explaining to distraught hotel managers why their lobbies had started to peel, or how it was hardly his fault if sheets of best Korean veneer had arrived corrugated at the dockside. At his dinner-party a woman burst into loud sobs at the word "spider" and disappeared in a cab. After an hour her husband left, too.

It is a small town—but a big city, with all the big city rewards. People pass through—you are an old Hong Kong hand after a year, and settlers, who have been here for three, talk of the speed with which you make friends in the city and lose them again. There is a lack of connection between the Chinese and the Westerners, who seem to move through each other's territory in gloves, leaving no prints.

I hadn't been in the city long before I began hearing about a Professor Tea. He had a real name, which nobody could quite remember; everybody seemed to have met him, but nobody could think where. I was advised to seek him out by a Dutch journalist, a German illustrator, a magazine proprietor, an art dealer, and an English lady of leisure.

"Professor" was a courtesy title which in Chinese could be applied to anyone with learning and wisdom. The Professor came from a long line of tea merchants who had followed the Kuomintang to Taiwan but continued to buy from China. In his shop, people said, he sold no Indian, Ceylon, or African tea at all. The gallery owner described him as a wild man, a sort of beatnik of the tea world; but the gallery owner was Chinese-American, and an Englishwoman at the Club raised her eyebrows. "Hardly," she said, when I repeated the description. "He's very serious, you know, and a real connoisseur. Tea is his work, of course, but it's really his life, too. He sits in his shop all evening with his friends comparing and appreciating teas from his cellars. Well, I don't know if there are any cellars, exactly, but that's how it feels. He strikes me as a gentleman, pretty old-fashioned but an absolute buff." I pictured the Professor as an elderly eccentric who charmed attractive women and spoke in riddles. Sometimes I was given a phone number, but not always the same one; all of them rang without an answer.

His elusiveness began to obsess me. I borrowed telephones in shops and bars. It was like scratching a bite—a moment's relief as the ringing began, followed by an inflamed desire to pin this character down.

The *taipans* still have their offices on the waterfront, from where they can watch the bustle of the harbour and stare across at Kowloon and the blue hills of China beyond. They sit high in their skyscrapers and speak as generals of free enterprise, eminent in every way, elevated above trivia to the commanding heights. So I would ask them about the tea trade and very often, after thought and maybe consultation, they would suppose that their last shipments left, oh, ten, twelve years ago, following years of dwindling returns, competition from smaller firms, or the retirement of the chap who ran that side.

The remnants of past civilizations are often revealed by the turn of a plough in an open field; only Hong Kong simply goes on ploughing. There's more money in that. So even the tea trade had been razed to make way for something brighter: concreted over and replaced by a bank and a fast food franchise.

"*What would the world do,*" 19th-century English clergyman, writer, and wit Sydney Smith asked in Lady Holland's Memoir, "*without tea?—how did it exist? I am glad I was not born before tea.*"

The Reverend Smith need not have worried about the horrors of a tea-less world because, as it turns out, a record of a time without tea is difficult to find: it has been grown in China and venerated by the Chinese for thousands of years. And long before the British engaged in the ritual of tea drinking, it was an essential part of Chinese culture.

—Amanda Meyer Stinchecum, "Pot Luck," *Departures*

Strange that a city built by traditionalists, the British and the Chinese, should be so mercilessly for the moment. Hong Kong's founders were agents, and Hong Kong is just an agent—financial agent, commercial agent, travel agent, secret agent—always doing, never creating, Janus-faced between client and supplier, between East and West, the mainland and the ocean.

I was looking for Professor Tea. I finally caught up with him in an underground garage hung with paintings of anguished baby-people and elongated women.

Across the tiling, with his arm around a sleek young woman, stood a surprisingly young man.

"You should have written in Sung dynasty," he complained. "In Sung dynasty everyone knows about tea. Young men and young women met for tea and music. They made poems, talked about tea, painted pictures. It was, uh, tea jamming?" He snickered. "They have famous tea competitions—to taste different teas. Beautiful life. Every art most refined. In mountains, in gardens, they were Beautiful People, jamming all day.

"Beautiful scenes, you know, they believe in nature. It was perfect life. Very difficult in city life. No poetry. If you wear Issey Miyake or Chanel, I know all about you, where you go, who you see. And in China, perfect life is finished.

"It was life of feeling, for anyone with right feeling, who un-derstand tea. You see, my best customer in the shop is a road sweeper. Every week he buys the best tea, a little amount. He gam-bles on the lottery. Sometimes he must have credit, but he always pays. He has strong feeling."

We agreed to go for dinner with a company from the gallery, but our numbers swelled by the minute, and when we reached the restaurant, I found myself sitting too far away to talk. Finally, in the scrum on the steps, I missed him by a few moments as I was bun-dled into a taxi heading my way.

In the taxi was a young Chinese who had been sitting near the Professor.

"Tonight, very quiet. Usually he is more drinking, and many songs," he remarked.

And he gave me the Professor's phone number.

The Assistant curator of the Hong Kong Museum of Tea Ware was called Rose Lee. "Rose is only my English name," she said seriously.

The Museum stood on a promontory of the Peak, possibly the lowest building in Hong Kong, a colonnaded villa in sparkling white which sailed upon a lawn of dull tropical grass with blades like dandelion. The traffic snarled about, invisible through trees, like a pride of hungry lions—and there must have been lions out there who coveted this unusual spot. Barely fifty yards from its low and tree-lined balustrade, across a network of carriageways, Hong Kong's newest Hong, the Bank of China, was rising to its seventieth floor. With pressure on land so intense, and buildings so high, each rhododendron in the garden had thwarted the activity of at least thirty offices. They must be the most valuable shrubs in the world.

Every few minutes a car turns up the drive and releases a bride and groom in full fig and plastic bouquets, accompanied by a pho-tographer. He adjusts his tripod, brushes a veil one way or another, waves the couple to and fro, calls for a smile which neither seems able to manage and finally snaps them against the one backdrop in the city which has nothing whatever to do with it—no lights, no mirrored glass, no press of people—and which has survived, by outrageous chance, as a place for wedding snaps and teapots.

Rose Lee loved Yixing. Yixing "purple" clay is unglazed and absorbs flavour, so that they say you may one day pour hot water into your pot and brew tea without leaves. Yixing pots should be judged, like any teapot, on their balance and the cleanness of the spout. In general they are no larger than a fist, and their shapes reflect a Taoist notion of harmony, the square and the circle reconciled, the straight line and the curve. They have practical advantages which Taoism, being the middle way, does not despise. Chinese teas can be brewed four or five times without spoiling the flavour, but in a porcelain teapot the leaves, if left too long between brews, will begin to rot. Tea can be left in a Yixing pot overnight because the lid fits so tightly. After Liberation in 1949 the price of antique Yixing had soared away from the new examples, whose quality declined. Now, Miss Lee was happy to say, the apprentice system was restored, the masters were free to create again and collectors had returned. It was a good time to buy, really.

Yixing, a city in Jiangsu Province between Shanghai and Nanjing, has been producing teapots associated with its name since at least the 16th century. The clay found there has unique qualities: its low shrinkage and remarkable plasticity are conducive to heat retention and the creation of a tight-fitting lid. This, together with its high porosity, is said to enhance the fragrance, flavor, and color of the tea better than other ceramics.

The earthy tones of Yixing stoneware stand in stark contrast to the colors and designs on the better-known imperial Chinese porcelains; and the beauty of Yixing teaware is subtle, which may be why it so appealed to the scholars and literati of Suzhou, the cultural center of the Ming Dynasty.

—Amanda Meyer Stinchecum, "Pot Luck," *Departures*

Clutching my Yixing teapot from the Museum shop (Rose Lee had examined the chop and pronounced it very good, the mark of a rising woman potter; but later I found that the pot dribbled), I sauntered into the garden. A man in a shirt and tie stood in the flower-beds hooking frangipani blooms from a tree with a long stick. He gave the stick a twist and caught the flower as it fell to

add to a small pile at his feet. "Very smell," he said, offering me one.
I sniffed. We both inhaled deeply. He lifted his nose and said:
"Inside every, small insect." A minute ant crawled out obediently
and started to run across my fingers. Another bride in a veil and
too much make-up was preceding her groom up the drive; he held
grey gloves. The frangipani man held up his bloom. "Smell for one
day only," he warned, and I thanked him for the present, and
walked back to the city.

Around 10:30 one evening the phone rang.

"Is there Mr. Jason Goodwin?" I recognized the voice of
Professor Tea. "Can you come over now?"

"It's quite late."

"I know, it's very good. It would be a time to drink tea. After,
we can hit some spots."

The address brought me to a stubby apartment block.
Struggling to the top, I met his wife emerging through the barred
outer door, the Professor standing behind her in a t-shirt and a pair
of blue shorts like a skinny schoolboy. "My wife goes to work now.
A nurse."

The Professor wore flip-flops. "Would you mind?" He gestured
politely to a little pile of shoes by the door, and with bare feet I
padded into the living room. There was a goldfish swimming in a
bowl on top of the TV set. The set was on; a Chinese princess was
tied to a tree and two clowns with kung-fu swords were approaching her crabwise through the undergrowth. "Chinese
Bertorucci," said Professor Tea, starting to watch it over my shoulder. With an effort he switched it off and put on the fan instead. "I
had it on for the kid. He has fever."

He was almost six foot, thin, and slightly hunched. The stoop
was the only real indication of his age; he had a childlike face, a
nose that curled like the scroll of a violin and a grille grin like
Charlie Chaplin. His teeth were dark, the lower row unattractively
brown. But Professor Tea wasn't worried. He was really proud of
his teeth, which he could flash like a membership card to the exclusive world of tea connoisseurs. That tannin stain had taken years

to create, like a proper English lawn. It was heavier upon his lower teeth because, like all serious tea-drinkers, he would pour the liquor into his pouched lip before swilling it back over his gums and teeth.

The *amah* went past with a cold flannel she had taken from the fridge. When she had gone, the Professor said: "She makes me feel, you know, shame, working so hard." He had begun almost with a laugh. "I don't work at all."

"I thought you had a shop," I pointed out.

"Yuh…Yuh." He paused, and his expression became abstracted like a child's, as if quiet cogs were whirring in his head and he had to strain to hear them. It was an expression he adopted often, pulling himself short to consider the effect of his words, as if only by a conscious effort could he keep control over them. English tended to overpower him, leaving him speechless and irritated, and he would begin anew, explaining his explanations, in rapid assaults from various angles.

"But I just go to the shop," he said at length. "I don't know what work is." He stared into his secret pond as if a sudden movement had attracted him.

> *When drinking tea, the Chinese custom is that the first person to pour the tea pays the bill.*
>
> —Larry Habegger,
> "New Days in Hong Kong"

"Tell me something about tea," I suggested.

"What," he inquired seraphically, "would you like to know?"

In the shop he had just discovered a chest of Yunnan pressed green tea. The tea, he explained, was pressed into irregular patties while the leaves were still slightly moist before the final firing. It looked like clods of earth. Yunnan Province borders on Burma, where the Shan tribes of the hill forests still eat pickled tea called *leppet* and where the tea bush probably originated. Yunnan is not pickled, but it does "ferment," blooming and darkening over the years, so that the very thought of the well-aged chest, some fifteen years old, which had been held over by accident, was enough to turn the Professor's mood. Economics is not generally kind to this tea. The cultivator sells his pickings to a factory for hard cash; the factory, to recoup, will not store the tea even in the expectation of a better price later, but sells to the dealers, who lack storage space. The tea is not well known; the dealers are unwilling to hold on to it without the certainty of getting the right price later. "It would be very, very expensive. So old tea like this is—rare.

"Perhaps we can have some sips," he added.

There is an account by Goslan of drinking tea with Balzac in an atmosphere of fervent connoisseurship:

> As fine as tobacco from Ladakh, as yellow as Venetian gold, the tea responded, without doubt, to the praise with which Balzac perfumed it before letting you taste; but you had to submit to a kind of initiation to enjoy the *droit de dégustation*. He never gave any to the profane; and we did not drink it every day ourselves. Only on feast days would he take it from the kamchatka box in which, like a relic, it was enclosed, and slowly unwrap it from the envelope of silk paper covered in hieroglyphic characters.
>
> Ever with fresh pleasure for him and for us, Balzac would relate the story of this precious golden tea. The sun, he would say, ripened it only for the emperor of China; Mandarins of the first rank were charged, as a privilege of birth, with watering and tending it on the stem. It was picked before sunrise by young virgins who carried it singing to the emperor's feet. China produced this enchanted tea in only one of her provinces, and this sacred province furnished but a few pounds destined for His Imperial Majesty and the eldest son of his august house. By special grace, the emperor of China, in his days of bounty, had a few handfuls sent by the caravans to the emperor of Russia. From the minister of that autocrat Balzac possessed the tea with which he, in his turn, favoured us.
>
> The yellow tea of gold given to Balzac by M. de Humboldt was sprinkled with human blood. Kirguise and Nogais Tartars had attacked the Russian caravan and it was

only after a long and murderous combat that it had reached
Moscow, its destination. You could say it was a sort of
Argonaut tea. The story of the expedition, which I have cut
very short, didn't quite finish there: added to it, astonishing
properties: too astonishing! If you took this golden tea
three times, Balzac claimed, you became *borgne*, dumb; six
times, you became blind.

But now, far from performing an intricate ceremonial, Professor
Tea reappeared with two shallow white bowls and saucers and a
thermos, from which he poured something that looked like coffee.
I said so. The Professor looked upset.

He took a pouched sip from his bowl, and found the inspiration.

"The flask is not the best. But coffee is coffee and water"—he
eyed the ceiling—"the coffee floats in the water. It just comes
through the mouth, leaves a dry taste, like bitterness." He swivelled
towards me, grappling with an observation. "Coffee—is—cold to
taste," he spelled out slowly.

We had taken some sips, as the Professor had suggested. The tea
was light.

"Tea and water give each other life," the Professor was saying.
"The tea is still alive. This tea has tea and water vitality," he added,
pronouncing the phrase like the surprised mother in a detergent
commercial. "Afterwards, the taste still happens. It is like, like,
like…it is this stuff, uh, with hairs upwards, silk upwards, uh…"
We contemplated the nature of this stuff together, very far apart.
"It comes up after your foot," he said lamely.

I thought of crocodiles, then dog turds.

"You push it one way, it rises again."

"Grass?" I suggested.

"No, not grass, A clothing thing. For chairs."

"Velvet?"

"It rises like velvet. Good tea—you move your tongue and it
rises afterwards. It starts here in one strength"—he dabbed his
lower lip—"and moves all the way. It changes. Then like—
what?—velvet. These are its, its…" We were stuck again. "Not a

drink. Not like coffee, cold. It is like the way to tell a story, or—
it acts." He was very serious now, pondering the structure of the
tea. "It is a performance."

We struggled. At last the Professor said: "The Chinese don't
have deep verbal knowledge. They have ways to understand without speaking. Lao-tzu says, if you understand you won't say.

"Whisky as a chaser?" He had an alarming command of English
in many respects.

The Professor went to visit his son, whose small coughs penetrated through the partition. It was fever weather—weather like a
fever, hot and clammy. Plain tiredness easily mimics fever, and
Hong Kong at night is a chequerboard of lights stacked one on top
of another, hard and gritty and deliriously clear-cut. The boy's
relief came in the flannels fetched from the icebox by his patient
amah, and perhaps from his father's visits. The Professor said he
would wait until three, and if the fever showed no signs of breaking, they would go to the hospital.

The Professor said: "We understand each other." I looked at him
warily. Lao-tzu seemed forgotten.

"You know who I think will dominate the next century?"
he enquired, with that queer expression of childlike innocence.
"Jews."

I felt tired and woozy of a sudden. I didn't want this lover of tea
and civilization to mouth the ancient prejudices of my European
world. I told him I thought the people dominating the next century
would probably be Chinese. And then, half an hour too late, I left.

The next day I telephoned the Hong Kong branch of the
Fujian Tea Association. "*Wei!*" bellowed the receptionist. *Wei* is
Cantonese for hello, so I said: "*Wei!* May I speak to—"

"*Wei!*" She shrieked.

I tried again: "CAN I SPEAK TO MR. WU?"

"*Wei*," she replied, matter-of-factly. Unable to make much
headway, or to retreat intelligibly, I put the receiver down.

The next attempt was made through a friendly interpreter at
Jardine Matheson. She put her hand over the mouthpiece. "They

say they haven't heard of you. Shall I try to make an appointment?" And so one puzzled tea-time, prudently armed with my invitation from Mr. Wu, I arrived at the association's headquarters.

Mr. Hu sat on a stuffed bench, shoehorned into a baby blue Mao suit made of thick cotton, his eyes buttoned into the puckered fat of his face. He smiled continually, a bland, uncomprehending smile. His interpreter was slight and wore big smoked glasses and a skinny brown nylon suit somewhere between Mao and demob. We sat around a low table and drank tea, Mr. Hu saying through his interpreter that he was pleased to meet me. I replied that I was pleased to meet him, too, and wondered about the tea. Fujian jasmine? They laughed indulgently and said I was quite right, and Mr. Hu mentioned that it came from his native county. I would very much like to go there, I said. The interpreter smiled, but did not translate.

"Mr. Wu very kindly offered me help in visiting tea gardens in Fujian," I explained. After a brief confabulation the interpreter said Mr. Hu was very sorry, but Wu Lao Sheng had left the Association.

It is customary in Hong Kong to pour everyone's tea if the pot is sitting near you. Legend has it that when a great emperor was travelling incognito with his servants, he reached for the teapot and began to pour. The servants were aghast as they were accustomed not only to doing all of the emperor's pouring but following this with deep reverent bows. In order not to reveal his true identity, the emperor suggested that each member of his entourage tap index and middle fingers at the same time as his tea was being poured—a symbolic bow. Even today when you look around a tea shop or restaurant in Hong Kong, you will notice people of all ages tapping their fingers in memory of this humble emperor.

—Iris Choi, "Pouring Tea"

"I don't think it was a personal offer. I understood that your Association could help me."

"Mr. Hu would like to know whether you have an invitation from our embassy in England."

"I have a letter of invitation from your Association, signed by Mr. Wu."

"I am afraid there is no recommendation from our embassy."

I produced the letter. The interpreter interpreted it, and they discussed.

"Mr. Hu is very sorry, but there is no record of this action."

Could Mr. Hu make the invitation himself? "I am sorry, but we need authorization from our head office."

"All right, perhaps we could ask them now?" Mr. Hu and his interpreter looked very doubtful, but eventually the interpreter left Mr. Hu and me to smile at each other and drink our tea. He was gone for three cups.

He came back holding a telex. "REGRET UNABLE TO ASSIST. NO HANDS AVAILABLE."

"You see," he explained, "everybody is working on the harvest. Very sorry."

Mr. Hu spoke and turned a crocodile smile on me.

"He says it is better you come after tea season. You can talk to our China Travel Service."

I took this to be the face-saver. The telex had come through very promptly, written in English, and for all I knew it had been composed by the interpreter himself. They could be fairly sure that I wasn't about to hang around for six months, but we could now part all smiles. I felt exactly what the Canton merchants of the 1830s felt—that their reasonable requests would be given a fair hearing by the highest powers, if lower officials were only willing to pass them on. It is in official nature to avoid troublesome communications with superiors, as it is natural for officials to use what powers they do possess to the full. Unable safely to say yes, Mr. Hu had a least the satisfaction of saying no.

I stomped onto the bus, fuming. Later on I discovered Robert Fortune had met the same men. "I had had too much to do with the Chinese authorities," he wrote, "to place any reliance in what they said, more particularly when their object was to procrastinate matters from day to day until I should be obliged to leave the district. When the Chinese have an end to gain, the only question with them is whether they are most likely to succeed by telling the truth or telling lies; either method is resorted to as may best suit their purpose, with a slight preference, perhaps, for the latter."

Fortune had a solution to the problem of delay. He just went, regardless.

Jason Goodwin is an award-winning author who has traveled extensively in the Far East and India. He is the author of two books, On Foot to the Golden Horn *and* A Time for Tea: Travels Through India and China in Search of Tea, *from which this story was excerpted.*

★

Governor Patten conceded he could only "speculate about China's understanding of the miracle ingredients of Hong Kong's success story, ingredients familiar to anyone who's lived in a free and plural society."

He found some grounds for optimism, however, in a speech this year by Li Ruihuan, a member of the standing committee of China's Politburo. Mr. Li compared Hong Kong to a well-used Chinese teapot, whose value lies in the unique flavor its dregs impart to its tea. Officials in charge of Hong Kong, Mr. Li warned, should be careful not to scrape the pot clean, lest they lose its most precious asset.

"What I can say is that at least we know that some Chinese leaders are saying, 'Look, they've got something very right in Hong Kong, and the stain in the old teapot does produce a hell of a good brew.'"

—Peter Stein, "Only China's Actions Can Ease Angst in Hong Kong, Colony's Governor Says," *The Wall Street Journal*

* * *

The Baghdad Connection

It wasn't just the English who came to Hong Kong.

A STIFLING AFTERNOON, THE HUMIDITY GAUGE SHOWING 99 percent, and the Orient is a slave to passion: label–lust, a particularly rapacious form of designer shopping. Nowadays from Tokyo to Taipei, from Singapore to Bangkok, Asia lives to shop.

Of course, Hong Kong is rather a special case. Stocking up on capitalist merchandise could be a sensible move if you are about to be handed over to the hard-line communist ideologies that, via CNN, gave Tiananmen Square to the world. In the arcade beneath The Peninsula, the city's most expensive hotel, people stand three deep before the Chanel and Hermès windows, while a few yards away, a group of men ogles an entire oyster bar of Rolex watches.

But is this really the feeding frenzy of people about to be plunged into Maoist austerity and gloom? Probably not. The affluent citizens of Hong Kong are spending hard, in apparent expectation that the bonanza will continue indefinitely.

High up in St. George's Building, a prominent tree in the forest of skyscrapers that gives Hong Kong Island its Manhattan–like appearance, I found Michael Kadoorie in a similarly confident mood. The Kadoories are an interesting family, their name being inseparable from the history of Hong Kong. Originally from

235

Baghdad, Michael Kadoorie's grandfather left the Middle East in
1880 to work for the Sassoons, another Mesopotamian Jewish
family, which had by then established itself as one of the leading
mercantile dynasties of the China trade.

More than 100 years later, his descendants preside over an empire that includes China Light and Power—the company that
keeps Hong Kong's neon burning—and Hong Kong and Shanghai
Hotels, Ltd., owner of The Peninsula Hotel in Kowloon and of
Peninsula hotels worldwide.

"We had a home in Shanghai," recalled Kadoorie, a man in his
50s who favors the expensively tailored, flawlessly suntanned look.
"My grandfather lived there most of the time. Not in Hong Kong.
Hong Kong was a backwater, an entrepôt, when Shanghai was the
third-largest city in the world."

In the '30s the Kadoories owned two of the smartest hotels in
Shanghai, the Palace and the Astor House. When the Japanese
bombing began in August 1937, the family had more to lose than
most. As the wealthy and the mobile soon moved out, Hong Kong
became one of the chief beneficiaries of the exodus.

In 1948 the communists seized power, and the industries that
had been the basis of Shanghai's wealth—particularly the textile
trade—all moved down to Hong Kong. Within a few years the
population increased from 600,000 to more than 2 million.

With the PLA poised on the border and the old guard still in
Beijing, the Kadoories must surely view the future with considerable trepidation. Is family history about to repeat itself? Kadoorie
shook his head and beamed with apparent equanimity. "I regard
the Chinese takeover as just another business risk. We've had difficult times before—in 1967, during the Cultural Revolution, we
had bombs outside The Peninsula—but we've always come
through. The reason for Hong Kong's existence is its usefulness.
Hong Kong is China's largest trading partner. And now, of course,
the world's economic focus is shifting."

Determined to find a flaw in his optimism, I pointed out that
China is still governed by the old Long Marchers, unregenerate
hard-liners, but he would have none of it. "China is not the same

as it was. Take our hotel in Beijing—the Palace—we're actually in business with the Chinese Army. The PLA owns 50 percent of it. Believe me, this is going to be the dominant economic region of the world in the 21st century. Absolutely no question."

Nowadays, I discovered, people call it the Triangle, by which they mean the area defined by Shanghai, Taipei, and Hong Kong. Already this region has been invested with some of the mystery of its namesake off the coast of Bermuda. It's not until you try getting on a plane that you begin to understand exactly what is happening on China's eastern seaboard. "To Shanghai? This week?" The travel agent clearly thought I was mad. "It's impossible. Don't you realize there's a gold rush going on?"

Arriving at Chinese customs with cameras and a laptop computer has in the past proved an uncomfortable experience. Not this time. After the two-hour flight, I was waved through by a pleasant young woman who actually smiled as I passed. A uniformed official in a communist country smiling! Further surprises were in store. Five years

ℋong Kong's Jewish community has thrived since the mid-19th century when merchant-prince David Sassoon and his Baghdadi family came to settle. Following him later was the global migration of Jewish merchants from Russia, Poland, Austria, Germany, Syria, Iraq, and other places. They came to Hong Kong—sometimes after difficult journeys, many times after outbreaks of religious persecution— to find their fortune....

Two waves of German Jews also infiltrated China. The first, in the early 1930s, included mostly professionals—doctors and lawyers. The bulk, perhaps as many as 20,000, escaped in 1938 and 1939. A few thousand Austrian and Polish Jews likewise sought refuge in the Orient, but they had little time to get settled before the outbreak of the Pacific War, and most remained in transit camps.

By the end of World War II, there were nearly 30,000 Jews in Shanghai and several hundred in Hong Kong. Ever riding on the coattails of history, many Shanghai Jews would make their way to Israel during the Chinese Revolution, although the diehard "Asia hands" preferred to remain in the Far East and relocated to Hong Kong.

—Debra Weiner, "Hong Kong,"
The Jewish Traveler

ago there were hardly any cars in China—a country of 1.2 billion people sensibly considered its railway network to be of primary importance—but now, within half a mile of the airport, I found myself sitting in a traffic jam. And the traffic police, struggling to bring some order into this newfound chaos, were consulting one another on portable telephones—in Shanghai, cradle of the Cultural Revolution.

After spending about 90 minutes snarled in traffic, I arrived at the elegant neoclassical entrance of the Garden Hotel, once the French Sporting Club, now a five-star deluxe capitalist temple managed by Tokyo's Okura Hotel. The art deco interior of the old building has been meticulously restored—including the glorious ballroom—and a tower has been built at the rear. In between its original and present-day functions, the building served as a residence for Jiang Qing, who, while urging the Red Guards to ever more lunatic excesses, lived in palatial *fin de siècle* splendor.

However, thanks to one of the more delightful ironies of history, the magnificent rooms once used by Madame Mao as her private apartment are now filled with conclaves of gray-suited executives plotting joint ventures with their earnest Chinese counterparts.

It's about an hour's walk from the Garden Hotel, down Nanjing Road to the Bund. Nanjing Road is Shanghai's chief thoroughfare, where every day a significant proportion of the city's thirteen million citizens are out shopping and trading and strolling. The atmosphere immediately struck me as relaxed and cheerful, utterly devoid of ideological fervor. Louis Vuitton and Ray Ban seemed to have been doing brisk business, and there was not a single Mao suit in sight. Doubtless as a reaction to communism's puritan ethic, the young girls were dressed mostly in clothes offering only minimal protection from the weather, while the boys seemed to favor a kind of mafiosi chic—the Palermo Triad look, altogether more comical than sinister.

Along the Bund, the waterfront of the Huang-p'u River, the crowds idled, chatted, and scolded their children in an atmosphere of serene normality. Revolution? What revolution? My guide stopped in front of one of the massive gray façades, constructed in the early years of this century. It was, she said, pointing to a red flag flying from the roof, headquarters of the Shanghai Municipal Party Committee. Confiscated in 1948, the building had originally belonged to the Hong Kong and Shanghai Bank. Rumor had it, she continued, that the bank was now negotiating for its return with the city's communist authorities. Oh yes, she thought, they'd get it back all right.

Andrew Powell is a travel consultant for Harper's Bazaar.

✳

Mao came into the room. He came so quietly that we were hardly aware of his presence. He wore a thick brown Sun Yat-sen uniform which seemed to have been woven of goats' hair, and as he stood beside the towering Peng Teh-huei he looked slighter and smaller than I had imagined him. I had suspected he was changeable when I saw him at the theater; now, once again, he assumed the appropriate disguise. There is hardly a photograph of him which resembles any other photograph, so strangely and so suddenly does he change. Today, he looked like a surprisingly young student, a candidate for a doctorate, and perhaps he played for the college: the shoulders were very heavy. The hair was very sleek and long, the eyes large, the lips pursed, and he had no mannerisms. There was about him a kind of quietness such as you will find among people who have lived much alone. But this quietness was delusory. It was true enough, and almost tangible, but it went oddly with the young student who seemed to be, not the giver of the party and the equal of the Emperors, but a young man who had strayed by accident from a university campus. He was 53 and looked 20.

Unaccountably, the room filled up. His wife came in, wearing black slacks and a sweater, and she said "*Nin hao?*" in greeting, with a classical Pekingese accent, and suddenly you realized that her long face possessed more beauty and expression than the face of the considerably more famous Mme. Chiang Kai-shek; also, she brought with her the scent of the flowers she had been gathering in the uplands. Chu Teh came in, limping a little, for the water in Yenan has a strange effect on the bones of the legs—I observed twenty to thirty peasants who limped in the same way. He had the face of a wise peasant and smiled broadly. God knows how many other generals there were at this time. It was like the opening scene of Tolstoy's *War and Peace:* you were continually expecting the princes and generals to enter, forgetting that they had entered a few minutes ago, disguised as university students and peasants.

—Robert Payne, *Mao Tse-tung: Ruler of Red China*

JOHN HOSKIN

✦

If You Knew Suzie

Life mirrors fiction as the author lives the life he dreamt as a child.

I FIRST DISCOVERED SUZIE WONG WHEN I WAS NINE. TWENTY years later I lived with her and discovered Wanchai.

The initial encounter at such a tender age took the form of a picture on the cover of a London theater program depicting a lovely Chinese girl provocatively dressed in a skin-hugging, thigh-split *cheongsam*. My parents had been to see the show *The World of Suzie Wong*, based on Richard Mason's novel of the same name, and, idly looking at the program the next day, I asked my mother what the play (or maybe it was a musical) was about. "Oh," she said, "you wouldn't like it." That typical parental brush-off coupled with the seductive picture made me pretty damn sure I would like it very much indeed.

For many years Suzie reposed in the back of my mind, only stirring when I made the occasional visit to a Chinese restaurant. But eventually fate and the offer of employment when most desperately needed brought me to Hong Kong. I don't know whether it was due to my meager salary or to some subconscious urge, but I soon found myself an expensively cheap "studio" apartment in Wanchai, Hong Kong's old bar district and home of the fictitious and perhaps, long ago, the real Suzie Wong.

Memories of that theater program came flooding back and I quickly devoured a copy of Mason's book. Unfortunately, I

241

couldn't find his Wanchai anywhere amid the strip of neon lights, cheap tailors, one or two tattoo parlors, and a string of seedy bars with curtain-hung doorways and plush plastic interiors. I even had to strain my eyes to see the famed waterfront since reclaimed land had pushed the harbor back several hundred meters, and even then the view was partially obscured by the towering Hong Kong Arts Center—and that had no place whatsoever in my mental picture of Oriental dens of iniquity.

Worse was to come. A diligent bar-to-bar search failed to produce even one *cheongsam*, not a single girl was dressed in the traditional costume and, sadly, I discovered much of Wanchai had gone topless. Instead of being sheathed in beautiful Chinese silk, the new Suzie Wongs were decked out in weird dresses that seemed as if the maker had run out of material by the time she reached the bodice. The female anatomy is fine but a boob in the eye while sipping one's beer was not my idea of a cozy tête-a-tête as enjoyed by Mason's hero.

Not all the bar girls were topless; some had good physical reasons not to be while the rest showed little imagination in the dress sense—mini skirts or jeans being the norm—and the average Hong Kong secretary was generally more smartly and seductively turned out.

The nearest I came to spotting Mason's Wanchai was the Luk Kwok hotel which was the model for the "Nam Kok Hotel" in his novel. But even this place had changed beyond recognition, becoming an ultra-respectable property specializing in middle-aged tourists and middle-class dinner parties for the extended Chinese family.

Nevertheless, if I hadn't found Mason's territory it was still Wanchai, and I was determined to make the best of it with all the sympathy an alcoholic could bring to a bar district. In finding my first Suzie Wong I had beginner's luck and in the first few days met a pleasant girl working behind one of the bars. She wasn't called Suzie as the tattoo emblazoned over her left breast informed me but that was no deterrent to asking her if she would like to come out after work. She agreed readily enough and so I said, "Fine, what time do you finish work, I'll pick you up?"

"Four-thirty in the morning," came the reply!

Surprisingly, the assignation was kept and everything was good fun, but it was no kind of life for a working man.

After this initial and untypical success I met a succession of the more usual latter-day Miss Wongs, Boozie Wongs. "Buy me drink?" "Buy me drink?" became the refrain that was to echo in my ears for the rest of my stay in Wanchai. The bar girls reminded me of those tableaux you used to find in old-time amusement arcades which sprung into action when you put a penny in the slot, only with these girls it was a "ladies' drink" that produced animation, or at least conversation. I call them Boozie Wongs but in fact their drinks were only cold tea or colored water, although from the price you thought you must be paying for at least a triple Black Label.

The extortionate price of the "ladies' drinks," however, didn't really upset me—everyone has to make a living and buying a drink here and there wouldn't have broken the bank—but what I did

My first glimpse of Hong Kong was a cinematic concoction: Jennifer Jones and William Holden climbing Victoria Peak with the world's most beautiful harbor as a backdrop. I was four years old, and my mother had taken me along to see Love is a Many Splendored Thing. *It was my first movie and the first time I'd seen my mother cry, which upset me so (according to her version of the story), that I too started bawling. We were asked to leave the theater.*

I didn't see the real Hong Kong for another 30 years, but when I did, I found it more extravagantly cinematic—and Cineramic—than anything Hollywood could have invented: a glorious, vertiginous, Technicolor city perched precariously on the edge of a continent and the future.

—Alan Brown, "Get There Now—It's in Its Prime: Hong Kong," *Travel & Leisure*

object to was the total lack of finesse on behalf of the girls' approach. Generally the Chinese are astute business people capable of great subtlety and patience. Not a bit of it with the Miss Wongs. They just followed a never-changing formula of "Hello. What your name? Where you come from?"…(slight pause…) "Buy me drink?" The latter being couched as part question and part threat, and no matter how you answered the first questions—and I made up hundreds of absurd identities for myself—it would never throw the girl off her patter.

Once, when I was the only customer in a bar, the one solitary girl there preferred to sulk alone in the corner simply because I refused to buy her a drink—to an outsider the scene must have looked like a lovers' tiff. Yet, if the girl had only had a better sense of business and customer service I would no doubt have eventually bought her a drink. Wanchai was on its uppers, the heyday of the '50s and '60s had passed and the temporary boom brought about by U.S. servicemen on R&R from Vietnam had also disappeared; yet instead of reviving flagging business by being more polite, there was just a crassness—whether resulting from a sense of loss of face or from thwarted greed if a drink wasn't forthcoming, I don't know—that produced an inevitable justification for the girls' favorite term of abuse, "You cheap Charlie."

Some girls even used the buying of drinks as a form of blackmail if you were hopeful of taking them out. Following the invitation, the typical reply would be, "I'll come to your place later but buy just one last drink now." That "last" drink would often become two or three once the hooks were in and, of course, the girl never turned up later. I was never really taken in by this ploy although for a while it amused me as a kind of gambling with the eternal hope that one last shot of cold tea would hit the jackpot.

In time I did meet Suzie Wong (that, naturally, was not her real name) with whom I was to share a flat in Wanchai for almost a year. It happened one Saturday afternoon when, hungover, I ambled into an early-opening bar for a drop of the "hair of the dog." As I sat down a woman in her mid-30s sidled up to me. The inescapable patter ensued but my head ached too much to refuse her a drink and I let the chatter pass over me until, after a standard follow-up question, "Where you live? How much you pay?" I realized she was offering me a cheap room in her apartment. It seemed a genuine offer, and the opportunity of finding somewhere to live at a reasonable rent in Hong Kong quickly aroused my brain. I brought her out of the bar and off we went to see the apartment—which was just around the corner.

Suzie's place was small and dark but clean. It was decorated in what can only be described as Nouveau Wanchai Kitsch—costume dolls in glass cases, gift calendars on the walls, two color TVs, a rattan bar in one corner of the living room but, disappointingly, no bamboo curtain across the entrance to the mistress bedroom. The room that was to be mine was minute, but as the deal included the run of the whole flat, and that did mean *every* room, I decided to take it. I admit that it was the cheap rent that really decided me, but the idea of living a life of Mason's hero was not totally absent from my mind.

My new home couldn't have been more Wanchai. It was in the very heart of the district and the apartment block held a topless bar in the basement and a night club a couple of floors above. I could hear the band at the latter until four in the morning although, due to strange acoustics, only the bass filtered up to my room and I would nod off to sleep to a monotonous boom, boom, with the rhythm completely absent. There were also other, more poignant reminders of my new habitat; often when I awoke in the mornings I would come across a strange briefcase and jacket lying on the living room sofa, and Suzie's door would be shut. It was a forlorn sight and my relationship with the working Suzie was regulated by open and closed doors—unspoken "do not disturb" signs.

Suzie did not have a heart of gold but it was in the right place and she was always kind and affectionate. She quested madly for a *gweilo* (foreign devil) husband, having been jilted by a Chinese in her youth. In truth it was a lost dream as she was not getting any younger, but she never bemoaned her lot and was always cheerful. She was a good sort, always warning me against the "no good young girls," and at an earlier age she could have done justice to Mason's heroine.

Our relationship never rose above mutual affection and often I wouldn't see Suzie for two or three days at a stretch if she hit a lucky streak and met some big spender. Yet there were many evenings when she wouldn't go to the bar and when I couldn't

face the booze-with-a-boob, and we enjoyed an intimate domes-
ticity that provided a temporary respite from the grotesque that
was funny and the beauty that was obscene of the Fellini-like scene
of Wanchai. We would watch old movies on TV, and I'll never
forget Clint Eastwood mumbling monosyllables of Cantonese in a
dubbed version of *The Good, The Bad and The Ugly*—there was a
metaphor there somewhere.

Only one thing would drive me away occasionally from Suzie
and the flat, and that was when she held one of her *mahjong* parties with three other bar girls. These generally lasted a whole
Saturday afternoon and often went on far into the evening, and the
noise of the tiles being thumped on to the table was deafening, let
alone the screeching when one of the girls won. And then the
large amounts of money that were being gambled were more than
my nerves could stand. *Mahjong* was the only thing Suzie and I
never agreed on despite her once trying to teach me the game.

Settled in the flat with Suzie I became more of a spectator in
the bars than a hunter after good times, although I still pursued
other Suzies from time to time. Such passing relationships did have
their amusing side. There was one girl who dropped me cold after
I had generously taken her for a weekend to Macau simply because
I did not put her up at the best hotel and so, unbeknown to me,
she lost face among her friends. The irony of it was that I could
have got a room in the top hotel free but, to my Western mind,
that place was too noisy and gaudy and I preferred to pay out of
my own pocket for a room in a European-style hotel that had
more character. Unfortunately, my sense of place did not translate
into Chinese.

Then there was the girl with a dozen tattoos, fewer than half of
which were visible even when she was only scantily dressed. A
succession of Felliniesque characters followed, all with their own
fascination, and I learnt that while the girls might be a more mercenary bunch than those in Mason's book, the variety of person-
alities he describes in the early pages still existed. Sadly, though,
genuine bonhomie had declined in direct proportion of Wanchai's
failing fortunes.

When at last the bar girls did become for me more extras on the scene—only the Suzie I lived with remained real to the last—I found endless entertainment in watching the other customers. Here it was not so much a case of the good, the bad, and the ugly but of the matey, the laughable, and the mildly aggressive.

The former abounded, and I had many a jolly drinking session with new-found friends whom I would never see again. One especially memorable instance was on a miserable Sunday evening when I had only HK$10 in my pocket, just enough for two beers and an enforced early night. That was not to be. In the course of nursing my beers I got chatting to some Scandinavian merchant seamen and one offered me a drink. I tried to refuse, explaining I was not in a position to return the courtesy, but in his jovial way he insisted. All of a sudden my quiet evening turned into another riotous night of carousing amid jolly company; the fact that I was temporarily broke made no difference.

The laughable incidents stemmed mostly from Japanese customers in Wanchai, not because that nationality is any funnier than the rest of us, but because the Wanchai "sharks" tended to single them out in the belief they had more money to lose than others. Two Japanese I happened to notice became the butt of a con that had a hilarious, if unfortunate for them, outcome. After they had consumed a couple of beers apiece the bar girl said the bill was "100 dollars" (the real price should have been HK$20). The Japanese were outraged over this obvious piece of extortion and an argument ensued. Eventually they agreed to pay half the asking price and plonked US$50 down on the counter. Of course, the girl had been conning in Hong Kong dollars, so while the Japanese had thought they'd beaten the price down by half they had actually ended up by paying HK$250!

Another bar I often frequented seemed to have an arrangement with a travel agency specializing in Japanese male groups which produced a scene that always amused me. Every night a group of nervous, grinning men would be led in, a quick round of drinks produced and then, before I could take another sip of my beer, I would suddenly find myself in a deserted bar. The Japanese had vanished as quickly as they had come, taking with them every single girl in the place except those behind the bar. It was as if a swarm of locusts had hit. Then, no more than 30 minutes later, the girls would troop back one by one wearing the same grins on their faces that the Japanese had sported a short while earlier.

True to the old times, Wanchai occasionally reverted to a sailors' bar district when the U.S. fleet was in. But unlike the old days, 5,000 frustrated seamen off a carrier that had been at sea for weeks found little outlet in Wanchai except through booze, rudeness, and mild aggression. Of course, most were harmless enough, mumbling into their glasses about "back home," but a few were unpleasant, calling out such things as "Hey Chink, give me a drink" or, looking at a girl's breast, "Where did you grow those?" All very unnecessary, and at such times I could well understand why the latter-day Suzies despised the foreign barbarian. Though sometimes a sailor would stick up for a girl in opposition to a shipmate and an amusing argument would follow with the play-acting of a promised fight that rarely took place.

That was one thing about Wanchai: it was safe. I never really felt physically threatened there and it held none of the street dangers usually associated with a seedy bar district. Even the one occasion when I did experience some aggro it quickly turned into a joke.

My antagonists were not, as might be expected, American sailors, but three members of that stalwart segment of society, the British Army. The soldiers in question, sitting on the opposite side of a round bar, tried to pick an argument with me, making up some story about my once having knocked over a mate's drink. In that wonderfully articulate way the British Tommy has, the conversation went something like, "Yeah, I know you. You're the one, ain't he, Mick?" "Yeah, me and you step outside…etc." I knew if I attempted to leave the bar it would be taken as an admission that I'd been scared by their bluff, so I sat where I was. Actually, I had no choice as my knees were refusing to support the rest of me, and I was forced to talk my way out of the situation and call their bluff. Eventually they recognized my mental fortitude and overlooked my lack of physical courage. We all agreed it was just a joke, they'd played their game and I'd played mine (the British are great sports-men) and we went on to spend the rest of the evening drinking together as the best of mates.

Wanchai was a kaleidoscope and I enjoyed it all, ups and downs. I met many characters and could find some value in all—with the notable exception of the *gweilo* cops who lorded it up, swanking with their perfect command of Cantonese. But cops in bars are the same everywhere.

Yet even the pale imitation of Mason's Wanchai that I knew was sinking fast. More and more "Chinese Only" bars were opening up. My Suzie eventually graduated to a famous bar on Kowloon side noted for its aging yet engaging bar girls, and I was forced to pull out to cure a condition that was rapidly developing into the DTs. So at last I stepped out of "The World," where "Suzie Wong" went who knows. Perhaps Mason was right when he wrote: "She came through the turnstile and joined the crowd waiting for the ferry."

John Hoskin is a writer who lives in Bangkok.

✳

For the mouth to desire sweet tastes, the eye to desire beautiful colors, the ear to desire pleasant sounds, the nose to desire fragrant odors, and the four limbs to desire rest and ease—these things are natural. But there is an appointment of Heaven in connection with them, and the superior man does not say of his pursuit of them, "It is my nature."

—Mencius

GEORGE ADAMS

✦ ✦ ✦

Mr. Leung

Romantic advice comes from an unexpected source.

MR. LEUNG TOOK ME BY THE HAND AND SHOWED ME HONG KONG.

Oh, Mr. Leung, how did we meet? We met in the staff room and you were marking books with the fans swirling and the microwave oven making someone their rehashed second rice meal of the day. You looked over to me and said something in a gentlemanly way, yes a very sweet and gentlemanly way, like the characters in the old films, the Cantonese films from the '50s I can only half understand even with subtitles.

It was something very important, if only I had known, but like so much that is important, it is forgotten, locked in some recalcitrant brain cell or maybe in one of the many that have succumbed to alcohol or nicotine or to sex. Yes, you looked over and said something, something comforting and which made me want to reply to your brilliantined hair and your ever so slightly browned teeth, brown from what I never knew. You suggested a meal, perhaps.

My next recollection of being with you is walking through the crowds of Kowloon one sticky afternoon in search of an afternoon snack. You had your jacket and your grey pullover on, despite all the heat, and you did not sweat. What an unlikely pair we made for I could not have been your nephew even after the genetic transmutation of several generations of mixed marriages. How can I put it? You were just a little, well, portly. I mean, not that you didn't carry it well in your Oxford bags so neatly ironed every day by who knows who. Through the crowds we strode, you with your incessant stream of excellent and select English, English from some time in those films, black-and-white English. I never knew local people could swear so well in English but you had made a study of it and you wanted to know more. Expletives flew as the infuriating hordes held up your magisterial progression. And then we were there, in the restaurant where everyone tipped their head to you, to your...*presence.*

"Do you like Chinese food? Don't you think it's slightly disgusting?"

I didn't, not even the chicken claws and the sea blubber and the more unmentionable things in the snacks brought to us. Fried rice and the pork was for me, with all the fat trimmed off, as you knew foreigners liked it, and you liked to please me.

"You can touch the local girls, anywhere. But don't sleep with them. They turn up in your lessons. Very embarrassing."

It was Mr. Leung's first rule. Was it from experience that you told me this? Did something lurk in your past, Mr. Leung?

I shovelled the rice into my mouth and watched your chopsticks move like fine pincers at the prawns and other delicacies I tried with caution.

"Chinese food is disgusting. Like making love. All good things are disgusting a little."

Mr. Leung's Rule Number Two. The rule of disgust. Grasp the nettle and smell the emetic odours of life. Then forget and live again. No guilt, no frustration, no unlived time. This was the essential, eternal secret and Mr. Leung's greatest rule, so difficult for a Westerner to follow but so persuasive. We die, you said, for such a long time.

"Chinese girls are like that. The shop girls want to be secretaries. The secretaries want to work in a hotel. The hotel girls want to be air hostesses. The air hostesses want to be models. The models want to be film stars. The film stars want to be public figures. They all want sex and daren't admit it."

Mr. Leung had been with the police and knew their tricks as well as the ways of Kowloon people, that swarming mass surviving somewhere between comatose desperation and unnatural frenzy.

Mr. Leung had The Knowledge.

In her novel A Many Splendored Thing, *Han Suyin described Hong Kong as a deep, roaring, bustling, eternal market "where life and love and souls and blood and all things made and grown under the sun are bought and sold and smuggled and squandered." That was the Crown Colony in 1950. Raze some slums, add some bricks and mortar, and it is that way today.*

—Lisa Gubernick, "The Crown Colony: Buisness as Usual," *Forbes*

"I came here in 1949 and I had nothing. I didn't even know that water came out of a tap and was drinkable. It was terrible at that time but everybody was the same. You worked, you ate, you slept with your girl, and when the babies came along you worked harder. Sometimes there was racing or a film or a good meal. And I made many friends. We were all on the take in those days. Policemen got lousy pay. Why not? You were criminal not to take the money. You took a whore if you didn't take the cash. So what? We survived. And now, *mahjong*."

The parlour was so loud that my ears rang painfully even hours afterwards. The passion of noise. Each man with his little box of money at the table in a drawer or else winnings were marked up for settlement later. Mr. Leung played like a demon, actually removed his jacket, his silk and mohair jacket, which fitted so tightly it suffocated him. I was harmless, he indicated. Not a cop despite my short hair. I was all right. Tea was brought, undrinkable, tasting of smoke and dust but a sip was all that was required. To fit in. To be accepted. To be always excluded but a part of it all. Conviviality. Mr. Leung always won, not too much, and then we were off again to see the girls.

The girls were his two sisters, both older than he, in silk pyjamas at all times, never hurried, bringing him tea and a snack of cakes or whatever soup was in the pan whenever he came home. His wife lived now in Shatin and his children, some of them, were in America. Up the stairs we went, past the cardboard boxes (sometimes inhabited) and the other debris of apartment block Kowloon before the buildings were transformed into Courts and Mansions and dwellers required property managers to clean up and provide fire extinguishers. The doorman never looked up from his racing page, if he was there at all, in his dimly lit cubby-hole with the cracked and sellotaped patterned glass and the ridiculous calendar from Dairy Farm always on the wrong month. Mr. Leung sometimes gave the doorman a bottle of beer to while away the time in his solitary confinement.

"You need a girl. Put her into a car and drive up to the Peak. Open up the glove compartment and that gives you all the light you need. Or ride around Tsim Sha Tsui. A man like you. You are in their fantasies. You need to go with a woman."

I already had a girl, I explained, but it was all to no avail. A woman was duly arranged.

Mr. Leung's niece, Catherine, was a tertiary student and stunning in a girlish way for it was hard to think that she was a woman—and I still had fixed ideas about such things—or would ever be one. She giggled at me across the table of Tea 42 in Jordan, a cosy place hovering between respectability and an air of cheap seduction. Even the waitresses flirted, one telling me she had a Green Card and was bored with her job before Catherine arrived. "Only couples come here," the waitress said. Her friend stood by her as she related the details of her life in the U.S.A. to me and I smiled as she imparted lascivious meaning to each fact from a bargirl's life in San Francisco.

Catherine arrived with books, looking as fresh and as innocent as a Waltons kid sister and causing me to gulp like a goldfish. Even the worldly clientèle of wicked Tea 42 was slightly scandalised and the giggling of the waitresses began afresh in the kitchen area where the unkempt boy, sullen by being deprived of his cigarette whilst working in full view (Tea 42 was more up-market than his last position) poured out *lai-cha* into steel pots from a grimy subsidiary jug and carefully cut the edges off our toasted tuna fish sandwiches.

"This is a date," said Catherine and smiled. "You are very strong."

That evening, we sat in the cinema arm in arm.

"I don't want a boyfriend," she said outside but kissed me good-night with more than a hint of Frenchness.

Mystery.

You Mr. Leung had told me not to expect straightforwardness and to practice caution but how to follow your precepts?

"She likes you."

"Then why is she telling me to keep my hands off?"

"It is their way. If she did not like you, she simply wouldn't see you again. You are in their fantasies. But remember, don't go too far. Great trouble."

Two days later, Catherine sat opposite me in the private karaoke lounge with just a hint of white panty showing below her high-crossed leg. The songs all sounded the same: dull monotones set to a metronome. Who needs this crap? And the room was so small that I felt like Gulliver.

"Do you know 'Unchained Melody'?"

"Oh, my God!"

I kissed her before the disc began its electronic warbling. This kiss was more than Gallic, it was a real tonsil tickler.

"Where did you learn to kiss like that?"

"Learn?"

Next day, over *dim sum*, Mr. Leung confirmed that I was getting somewhere.

"It's dangerous. But you are young. Many people forgive the young."

"I think something must happen soon or else I'll go mad."

It did happen—the next Saturday evening in Catherine's friend's cramped room full of Snoopy toys and posters. It was harmless and very nice but I could not believe that Catherine could look so innocent as we walked to the MTR afterwards. Perhaps it is their way.

The next morning at *dim sum* Mr. Leung asked me if I was satisfied. I looked at him not quite believing what I was hearing and said, "Yes."

"Satisfaction is dangerous," he said. "It is always better to be slightly disgusted." Rising from the table with a half smile on his lips, he walked from the room.

Dr. George Adams is the author of several books about Hong Kong. This story was adapted from a chapter in his book Wicked Hong Kong Stories.

✳

A pervert is a man who prefers sex to money.
—Old Hong Kong saying

KELLY SIMON

✦ ✦ ✦

Man–Made Uppers

How to get even.

THERE THEY GO AT THE STROKE OF NOON, THE CONSUMERS From Hell, freed as if by the school bell from Madame's kitchen. The women cluster, blabbing with each other in Cantonese, pumping adrenaline for the upcoming Battle-of-the-Bargain. The men stand silent, hands thrust in deep pockets, quivers for their wives arrows. They line up, two by two, beneath the Golden Arches for a Big Mac fix to fortify themselves for their next shopping spree.

This past week, Madame Fu Pei Mei, the Julia Child of Asia, deftly demonstrated for us how to carve a mango into a hand grenade, a sea bass into a pineapple, how to prepare such delicacies as Mold Pork in Brown, Assorted Dish with Hot Sauce, Two-sides Brown Noodles, and Rinsed Mutton in Chafing Pot. The men snored and the women crocheted through the lessons. Then they rushed out to McDonald's.

"Why do they eat hamburgers if they came here for Chinese food?" I ask Sunshine, who has a lot of tour savvy, having been on thirteen of them.

"It's a cheap way for them to get here and shop."

We are on a Chinese Cooking Tour. Every afternoon for the last week, my tour mates have stripped a wide swath through the boutiques and factories and electronic marts of Taiwan, scooping up everything in their path leaving in their wake scorched earth and a passel of grinning shopkeepers, not to mention the happy tour guides, who collect a healthy commission for every item.

This is my first tour. "It's Bangkok," I envisioned some tour guide shouting through a megaphone. "You've got forty-five minutes."

But this tour sounded different. Surely I'd fit in with people whose passion, like mine, was food.

To avoid a single supplement, Sunshine and I have been assigned the same room. Sunshine is a rad, second generation Chinese-American flower-child half my age who thinks Asia is a "happening thing." We have little in common except that we're both single women. The rest of the tour members are Chinese-American couples in their Golden Years who seem to have closed ranks against us.

She and I are the only non-shoppers. Unlike the rest of the tour members, we bring no hard or soft ware, no printed circuitry, no shrink-wrapped, bar-coded, fiber-optical treasures to the nightly show-and-tell. The tour guides get no commissions from us. We are pariahs. (Who knew shopping was the point?)

Oh well, maybe this coming week in Hong Kong will be different.

We're assembled at the front desk of our Wanchai hotel to meet Nelson, our Hong Kong guide. He sports a pomaded crew cut and thick-soled wing tip shoes. He'll take us to factories and stores with the best bargains in town.

"Guarantee," he says. Bestowing a meaningful look on the consumers before him, he shoots his cuff, mesmerizing the group with his golden Rolex and its glittering diamond bezel. "Happy customer gib to me." He taps his watch. "Tomorrow, eight a.m. on dot. You late, we go without you."

At 8:01 the next morning, the bus doors close and we head for Jumbo Floating Restaurant in Aberdeen, where the chefs will show us their secret techniques. But surprise, surprise, we stop at a Ray Ban factory for a pre-prandial buy. Nelson, rubbing his hands, huddles with the owners, whose eyes are hidden behind mirrored Ray Bans. We have an hour to spend—so to speak—before the bus leaves.

One man had filleted his fish, about a dozen of them set in a sloping incline in front of him. Each fish had a red spot on it. The red spot pulsed. I couldn't imagine what that was. I looked more closely.

He had filleted each fish with such skill that he had left the hearts in tact. These exposed fish hearts were now beating, as a kind of visual display, and as a proof that his fish were fresh. I was looking at a dozen beating fish hearts. I had to go lie down.

—Michael Crichton, *Travels*

Sunshine and I slip away to a nearby food market where glazed mahogany-colored ducks fragrant with aromatic anise hang from hooks and bins display all manner of crustacea and mollusks, the likes of which I've never seen. Glass tanks alive with crystalline shrimp and shimmering carp and gossamer swimming prawns translucent as chiffon line the walls. Stacks of wire cages house squawking ducks and hopping frogs and turtles scrambling up one another's backs as if to flee the wok.

Our conversation goes like this:

Me: "Look at those fish!"

Sunshine: "Scope out that dude."

Back on the bus, Nelson points around the cabin like a kindergarten teacher, encouraging us to hold up our purchases. I'm the last. I hold up a carved wooden opium scale I found in a dark corner of the market.

"You smoke opium?" he asks, deadpan. He winks at the passengers and holds the scale up for them to see, flashing his Rolex. "She smoke opium. How much you pay?"

"Seven dollars," I say, proud of my bargain.

"You last of big time spender," he says. My tour mates giggle. I force a smile. Being the butt of jokes isn't my cup of oolong.

The next day, while the rest of the group is in a textile factory, I find an intricate brass betel nut cutter in a dusty antique store.

Back on the bus, Nelson scrutinizes it.

"Is old. Why you buy old? This have screw loose. You know what mean screw loose?"

I laugh with the rest of them. I feel like I did in grammar school when the teacher called on me and I didn't know the answer.

By the fourth day, my stomach clenches as show-and-tell time approaches. Is he a jerk? Am I xenophobic? All of the above?

"Hong Kong dudes are weird," Sunshine says. "They think they're being funny when they make you squirm."

On the hydrofoil to Macau, chewing bitter cud, I mull over what I can say to make him stop, but everything I come up with sounds like grist for his mill. Keep it light, I tell myself. Normal, corn-fed folk would smack him on the back and tell him to knock it off, but I'm not normal and corn-fed. I'm psychosemitic, a simmering stew of paranoia. "Knock-off?" Nelson will say, pretending to miss my point. "I gib you knock-off. Gucci? YSL? Fendi?"

The jetfoil skims the surface of the Pearl River, hovering above the water on a pillow of air. Connaught Road and the skyscrapers of Hong Kong Island recede in the distance. The men inside the cabin are absorbed in the *South China Morning Post*. The women look straight ahead, embracing the handbags in their laps. Every now and then a sampan looms in the frame of the window, gunnels in the water, poled by a woman in a conical bamboo hat, her leathered face impassive as she swerves to avoid colliding with us.

Looking out at the dramatic skyline, a pastiche of modernity and tradition, reason returns. If I didn't fit in in my own country, how could I expect to fit in in someone else's? And if I knew I wouldn't fit in, why did I choose a tour? The answer was, of course, that I hate to eat alone.

The rhythmic vibration of the boat's engine lulls me. I'm halfway asleep when the air is ripped apart by a clangorous explosion, followed by the grinding scream of metal on metal, all the louder since the engine has suddenly become deathly silent.

The craft stops dead and wobbles from side to side as the pillow of air beneath it deflates with an ominous gurgle. The view of the cathedrals and lighthouses and casino of Macau is supplanted by rising water. It's as if we're in an aquarium, looking out. Immobilized for a split second by panic, we look around, seeking reassurance in each other's eyes.

The red emergency light flashes on, off, on, off like a hotel marquee. A bullhorn blasts an intermittent alarm. A voice of authority barks from the loudspeakers in Cantonese. The passengers spring to attention and I follow suit. We rush to the aisle en masse. Swept along by terror, we swarm the narrow gangway, pushing and shoving, clambering up one another's backs, trying to claw our way to the upper deck.

Panting with fear, we burst from the narrow passageway onto the deck like a freed impaction. There are no bulwarks or railings to contain us. Only an ankle-level rope strung through stanchions six inches above the slippery varnished deck.

The craft makes a slow-motion U-turn and heads back to Hong Kong Island, chugging asthmatically through the oily water. The deck is slippery with varnish and wash. The passengers are livid. They want to be in Macau, not back at the ferry terminal. They mutter among themselves and collect in a sullen knot at the bow, preparing to jump ship the instant it docks. A few of us huddle in the gangway. Power gone, The Little Engine That Couldn't laboriously breasts the swells of the passing boats, whose crews jeer at us as we bob helplessly in their wake.

We limp into the narrow channel. Champing at the bit, the passengers above deck surge forward to debark but, for some reason, the dockswain bars our way. There is a collective outcry from the passengers. The men glower and curse and shake their fists. The women emerge from the gangway yelling shrilly. A tough-looking character in a watch cap—the kind you'd hate to meet in a dark alley—makes menacing gestures at the dockhand, drawing his hand across his throat. I have no clue why we're being detained.

The crowd grows increasingly surly and rebellious, cursing and railing at the stevedores, who block our way with a chain of outstretched arms. They want to be paid for a round trip, it seems.

We are hours late by now. The hydrofoil trip to Macau was to have taken fifty-five minutes. The return to the terminal has taken two hours and fifty-five minutes. The passengers push forward, an amalgam of flesh, bodies glued against one another. Now a mob, they forge ahead using one another as ladders. At any moment, any one of us could lose our balance and be trampled to death.

Weak with fear, propped upright by the bodies next to me, I'm swept along like flotsam by the tide of passengers surging toward the narrow gangplank, my feet skimming the deck. A sudden shove knocks me sideways and I stumble against the stanchion. There is nothing solid to hold onto. My moorings are gone and as I am about to topple over the side, a hand reaches out and yanks me back from the brink.

"Is okay, is okay," the tough-looking character in the watch cap says as he pulls me to safety. His voice is soft as a mother's. Another passenger puts himself between me and the water. Blocking for me like linemen, the two ease me through the crowd and down the narrow gangplank and, before I have a chance to thank them, they disappear into the ferry terminal.

There's not even time to wash up before dinner. Sweaty and disheveled, I burst into the dining room. Nelson looks me up and down, registers my tear-streaked face and sopping clothes.

Then he taps his watch and says, "You six and a half minutes late."

Tomorrow is our final day in Hong Kong, the big one, the last chance to buy. "Eight a.m. on dot," Nelson says.

On the bus the next day, he calls for us to show off our purchases. The winner gets a prize at the big banquet tonight.

"Where your frien'? She late three minutes." The seat next to me is empty. Sunshine is nowhere to be seen. I shrug.

Bella holds up a brand new Rolex with a diamond bezel. Nelson beams, his eyes vanishing into his cheeks.

"We twins." He points to his own.

"Me, me," says Hyacinth Yee, holding up a Vuittonesque make-up case.

P.P. holds up a Hasselblad camera.

"How much you pay?" Nelson calls to him.

"Fitty fi' hundred," P.P. shouts. The thought balloon over Nelson's head reads ten percent.

Suddenly, there is a pneumatic sigh and the bus doors open. It's Sunshine, breathless, beaming.

"You late fi' minute," Nelson accuses.

"I'm right on time, Dude."

"You Timex, I Rolex. End of subject," Nelson says.

Sunshine shrugs. From her bag, she produces a package wrapped in twine. She unties the twine, reverently removes a shrink-wrapped box from the bag and holds it up for us to see.

"What is?" Nelson says.

"A camcorder." Triumphantly, she holds it in the air, color creeping to her cheeks. There is stunned silence. Then, everyone cheers and claps. The sound rocks the bus. There is a lot of back-slapping as the convert is welcomed into the inner circle.

So now it's me, alone, a retro David against the Goliath of technology. Call me a throwback but I like old things, the kind that have been handled and used and passed around, things that have held precious simple cargo.

Nelson aims his pointer finger like a rapier. Everyone turns toward me, sly smiles on their faces. I cradle my basket. I bought it on the open market for thirteen dollars. No factory store. No commission for Nelson.

It is old and graceful, a circu-

One of the commonest pastimes in everyday conversation in Hong Kong is "I Can Get It For You Wholesale" in which the better connections of he who can get it cheaper are paraded for the poor unfortunate who has, for example, paid two hundred dollars more than he might have done for a video recorder ("and it doesn't even have Nicam!"). Hong Kong people are obsessed with cheaper prices, a fact of which the Government is only too aware. It maintains a very cheap transport system to keep local people happy (as well as cheap hospitals and schools but you actually get what you pay for). Local people will even go shopping in Shamshuipo to get a better price. All this money saving inspired the well-known joke of the Hong Kong person entering Heaven where he complains about all those foreigners on earth and "why did God create them anyway?" "Well, someone has to buy retail," was God's reply.

—Dr. George Adams, *Games Hong Kong People Play: A Social Psychology of the Hong Kong Chinese*

lar, tightly woven lidded affair with a sturdy handle. It has no moving parts, no batteries. It has been touched by many hands, burnished with the patina of use. It will look lovely filled with glistening strawberries, their bright green calyx's wet with dew, or strewn with slender onion bulbs and purple garlics with skin as fine as rice paper. I can see it as a sewing basket, crammed with spools of bright thread the color of crayons.

"What you buy?"

I slump in my seat.

"You. You. Miss Kerry," he stabs the air over my head so there will be no misunderstanding. When my name rings out, I cower.

"A basket," I mumble.

"Show," he orders. I raise the basket tentatively. "Higher," he says, boosting air with his palms. He narrows his eyes, appraising it from the front of the bus. "Is for betel nut!" He snorts as if this is proof that I'm retail-challenged.

"How much you pay?"

"Thirteen dollars."

My bus mates turn from me tittering, their trousers and skirts hissing judgments against the vinyl seats.

"Ho, ho," Nelson snorts, prodding the air with his forefinger. "You shrep home worthress basket. My mother have one like that," he says. "She pay you to take it."

Tonight is the farewell banquet. To go or not to go. I mull it over over a couple of Singapore Slings. On my way back from the bar, I notice Nelson's door slightly ajar. I peek in. The room is empty.

Emboldened by the alcohol, I slip inside and close the door behind me. His clothes are laid out neatly on the bed—the same too-shiny, too-blue suit and the lizard patterned tie he has worn for the past five days, but tonight he has set out his brown wing-tipped shoes instead of his black, which rest on a shelf in the open wardrobe. I feel his presence as palpably as a bone in my throat.

I hear water running and I realize he's in the shower. His Rolex is laid out on the night stand, the silvergold band perfectly parallel with its edge. I pick it up. The diamond bezel catches the light and casts a dazzling rainbow on the wardrobe door. I could tuck it into the tip of the black shoes and give him a scare. I reach up, slide out one of the shoes and peer inside it, hoping to find some loathsome secret like Odor-Eaters. Man-Made Uppers, reads the inside of the heel. I shove the shoe back in place.

The room is humid from the shower, I lean out the window. Below, the mad roil of Hong Kong traffic surges and swells. I hold my arm out the window. The Rolex feels heavy and solid in my palm. I imagine tilting my hand, the cool quicksilver rush as it slithers off, the band twisting like wings as it tumbles, the diamond bezel catching the light and shooting prisms against the opposite wall, the cracking sound as it fractures on the pavement spitting tiny springs and shards of crystal and splinters of quartz.

But, as satisfying as that might be in the short run, in the long run it would backfire. The happy customers would surely band together and buy him another in lieu of a tip. True revenge would be to make him a laughing stock, an outsider. How satisfying it would be to see his superior smile dissolve, his authority crumble. What sweet justice to join in with the others on the ridicule.

I reset his watch and place it back on the end table where I found it, line it up exactly parallel with the edge. The shower is still running as I close the door behind me, imagining the look on his face when he walks into the banquet room seventeen minutes late.

Kelly Simon has been eating around longer than she cares to admit. She has published a Thai cookbook, and her work has appeared in The Washington Post, The Quarterly, Ellery Queen Magazine, *and other publications. She lives in San Francisco.*

✳

No matter how many times I visited Hong Kong, I could never get used to the tourist side of the city—Ocean Terminal, Harbour City, the miles and miles of designer shops side by side. I hated the crowds and the sheer overwhelmingness of so many clothes, so many choices. Too many people moving too slow; too much noise; too much excess. I'd O.D. on the whole scene and run off to buy myself an egg custard from a street stall somewhere—my only purchase. My shop-till-you-drop friends think I'm crazy, of course. This is Nathan Road in Kowloon: camera shop, jewelry shop, clothing shop, audio shop; then rewind the block and play it over and over again. I walked 46 blocks one day and the pattern stayed the same.

The part of Hong Kong I've always loved best is the ratty, smarmy part, high up, around the tenements. "Barefoot doctors" doing acupuncture and moxibustion on the street, patients lying on tables on the sidewalk while the heated glass suction cups are attached to their backs, then pulled off with a loud "thwuck." Crowds of locals standing around watching the treatments. Noodle stalls, flower markets, pans of swimming eels outside tiny restaurants. Real people, not bored shop clerks.

—Paula McDonald, "South China Sea Journal"

RAJENDRA S. KHADKA

Chungking and Other Horrors

Behind the glitter and economic razzmatazz lies another world.

I HAD NOT HEARD ABOUT CHUNGKING PALACE—SOMETIMES ALSO known as Chungking Mansion—until I told a Nepali friend, a businessman, that I was planning to visit Hong Kong. Could he recommend a cheap hotel?

"Chungking Palace," he answered immediately. "It's not only cheap, it has everything—shops, Indian restaurants, and guests from Nepal and India, so you feel at home. It's on Nathan Road where you can get anything you want very cheaply."

"What's the best way to get there?"

"It's very simple. At the airport, just get into a taxi and tell him to take you to Chungking. Every taxi-driver knows it."

In the airplane, I sat next to a Filipino businessman who said he used to be the late Philippine president and dictator Marcos's class-mate. He ran a successful catering business with some of the Asian air carriers as his main customers, but he was not happy when he compared himself to Marcos and other classmates and contempo-raries. They had become presidents and ministers, and he, well, he was just a damn caterer. He had made the wrong choice. He should've gone into the army. He suddenly had a faraway look. Then, abruptly, he asked me, "Where are you staying in Hong Kong?"

"Chungking Palace. Do you know of it?"

I thought he shuddered briefly. He said in a flat voice, "It's a firetrap. Don't stay there. Every crooked businessman from the Third World stays there. Bad place. Don't stay there."

He excused himself, punched the airline pillow, turned his back on me and pretended to fall asleep. I thought by mentioning Chungking Palace, I had suddenly lowered myself in his eyes. Instead of being an international traveler, he perhaps saw me as yet another grubby, sneaky, Third World smuggler, with my inevitable appointment at Chungking.

My Nepali friend was right. The taxi driver at the airport nodded when I said "Chungking Palace." In the crowded, brightly-lit, billboard-choked Nathan Road, the driver stopped and dumped my two pieces of luggage at the edge of the street. Before I had even paid the driver, a man picked up both my bags. I had visions of arriving at an Indian railway station. Even as I paid the driver, I told the man to drop my bags. He ignored me and asked me if I had a hotel room.

"Chungking Pal——," I started to say.

The man began walking rapidly, a bag in each of his hands, and I tried not to lose him in the crowd. A moment later he led me into what looked like a tiny lobby where several Asian and African men were waiting for the elevator. I saw no white skin. My escort dropped the bags and waited too. I looked at the elevator entrance where a crude, hand-written sign in red ink said "Beware of Pickpockets."

I felt I was not in Hong Kong, the sleek, sophisticated metropolis I had imagined, but in some lurid section of Delhi or Calcutta. We Nepalis had always rated Hong Kong above Bangkok, and certainly above Bombay and Calcutta, but now I felt that Bangkok was vastly superior, at least comparing this to the places I had stayed in Bangkok.

The elevator arrived, a tiny cubicle in which all dozen and more of us jammed in. Many of the men wore tank-tops or were bare above the waist. No one had bothered with deodorants. The elevator creaked upwards slowly, threatening to plunge down as the strain of ascending became more labored. I held my breath.

At one of the stops, my escort barked at the sweaty bodies; they separated just enough so we could squeeze out. He led me to a room with two beds and an open window with iron bars that looked out onto other square, barred windows. I glanced outside and saw the ground below; we were perhaps on the sixth or seventh floor.

So far, we had not discussed money. My escort laid the bags on the floor next to one of the beds and asked for what I thought was too much money. We were both Asians. He expected me to bargain, which I did weakly, since I detest bargaining. We agreed upon a price. I said I was paying for the whole room not just my bed. He shook his head rather violently and said I'd have to pay more. I asked where is the bathroom. Down the hall. Ah! If I had a room with attached bath, I'd pay more, but not for this—and I made a sweeping but disdainful gesture with my open palm—no, not for this. I paid him and shooed him out of the room and told him I was going to lock the door so he could not bring anyone else in during the night. He grinned, and I knew I'd been had. Only a novice, naive tourist ever believes that he or she has gotten a better bargain in the bazaars of Asia.

I locked the door and began to unpack. A very large cockroach scurried across the cemented floor. Fortunately, I had seen cockroaches like that before so I did not panic. I did not even attempt to crush it. I knew that there were thousands—if not millions—of them. I did not want to spend my night locked in a futile battle. I made a mental note to sleep with the light on and move out the first thing next morning. The bathroom at the end of the hall had a bucket and a tap and a temperamental toilet that flushed after several attempts. The floor was wet and I don't think ever got a chance to get dry.

I lay on the bed, thankful the sheets were at least clean, stared at the walls where various creatures darted from unseen cracks and holes at indefinite intervals. From the open but barred window a gentle breeze drifted in, fanning away the moist, oppressive air. Soon it began to rain, a gentle rain that became a downpour.

Next morning, the lobby was busy with various Asian and African businessmen, standing guard over enormous duffels bursting with goods to be taken back to Kathmandu, Calcutta,

Dhaka, and probably Lagos or Kampala. I looked for an Indian restaurant but found none. I walked around the mall-like building and looked into various stores, some run by Indian merchants. A young Indian woman attracted my attention so I went into her store, pretending I was interested in buying a sari. She immediately unrolled several fabrics for me to appraise. She asked if it was for my wife. I said no, my sister or mother. She convinced me to buy a sari of the "latest fashion, computer designed." She would give me a special price since I was her first customer of the day and a young man buying a gift for his mother. She asked for forty U.S. dollars and finally agreed on thirty. Later my sister complained. During the first wash, the "computer designed" patterns had fallen apart and the fabric of the sari was so cheap that it wouldn't even work as a wash rag.

Certainly the prospect of cheaper rents, more than anything else, draw the bohemians to Lamma Island. It is a decidedly British crowd full of artists, writers, musicians, and various street performers. Quite a few aspiring journalists also seem to have landed there after catching on with one or another of the local English language papers. Many short-termers, backpackers trying to save up enough cash to continue their travels, English teachers, bartenders, waitresses, the lot, drift in and out. It is the next step up once you've graduated from the crash pads at Chungking Mansions.

—Jonathan W. Maffay,
"Lamma Island"

I was not surprised. After all, among the more sophisticated Nepali travelers, Hong Kong had a reputation as a "Thief's Market." One never bought name brands or expensive jewelry and watches there. They were all fake! An uncle of mine had once bought an "Omega" watch in Hong Kong. Even though it gave accurate time for several years, my father, the sophisticated traveler, was dismissive of that watch and my uncle's gullibility. He was convinced one could not buy a genuine "Omega" or "Rolex" watch in Hong Kong, that the watch was an imitation. "Not even the 'O' in the 'Omega' was genuine," he insisted.

So now, his stupid son had been cheated by a crafty Indian girl in the alleys of Hong Kong.

I finally found an Indian restaurant, but it did not open until noon, so I went out to get something to eat. I found a noodle shop and went in. It was busy but not crowded so I sat down. An elderly gentleman slapped down the menu, poured tea and left. I couldn't decide what to eat. When the gentleman returned, I sought his suggestion. He became irritable. Why didn't I know what to order. He thrust his index finger at an item in the menu and snapped, "Eat this!"

"Is it good?" I asked, quite appalled by such rude behavior.

"Yes, good. Very good. You eat." He picked up the menu and left. And I did something I have never done before or since—I walked out of the noodle shop, the man shouting behind me in Chinese, which I thankfully did not understand.

Once outside, I made up mind. I had planned to stay a few days in Hong Kong, but it had become clear I was no match for its aggressive brand of hospitality. I felt I would be swallowed whole and excreted if I hung around any longer. I called my airline, found there was a flight leaving that night to Bangkok, a city I loved and whose citizens I admired for their smiles and unobtrusive behavior.

I went back to my room, packed, and checked out. My escort, also the owner of that single-room "hostel," seemed surprised I was leaving so soon. He said it was the best bargain in all of Hong Kong. I told him I agreed, but I was no longer interested in the best bargain available in Hong Kong.

Outside, on Nathan Road, I hailed a cab. It stopped almost in the center of the road, blocking the already choked traffic, and the driver calmly placed my bags in the trunk of the car as others honked and screamed. He was unperturbed, the calmest gentleman I had yet encountered in my very brief stay in Hong Kong.

On the way to the airport, he asked where I had stayed.

"Chungking."

"Oh, good place. Cheap. You enjoy your stay?"

"No, I did not." Seldom have I been so brutally honest in my life.

"No? Why? Which wing you stay?"

"Wing? What wing? The 'D' wing, I think."

"Oh, 'D' wing bad, very bad. You should've stayed in 'A' wing. Very clean, very nice, very cheap."

"Next time," I said, knowing full well that there would be no next time.

Rajendra S. Khadka, born in Nepal close to the birthplace of Buddha, was educated by American Jesuits in Kathmandu. He then attended Williams College in the U.S.A. and has been living and working in Berkeley, California since 1981. Among other things, he has been a book reviewer, waiter, freelance writer, travel agent, cappuccino maker, and dictionary research assistant. He is the editor of Travelers' Tales Nepal.

*

The ancients in prosecuting their learning compared different things and traced the analogies between them. The drum has no special relation to any of the musical notes, but without it they cannot be harmonized. Water has no particular relation to any of the five colors, but without it they cannot be displayed. Learning has no particular relation to any of the five senses, but without it they cannot be regulated.

—Confucius

GEORGE ADAMS

* * *

Lucky Money and Blood on the Pavement

What would you do?

THE PROBLEM WE ALL FACE IN HONG KONG IS HOW TO KEEP A grip on reality. Reality is at times so fictional that we need to escape into a world of order—the world provided by Singapore news editorials or North Korea's next Five Year Plan. Stories from every-day life in Hong Kong present us with a chaotic and anarchic world which is impossible to take seriously for very long. Two recent true stories bear this out:

An impecunious delivery man walks into his bank one day dressed in singlet and dirty jeans to discover that $780,000 have been credited by mistake to his account. This balance is markedly more than the $1,500 he usually has in the bank. What does he do? Well, if you are poor in Hong Kong there is only one choice. Take the money and run. The gods have spoken and we must follow their directives. This kind of event is the one Wong Man-fai has probably dreamed about in his daily rounds, as he calculates how many Mark Six lottery tickets he can buy and which are the likely runners and riders at Happy Valley racecourse. How wonderful to be given such a chance! He withdraws half a million immediately.

The sum asked for is so large that the bank has difficulty finding enough $1,000 notes. The staff loan him a large plastic bag to stuff his booty into. And no one suspects anything. Men in singlets and jeans often withdraw fortunes it seems. Mr. Wong leaves the bank. A few hours later he returns for another $200,000. Again no questions are asked.

But now, as he heads for the Macau ferry terminal with the loot in his trembling hands there is a moment of indecision: "I will certainly be found out," Mr. Wong thinks, "what can I do?" Mr. Wong decides to gamble the money and repay the amount with his winnings. Nothing could be easier to believe for a desperate man. If you suddenly have the luck to find $100,000 (US) in your account, the gods will almost certainly have more luck in store for you.

What thoughts run through Mr. Wong's mind as he sits in the hoverferry, clutching the money tightly in his lap? Does he feel guilty? Hardly. Does he feel afraid? I don't think so. So how does he feel? I think he feels

A wide range of games is offered at Macau's casinos—baccarat, blackjack, roulette, boule, "big and small," fan-tan, pai kao or Chinese dominoes and, of course, there are hundreds of slot machines or "hungry tigers."

Even for those not interested in gambling, the casinos merit a visit for people-watching. The vast majority come from Hong Kong—people from every walk of life, ranging from taxi drivers and housewives to society matrons, sales clerks and tycoons.

—JO'R, LH, and SO'R

elated and curiously existential. He is the true man of Sartre's and Camus's imaginations. He has made a choice to be wicked, to make his own destiny, and he lives forever in the moment. Morality? It is an illusion. Apologise? For what? Regrets? Condemned by his background and his society into a role of perennial mediocrity, he has at last seized the initiative.

Nothing is more existential than the feeling he has when sitting down at the gambling table with a pile of chips before him. The potency of his existence courses through him. It is all in the turn of a card now, the tumble of a ball into a slot. No set of precepts can guide him. No saviour looms up in his imagination with the promise of salvation. His past has disappeared and is symbolised by the haze of smoke around him. His future is a vague blur just beyond his present heartbeat. His present is everything, an incandescent blaze of light represented by the stunning chandeliers above his head. Now, he thinks always, now is when I feel alive.

Les jeux sont faits. Place your bets Mr. Wong. Free yourself from your humdrum existence, choose to lose your life in the green baize of tables, more colourful than Hong Kong streets. Give your soul to the gambling chips, sleeker, more sensuous and more honest than all the women of that city. And when you lose…try to be indifferent. But it is difficult to swallow for a moment, the harsh defeat. Yet as Mr. Wong heads for the ferry pier once more, after 23 hours on the tables, he is not crushed although he has only $2,000 in his pockets. He knows that the police will meet him in Hong Kong and that he will serve time. Nothing is sadder than night in prison says Meursault. But what a time Mr. Wong has had! He has made his bet with his existence. He has woven the fabric of his own life. For one day at least, he was free!

The next story is more macabre and, for me, even more real than the last. It happened just 50 yards from my home. Twenty young men of the triad community marched into our local lobster restaurant and chopped up another group of men who were sitting at a table, innocently enjoying their portions of recently demised crustaceans. Two men died and a number of others are on the critical list. One dying man ran down the steps of the restaurant into King's Road and tried to hail a taxi to take him to the hospital. The other made it into Cheung Hong Street and

> *Secret Chinese criminal societies, known as triads, were originally formed as resistance groups to the Ching Dynasty that ruled China from early in the 17th century until 1912. The word "triad" is an English term derived from the societies' sacred emblem—a triangle whose sides represent three basic powers: heaven, earth and man.*
>
> —Linda L. Keene, "Asian Organized Crime," *FBI Law Enforcement Bulletin*

died on the pavement. The killings happened late one afternoon whilst I was calmly sitting in a hotel in Wanchai sipping the house white. I might have witnessed some of it if I had taken a walk down the street as I often do at that time. What would I have done as I saw the man stagger past the lobster aquarium, covered in gore and bleeding from every pore? How would I have reacted if the mob had passed me in the street wielding choppers, their faces contorted by hatred and fear?

The man who made it into Cheung Hong Street died on the pavement. At seven in the evening I walked past the restaurant thinking about Christmas shopping. I never go into the restaurant because I don't like the loud noise of crunching lobsters dying on the chopping boards outside the restaurant. I always hear that sound when I walk past. It seems to drown out every other sound. Possibly, the guests did not hear anything unusual that afternoon for the same reason. This might explain why the restaurant is still full, lights blazing, and people are filling their bellies with Canadian *homard vivant*, fried rice, and pork. After all, food in Hong Kong stops for no one and nothing.

I ask the photographers what is going on. They give the unusual reply that they do not know. When people say this in Hong Kong it means that they don't want to tell (or that they can't say it in English). But when I insist I do learn that it is a homicide. The photographer pronounces it strangely: HOM AH CIDE. Oh, well, I think. Just another Hong Kong gangland killing. But then I see the puddle of rich red in Cheung Hong Street, the jacket still lying there stiff with blood, almost standing up, and then one soiled plimsoll (the dead man was not rich, it seems). I begin to cry a little. It is all too pathetic.

But the crushing and the munching of the lobsters goes on.

Once home, I telephone an English language newspaper and find out they do not know about the murder yet. I tell all the details as well as I can. Next day the story is on the front page. Will I get a bounty?

Also next day I am walking past the spot where the man died in Cheung Hong Street. It has been scrubbed clean. The bleached pavement tells all. But in King's Road the drips and smears of blood are everywhere. In my mind I see the man rushing from the restaurant and picture him standing by the roadside, his eyes blinded by blood as he desperately seeks a taxi. The air is marked by him. The place is his forever.

But all around it is business as usual. The vanilla ball seller is pouring out his custard into the mould. The newspaper vendor is extending his pitch one more square foot. The jeans shop is opening and the sales assistant mounts her ladder to blast forth news of the closing down sale through her portable megaphone.

Some days later I see a strange ceremony of incense, oranges, and barbecued pork offerings near the site of the scrubbed dying place in Cheung Hong Street. Is the ceremony for the departed soul or is it for the staff in the restaurant, to expiate themselves from hungry ghosts and lost souls? Not a bit of it.

On Sunday, a new shop is opening next to the restaurant and the offerings were to assuage the gods and to bring good luck for the new venture. Wreaths and flower arrangements with bright red proclamations and dedications crowd the pavement and a throng of smartly-dressed people are standing about, sipping champagne and eating curry puffs. One of the shop owners, I notice, is standing on one of the bleached flagstones. "A man died there," I say and I am pleased to see that the blood is once more visible under the scrubbed surface.

The man winces back with real worry on his face. Perhaps it was more than the fear that his business would pick up bad omens. Perhaps it was real respect for the dead.

Dr. George Adams also contributed "Mr. Leung" in Part III.

★

I like Americans best when I see them breaking laws and regulations, when I see at a movie theater that the audience's sympathy is with the stowaway and not with the law-upholding captain, and when I see on the trains between Washington and New York people smoking in every car marked "No smoking." These are born democrats, I say. When the situation gets bad enough, it is not the Herr Conductor that will stop it, but the public, by somebody writing to *The New York Times* pleading against the danger of ashes burning babies' arms. If the public does not mind, neither will the American conductor. But imagine a Prussian crowd smoking in a car where smoking is *verboten!* They just can't do it, and that is why the Weimar Republic fell and the *Frankfurter Zeitung* turned tail and they needed a Hitler. Put a Hitler over an American crowd to tell them not to do this and not to do that, and see the result. Life would not survive three months before his head was smashed. Democracy's reply to Prohibition was the speakeasies. The history of the speakeasies is the glorious history of exactly how much the American people would stand for *verbotens*, and of how they would obey even laws passed by themselves! I take off my hats to these Americans, because they are like my own people, the Chinese. You can't "prohibit" the Americans, nor can you the Chinese. An official prohibition to do a thing is an invitation to a Chinese to do it. Long live the identity of our causes!

—Lin Yutang, *Between Tears and Laughter*

⋆ ⋆ ⋆

Shipping Out

Temporarily stifled in his attempt to circle the globe without using aircraft,
the author explores the Hungry Ghost Realm and other states of mind.

SCORES OF SHIPS SAIL EACH MONTH FROM HONG KONG'S HUGE
containerport, but finding passage on even one of them is virtually
impossible. Hong Kong is a city consummately without a sense
of humor, a habitat belonging to the no-nonsense school of
enterprise. I grew accustomed to the look of blank bewilder-
ment in people's eyes when I described my mission. Go home by
ship? Why?

The fact that I was now in the air terminus of East Asia made
my plight surreal. Day and night, the sky was filled with airplanes.
Ferrying between Kowloon and Hong Kong Island, watching an
endless procession of jets bank eastward across Victoria Harbor,
I felt like a pelican who'd been caught in an oil spill. Every 747
was full of weary travelers heading for Seattle, San Francisco,
L.A. They'd be snug at home, unpacking their socks, before I ate
my next Egg McMuffin.

I spent my afternoons in an air-conditioned cubicle at the
Foreign Correspondents' Club, poring through the *Shipping Gazette*,
pounding out faxes and calling every single shipping line servicing
the West Coast. Hyundai, "K" Line, Maersk, Mexican, Mitsui, NYK,

Sea-Land, Hapag-Lloyd; I tried them all. Few of the operations managers said no directly. It was always a matter of calling back after a few days, and a few days more than that, for my paperwork to creep up and down the chain of command. The main obstacle, as ever, was liability, but there were other alibis as well. The new containerships were designed for reduced crews and had no extra beds or life preservers. Sea-Land—leaving for Oakland in a week!—had a dozen extra rooms, but was training a group of seamen from Shanghai. The Japanese and Chinese lines simply didn't want any Yankees on board; the Koreans were afraid I wouldn't like their food. The cruelest blow of all came when American President Lines, based in my own home port, stonewalled me completely....

The days went by. I passed my second Tuesday in Hong Kong without speaking to another human being, except for various robotic service personnel.

This put me in a quandary. All day long I'd been looking forward to my Event of the Week: getting home early, switching on the Pearl Network and watching *NYPD Blue*. Then I'd watch half an hour of *Twin Peaks*, read another hundred pages of *Fearless* and spend an hour or two writing. The problem was, I had nothing to write *about*.

But there was something going on in Central, as I guiltily knew. The Fringe, Hong Kong's only alternative theater and performance space, was hosting their bimonthly "Partners in Rhyme" night. The event began at eight, thirty minutes before *NYPD Blue*.

The conflict annoyed me. Was I so desperate for something to do that I'd actually go to a poetry reading...in Hong Kong? All right, in New York or Chicago

One of the hits of the Hong Kong Arts Festival was a new Chinese-language production of an American stage classic, Tennessee Williams's Women in a Rich Household with a Lot to Complain About. *You remember, it's the one about "Maggie the Wildcat" and her alcoholic husband, Brick, and his nightmare family, including "Venerable Daddy" and a grasping brother and sister-in-law, whose ill-mannered children Maggie calls "the necklace ghosts." You probably know it by its original title,* Cat on a Hot Tin Roof.

—Jamie James,
"Acting Globally," *Hemispheres*

or San Francisco, sure. But poetry in Hong Kong would be like pizza in Kunming. "Partners in Rhyme!" For the first time in my life I was torn between live performance and television. What finally resolved the decision was my hope, albeit slim, that I might meet other writers at the event. My life-in-waiting, a one-act drama set within the fluorescent funk of a seemingly endless low-pressure system, was undermining my usually infectious *joie de vivre* and addicting me to KitKats.

I rolled into the Fringe at quarter past eight, bought a pint, took a table near the stage and waited. At eight-thirty sharp the MC, a tall blond chap who resembled a goat, took the mike.

"We've got a mercifully short reading this evening," he announced. "We're competing with some great television tonight…"

The MC read first. His poetry was so bad it rhymed. He was followed by a Canadian with a misleading resemblance to Eric Bogosian who seemed to believe that high-volume garrulity could compensate for the vapidity of his verse. His poems, hurled at the audience like Greek traffic insults, were incomprehensible, though an undertone of misogyny emerged skunklike from the thicket.

The third reader was a Texan named Willis. Despite extreme stage fright he orated well, with a clear, strong voice. His poems narrated concise, honest episodes of devastating romantic failure with adolescent Chinese girls who wore too much eyeshadow and had never heard of Camus. He was a soulful kind of guy, one of those perpetual outsiders who sometimes surprise you by having a sense of humor about their plight. I invited him over for a beer, but after ten minutes my attention flagged. I was looking for someone dangerous, or at least surprising. A woman, preferably, with black eyes and a cat and some idea of how to have fun in this empty place.

But finding a soul mate in Hong Kong was like looking for a bagel in Riyadh. I left the Fringe despondent and strolled down Lan Xwai Fong to pick up some fried chicken. The streets were crowded with trucks, lights, and cameras. Women in halter tops clustered around tables, attending to their makeup with yogic concentration.

An Italian-looking man with swept-back hair was sitting alone at a falafel kiosk, reading Bruce Chatwin's *The Songlines*. I asked him what was going on.

"They're filming a movie. A British spy flick with an American crew. I'm one of the extras." He gazed philosophically down the block. "We're all extras."

His name was Nuncio. He'd been in Hong Kong three years, working on an odd assortment of Chinese and Western flicks, never making the big time but eking out a living. I bought a couple of beers and sat back down, waiting to be discovered.

"Acting is a big part of the expatriate subculture here, the way teaching English is in Japan. There are hundreds of foreigners who make their rent by feeding on the bit parts that drift down from the bigger fish." Nuncio's one big break had come a year earlier, when he'd played a bad guy in a Chinese movie ("Westerners always play the bad guys,"

It must be said that the production values of Hong Kong films are not always the best. Budgets are minuscule by Hollywood standards: a million United States dollars is average, and four million is very big. Film companies are able to churn out features from start to finish in seven or eight weeks. Movies are edited as they are being shot, and post-production time is astonishingly brief. (I was told of one major film for which the shooting ended four days before the sneak preview.) Most Hong Kong movies are filmed without synchronized sound, the entire soundtrack is created afterward in a recording studio. Often, top stars, including Jackie Chan, don't even bother to dub in their own voices, but instead use voice doubles.

—Fredric Dannen, "Hong Kong Babylon," *The New Yorker*

he observed). He got to kneel at the end of Lan Kwai Fong and fire an M-16 up the streets as windows shattered, signboards collapsed, and a big white van exploded into flames.

"It took hours to set up for every new take. The explosive charges, the van, everything had to be put back together like some intricate puzzle. Then we'd blow it all up again. It was fun." He sighed. "Fun for Hong Kong, anyway."

I took the long ride home in the bright bluish brushed aluminum glare of the MTR, cleaning my nails with my magnetic ticket. A girl was standing next to me, wearing a solid gold Mickey Mouse ring and clutching a canvas tote bag—clearly of Japanese pedigree—with a large red slogan on the side:

MR. FRIENDLY
YOUR BEST ALLY!
HE ALWAYS STAYS NEAR YOU,
AND STEALS IN YOUR MIND,
TO LEAD YOU INTO A GOOD SITUATION

Where was this guy when I needed him?

Typhoons rolled up the South China Sea, skirting the Philippines, dumping their accumulated rain along the beleaguered coast of Guangxi. Large jets thundered over the Admiralty arcade, windows illuminated, their full cargo of relaxed and happy passengers drinking Absolut from tiny plastic bottles and watching Meg Ryan on small video screens. I craned my neck to follow them.

Ships continued to arrive and depart, but none of them had a place for me. I rented an apartment in Kowloon and bought a motorcycle. A month later I went to the Humane Society and bought a dog, a white terrier that symbolized my final divorce from any of the preconceptions about the future that I might have harbored during those first two weeks, those first naïve and hopeful weeks after my arrival in Hong Kong.

It took me months to get used to the idea of going out to bars to meet people, but there wasn't a lot of choice. I joined the Fringe Club and started reading at the "Partners in Rhyme" series, taking chances, my desperate elocutions uncomplicated by any hope of rescue or fame. For the first time since adolescence I began to write purely for myself, for the rhythm of the words. One Tuesday night in November I met a Burmese expatriate, a 30-year-old woman who had escaped her country's despotic regime and fled to Hong Kong to raise money for a small band of freedom fighters encamped on the Laotian border. I took her home. She moved in with me three weeks later, and brought her cat.

The moment continued to expand, blossoming into space-time like baking bread, the yeasted miracle of Now growing endlessly out of the pan. I was just another raisin, carried along in the cinnamon loaf of Creation. It was not a bad thing to be....

＊

The line between reality and fantasy, hope, and fear was blurring. The sense of finality I had enjoyed leaving Canton was pure illusion. It could take months, years even, to find my way home. Still, there was no debate about it. I would take a ship, or I'd rent an apartment. No way was I getting on a plane.

After two weeks of research, every shipping company save one—Hapag-Lloyd, whose chief op was on vacation—had turned me down. I telephoned Allen Noren, my stateside contact, aware that it might be our last contact for many moons.

"I can't believe you called," he said. "I was just about to fax you…"

"No need to rush. I'll be here at least a couple more months. My plan is to sell my passport on the black market, and use the money to buy a sea kayak. If the currents are good I'll be home by next June…."

"No. Wait." His usually equable voice held a note of urgency. "Call your friend"—I could hear him shuffling papers—"Dwayne. Immediately. You have his number?"

"Dwayne? You mean Newton? Is everything okay?"

"You might say that. He called me this morning. Said he may have found you a ship."

It was incredible, but true. Newton—Mr. Friendly incarnate—had come through again. The *Micronesian Pride*, part of the China Navigation fleet, would leave for Oakland on September 6, Captain Dennis Mitchell, the company's operations manager, was agreeable to signing me on.

The *Pride*, a small and oddly designed container vessel (the superstructure was close to the prow, improving visibility but guaranteeing a rough ride), would take 25 days to get to Oakland, stopping at Saipan, Guam, and Hawaii. There was just one catch— it would leave from Manila.

The passage to Manila takes two to three days, depending on weather and currents. I went back to the *Gazette*, phoning the half-dozen companies ferrying cargo between Hong Kong and the Philippines. After a few days of back-and-forth negotiations, I'd landed myself a ship. The M.S. *Infinity*, a Fleet Trans vessel commanded by Captain Ricardo Janeo, made the round-trip once a week.

But it was too late to qualify for the next departure, leaving that afternoon. I'd have to stay in Hong Kong one more week.

Hong Kong's Festival of the Hungry Ghosts takes place during the seventh lunar month. The event is remarkably similar to Mexico's Dia de los Muertos, during which the spirits of the dead visit their progeny for a nostalgic feast. The two festivals originally occurred at the same time of the year—late summer—until Catholic missionaries coopted the Aztec ritual and moved it up to coincide with All Saints' Day.

I got off the MTR stop at Wong Tai Sin and followed the signs up to the Taoist temple. There were a dozen old ladies outside the gate, begging for coins with paper McDonald's cups. Kiosks sold incense, gaudy good-luck ornaments, and bright foil pinwheels that stood motionless, like silver lures in a still summer pond.

The temple was a new building, erected in 1973 in the traditional dragons-by-the-dozen style. There was a turtle solarium, an obsessively neat "Good Wish Garden," and a row of aluminum drinking fountains offering Hygienically Filtered Water. The Wong Tai Sin housing complex towered above the complex, a forest of bleak gray monoliths covered with an acne of dull balconies. Drying clothes fluttered from their high railings like battle-worn flags.

There were hundreds of people at the temple, laying out baskets of suckling pig, barbecued duck, ripe fruits, and fat red candles. The

Hell money

air was thick with smoke. Scores of devotees kneeled before the main prayer room, igniting small bonfires of rectangle-shaped origami and putting the match to flat folded constructions that resembled terminally overstarched shirts. I'd seen these paper inventions for sale by the gate, and couldn't figure out what they were. Equally puzzling were the thick-wristed bankrolls of "Hell Bank" notes, always in astronomical denominations.

The refuse bins at every corner of the temple courtyard overflowed with sheaves of brilliantly colored papers, emblazoned with bold Chinese characters and faux gold and silver leaf. My friend Paula, an Oakland collage artist, would relish these découpageable scraps. I had scavenged an impressive stash when a middle-aged Chinese man wearing Ray Bans and a point-and-shoot Canon stopped me. I glanced at him guiltily, wondering if it was some sort of sin to steal religious garbage.

But the man was grinning. "Do you know what those are?"

I sheepishly admitted that I didn't.

"Look." He took a sheet from my pile and, with a few deft folds, transformed it into a lightweight replica of a gold ingot. "You burn these," he explained, "and they become like real. We do this for our dead families." He gestured at the ground. "Down there."

"Down there? You mean in Hell?"

"Of course. The spirits of our ancestors stay there, but one time in a year—starting today, for two weeks—the gateway between Hell and Earth is open. Then the ghosts can come visit—but they must have money to spend. So we burn this paper money, and it goes to them. We also offer them food. The ghosts don't eat it, they just enjoy the smell. We bring it home and eat it ourselves."

"Why," I asked, "do you assume that your dead relatives are in Hell? I mean, couldn't they be in Heaven?"

"Ha, ha, ha! I don't know." He became suddenly serious. "I think, maybe, Hell."

I found this Chinese perspective an intriguing reversal of original sin. We're not necessarily born evil, but by the time we die...

The man gestured to the starched shirt patterns in my hand. "Sometimes," he said, "some ghosts, they haven't got anyone to offer them food or money. They have nothing, not even clothes. What to do? So some generous people, they burn these. That way, even the hungry ghosts without family will have something to wear."

Taoism, as practiced in Hong Kong, contained many elements familiar to me from Nepali and Tibetan Buddhism. On the Wheel of Life the Hungry Ghost Realm is one of the six realms of existence, a dry piece of spiritual real estate situated between Hell and the Animal Realm. While not subject to the torments of true Hell, beings trapped in the Hungry Ghost Realm suffer terribly. They are afflicted with a continual, gnawing hunger, and although mountains of food surround them, their mouths are the size of pinheads. They can never assuage their hunger, can barely slake their thirst. Greedy consumption is the whole of their existence.

All of the six realms (even the Human one, real as it seems to us) are illusory states, waystations visited by consciousness on its long, slow climb toward nirvana. Each has its own specific quality. Anger scalds the Hell realm, while greed torments the Hungry Ghosts. The Animals suffer from ignorance, the Demigods are afflicted by jealousy and the Gods themselves are crippled by pride. Chokyi Nyima Rimpoche once pointed out that the unenlightened mind visits all of these realms each day, spinning haphazardly from ignorance to pride, from jealousy to anger. But desire is a sword that cuts two ways—for it is the desire for liberation that leads, ultimately, to freedom.

And what, I wondered, was the buzzword of my own pilgrimage? Not anger, certainly, although I'd experienced my share. Not ignorance, despite the fact that the main thing I had learned, in nearly eight months of travel, was how little I knew about the world. It was not jealousy, certainly, even though the sight of roaring jets made my heart itch, and there had been too many balks and fouls for me to feel overwhelmed by pride.

Desire, of course—the desire to honor my vocation and my planet—had motivated my global Kora from the start. But if anything had interfered with those best of intentions, it could only be greed. Greed for experience, sensation, and exotic visas.

This was nothing new. Growing up on Long Island, I was af-flicted at an early age with "map fever." This was more than a compulsion to cover my walls; it was a need to possess the places those maps represented, to accumulate destinations. In the tribal rituals of the ancients, a boy was hiked into manhood by vision quests or by bagging a difficult pelt. My American initiation, a coming-of-age in the land of consumerism, had combined aspects of both. I wanted not only to experience mysterious new places, but to collect them as well. Nothing had symbolized this better than my huge map of the United States, stuck full of pins, heavy with the destination voodoo of the post-Kerouac generation.

And like the Hungry Ghosts I could never be satisfied, even after a trip that had taken me the better part of a year and carried me to the soil of 23 countries.

It was time to let that greed go. Never again would I organize a banquet as vast or as varied as the one I had devoured during my time abroad. If my hunger was yet unfulfilled perhaps it was time to seek nourishment elsewhere.

The hubbub of the temple crowd surged back into my ears as a babe in arms—held over the shoulder of its mother, standing beside me—grabbed a fistful of my hair. I disengaged myself as gently as possible.

If the hungry ghost inside me still wanted the world, he could have it. I swung off my daypack, opened the flap and pulled out the 1:30,000,000 scale Peters projection that had accompanied me through my entire journey.

The man who had stopped me by the trash bin had worked fast, but I was able to recall his movements. I folded my world map into a huge gold ingot and made my way through the crowd to the smoke-shrouded offering table.

One memory that will stay with me forever is the image of scores of glassy-eyed men and women—riding the MTR, walking along Ice House Road or driving sleek German cars—muttering into the slim fold-down jaws of cellular phones. To a Luddite like me, who thinks that even Walkmen are escapist, these phones are the harbingers of a new Age of Isolationism. The fact that these people are talking to other people is inconsequential. The reality is that they're utterly removed from their environments, walking down the avenues in electronic comas. They glide through the masses of humanity debarking at Admiralty and Tsim Tsa Tsui like pod-people, responding to voices as ethereal as those that beguiled Saint Joan.

Pocket phones are one sign of technological affluence—there are others. Woe to the child who only can afford a Walkman, or a Game Boy. Here in Hong Kong, even sixth-graders carry beepers. "Oh, it's very important," a ten-year-old assured me before flying off the MTR at Central. But *why?* No elaboration was forthcoming.

I'll venture a guess. Beepers, I believe, are symptomatic of the peculiar neurosis of our Neosilicate Epoch, the conviction that one dare not, even for an instant, disappear from sight. "At any moment," a New York Yankees billboard once chortled, "a great moment." It was a slogan calculated to bond you, with the Krazy Glue of perpetual anticipation, to your radio or TV set, and it's a sentiment that the young and restless of Hong Kong seem to share. In a world so thinly schmeared with great moments, no one wants to risk missing theirs.

But the trend has alarming consequences. What was once dignified as "personal space" is now damned as unsociability. Patience, already scant as helium, is evaporating by the hour. There was a time—I dimly remember—when, if a friend's line was busy, one tried back later. If there was no answer, it meant the party was out. One would call again or, if it wasn't critical, drop it. No longer. In the very near future, the inability to find someone within 120 seconds of dragging their name into one's id will be seen as a form of betrayal. *"Where the fuck were you? I've been calling for two minutes."*

The era of sweating it out by the phone has faded into adolescent history, along with "mad money" and goldfish gulping. The classic "I tried to phone but you were out" (or the more contemporary "I called but your answering machine wasn't working") doesn't cut it in Hong Kong—The City Where No One Misses a Call.

✳

Hong Kong is a strange beast, a schizy megalopolis with an awful lot of money and very little soul. At eye level it's shops and bars, but up above it's strictly business: giddy monoliths of marble and steel drip air-conditioner water on pedestrians below. Typhoon season brings rain and mosquitoes, and the humidity makes clothing stick to the skin like Colorforms. Climbing out of the Quarry Bay MTR station into pork-bun-steamer heat, I slogged past department stores blasting meat-locker cold. Sweat froze to ice on the nape of my neck, only to boil off again a few seconds later.

My ascent into the inferno had a motive. On assignment for a magazine, I was looking for the coolest man in town. Five minutes later, buzzed through new security doors into the offices of *Next* magazine, I found him.

I started to miss Vietnam, the smiles, the all-in one-breath, "Hello how are you where you from?" One morning, as I had walked down a back street in Hue, a young woman had passed and whispered, "I love you." I knew it was a throwaway line, a sentence pulled from a recent English lesson or Tom Cruise movie, but it seemed what every tourist who's been on the road awhile needs to hear. And something told me that I wasn't going to hear it here in Hong Kong. I had gone, in 48 hours, from being loved to being invisible.

—Thomas Swick, "The Invisible Man in Hong Kong," *Fort Lauderdale Sun-Sentinel*

Jimmy Lai sat at a round table, hands folded. His crew cut was thick as a carpet, without a single gray hair. I couldn't see a line on his cherubic, almost beatific face, or a sweat stain in the pits of his tailored shirt. It was hard to believe this was the same guy who was being hounded by vandals and threatened by organized crime.

Lai is a legend in Hong Kong. A twelve-year-old street urchin in 1960, he'd been smuggled into the Territory from Canton in the hull of a boat. He took a succession of jobs in garment factories, picking up English along the way. Smart and ambitious, Lai rose through the ranks until, in 1975, he started his own clothing line. Today Giordano's three hundred stores, scattered throughout Asia, do $350 million in annual sales.

But Lai became bored with retail, and lusted for a change. The offspring of his ennui was a weekly magazine called *Next*, conceived on June 4, 1989, as Lai sat in his Hong Kong living room glued to CNN's coverage from Beijing.

"I got the idea to do this magazine during the Tiananmen massacre," he said, nodding. "The fact that the Chinese government was responding to the demand for democracy by shooting people—that they were completely unable to deal with the demonstration—showed me just how desperate and doomed they were. I realized right then that there was no reverse role for China. It would have to open up to the free flow of information. And when it did, it would be the biggest market in the world."

Lai's response to Tiananmen was to twist the knife. Using information as a weapon—more accurately, a crowbar—he decided to jimmy the lid off one of the world's most xenophobic and information-starved nations.

"The events of June 4th gave me the inspiration I needed. Now I'm in a business that delivers information—and information is freedom. That's a great motivator for me. I've never been able to relate to my home country, yet now I'm directly involved in bringing more freedom to the Chinese people."

Lai's idealism initially struck me as naïve, but the situation in Hong Kong demands it. Free-market visionaries like Lai have a vested interest in preserving freedom of information—and what better way to trump the incoming regime than establishing a popular, fearless magazine?

The first issue of *Next* was released in March 1991, less than two years after the Tiananmen bloodbath. Subsequent issues had included exposés of the powerful Triad gangs, reports on prostitution, and investigations into official corruption. The latest issue, Lai's boldest by far, featured a cover story on how communist China enforced its "one family, one child" policy with arrest, blackmail, and forced abortions.

Next's readership of more than one million makes it Hong Kong's largest-circulation weekly, remarkable in light of the fact that it's published exclusively in Cantonese.

"*Next* is for the educated Chinese middle class," Lai explained. "If English speakers want information they don't need a local magazine. They can read *Fortune*, or the *International Herald Tribune*."

For many Hong Kong residents *Next* is a godsend, an indication of what might still be possible in a country where idealists are few and the obsession with getting rich (and getting out) dominates contemporary thought. Not everyone, however, is as ecstatic. A year ago, Triad thugs broke into the offices and smashed the magazine's computers. Giordano windows were spray-painted, and Lai's house has been targeted by firebombs. But Lai grew up in the ghetto, and laughs off the pressure. "If they threaten me, they won't kill me," he observed wryly. "If they want to kill me, they won't threaten me."

Still, it seems unlikely that the Chinese, never known for their open-mindedness, will continue to tolerate a magazine that openly busts their chops.

Jimmy Lai shrugged. "They can physically stop the presses," he admitted, "but they can't stop electronic media." He smiled and leaned forward. "There are two reasons I'm optimistic about our chances for survival after 1997. First of all, within three years we'll probably see the death of Deng Xiaoping. What kind of changes will that bring? Nobody knows. Secondly, by 1997, what new tools will exist for disseminating information? Again, nobody knows. But I guarantee you that they won't be able to stop television. And if they can't stop that, what's the point of trying to stop us?"

Nothing short of bankruptcy is going to stop Lai from becoming the top information broker of the new China. He's already announced his intention to expand into the new economic zones of South China—a move that could increase the magazine's circulation tenfold. His dreams are more ambitious still.

At the World Free Press Conference in 1993, Lai proposed creating a "United Nations of Free Media." He envisioned the quasipolitical collective as a multimedia task force, modeled on the UN and dedicated to preserving freedom of information. Under the UNFM's charter, governments seeking to curtail such freedoms (e.g., China) could be saddled with crippling "information embargoes." A sideswipe onto the cold shoulder of the information superhighway, observed Lai, might be even more effective than an embargo of material goods.

"And where," I asked, "do you envision the venue for this organization?"

Slyly: "Hong Kong. Why not? Locating the planet's top information watch dog in Hong Kong—months before the region rolls under the wheels of the PRC—would put China's leaders in a real fix. Either they virtually guarantee free press in the region, or face loud protests and international suspicion."

I left the offices of *Next*, reemerging into the furnace of summertime Hong Kong. Chinese businesswomen tweaked their beepers, while harried bankers and *gweilo*—a Chinese term meaning both foreigners and ghosts—rushed from air-conditioned offices into air-conditioned taxis. I had to laugh. Six million people obsessed with keeping cool—and Jimmy Lai, turning up the heat.

Approaching the *Infinity* was like coming upon an ancient, active Egyptian tomb, or the launchpad of a space shuttle. Spotlights flooded the area, and tremendous cranes danced in the sodium glare. The moan of winches filled the night with a siren's song, punctuated by the hollow roar of containers falling into place. I climbed the gangway and spent a long time on deck, watching, listening, following the catwalks.

We were supposed to set sail at midnight, but the loading was behind schedule. I stood on the bow of the ship and watched as huge steel boxes, dangling from heavy-duty cranes, swung through the air and into our hold. Steel cables swung across the sky, slicing the moon like a hard-boiled egg. It was a noisy place to be. Steam hissed, cranks and pulleys moaned and squeaked, and every few minutes arose the thunder of one steel container colliding heavily with another.

I clung to the handrail as I walked along the rain-slicked deck, roaring drunk after drinking two San Miguels on an empty stomach. Above my head, mammoth cargo containers rocked in the air. The crane operators, bare-chested teenagers, couldn't see the boxes once they'd been lowered into the hull and had to rely on elaborate hand signals from stevedores squatting below. The precision of the process amazed me. Every container must slip exactly onto four anchor pins, located at each corner of the container below. The work was performed with surgical skill, despite the behemoth size of the cranes and the fact that both ferries—as well as the *Infinity*—were rocking crazily in the windy harbor.

It was a scene from Conrad, timeless and raw, played out against the pulsing neon skyline of modern Hong Kong.

Jeff Greenwald is a contributing editor for Wired *magazine and the author of* Mr. Raja's Neighborhood *and* Shopping for Buddhas. *His book,* The Size of the World: A Global Odyssey—Around the World Without Leaving the Ground, *is based on his around-the-globe tour without the benefit of aircraft.*

✳

Finally, in a diplomatic or government negotiation, in which the Western negotiator will naturally have his own principles of proceeding, it is important never to forget the principles which will be guiding matters on the Chinese side. There will probably be no visible signs of it, but the Chinese officials will almost surely be sticking closely to their own maxim of the three principles, or duties, of sound government. There are:

to simulate friendship;

to express honeyed sentiments; and

to treat your inferiors as your equals.

Thus when a diplomat in China—or indeed any Westerner engaged in formal business—finds himself being treated on terms of delightful equality, let him be on his guard, he is almost certainly being used for some ulterior purpose.

—Austin Coates, *Myself a Mandarin*

★ ★ ★

Hong Kong Pedigree

The author looks for his roots in Hong Kong.

GENERAL HO CLAPPED HIS CUPPED HANDS SOFTLY BUT EMPHATICALLY for a servant to refill the glasses. After issuing a brief command in Cantonese, he reverted to English and memories of his childhood, long ago. "You couldn't use a ricksha up here," he reminisced. "The only way to get about was by sedan chair—there were no roads, you see."

"Up here" was the Peak, the steep green hill that dominates Hong Kong geographically and socially. It has been a very long time since anyone traveled by sedan chair up here, as the British expatriate rulers and General Ho's parents used to do. Half an hour before, my taxi had fought its way out of Central, the main financial district, in the company of fleets of Rolls-Royces and Mercedes that steadily peeled off to deposit their passengers in widely spaced houses and apartment blocks set well back from the steep road. At the end we had been alone, for the great gray house of the Ho Tungs is almost at the summit. Fifteen hundred feet below us, the workers jostling along the impossibly crowded sidewalks were eagerly discussing that day's 200-point market drop on their cellular phones, but up here the early spring mist swirling around the Peak hid the great bank buildings that tower over Central. As I climbed the wide stairs in the silent house and entered the drawing room, with its family portraits and teak inlaid furniture, I felt I had traveled back 90 years to a Hong Kong I knew only from stories and photographs almost three generations old.

The stories and pictures, not to mention shelves of Ming vases and other mementos, had come into my family from the days when my great-grandparents ruled Hong Kong. Sir Henry Blake had been a professional colonial governor—a career now utterly extinct—and as such he had been in charge of this place between 1898 and 1903. He seems to have had an interesting and possibly profitable time. When he arrived, his little kingdom amounted to no more than Hong Kong Island and the Kowloon Peninsula, on the tip of the mainland opposite the harbor (these had been extracted from the Chinese as fruits of the two opium wars fought earlier in the century, fought to force the Chinese to allow the British to sell them opium). Blake left Hong Kong a much bigger place, having taken over an area north of Kowloon known then and since as the New Territories under a 99-year lease from China.

Coincidentally or not, he and my great-grandmother Edith made Chinese friends, a most ungubernatorial action in those days. The closest of these friends, legendary in our family for his wealth and the lavishness of his presents when he came to visit, was a Eurasian entrepreneur called Sir Robert Ho Tung, the father of my 87-year-old host in

As I cannot believe that the British empire will ever acquiesce in the retrocession of Hong Kong to China, it behoves us to offer, and the sooner the better, terms upon which the Chinese can honourably agree to the cession of the New Territories in perpetuity to Great Britain.

—Sir Cecil Clementi (1936)

the big house in the mists of the Peak. In Hong Kong, where really big money tends to be new and, as often as not, ostentatious, the Ho Tungs count as old aristocracy.

The general got his rank in the Chinese Nationalist Army of Chiang Kai-shek. During dinner he reminisced on the hidden history of great events and people, long dead, he had known—"I remember MacArthur telling me why he invaded North Korea"—

before his thoughts drifted back to the days when he was a small boy and bereft of playmates among the neighbors because he had Chinese blood. In those days and for long afterward, the Peak was reserved for whites only. When his father had first tried to rent a house there, the governor of the day had firmly vetoed the notion, observing in a note that it would be impossible to have a "half-caste with four wives" living on the Nob Hill of Hong Kong.

My long-departed ancestors lacked the Neanderthal attributes of that governor, which was why I, a descendant of the Blakes, was welcome at Ho Tung Gardens. The general raised his glass. "The Blakes were the first to receive Chinese at Government House," he declared. "My family always remembered that the Blakes had been friends, and remained friends. Welcome back!" As I drank to the toast, my napkin slid off my lap. A servant advanced on hands and knees to retrieve it.

In a way, it was not surprising that Governor Blake and the original Ho Tung had hit it off. Both had had to make their own way in life. Despite his later viceregal status, Henry Blake had started off as an Irish policeman in the backwoods of County Galway. His luck changed when he eloped with my great-grand-mother, the heiress to the local big house. Marriage did not bring any immediate financial benefit, because she was promptly cut off without a penny by her indignant parents. But Edith's sister had more acceptably married a duke, who loyally jerked enough of the right strings to get the then Inspector Blake a job as governor of the Bahamas. A tough and capable fellow, Blake was thereafter promoted to the rule of progressively more important slices of imperial real estate. Before Hong Kong, he had had Jamaica, and afterward they gave him Ceylon. The couple never seemed to have liked their white expatriate subjects much. Lady Blake used to pretend she was ill whenever they called, preferring to confer with interesting "natives" in their own language.

Hence the friendship with Ho Tung, who came from a back-ground even more obscure than Blake's. He was the son of a Dutch sea captain and a woman from Shanghai, about whom little is known. Nevertheless, at the age of eighteen, he became comprador—Chinese business agent—of Jardine Matheson, the Scots trading firm that had helped found Hong Kong, the better to smuggle opium into China. After a few years he had gone into business on his own account, and by the time Blake showed up, he was already almost as rich as his erstwhile employers, though not, of course, permitted to live among them.

It is not clear whether the Eurasian and the Irishman came together socially or on business. Nowadays, Hong Kong is a world-class financial power, with foreign exchange reserves of $28 billion and a regular government surplus. Back then things were simpler, and the government depended for a sizable chunk of its income on its monopoly of the opium market, known as "the opium farm" in Hong Kong. The monopoly was rented out to the highest bidder, and Sir Henry's diary entry for March 29, 1899, notes that "Ho Tung is

The growth and sale of opium was officially organized in British India, and traders brought vast quantities of it up the Pearl River, selling it at a handsome profit to Chinese entrepreneurs. As a matter of fact, there was not much else British traders could sell to the Chinese, who were self-sufficient in most things and scornful of Western innovations, so that the opium traffic was developed with relentless energy. The drugs illegally sold to China were worth twice as much as all the legal commodities put together, and without them Britain's imports of China tea could have been paid for only in specie. Opium became, so it is said, not only the principal export of the Indian empire, but actually the largest single article of international commerce anywhere in the world.

—Jan Morris, *Hong Kong*

prepared to give $300,000 a year for a five-year term of opium farming...2½ chests a day consumed here." (Two and a half chests amounted to 450 pounds, suggesting that the local population had quite a habit.)

Despite his military background, the general has reportedly inherited his father's acquisitive faculties. "He runs the family business with a rod of iron," said one denizen of the financial district. "No one dares make a move without him." So discreetly indeed is the family fortune handled that it had not even made Ong Chin

Huat's feature on ten anonymous Hong Kong billionaires, which the editor was busy preparing for an upcoming issue of *Tatler*. A coolly elegant figure, Chin Huat qualifies as a social arbiter in Hong Kong. His magazine consists broadly of a monthly tribute to the rich and, if possible, glamorous inhabitants of the colony. Following the traditional format of such journals (clones of the English original have sprouted all over Southeast Asia), much of the text consists of names ("...it was then farewell to some guests—Li Ka-shing, Michael and Betty Kadoorie, Ho Tim and Dennis Ting, included—who could not stay for the evening party.").

While monitoring the money/cultural heartbeat of Hong Kong, Chin Huat also embodies a process that goes back at least as far as Robert Ho Tung's first attempt to move to the Peak. "Up until a few years ago, the *Tatler* mostly covered the expat scene," he explains. "Then they thought that since so many of the people on the social circuit were Chinese, perhaps they ought to have a Chinese reporter, so they hired me."

The British still have a lot of power and money here, a fact made evident by the skyline of Central. The Hong Kong and Shanghai Bank looms over the harbor, its chairman, Sir William Purves, reigning simultaneously over the Jockey Club. The great 19th-century British trading firms are still very much a physical as well as a financial presence. In Central, Jardine House, named for Jardine Matheson and known locally as the House of a Thousand Assholes, thanks to its round windows, stares out at the harbor from just behind the post office, while Swire House, so called for the Swire family—one of the richest in the world—rises from the other side of Connaught Road.

Once there was a belief that all this would come to an end when the Communists took back what the British had extracted at the point of a gunboat. But the Chinese themselves have signed on to what might be called a Hong Kong ideology of unrestrained capitalism. There may even be a hardheaded capitalist maneuver behind the denunciations regularly hurled at Chris Patten—Fei Pang, or "Fat Patten" as the locals call him—and the occasional conciliatory announcements indicating that perhaps something could be worked out. Two local Communists with excellent contacts in Beijing assured me, for example, that one such conciliatory statement, which had sent the stock market up by 200 points, was preceded by heavy buying orders from the mainland. "They know they can move the market," said one. "Maybe that's what the whole row is about." Perhaps the game is being played on both sides. When Patten went before the Legislative Council to announce that he was pressing ahead with his plans for electoral reform—a move guaranteed to send the market into a tailspin—heavy selling commenced ten minutes before he spoke the fatal words.

The clash with Beijing has turned Patten into a world-famous figure—profiled in *The New Yorker,* featured on the Larry King show—so it would be ironic if he were merely a pawn in a gigantic game of insider trading. But at Government House, the Victorian mansion on Upper Albert Road once occupied by my great grandfather, there are suspicions that even darker forces, emanating from just over the garden wall, may be at work.

Sir Henry could look out the window of his study and see quite a lot of the colony he governed. Across the harbor, then as now brimming with everything from tiny fishing junks to huge liners, there straggled the city of Kowloon. In the foreground the land fell away steeply almost to the water's edge, but along the shore there ranged traditional manifestations of the British Empire: the Anglican cathedral, the Hong Kong Club, the Supreme Court, the cricket field, the naval dockyard. Not everything is gone now, but they have nearly all become invisible from the study window. "You see, we're surrounded by banks," remarked Louise Cox, the governor's social secretary, as we admired the azaleas in the garden in front of the mansion. She was stating the obvious. From just the other side of the garden wall there rose the ramparts of the gigantic financial edifices, line upon line of them.

Over to the right, the Bank of China building pierces the clouds. The bank is of course owned by the mainland government, and when it decided to build a new headquarters in Hong Kong, it opted for prestige and reached for I. M. Pei. He gave the People's Republic something tall, the tallest in town, slim and aggressively angular.

In Blake's day, before the concrete barriers went up, it might have been possible to see beyond Kowloon into the edge of the New Territories that he took over under the terms of the famous lease. He noted the big day in typically laconic fashion: "Monday, 17th April, 1899...Place is handed over to colony. Edith hoisted the flag...Then the interpreter...read my speech, which seemed to satisfy them....Afterwards distributed a pound worth of ten cent pieces to the children." Naturally, he hung on to the flag.

Back then the area was a relatively bucolic landscape of low green hills and paddy fields, fertile enough to have been called "the Emperor's rice bowl." But the exploding population of Hong Kong—now almost six million people—meant that the paddy fields and their peasant farmers had to give way to the grim vistas of high-rise apartment blocks interspersed with mountains of empty shipping containers and auto junkyards that one sees today. Here and there a hillside sprouts tar-and-paper shacks, home to the half-million squatters still on the waiting list for paradise.

There are, however, some vestiges of the old life still remaining in the Territories, most notably the walled villages of Kam Tin, built in the 17th century with stout defenses against pirates and other hostile elements and the scene of Sir Henry's looting instinct at work.

When his officials turned up to announce to the inhabitants of Kam Tin that they had been leased to Queen Victoria, the locals, all members of an ancient clan known as the Tangs, took a dim view of the news. After venting their feelings with shouts of "foreign devils" and a shower of rotten eggs, they retreated behind their walls and moats. Only after a party of military sappers had blown a hole in the walls did the Tangs cave in. To complete their humiliation, the villagers were forced to carry their gates, heavy wrought-iron affairs, and lay them in submission at Sir Henry's feet. He promptly appropriated a set and sent them home to Ireland to be installed in his walled garden.

For years the Tangs brooded over the theft of their gates, and in 1925 they finally asked for them back. Sir Henry was dead by then, but his widow obligingly crated them up and sent them halfway around the world to their original home. Two years later, an enormous crate arrived at Cork, the nearest port to my family's home, and broke the crane as it was being unloaded. The villagers had sent a replacement set.

At least the Tangs have a sense of history. In urban Hong Kong, history is yesterday's closing prices. In fact, as Hong Kong author and journalist Frank Ching points out, "The Chinese population here has no history. The only history that has been recorded here is the story of white expatriate Hong Kong. For example, the court documents from a hundred years ago refer only to 'Chinaman number one, Chinaman number two,' and so on. There was a Chinese press, but it was ruthlessly censored by the British."

For the longest time, most people here came from somewhere else anyway. During the first fifty years of this century, the mainland was wracked by civil war, invasion, and revolution, leading to successive waves of refugees seeking the relative security of the colony. This culminated in the torrent that poured over the northern border when the Communists finally took power in 1949. "They were exiles," Ching points out. "They never regarded Hong Kong as their home. They formed what they called sojourners societies, groups from Shanghai or Wuhan or wherever they had come from. The first time the census showed that a majority of people in Hong Kong had actually been born here was in 1971, and they were mostly children. Only now do we have a majority of people, like me, who were born and grew up here and have a stake in the place."

It is this group that has been demanding that the people of Hong Kong, long excluded by the British from any political role, be given some direct say in their future. Unfortunately, they found their voice just as the British had arranged to hand the real estate back to the mainland Chinese, who, despite some solemn declarations, show even less regard for local sentiment.

The mainland rulers have indeed a keen sense of history, vividly recalling that Hong Kong was forcibly peeled off by the "foreign devils" in the first of a series of humiliations that they are determined to reverse. The depth of this feeling can sometimes take locals aback. The wife of a director of Jardine Matheson described to me a meeting with Zhou Nan, the de facto Chinese ambassador in Hong Kong: "Hardly had we plonked our bottoms down on the chairs when he started right in, shaking his finger. 'We remember Jardine's pushing opium on the Chinese,' and so on and so forth. Did you know he learned his English interrogating prisoners in Korea?"

Only recently did the British, in the portly shape of Chris Patten, take note that "Hong Kongers," as they are inelegantly called, might be properly represented in decisions over their fate. Christine Loh, an attractive as well as high-powered executive, is one of the more vocal representatives of the pro-reform group in the legislature. "We were the first Hong Kong generation," she declares. "We were the first to be educated, the first not to worry about food. The opium wars and all that ancient history that so obsesses the mainland people, that doesn't matter to us. The trouble is," she continues with brisk intensity, "Hong Kong still likes to project a 'Chinese junk' image of itself. That's really shortchanging ourselves."

"Chinese junks" do indeed feature prominently in the marketing of Hong Kong. It is certainly worth taking a harbor tour, perhaps as far as Aberdeen, around the west side of the island to see

Hundreds of men have borne the title of emperor, huang-ti, *in China's long history. Few have exercised more power, personal and political, than Mao Zedong and Deng Xiaoping, true* huang-ti.

The first huang-ti *was the Yellow Emperor, the legendary ruler who founded China on the rich loess floodplains of the Yellow River. Mao led his Red armies, with Deng at his side, out of these plains to found his New China at Tiananmen in 1949....*

In Chinese custom, dynasties and bloodlines are not so important as power. The great Chinese dynastic scholar Zhang Zhi says of Mao, "He founded the first peasant dynasty in 600 years." In Chinese history a capable minister or victorious general has often won the Mandate of Heaven. Deng Xiaoping fit the concept perfectly. Both men earned the title of huang-ti *despite the fact that both considered themselves Marxists. Both were Sons of Heaven, rulers by a kind of divine right.*

—Harrison E. Salisbury,
The New Emperors: China in the Era of Mao and Deng

the fishing community living much as it always did. Nevertheless, the junks—along with photo opportunities of old ladies wearing what appear to be lampshades on their heads—do not seem to have much to do with what makes this amazing city-state tick. It is most emphatically not a museum. Yet, if Dr. Doom is right, it may become one.

The local financial press has given Marc Faber that title because he defies a deep Hong Kong belief, held equally by billionaires with business partners in Beijing and optimistic young professionals like Christine Loh: whatever happens to Hong Kong politically, whatever effects the Chinese takeover may have in other ways, the place will continue as a great, rich trading metropolis for decades to come.

Faber is an erudite and highly successful investment adviser, Swiss by origin, with a Germanic accent perfectly suited to his acerbic observations. His desk in his highpriced office 27 floors above Queen's Road Central, the Wall Street of Hong Kong, is as likely to be littered with first editions of 17th-century economists as Merrill Lynch reports.

"They talk about Hong Kong becoming the Manhattan of China, which is supposed to become richer than the United States in a generation," he rasps scornfully. "I think that the 'Monaco of China' would be a more appropriate comparison. These kids around here have never seen a real bear market, but all the fundamentals point to a significant long-term decline. Hong Kong is still a trading economy, but most of the wealth here is in the stock market and property. Yet the property market, particularly in small [apartments], is already showing signs of topping out." (Any speculative endeavor is sure to find takers in Hong Kong. At the wonderful Happy Valley racetrack, a Chinese friend observes, "Have you noticed everyone is smiling after the races? The winners are smiling because they've won, and the losers are smiling because they think, 'I will win next time.'")

The fabulous wealth of Hong Kong, he points out, is based on a historical accident. The Communist victory in 1949 closed off China, including the preeminent financial and industrial center of

Shanghai, from the world economy. The only outlet was Hong Kong, which in the meantime picked up most of the money and brains fleeing Mao. Two incredible strokes of luck followed in the 1980s: the Taiwanese decided that they would at last deal with the mainland, but only through Hong Kong, and Deng Xiaoping set up the first of his free-market New Economic Zones right next door in Guangdong.

But all that is about to change, as the Taiwanese deal directly, China opens up further, and Shanghai in particular rises again. Faber draws an ominous comparison with 15th-century Venice. Then the world's greatest trading city, it went into decline when trading routes shifted and ultimately became a museum catering only to tourists.

As I sit in Faber's office listening to the even flow of his arguments, laced with sardonic references to the 17th-century speculative bubble in Dutch tulip bulbs, or the German stock market of the 1920s and its relevance to the near future in South China, I realize what brand of nostalgia the Hong Kong Tourist Association ought to be peddling. Not traditional China, not the bygone days of imperial governors raising the flag over yet more territory, but, rather, a

"Hong Kong people are not a jealous people," Sir David Ford, the colonial secretary, remarked once—and when it comes to the attitude to wealth (though he was actually talking about something else), this is no doubt true. The ordinary Chinese who gazes enraptured from down among the gibbons and the Palawan pheasants, who sees the twinkling lights up in The Albany penthouse and wonders idly how the Baroness and her consort are living above, will have no truck with envy: quite simply, he wants what the Baroness has, he vows to acquire it and is quite certain that he can acquire it— either by work, by stealth, by chicanery, or by cunning.

He feels none of the lip-curling resentment that such good fortune would engender in Britain: Lady Dunn, he knows only too well, came from China to Hong Kong and made good—and so can anyone else. This is the dictum by which the territory has lived for 150 years, and it applies across the board to all fortunate enough to live within.

—Simon Winchester, *Pacific Rising: The Emergence of a New World Culture* more recent time that seems so distant now in the United States: the 1980s. Here you can experience one more time the thrill of roaring stock and property markets, the glowing optimism about the business future, and the unabashed glorification of wealth of a kind unimaginable in our own austere nineties. But hurry.

Andrew Cockburn is the author of Dangerous Liaisons *and* The Threat: Inside the Soviet Military Machine.

★

Do not move unless it is advantageous.
Do not execute unless it is effective.
Do not challenge unless it is crucial.

An intense View is not a reason to launch an opposition.
An angry leader is not a reason to initiate a challenge.

If engagement brings advantage, move.
If not, stop.

Intensity can cycle back to fondness.
Anger can cycle back to satisfaction.
But an extinct organization cannot cycle back to survival.
And those who are destroyed cannot cycle back to life.

Thus, a Brilliant Ruler is prudent;
A Good Leader is on guard.

Such is the Tao of a Stable Organization and a Complete Force.

—Sun Tzu, "The Ultimate Restraint," *The Art of Strategy,*
a new translation of *The Art of War* by R. L. Wing

AMANDA MAYER STINCHECUM

✦ ✦ ✦

Suitable Advice

The quest for the perfect fit.

IF YOU THINK HAVING A SUIT MADE IN HONG KONG IS AS EASY AS falling off a log, think again. At least, if you have visions of a beautifully made, perfectly fitting suit with the construction, fit, and hand-sewn touches that only come with custom work.

Maybe it's easier if you happen to be a man. There are certain accepted standards for men's suits made in Hong Kong. There should be no question about the hand stitched lapels and the pad-stitching on the underside of the collar to give it that soft roll. Narrow cotton tape should be applied along the lapel seam and down the front of the jacket to keep it from stretching out of shape, and wool canvas (called hair canvas) must be used to give body to lapels, collar and shoulders.

But for women's suits, there seem to be no general standards of workmanship. In general, women's tailors know how to fit jackets that hug the waist and expand at the appropriate spots, how to cut a variety of collars and front closings, and how to cut and fit a skirt. Men's tailors, on the other hand, are used to making more-or-less boxy jackets and trousers (not that the cut and fit are any less precise, just different) and are reluctant to take on a woman's suit, because doing work they are not used to might damage their reputations if the work is not done perfectly.

Because I wanted all of the fine workmanship that normally goes into a man's custom-made suit, I decided to look for a man's tailor to make mine.

MONDAY: The first shop I visited was chosen from a guide that noted it was one of the few shops in Hong Kong that still employs tailors from Shanghai. In two shopping bags I had dragged my four yards of heavy Scottish tweed, carried by my very own hands from the Highlands of Scotland (from Campbell's of Beauty Purveyors of Tweed to the Queen Mother, to be precise) to Brooklyn. I took the fabric from Brooklyn to Tokyo to Hong Kong, along with matching silk thread and rough staghorn buttons from the Scottish village of Bonar Bridge.

I had also brought with me my most precious suit, probably 40 or 50 years old, from the long-defunct Tailored Woman at the corner of Fifth Avenue and 57th Street, to be copied as exactly as possible by the Hong Kong tailor of my choice.

In the heat of noon I pushed through the crowds jamming Nathan Road, Hong Kong's main shopping street, carrying all these things to a certain hotel. The chosen shop was located in the lobby.

Feeling a bit faint due to the heat, crowds and the heavy plastic bags cutting into my hands, I was overwhelmed by the cascades of mirror strips and dripping chandeliers hanging from the low ceiling, and by the dazzling light fixtures and the glowing emerald-green glass bricks forming a serpentine wall around the Prince Garden Terrace cocktail lounge, in the middle of the lobby.

After resting a few minutes on one of the Leatherette banquettes, I gathered up my courage and went into the narrow shop, eyeing uneasily the photographs in the display window of the proprietor, Mr. H. with Frank Sinatra, Mr. H. with Pat Boone, and Mr. H. with Sammy Davis Jr.

A woman's blazer of red wool crepe hung on a steel rack by the door. The uneven machine stitching around the lapels caught my eye, which then traveled to the underside of the lapel, both stiff and flimsy to the touch, suggesting that the tailor had used a synthetic interfacing. The underside of the collar showed none of the rows of parallel pad-stitching needed to give the collar a perfect roll.

I dismissed the red blazer and turned to a half-finished man's jacket hanging nearby. Before I had a chance to examine it properly, Mr. H. pronounced, "That's not a lady's jacket," and hastened to put it out of my reach. I explained that I was looking for someone who would give me the quality of tailoring found in a well-made man's suit, modeled on the suit I had brought with me. That was not possible, he said, and I left the shop bearing my ever-heavier burden.

TUESDAY: A fresh start. I called on a tailoring establishment in the Mandarin Hotel, where a salesman in an exquisite white-on-white batiste shirt (no doubts about sensibility here) said they did not do women's suits, but graciously consented to take a look at mine. And indeed he inspected the jacket very carefully, pointing out to me that the shaping darts were not in the same places as in a man's jacket, that it was much more fitted, that they were not used to making skirts and did not think they could do justice to it. In short, sorry, no.

One more phone call led me to Jimmy Chen & Co., Ltd., on the mezzanine of the Mandarin Hotel. This was one of a chain of shops—there are two more in the Peninsula, one which goes by the name Italian Tailors, and the main shop in the Hong Kong Hotel—all linked to one workshop in Kowloon.

This turned out to be a considerable advantage, because I was able to have two of my fittings at the Peninsula when I had business on the Kowloon side. My young salesman, Danny Kon, assured me that both their men's and women's tailors (about 20 of the former and 25 of the latter) did fine work. Maybe 65 percent of them were from Shanghai, he said.

What was this mystique about Shanghai tailors? "Shanghai was an international city for a long time," Kon said, "with many ambassadors and consuls, so people had to wear suits all the time. But the Shanghai tailors," and this must mean tailors trained in Shanghai before the revolution, "are getting old now, and there is no one to replace them, because the younger ones don't want to do all that hard work. Tailors in Hong Kong now learning to make a suit for the first time don't do such good work."

The explanation was not entirely convincing, but, recalling the old hand-sewn silk underwear from Shanghai still available in a certain shop in San Francisco's Chinatown (though apparently no longer made, for I could not find it anywhere in Hong Kong), the connection between Shanghai and fine sewing seemed reasonable.

Kon measured me carefully and examined my suit, the silk thread and staghorn buttons, expressing neither scorn nor surprise. We discussed the construction of button-holes (I demanded bound button-holes throughout, including real ones on the cuffs), the use of hair canvas interfacing, my next fitting (I had asked for three fittings), and the cost. A week would be plenty of time for the whole job.

Hong Kong had a reputation for tailoring long before it saw its first cruise ship or Boeing 707. More than a century ago, important Chinese warlords had their most elegant uniforms made in Hong Kong— by Chinese tailors who had learned their trade in Japan.

—Charles N. Barnard, "The Hong Kong Suite," *Travel & Leisure*

I asked about lining material. Kon showed me the inside of a man's jacket, a twill-faced fabric of 65 percent silk and 35 percent polyester. He said pure silk was too fragile. I agreed and asked to see color swatches.

The day before the fitting, I called Kon to confirm the time of my appointment. How would I feel, he said, if the skirt was cut in four gores or panels instead of six like the skirt I had brought in? I wanted the softness of a six-gore skirt.

THE FIRST FITTING (Wednesday evening): I met Kon and the cutter who was assigned to me at the Italian Tailors in the Peninsula. My suit, basted together with generous seam allowances to permit a looser fit if necessary, emerged from a gray plastic bag. When I put it on, it looked OK, but somehow it didn't knock me out. The cutter had the general idea right, but the jacket was too long, the sleeves were also too long, the slash pocket was placed too high, the pocket itself was too large and the single button-hole at the waist was a bit high (buttonholes and pockets were indicated by strips of white cloth and would be cut when their final position had been decided on).

"I don't like these foam-rubber shoulder pads," I whined. Foam rubber, in addition to creating a kind of pneumatic look, dries out and cracks with age. "You want wool? No problem." But he should have known without asking, I thought, from my obvious concern with details of workmanship and material. The skirt had, against my instructions, been cut in four gores. I suspected it had already been cut when Kon asked me about it on the phone. "But we can change it if you want," he insisted. In the end, I agreed with his judgment that because the tweed was heavier than my old suit and the windowpane check quite large, the simpler and slightly narrower form was more suitable. We adjourned after nearly an hour.

THE SECOND FITTING (Friday): I went to the shop in the Mandarin at nine. The cutter was to stop by on his way to the workshop in Kowloon (he lived on the Hong Kong side). My suit was still only basted together. The foam-rubber shoulder pads had been removed, but nothing had been put in to replace them. "How can I see how the jacket hangs if there are no shoulder pads?" I grumbled. The cutter good-naturedly stuffed in a pair of wool-and-cotton pads. All the corrections I had requested had been basted in. I decided the tailor had been right after all about the buttonhole placing.

Neither Kon nor the cutter showed any irritation at my demands and crankiness, or looked askance at my rubber sandals. At the same time, I felt that if I didn't pay attention to every single detail I would end up with something quite different from what I had ordered.

Kon brought out a bouquet of three small strips of silk crepe in the general range of colors I had suggested might be good for the lining. "But this isn't the lining material you showed me," I said.

"That was lining for a man's jacket. This is what we use for ladies suits," Kon explained.

"But I want the heavier lining. I expect this suit to last at least thirty years."

"But you can choose the colors," he almost begged, "they're the same."

"Are they the same, or similar?" I insisted.

"Well, similar."

"I want to see the actual material you're going to use."

"But we don't have a set of swatches. We'll have to cut them off bolts of cloth in the workroom."

"Fine, I'll come in to see them tomorrow."

Kon then said my suit would be finished Monday. Perturbed, I asked. "But what about my third fitting?" Oh of course, the third fitting. But if I hadn't asked, I wouldn't have had a third fitting.

The next day I stopped by the Mandarin to see the lining swatches. Kon had brought the entire color card sent out by the fabric company. The suit was in the workshop, so I had nothing but my memory with which to compare colors. The choice I made turned out to blend well with the beige, brown, rust, and Lovat of the tweed, much to my relief.

Since Saturday was a holiday, we agreed on Sunday morning for my last fitting.

When I returned to the YWCA after an early dinner Saturday, I found a message from Kon. I called, but it was two hours past closing time. About twenty minutes after I got back to my room, the phone rang. It was Kon. "How did you know where I was staying?" I asked, a bit surprised. I hadn't mentioned where I was staying.

"I called all the hotels on the Hong Kong side until I found the right one." I was speechless. "Sunday the tailor doesn't work because of the holiday," he explained. "I thought you would be mad if you came at nine Sunday morning and there was no suit. Since he won't be working Sunday night either, we'll have the fitting late Monday afternoon and then deliver the suit to your hotel in the middle of the night." (I was leaving Hong Kong Tuesday morning.)

THE THIRD FITTING (Monday, 6 p.m.): I was having dinner with friends staying at the Peninsula, so I met Kon and the cutter there. All the seams were stitched, the shoulder pads were in place, the top-stitching with my silk thread (which actually didn't show up much on the tweed) was completed and the skirt was hemmed. It looked great, I had to admit. I couldn't wait to see it with the three hand-embroidered silk blouses I had bought, and my new custom-made shoes.

"The sleeves are uneven," Kon said. "Another quarter of an inch on this one," he directed the cutter.

I said, "I think I've gained weight since the last fitting"—which in light of what I had consumed over the weekend, seemed entirely possible. Kon thought it was fine, it would stretch out a little, but I was worried. He could add a quarter of an inch on each side, just at the hips. An extra half inch should be plenty. We agreed on that. There were no other changes.

"We'll deliver your suit late tonight. Don't worry about it," he assured me. We settled the bill and shook hands.

I left the shop and started down the stairs to the lobby, but turned back and entered the shop again. He was right, after all. The skirt hung perfectly as it was. If the side seams were tampered with, wouldn't it interfere with the fall of the skirt? I told Kon to forget the extra half inch. I would lose weight. He smiled. We shook hands again.

Kon said, "Come back to see us the next time you're in Hong Kong." Could he really mean it? I knew my suit would be exactly as I had envisioned it when I made the trip from Inverness to Beauly to buy the tweed four years previously. And so it was.

That night I didn't get back to the Y until 11:30. My suits, and the leftover tweed, had already been delivered, folded into a couple of plastic shopping bags. At least they could have given me a suit bag, I thought. I went up to my room, hung up the two suits, packed my bag and set my alarm for 7:30.

About half an hour after I went to bed, I realized I hadn't checked the buttonholes on the sleeves. Were they real button-through buttonholes? I turned on the light, opened the wardrobe and took out my new jacket. The buttonholes were fine.

Amanda Mayer Stinchecum is a textile historian, Japanese translator, and travel writer. She is the author of Kosode: Sixteenth Through Nineteenth Century Textiles from the Nomura Collection *and* Taxation and

Textile Production In Ryuku: Four Hundred Years. *She also contributes to periodicals, including* Natural History, Northwest, *and* Travel & Leisure.

✷

The time-honored practice of haggling now has countermeasures designed by suitmakers. The scenario might go like this: you find a material you want for a suit and whittle down the price with the appropriate moaning and gnashing of dispositions. All is well—you are pleased with your wily bargaining—but when you get your suit—beware. The shopkeeper may have substituted an inferior lining, the buttons are a cheesier quality than you seem to recall and, indeed, many small quality downgrades observed do not bode well for its longevity. The moral of the story: settle for a fair price and insist that buttons and lining etc. are to be the same as what you have been shown.

—David E. Scott, "Hong Kong Observations"

PAUL THEROUX

* * *

Going to See the Dragon

Welcome to the New Revolution.

THERE IS NO BETTER PLACE FOR THE TRAVELER THAN A LAND outside the scope of guidebooks, beyond the reach of maps, where only local knowledge matters and word of mouth is everything. China is just such a place now. You have to go there to find out what is happening. In my travels around China's southern provinces of Guangdong and Fujian in April of 1993, I discovered that roads are being built so fast, in so many new directions, that no maps are accurate. The guidebooks cannot keep up with the hotels and restaurants that have opened—every one is out of date. So are telephone directories and company listings. These explosive changes make China terra incognita.

I first visited China in 1980. Since the death of Mao in 1976 a power struggle had been going on between the Maoists, led by Hua Guofeng, Mao's handpicked inheritor, and the reformers, led by Deng Xiaoping, now the ruling patriarch. Hua's portrait was displayed everywhere with that of his benefactor, Hua's cheek next to Mao's jowl. Deng's face was nowhere, and yet from the shadows of the Chinese hierarchy he was sketching his master plan to revitalize China. This was not yet obvious. I sailed down the Yangtze and visited ten cities. China then was all struggle, people in blue suits and cloth slippers riding bicycles down muddy streets, workers going blind in poorly lighted factories, waiters refusing tips and chanting, "Serve the people!" The only bright colors were the ribbons the more daring women and girls wore in their hair. Near Guangzhou (Canton) I visited a Maoist model commune called Da Li. It was like a good-natured prison of reluctant sloganeers and suppressed ambitions—71,000 people working 6,000 acres of rice fields and making Whistling Cicada brand firecrackers. It seemed at once appalling and wonderful for its unity and its innocence. Every job was carried out with crude tools and great spirit. It was a society of intimidating and ingenious frugality in which everything was mended—shoes, clothes, vehicles. The Chinese were poor, but their ingenuity made them seem indestructible.

In the spring of 1986 I made another visit to China, taking the train from London through West and East Germany, Communist Poland, the Soviet Union, and the People's Republic of Mongolia— all of them gone now. I was astonished by the changes and new attitudes, the communes either closed or changed—the charade over, the rice fields buried, the people turned loose to find employment at large. Late in 1986 there were student demonstrations in most of the largest Chinese cities. Shanghai was shut down for two days. No one outside China took any notice.

In the spring of 1993 I returned to China for the third time, to have a look at what the newspapers were calling the "Chinese miracle." What I had read did indeed suggest that something miraculous was afoot. Almost overnight, while few people were paying attention, China had emerged as the world's third-largest economy, according to the International Monetary Fund, and as America's largest trading partner after Japan. In the first quarter of 1993, China's GNP grew at an annual rate of fourteen percent, outstripping every country in the world; in contrast, America grew, in the first quarter of 1993, at a one percent annual rate. The engine driving most of China's growth is centered in the southern provinces, a region of 290 million people, where the government has established five Special Economic Zones. From what I'd read, it sounded as though China had embarked on its own version of the type of industrial revolution that transformed England and America.

*S*ince Deng Xiaoping took over in 1978, the Chinese economy has enjoyed an annual average growth rate of a bit more than 9 percent. That is triple the average growth rate of the United States in that period, and about 70 percent more than the growth rate in India or Indonesia.

China is now the biggest producer in the world of coal, cement, grain, cotton, meat, and fish. It ranks third in steel production, after Japan and the United States, and fifth in crude oil output, after the United States, Saudi Arabia, Russia, and Iran.

—Nicholas D. Kristof, "China's Rush to Riches," *New York Times Magazine*

Viewed from a distance, such changes seem wondrous, but up close the story turns out to be messier and more complicated. Like the dark, satanic mills of William Blake's "Jerusalem," the Chinese economic miracle has been a deranging process and an ecological disaster, as demonstrated by the chemical blast in Shenzhen in August 1992 that killed an estimated seventy people and destroyed eight warehouses. In some places air quality is the worst to be found on earth. To make way for cities erected in a matter of months, mountains are being moved, rice paddies filled in, forests cleared—a process that has caused devastating floods in south China. The dynamo of capitalism has been loosed, and the "creative destruction" that economist Joseph Schumpeter called the defining feature of 19th-century American capitalism is on display in the China of 1993. It is a sight the likes of which few people alive today have seen.

There was once a time when all American cityscapes looked like south China's new industrial zones—most of us in the West live at the relatively tranquil terminus of a very messy economic process that had its start in a raw cityscape like Shenzhen or Guangzhou. Here is street after street of large, new factory buildings—structures similar to the factories I grew up with in Massachusetts, factories that fell into dereliction after World War II. Fall River had them, and so did New Bedford, Lawrence, and Brockton; they still have them, but the structures have been revived now as "factory outlets," selling designer-label Chinese-made goods. The cities of south China are functioning versions of the towns that are familiar to anyone who has lived in an urban area in Europe or America where the factories are now empty and the machines have stopped. Not just Boston and Chicago, but Bradford and Manchester in England, and Derry in Northern Ireland, and so many others. They have shut down.

China is succeeding because China is at work. The world has put the country to work and has invested in it, and the world has received a return on its investment. Most people reading this article are wearing a Chinese shirt, or sweater, or trousers, or pair of shoes. "Traditional" English baskets are Chinese. Carved Christmas decorations are Chinese. Our do-it-yourself tools, hammers and screwdrivers and socket wrenches, are Chinese. Our children's toys are Chinese. Our bikes. High-fashion beaded dresses are Chinese. Ninja Turtles are Chinese. The tires on our cars are Chinese. Many of the Japanese electronic goods we buy are actually assembled in China. The Chinese sell AK-47 semiautomatic rifles to wholesale buyers for $200 per unit, making war all over the world cheap, deadly, and endless. In recent years China has sold Silkworm missiles to Iraq, and in August 1992 was suspected by the Clinton Administration to be shipping the chemicals used to produce mustard and nerve gas to Iran. The Chinese sell tin pots in African countries and baseball caps in America and, ever since the pit closures in Britain, might well be shipping coals to Newcastle. There is hardly a gift shop in America that is not stocked from top to bottom with candles and carvings from the many kitsch-producing provinces in China. Those pretty masks and doormats and mailboxes and Santa Clauses and almost-Hummels and porcelain dragons and classic cars that are so sensibly priced in any Olde Worlde Gyfte Shoppe? They're from China. And so, too, are high-tech aircraft parts now being made in Fujian Province, a place that for 6,000 years was known only for its cork paintings and oolong tea.

"In the 19th century," Michael Lind recently wrote in *The National Interest*, "corporations in European lands of settlement would actually import coolie labor from China and India by the thousands to compete with home-country nationals for jobs, driving down wage rates. In the 21st century, corporations may take the jobs to the coolies, as it were, rather than bringing the coolies to the jobs."

The Chinese dragon, scorned in the Maoist era as a superstitious symbol, is China's favorite creature, one of its friendliest and most enduring guardian figures—a good omen representing power and prosperity. Now the dragon had risen again. It was breathing fire. I wanted to see it....

Suddenly, on a road in eastern Guangdong—all bulldozers and buffaloes—my driver, Li Zhong Ming, veered left and began driving on the wrong side of the road. Was it the freshly dismembered human corpse, all its separate parts splashed Chinese red, scattered widely like a load of fresh pork off the back of a truck on our side of the highway—and the ensuing traffic jam—that made him do it? No. Mr. Li *liked* spinning the steering wheel and whipping over to face the oncoming traffic. He had hardly glanced at the mutilated body. "This is quicker," he said. Of course, the risks were enormous—trucks and buses bore down on us head-on—but he got in front of everyone with an eat-my-dust expression on his face, his teeth ajar in aggression.

> *The concept of emperor in China is intimately associated with that of the dragon. China's dragons, guardians of the throne, are unlike those of the West. They are benign and protective but can turn like terrible emperors on the people. If they do so, it is the fault of the people, not the dragons. They breathe fire and thrash their tail only if betrayed, a convenient concept for an emperor.*
>
> —Harrison E. Salisbury,
> *The New Emperors: China in the Era of Mao and Deng*

Mr. Li was so persistent I began to think of his driving on the wrong side (and the carnage on the right one, of the numerous auto accidents I saw in an average day) as a metaphor for modernized China. He booted our assembled-in-China Audi down the main road to Shantou (old Swatow), past the red hills being shoveled apart and bulldozed to use for filling rice fields and making room for tenements and factories. The entire landscape was being leveled for hundreds of miles, and when it began to rain, water coursed down the clawed, eroded hills, washing silt into the sewers and flooding the roads, causing another traffic jam.

Into the wrong lane Mr. Li went again, playing chicken with oncoming dump trucks and tractors and bikes. He did not dodge them. He just blew his horn and surged forward against the flow of cockeyed headlights. Bolstering Mr. Li in his luck was a portrait of Mao Zedong on his dashboard. This gesture, wholly nonpolitical, was a recent fetish for drivers in China. Just a year before, a taxi driver in Beijing claimed in the *People's Daily* that he had been spared in a car crash, in which there had been many fatalities, because he had kept a picture of the old man on his dashboard. Many Chinese drivers began using the picture for spiritual protection. This reminded me of the images of St. Christopher that I saw in cars when I was growing up in Massachusetts in the 1950s.

Mao kitsch is popular in China again. You can buy Mao badges and Mao portraits, and embroidered knickknacks of the great man in baggy pants. His speeches are back in print. I often thought of them, of one in particular, his "Report on an Investigation of the Peasant Movement in Hunan," written in 1927, after he had traveled around the countryside, noting abuses, jotting down wisdom, and making suggestions. That was what I told myself I was doing now—simply looking around, gathering impressions for my "Report on the Factory Workers of Guangdong and Fujian in this Era of Chinese Prosperity." And, in fact, I was traveling to the music of Mao. In a dusty shop in a small town in rural Guangdong I had bought some Mao playing cards and some Mao cassettes. *Memories of Mao* was playing on Mr. Li's tape deck, the tuneful "Dong Fang Hong":

The East is Red!
The sun rises!
China produces Mao Zedong!

We passed two men on a big red 350-cc joint-venture Wy Yang-Honda motorcycle, and the man on the rear seat was talking wildly into a cellular phone—making a deal without a helmet at 70 miles an hour. Gunning his engine, Mr. Li was happy. And everywhere I looked I saw ruined hills and abandoned paddy fields and bamboo scaffolding where just months before there had been bamboo groves. These were the only landscape features apart from the freshly robbed graves, one of the more recent growth industries in rural China (ancient artifacts such as pots and clay animal figures are unearthed to smuggle and sell for good prices in Hong Kong), and the odd forlorn pagoda, almost certainly doomed. But nothing ancient, nothing notable, nothing but new brown, crumbly buildings— factories and tenements—rising from the filled-in rice fields.

I penetrated farther east into Guangdong, beyond the red hills and paddy fields and stands of bamboo, the muddy ditches and hot boulders, the haunts of snakes and eels and lizards and frogs, pop- ular in the restaurants in these parts. In spite of all the new wealth, some things in China never change: the small side roads made by hand, squatting people pounding the asphalt flat with mallets; the rice-growing process—women scooping water into the ter- races using large wooden ladles, others bent double planting the rice shoots, the men plowing with buffaloes, up to their knees in water. We passed cyclists transporting squealing pigs or lengths of steel reinforcing rods on their bike racks, and edge-of-town dump pickers, usually a man and a boy, studiously sorting junk into piles—glass, metal, rags, paper. There were barefoot men kneeling by the side of the road welding metal without masks or eye pro- tection, sparks flying; on the highest and most ambitious buildings, men erecting scaffolding of poles and tying them together with string or split cane stands instead of using metal clips; gardeners lugging heavy buckets on yokes and watering their beautiful veg- etable gardens; men fishing for tiddlers in canals. "The principle of diligence and frugality should be observed in everything," Mao said, though it hardly needed saying.

Although I have a basic grasp of *Putonghua*—Mandarin—I was traveling with a translator in case the conversation became abstract or contentious. We came to a town. What was its name?

"I don't know," my driver answered.

We asked. It was Bou Lou.

"It was just a small place last year."

It would be a city next year.

We then passed what appeared to be a movie set, all bamboo scaffolding and rising buildings, another city being created in the middle of nowhere, with an archway lettered WELCOME TO ZHANG MOU TOU.

"So this is Zhang Mou Tou," I said as we drove through the flying dust. "It's not on the map."

"It is new."

Last year it existed as a mud-and-buffalo rice-growing village of ten huts. The buildings are rising, and to fill in the rice fields they have had to pull down all the surrounding hills, an amazing sight, just like the Maoist fable, quoted in the Little Red Book, of "The Foolish Old Man Who Removed the Mountains."

It was on the road that I had a vision of the new strangeness of China. Perhaps it was the twilight, perhaps it was the dust. Whatever, it was the apparition of a city-in-the-making. For days I had been seeing additions, enlargements, new subdivisions, and districts, but this was something else—skeletal, unfinished, all of it brown with blown dust and dried mud. Everything was being built at once—the roads, the pedestrian bridges, the apartment houses, the factories, the stores. The buildings were 30 or 40 stories high and still clad in spindly scaffolding. Because of the time of day, twilight, no one was working, and only workers were involved in this. No one lived here. Except for detour arrows, there were no signs. There was no color, nothing alert or alive. I had never seen anything like it in China, or the world, a whole city under construction, and what made it strangest of all was that no heavy machinery was in evidence—no bulldozers, no cranes, just the odd wheelbarrow or ladder and the stitched-together scaffolding covering every structure and making the city seem fragile. We drove through, looking for someone to ask about it— perhaps its name. But there was no one around. Then it was behind us.

But this was south China. In a short time—months maybe—the town would be inhabited and brightly lit.

As soon as you get to China you hear the success stories. Everyone tells them, affirming the Chinese miracle. The $8-a-week driver for the company in Shanghai who spent his nights at the free market flogging defective shirts with designer labels, used the profit to get involved in a joint venture, and is now making $60,000 a year and is the owner of a house in Australia, having paid for it in cash by sending his cousin to Sydney with the purchase price in a brown paper bag. Or the man who recognized a need for cycle helmets. His were very cheap, because his were very unsafe—just a plastic shell, but never mind, you could have one for ten *yuan*. This entrepreneur became a multimillionaire and prospered until he died in what was described to me as "a bizarre fishing accident." Foreigners tell these stories even more than the Chinese, and always in a tone of admiration and amazement, because anyone who was in China ten or more years ago knows that this bountiful place exploded from a monochrome country of faded clothes and gruel, a scrimping, saving, mend-and-make-do society of toiling comrades. These days, however, the stories are of decadence and wealth: "Last year ten new Rolls-Royces were imported into Guangdong by Chinese businessmen—"

"The most popular dish in Canton these days is lobster sashimi—"

"There's a massage parlor in Shenzhen staffed entirely by Russian girls—"

"There is a Chinese businessman in Zhuhai who buys ten bottles at a time of Louis XIII brandy, and it costs thousands of dollars a bottle—"

"It's a feeding frenzy—"

Some of the new fortunes are now made at the China Export Commodities Fair in Guangzhou, often called the Canton Trade Fair. The first official fair was held in 1957. A frenetic bazaar, the fair fills one of the largest buildings in Guangzhou. The trade fair was once the only way foreign businessmen could do business in

China, since they were forbidden to pass beyond the Guangzhou threshold into China. These days foreigners travel to factories around China to place their orders, and yet the trade fair remains the main focus of Chinese commerce. Here, buyers for Western corporations, middlemen, suppliers, and even individuals converge, buying goods by the container-load. In past years the fair's areas have been demarcated by varieties of merchandise—carpets here, electrical appliances there, hairpieces and bikes over here, and so forth. But this year, for the first time, the fair's stalls and stands were divided by provinces: Jiangxi here, Shandong there, Inner Mongolia right down the stairs. It costs about ten dollars to register as a delegate and have your picture inserted into an I.D. badge, and the rest is easy, like a long vulgar trek browsing through the biggest market on earth, a gift shop almost without end.

In the lobby is a musical fountain, with lights flashing to the piano of Richard Clayderman playing "Don't Cry for Me, Argentina." The buyers are bussed in from their hotels; they are mainly huge sweating men and feverish-looking women from all over the world, squinting and poker-faced, like most bargain hunters.

"Zis bench grinder—tell him I want two sousand pieces," a Frenchman is saying to his interpreter.

"When these shirts arrive Lebanon?" a Levantine woman is saying.

A man is buying an orange lifeboat, another haggling over cotton baseball caps made in Shanghai, which cost $7 a dozen, at 1,000 dozen per color, minimum order.

A German is ordering sleeping bags, made in Tianjin in a factory that employs 2,400 workers. Two million are exported annually, a great number to Germany. The wholesale price for these well-designed ones—warm, light, easily compressible—is $11.80 a bag.

I drifted over to a stall where a sign read FOSHON HARDWARE & PLASTIC FACTORY, and in this one small space I saw fishing rods (eight sizes), mortise door locks, hammocks, pipe joints, cups, plastic flowers, brake shoes, welding electrodes, hinges, washers, faucets, windshield wipers, spoons, small toy dogs that jumped and yapped, and an assortment of cigarette lighters—fifty or more—

one of which was a panther whose eyes lit up as its mouth expelled a jet of fire.

In other stalls you could get a floor-length raccoon coat for $418 (including delivery to California); a "Chinalight New Magnetic Massage Cushion" ($14); Black Dragon brand rollerblades made in the remote northern province of Heilongjiang ($13.60 a pair, delivered); a wig made of Chinese human hair, dyed blonde, Shirley Temple-style, for $10.25. A mountain bike was $50, cashmere scarves were $8, herbal remedies and surgical tools were all reasonably priced, and a Xing Fu 250-cc motorcycle was $663. The WuYang I had seen on the road with the passenger riding and talking on a cellular phone was $2,000 wholesale. There was every machine tool known to man. There were inflatable toys. There were more Virgin Marys and plaster saints and crucifixes than you would see in a whole year's pilgrimage in Italy.

I spent two days at the fair. My most productive time was spent at the tea stalls, where all the varieties of tea in China are displayed. My preferred type of tea is Long Ching (Dragon Well), from Hangzhou. It is green tea, and its flat smooth leaves resemble the needles of a fir tree. "Why is this tea so expensive?" I asked the tea company's representative, Mr. Jin.

"This tea is picked in a small area," Mr. Jin said. "The best is found on just one hill. There are not many trees, the season is short, only two tons a month of the best quality are picked in the harvest season." I discovered it on my first visit to China in 1980 and have drunk it ever since, buying it in Friendship Stores or else in New York, where the best quality sells for $50 for a box of two cans. But "expensive" is an impression you get only if you buy it outside China. This same tea at the trade fair can be bought for roughly $2 a box from the China Tuhsu Zhejiang Tea Import-Export Corporation.

> *The best quality tea must have creases like the leathern boot of Tartar horsemen, curl like the dewlap of a mighty bullock, unfold like a mist rising out of a ravine, gleam like a lake touched by a zephyr, and be wet and soft like fine earth newly swept in by rain....*
>
> —Lu Yu

Walking through the exhibition hall, I came across a provincial stall selling herbal remedies, which included ginseng, royal jelly, anti-cancer pills (made of "myrrh, muschus, mastix, and calculus bovis"), and my eye was caught by something called "Love Solution." It had something to do with health and sex, and the box claimed that with it "100% of AIDS virus and chlamydia can be killed within two minutes." There was a spray version for men, a plunger for women.

Many of the products at the fair are lovely and finely made— the carpets, the embroideries, the lace, the silks. The tools are among the finest and cheapest in the world, and have put many American tool companies out of business. But if there is one business that the Chinese now monopolize worldwide it is Christmas decorations. Hardly a Santa or a hanging ball on earth is not produced in the People's Republic, and even the Christmas lights that were formerly made in Taiwan are now made in China, many of them in joint ventures with Taiwanese partners who are looking to find cheaper labor as wages have risen in Taiwan.

"Are they any good?" I asked an Italian, Mario from Modena, who was in Guangzhou for no other reason than to buy Christmas lights to sell in Italy.

"They are very good," he said. "They conform to Italian standards. They are cheap. It's perfect."

And he smiled.

"But this place"—and he made an Italianate gesture, his hands and face simultaneously expressive, to take in not only the fair but Guangzhou and perhaps the whole of China—"is 'orrible, eh?"

As the Chinese sometimes say when foreign business executives gush about the boom in their country: lu fen dan, biaomian guang—on the outside, even donkey droppings gleam.

—Nicholas D. Kristof and Sheryl WuDunn, *China Wakes: The Struggle for the Soul of a Rising Power*

Yet Mario knew better than to dismiss what was before us. We were talking about how China made everything and shipped it everywhere. "China," he said, "is the manufacturer for the world."

Browsing through items at the fair, I understood why the

Chinese are considered to be masters of the art of copyright in-
fringement and have found it an effective way to generate business,
make enormous profits, and earn hard currency. Despite being
closely monitored in Hong Kong by people representing the
brands and labels that are assiduously pirated, the infringers get
away with murder. "Take running shoes," a Hong Kong lawyer told
me. "It is a billion-dollar business. I am not exaggerating when I
say a billion. They make the shoes and label them NIKE or PUMA,
they put them in boxes printed MADE IN KOREA, and they ship
them all over the world."

The Chinese purloin trademarks and labels and logos willy-
nilly. You don't have to be in China very long to recognize the
rip-offs. Mickey Mouse is gallivanting all over China without a
license—on every conceivable consumer item—and sometimes
Mickey wears a curiously almond-eyed expression. The Playboy
bunny appears on any number of products without the approval of
Hugh Hefner. Knockoff Swiss Army knives are fairly common.
Lux soap has been popular in China for so long that there are a
dozen pirate versions, with the same colored wrapper and often
the same name or a similar one—"Lid," "Lix," "Lud," "Lus." These
items are exported to Africa and Southeast Asia, where they may
be found stacked near "Goldgate" toothpaste and "Rodigate"
toothpaste (the same Colgate colors, no relation), "Pepsi-Cola"
biscuits, or fake and almost unchewable Chiclets.

False labeling—especially regarding the label of origin—extends to clothing exported worldwide but especially to the United
States, which last year purchased four and a half billion dollars in
clothes and textiles from China, this despite certain quotas that are
reached by negotiation between the two countries. China's production far exceeds its quotas, so many Chinese products are given
labels such as MADE IN HAITI or MADE IN MONGOLIA and trans-
shipped through those places, the third-country connection, where
a fax machine in a dusty office may be the only apparent chinois-
erie. MADE IN MONGOLIA has been very popular on Chinese labels
because little is manufactured in that country of grasslands and
yaks and nomads.

★

Why is the MADE IN CHINA label now so commonplace? There are many reasons: the collapse of Eastern Europe and the fragmentation of the Soviet Union created new markets and diverted investment to China. The world recession inspired manufacturers to look for cheaper labor and more consumers—China, these businessmen discovered, not only can make electronics and Ninja Turtles at a fraction of the cost of making them elsewhere, for even less than in traditional cheap labor centers such as Taiwan and Korea and Hong Kong, but also can supply an immense new domestic market. That 70 percent of urban households in China now have color televisions and 81 percent have washing machines suggests a growing middle-class market; that there are 750 million people in China under the age of 35 foretells a 21st-century economic juggernaut. In 1992 the government approved 48,000 new foreign investment projects, and foreigners invested $11.2 billion in the country, up from $4.4 billion the year before.

So suddenly China is no longer a sprawling, monolithic gerontocracy of enigmatic ideologists but rather an enormous if somewhat clumsily businesslike place that inspires confidence among the world's venture capitalists.

Perhaps it is this simple: foreign investment was invited. Factories got built. The Chinese workers accepted the lowest wages in the world. They didn't argue. They were not religious. Because of their peculiar political indoctrination, they were totally materialistic. And they showed up on time.

As recently as 1971, Shenzhen was no more than a railway platform lettered SHUMCHUN twenty miles north of Hong Kong in

Robert Theleen's theme is investing with entrepreneurs in "Greater China"—by which he means the region of 120 million Chinese encompassing Taiwan, Hong Kong, and China's two southern provinces of Guangdong and Fujian, all of which are rapidly becoming one integrated economy. "You can't find a better model for growth than the overseas Chinese entrepreneurial mind," asserts Theleen, a professorial former banker. To put it another way: invest in people, not in fixed assets.

—Andrew Tanzer, "Greater China, Greater Profits," *Forbes*

the province of Guangdong. In 1980, I described it in my diary as
a wilderness of barricades and barbed wire; it had just been designated a Special Economic Zone. Now an ancient-seeming metropolis, Shenzhen is vast, with a railroad station almost as large as
New York's Grand Central and scores of hotels. It is a city of 2.5
million, nearly the population of Hong Kong, and sprawling in all
directions. Looking older than its years, the city is as famous for
its prosperity and buoyant stock market as it is notorious for its
massage parlors and prostitutes, its organized (and approved) gambling, its bustling streets and busy factories brilliantly lit by blinking signs. On a visit to Shenzhen in 1992 Deng had said, famously,
"I like this."

Mao's legacy is all those communes and collective farms that
have been reconstituted as manufacturing villages or else plowed
under, their people dispersed to find their niche in the labor market. Deng's creation is Shenzhen, for he set into play the forces that
allowed its seemingly spontaneous birth. Deng is often rumored to
be near death. His face appeared on a billboard in Shenzhen looking ghostly and cadaverous. A lifelong chain-smoker who has carried an oxygen bottle for the past eight years, he has emphysema,
which was evident in his sucked-in checks and popping eyes. On the
billboard he was making an admonishing gesture with his fingers:

> If you don't adhere to the Socialist Road
> If you don't follow the Reforms
> If you don't develop the economy
> If you don't improve your livelihood
> Then the only way for you is death.

In a simplified history, China's prosperity may be charted by the
rise of Deng, whom from an early stage Mao had sniffed out as a
"capitalist roader." Later, Deng was described with more elaborate
contempt as "an arch unrepentant capitalist roader and harbinger
of the right deviationist wind." Yet this comrade in arms turned
pariah is someone who, politically speaking, came back from the
dead—and not once but three times.

One of the many goals of the Cultural Revolution was to rusticate the bureaucrats and "class traitors," to sweep aside such bourgeois notions as modernization, and take the starch out of the people who had become known as revisionists. Deng, the son of well-to-do landlords, was put under house arrest. One of his sons, Deng Pufang, is said to have been thrown or dropped out of a fourth-story window (he is still in a wheelchair).

After the death of Zhou Enlai in 1976, an event that provoked greater grief and more intense emotion in China than the death of Mao later that same year, the Maoist Gang of Four were arrested for conspiracy. They were blamed for (among many other things) the excesses of the Cultural Revolution, and Deng was reinstated to the party and to all his posts by the Eleventh Party Congress in 1977. In 1979 and 1980, Deng consolidated his power and put his friends and like-minded associates and bridge partners and hatchet men in key posts.

Any illusion that Deng was a high-minded Jeffersonian at odds with the forces of Marxist-Leninist darkness was shattered in 1980, when, for political convenience, he proposed deleting the four freedoms from the 1978 constitution: speaking out freely, airing views fully, holding debates, and writing big-character posters, the traditional form of political protest. Deng's proposal was endorsed in the fifth plenum in 1980.

In the same year, Deng established the Statute of Joint Venture and the new Commission for Foreign Investment. Although business with the outside world had been going on since the visit by Richard Nixon in 1972, these two policy changes marked the beginning of contemporary China's prosperity. They meant that foreign companies could start factories in China with Chinese partners, that capital and technology could be easily transferred, and, perhaps most important, that foreign loans (both government and private) were permitted. Just as crucial, it meant that business affairs were decentralized. Now foreign businessmen could negotiate directly with factories, bypassing the bureaucracy (and bribery) entailed when every deal had once had to be routed through the ministries in Beijing.

With this start of China's Open Door Policy came some practical steps to develop China. One was the concept of Special Economic Zones—sealed zones where foreigners could transact business without stinking up the rest of the country with their decadent or subversive notions. Special money also was created, not *ren-minbi* (people's money) but Foreign Exchange Certificates. So, just over the Hong Kong border station of Lowu, in a village on the railway line fringed by bamboo groves, at a place then known in its Cantonese form as Shumchun, a new city was planned.

Stung by the ferocity of the Cultural Revolution, and receiving mixed signals from the right and the left of the party, the Chinese people were at first tentative in carrying out Deng's exhortations. His cry "To get rich is glorious!" remained little more than a yearning. What I saw in China in 1986 and 1987 was mainly confusion, tentative movement toward a free market, and severe official punishment for crime (10,000 people were executed for various crimes between 1983 and 1986). After the 1989 Tiananmen Square massacre, it appeared that China was in the economic doldrums. This was an illusion. As we now know, a serious businessman is unlikely to be deterred by a little thing like a massacre.

Deng himself was unrepentant about the killings. "Kill a chicken to scare the monkeys," he said, quoting a Chinese proverb to justify the massacre he had ordered. It is a standard military tactic in Sun Tzu's *The Art of War* to hack a soldier to pieces in front of his regiment in order to make a vivid and memorable point about discipline. The feebler the pretext, the sterner the lesson. Deng is often described as "pragmatic." His desire to host the Summer Olympics in the year 2000 was strictly to give China an aura of international respectability and had nothing to do with the Olympic ideals of fair play and brotherhood. Mao, by contrast had a sort of monstrous style. He was a romantic, a poet, almost Byronic, and yet someone who rather enjoyed his reputation as a demonic manipulator. He was happy to hand power to the Red Guards and turn the country upside down for ten years just to see what would happen. Deng is without charisma—doesn't have it, doesn't want it. No cult of personality has grown up around him, nor will it in what remaining time he has left. His briskness and frankness are a reaction to the time-wasting and secrecy of the past. Mao—arrogant, ruthless, serene—was an emperor whose image was iconographic. Deng is a sort of blandly non-ideological CEO and is almost faceless. One of his main dictums of reform is "Tight on the inside, loose on the outside."

I went to the market in Shenzhen with a friend of a friend, Mr. Lu, who told me, "I would much rather live here than in Hong Kong. I have a larger apartment here than I would have in Hong Kong. Shenzhen is cleaner and better organized."

When I asked Mr. Lu about his family he said, "They were very red," meaning they'd had power but no money, had never been landowners, and were party members. I took this to indicate that their credentials were perfect during the Cultural Revolution. Mr. Lu said this was so. I asked him whether he had been active himself—he was 48, just the right age. He said yes. Had he been a Red Guard? He said yes.

"What was your unit?" I asked.

"Revolutionary Revolt—the reddest," he said, and smiled, as though having been a member of this fanatical ultra-leftist unit had been a youthful indiscretion. Mr. Lu had been teaching English in 1966, but after being subjected to intense self-criticism (essays, confessions, recitations), he had become a Red Guard. His unit fought regularly with other units, mostly throwing chairs at one another, over which unit was the truest guardian of Mao's thought.

> *The global economy is sometimes said to be tripolar, revolving around the United States, Japan, and the European Community. But Greater China is rapidly becoming a fourth pole, a new pillar of the international economy. According to to World Bank projections using comparable international prices, Greater China in the year 2002 is projected to have a gross domestic product of $9.8 trillion, compared with $9.7 trillion in the same year for the United States. If those forecasts hold, Greater China would not just be another economic pole. It would be the biggest of them all.*
>
> —Nicholas D. Kristof,
> "China's Rush to Riches,"
> *The New York Times Magazine*

In 1969, Mr. Lu was chosen as a model Red Guard, having worked for a year at a lathe, making parts for machine tools, in a factory in the countryside. Machine tools during the day, Marxist-Leninist study at night. He was selected to be a propagandist, traveling the country, galvanizing Red Guard units, and leading political pep rallies from Mongolia to Shanghai. In his spare time he studied revolutions around the world. Then, when foreign visitors began arriving, Mr. Lu, whose English was now an asset, was appointed to take them around. Many were well known. John Kenneth Galbraith was one.

Just after Deng took control, Mr. Lu was sent to study in the United States and Canada, and that experience, the sight of prosperity, transformed him. "It was the way people lived," he said. "I wanted that for us." Mr. Lu became a passionate reformer. In June 1989 he was at the barricades in Tiananmen Square. "It was too bad that some students died," he said, obviously chastened by the violence. "But that is the past. We have to be optimistic."

I asked him about the man whose speeches had incited the students, Professor Fang Lizhi, now in the United States.

"The great number of Chinese people don't care about his ideas. He is better off in America, anyway—he is more American than Chinese."

Mr. Lu seemed the perfect person to walk around Shenzhen with. He was small and slight of build but he said that, having been through the Cultural Revolution, he was not daunted by any adversity, whether it was walking a long distance or carrying a heavy load. As we passed the railway station, I mentioned that we could nip through the turnstiles, hop on a train at Lowu, and be drinking a beer in Hong Kong is less than an hour. I had made the trip myself from the other direction one rainy morning—caught the subway train outside the Sheraton Hong Kong, changed trains in Kowloon Tong, and was at the border before I had finished reading the *South China Morning Post*. I had gotten back to Hong Kong Central in time for lunch. ("I wouldn't mind seeing China," the English poet Philip Larkin had said, "if I could come back the same day." That was now possible.)

"I don't like Hong Kong," Mr. Lu said. "It's too crowded."

"Is it too full of *gweilos*?" I asked, meaning foreigners.

Mr. Lu laughed politely, so I asked him about something that had been on my mind for a while. If he happened to be with another Chinese person and one of them called attention to an American in the distance, would they normally use the term "foreign devil"? ("That foreign devil is very tall," for example.)

"Yes. If he was a man. If it was a woman we would say *gweibo*."

"Devil-woman."

"So to speak." There were, however, no *gweilos* here, no tourists at all. Why would they come here? I had seen no tourists in Guangzhou. None in the pro-vincial towns. There was a park in Shenzhen, but it was not for foreigners; it was for the Chinese, a China theme park, Splendid China, with replicas of every "sight" in China: a Great Wall section, a temple, a pagoda, a group of terra-cotta warriors, and so forth. Tourists, I realize, are an irrelevance in these economic zones; there is no place for them, everything moves too quickly for them, and really, there is nothing to see.

The term hua-ch'iao *is almost always rendered as "overseas Chinese" and employed to refer broadly to all Chinese living outside China, but its epitome or model was a sojourner who enjoyed the protection of the Chinese government (through its embassies or consulates), and who lived in spirit in China, politically, culturally, and emotionally attached to his mother country. The notion was of comparatively recent coinage, and the pattern it embodies had its heyday in the period between about 1900 and 1950, the years of overseas Chinese nationalist upsurge.*

When a Chinese called himself a hua-ch'iao, *he did so with pride, for it signified his inclusion in the great Chinese political family; he was somebody that the Chinese government recognized for one of its own and, what was more, somebody whose money and expertise China needed and courted.*

—Lynn Pan, *Sons of the Yellow Emperor: The Story of the Overseas Chinese*

The Shenzhen market covered six acres or more. At the butchers' stalls the cheapest meat was chicken at $1.20 a catty (500 grams), beef was $1.20, pork was $1.40, dog was $1.75, and snake was $18.75. The dogmeat section of the market was no different from any of the others—a series of long stone slabs smeared with blood, with blood-flecked Chinese working their cleavers through stringy bone joints. The creatures themselves were either gutted and strung up on hooks or else piled in cuts, and even headless they were recognizable as dogs, from their long narrow muscles and their lean haunches.

It was said of Hong Kong long ago that by its acquisition the Victorians had cut a notch in the body of China, as a woodman cuts a notch in a great oak he is presently going to fell. But the oak has never fallen, and actually Hong Kong no longer feels an alien mark upon the coast of China: it has been notched there too long, it is too Chinese itself, its affairs have been too inextricably linked with those of China, and its return to the great presence, however ominous or bewildering the circumstances, seems only natural.

—Jan Morris, *Hong Kong*

As I drifted around the city with him, it was clear that Mr. Lu had put his Red Guard past behind him. He was proud of this proliferation of factories and housing blocks. Shenzhen was undoubtedly the best organized city in China. The authorities tried to keep crime to a minimum—although this had become a major challenge. Eighty-two men in Shenzhen had recently been stripped of their party membership for being "prostitution patrons" (and a "half-year re-education" was also part of their punishment). But young women still quietly solicited in many bars—they wore the current Chinese hooker fashion of very short shorts, once known in America by the evocative name "hot pants." The women were pretty. There were brothels too, many of them using the cover of barbershops ("I got suspicious when my husband needed a haircut every day," a wife says in a current Shenzhen joke). The women did not bother Mr. Lu. He called them "flies."

"If you open a window, you get some flies," he said, and he might have been quoting one of Deng's speeches. Whenever we saw something decadent or jarring in Shenzhen, Mr. Lu said, with the Chinese gift for euphemism, "More flies."

One night in Shenzhen Mr. Lu and I were in a restaurant that at ten o'clock was abruptly turned into a disco, the sort of place that would have been unthinkable in Maoist times, when one could be sent to a pig farm in Mongolia for listening to Western music. There we were, talking about the future of Hong Kong over our shrimp and bamboo shoots, and the lights dimmed and young men began setting out sound equipment and tuning their guitars.

"Hong Kong will be handed over. China will give no assurances. These people in Hong Kong who are asking for elections and referendums are wasting their time," Mr. Lu was saying.

Then the lights were dimmed, the youths appeared, and the music started; and it was so loud we could not hear each other. The guitarists wore silver joggings suits, the lead singer was in blue. I recognized one or two of the songs—Michael Jackson was obviously popular here. Then the singer started hectoring the audience and waving green slips of paper.

"What's he saying?"

"He's asking for requests."

The idea was that you would write down your request and hand it over to him. I took a slip of paper.

"I have a request. I want him to sing 'Dong Fang Hong.'"

Mr. Lu, delighted, copied down the Chinese characters and we passed it to the singer, who glanced at it and called out to his musicians. And without batting an eyelash, he began marching in step and singing "*Dong fang hong! Tai yang shang.*"

The East is Red!
The sun rises!
China produces Mao Zedong!
He works for the happiness of the people
He is the savor of the Chinese people
The East is Red!

When the musician was finished, he went back to singing rock songs.

✳

When countries modernize these days, they become Americanized, and often lose their cultural identity. China is the exception. The more China develops, the more it seems to be turning back into old China, just as regional and unequal, ambitious, busily self-sufficient, and hard to read as China in the Tang dynasty. As it modernizes, it reveals a greater complexity and a deeper Chineseness. And yet there are differences. Whereas the old China was informed by Confucianism and, in some places, Christianity, China now seems totally materialistic, cannier, wiser, even selfish. The provinces of Guangdong and Fujian may have the oily, muddy look of old China, but except for filial piety they have few of China's old reverences, the Confucian virtues of refinement, gentleness, decency, and good order. And there are the throwbacks that show in something as simple as tipping. In Maoist times it was not done. Then, with the tourists and businessmen of the 1980s, some tips were given. Now in the 1990s a tip is expected when a transaction takes place or service is given. There can be a real ugliness when a tip is not offered, and there is a new permutation—for many services the tip comes before any act is performed. In a very short time in China tipping has turned into

A new civilization is in the making. It is, like all the grand enduring eras in the chronicles of human endeavor, a hybrid creation. From Aryan India to the Roman Empire, from Genghis Khan's Beijing to Suleiman the Magnificent's Constantinople, the civilizations that flourished for centuries were vibrant blends of different cultures. Now Asia and America are fusing into a commonality of shared goals and values that will create the next century's great arc of peace and prosperity. Whether "Asia-merica" is formalized by today's leaders or their successors is not all that important. Nothing can stop it. America is turning its back on Europe and tumbling into the arms of a waiting Asia. Meanwhile, Asia is opening to the intellectual vigor of the Americas. Politically, economically, commercially, socially, culturally, the Pacific is evaporating. Soon it will be as easily stepped over by a Chinese in Los Angeles as an American in Hong Kong.

—Asiaweek

bribery. Or is it bribery? After all, this is the East. Perhaps a tip has turned back into what it has been in this hemisphere for thousands of years—*baksheesh*, not a reward, but merely the cost of doing business.

The pressure to get things done quickly has bred crime. With bad roads and slow services and backed-up deliveries, grease helps. Many people I spoke to in China, foreign and Chinese alike, said that grease was an absolute necessity for a smooth business operation. Their view was that prosperity without crime is almost unthinkable. Corruption is not new in China, but it has become pervasive, and China's biggest single social problem will continue to be crime. The triads, crime syndicates, and secret societies that flourished in China for centuries and seemed to be stamped out have returned, many from Hong Kong and Taiwan, where the ritualistic brotherhoods and protection rackets were reconstituted. And the highwaymen and cat burglars are back. As recently as seven or eight years ago, you could with confidence have sent your seventeen-year-old daughter traipsing all over China alone. No longer. China has become unsafe; I feel it is likely to become even less safe. But then, it was for thousands of years a country famous for its defensive perimeters—behind the Great Wall were more walls, walled compounds and fortified cities. These days, look at any new housing development of condominiums or apartments or single-family dwellings and you will see high perimeter walls.

Outside these walls there are the poor, some of them predatory, most of them simply pathetic. They are the rural poor of subsistence farmers in neglected provinces that have never known prosperity in the whole of Chinese history. It is doubtful that life will change for them. In the cities the struggle will go on, but such extreme class divisions will re-create even more of the old China, more conspicuous wealth and ownership and a deeper oppression, of which the client and his prostitute are just one version, and the factory owner and his sweatshop are another. No one owned gold in Maoist China—there was none to buy—but before Liberation, the Chinese had always been great buyers of gold and jewelry. The habit is back and was one of the factors in the spectacular worldwide rise in the price of gold in the first half of 1993. It is not

greed; it is another technique of survival, a Chinese way of concentrating wealth, protecting against inflation, and hoarding against
the inevitable hard times ahead. Deng, they know, is not long for
this world. His chosen successors are, like him, believers in economic progress, not political change. But it remains to be seen
whether they prevail.

In the past, whenever times were bad, in periods of famine or
war or repression, the Chinese—the most portable of people—
picked up a small bundle of their belongings and fled for their
safety and well-being. Not all Chinese have gold in their little bundles, but some do. The others pay it in advance to men who smuggle them out of China and into other countries. As recent events
have shown, even in a time of Chinese prosperity, people wish to
leave China, many of them for the United States. China's growth
and destabilization may come to have important consequences
here. American immigration officials estimate that as many as
80,000 undocumented Chinese are arriving each year on America's
shores, and the number is rising.

Until recently, Chinese life was not so much engimatic as unknown. We did not have a clear perception of Chinese stubbornness,
tenacity, or materialism; the Chinese lack of illusions; their strong
sense of family; their powerful survival instinct; their hatred of
complainers; their passion for secrecy. More than any people I have
ever come across, the Chinese are obsessive about living in the present. They don't look back, because in the strange interplay of light
and shadow, splendor and misery, of their history, there is too much
to look back upon—and so it is fatal to be sentimental. Chinese
life is both active and hesitant, like a creature being pursued, now
in motion, now stopped and tremulous, never at rest, always alert.

The Chinese clock has a tick unlike any other on earth, sometimes fast, sometimes slow, contracting, expanding, with an alarm
that might go off at any moment. We Americans expect tomorrow
to be pretty much like today, and perhaps a little better. We find
it strange that a people should perpetually anticipate disasters. But
then, 6,000 years of disasters have made the Chinese skepitcal and
somewhat untrusting. These days everyone speaks of the Chinese

miracle, but when has the world taken much notice of Chinese catastrophes, of which the Japanese rape and plunder of China before and during World War II and the earthquake that instantly killed a quarter of a million Chinese in 1976 are but two instances? The Chinese people know they cannot count on the future, since "future" in Chinese terms might mean a brutal decree or sudden reversal enacted in the dark hours of tomorrow morning. What they are doing now was illegal yesterday, and might be proscribed once again. Understanding the uniqueness of the Chinese clock, you begin to get an inkling of Chinese hope and the attentiveness of Chinese labor. Their sense of survival is not a racial but a political imperative, for Chinese life is full of instances of people who lingered and looked back and were lost, overwhelmed and buried by one avalanche or another in their country's long, unpredictable history.

Paul Theroux is the author of many works, among them travel books such as The Great Railway Bazaar, The Old Patagonian Express, Riding the Iron Rooster, *and* The Happy Isles of Oceania, *and the novels* The Mosquito Coast, My Secret History, *and* Millroy the Magician.

*

A loose list of Chinese inventions from earliest times in fact covers an astonishing variety of everyday gadgets and their working principles. When the Roman legions were still in Britain, the Chinese were making wheelbarrows (which did not appear in Europe for another thousand years), watermills, seed-sowing mechanisms, and crank-operated rotary-fan winnowing machines that were not to be seen in the West until 600 years later. In A.D. 132, the Chinese produced the first seismograph. On the cylindrical outer casing of this "earthquake weathercock" were eight dragon heads, each one facing toward one of the eight divisions of the compass, while beneath it squatted one of eight open-mouthed toads that sat in a ring around the instrument. Suspended inside the casing, it appears, was a pendulum which was connected by levers to each of the dragon heads and could therefore move in the direction of any one of the points of the compass. When there was an earthquake, the pendulum tipped in the direction of the tremor and tilted the dragon's head that pointed in the same way, whereupon the dragon vomited a ball into the mouth of the toad below. Earthquakes which no one had felt were recorded in this way.

—Dennis Bloodworth, *The Chinese Looking Glass*

PART FOUR

IN THE SHADOWS

ISABEL TAYLOR ESCODA

✦ ✦ ✦

In a Hong Kong Prison

A broadcaster uncovers a very personal story of street crime.

I WENT TO JAIL LAST SUNDAY. AN ENGLISHWOMAN I KNOW SENT me there. Hong Kong's Victoria Prison is not far from my small flat, up a hill in the colony's Central District. Around the prison block are art galleries, antique and furniture shops, and on the same street as the jail entrance, down the hill a bit, is a cozy French restaurant.

I went to Victoria Prison not just because my friend Ann Smyth (not her real name) told me to visit one of my compatriots, but because I was curious. I'd never been in a jail before even though I could have gone some years ago. This was when a British photographer had rung me up saying he had heard me during my radio broadcasts. He was desperate—his Filipino girlfriend was locked up in Victoria Prison for having overstayed her visa.

I was flattered that anyone would think I could intervene in such a case, but I begged off, saying I was nobody, just someone who talked about the Philippines over Hong Kong radio. I didn't pretend to possess any clout with the Hong Kong Government, which is notoriously biased against Filipinos.

I didn't get to see the jail then, so now was my chance. I was also curious about my compatriot because I had seen her downtown soon after she had committed her "crime."

I stood in line outside the prison gate, with a group of Chinese waiting to visit the inmates. Once inside the gate I handed over my ID card and told the officer I wanted to see Clara Cruz (not her real name). I was told to go to the next room where a young, stern-faced woman officer asked if I had made an appointment. I said no, but that my friend Ann Smyth had told me I could go anytime.

"I'm sorry," the officer said flatly. "You cannot see her."

"Oh please," I begged (Ann had told me to act abject—"kiss her boots, if need be, they enjoy that"). "I am going to Manila tomorrow and I want to tell her mother I've seen her." I was lying, of course.

After consulting with another officer, she told me I had special permission this once, and I was made to wait twenty minutes after writing down my name, address, and ID number. Then I was ushered into the "Open Visiting Room" and told I had fifteen minutes (everyone gets only that amount of time).

There were about a dozen square tables in the room, with people sitting and talking to the inmates. There was one woman inmate nursing a baby.

I recognized Clara at once. She was small and pretty but looked worn-out, sitting at one of the tables. She did not know me, of course. I sat down across from her and asked, *"Natandaan mo ba ako?"* (Do you remember me?) She shook her head. I noticed she had lipstick on and some eyeliner.

I refreshed her memory. Three weeks ago I had been walking along Des Voeux Road to go to an eye doctor. I suddenly came across a crowd of people on the sidewalk, all staring at two tall Europeans. I went closer and saw a European man talking into his mobile phone, "Please send the police to the corner of Des Voeux Road and Pedder Street immediately."

Next to him was a tall European woman. I edged closer and saw that between them was a small dark woman, with her arm firmly in the grip of the man speaking into his mobile phone. I asked a Chinese man in the crowd what it was all about. *"Filipanyan* pickpocket," he smirked as he walked away.

I went up to the European woman and asked, "What's going on?"

"This woman snatched my wallet," she replied. She sounded American but she could have been Canadian. The man sounded British.

Like an idiot, I addressed the poor frightened girl, "*Kinuba mo ba talaga ang wallet niya?*" (Did you really snatch her wallet?)

"*Hindi po*" (No, Ma'am), she replied and hung her head.

I've done some dumb things in my life, but this must have been the dumbest. It would have been like asking Imelda Marcos if she'd indeed stolen the nation's wealth—she'd deny it as surely as night follows day.

I hung around the crowd to see what would happen, and the police arrived soon after and took the girl away, with the couple following. I rushed off to my doctor's appointment.

Ann Smyth is, like myself, a longtime Hong Kong resident. I met her because she rang me up one day after someone who had read my book *Letters from Hong Kong* told her about me. Ann has been trying to help Filipino domestics in trouble in Hong Kong, and she is looking for other Filipino women to help with a project she has initiated.

Ever since she first called me up, we have chatted regularly and I have been amazed at her energy and resourcefulness. She is a mover and a shaker in the truest sense of the word, and she knows many people in the colony who can help her.

She has made me somewhat ashamed of the fact that it has taken an Englishwoman to do something to help disadvantaged Filipino women when there are a number of Filipinos in the colony, well-off and comfortable, who should be the ones helping their underprivileged compatriots. But, sadly, that small percentage of well-off *Pinays* in Hong Kong seem to hate the fact that most of their compatriots are servants and they like to pretend they don't exist. A number of these wealthy women regularly attend religious meetings, and they seem to think attending to spiritual matters is more important than caring for the material needs of their compatriots.

After witnessing the arrest of that pickpocket, I mentioned it in passing to Ann when we next spoke. "Oh please, Isabel," she said, "tell me where this happened and at what time. Did you get the girl's name?"

I said I hadn't. It hadn't occurred to me to ask—I'd only asked if she was guilty.

"I must find that poor girl," Ann said and rang off hurriedly.

At that point I shook my head. I knew Ann was a do-gooder possessed of a great big bleeding heart (she has worked among Ethiopian refugees and engaged in other philanthropic projects), but I thought she was going off the deep end when she said she'd track down the pickpocket without even knowing her name.

The next day she rang me up to say she'd found the girl, learned her name, and was on her way to visit her at a remand center in the New Territories. This is where they detain people before they are charged and sentenced.

"How on earth did you find her?" I asked.

"I just rang up Western Police Station and asked if they'd picked up a woman pickpocket at the time and place you told me, that's how I got the information. And I've asked my lawyer to help me out," said Ann.

Just like that. During the following weeks I received reports from Ann about Clara, whom she'd visited. Ann said she was guilty as hell, having admitted to the pickpocketting, but Ann said she would do all she could to see that she was not deported or jailed (three months is the minimum sentence). If need be, Ann said she'd hire Clara as her maid.

> *After three and a half years as expatriates in Asia, only in Hong Kong have we seen Filipino maids walking their master's dog and talking on his cellular phone at the same time. It is an enduring image that sums up many aspects of expatriate life: the master wants to live life with the same creature comforts as at home, therefore the dog (which suffers miserably in the summer heat and humidity), but he is too busy or too lazy to walk the poor beast himself so the task is handed to the maid. She in turn is lonely, being at his beck and call 24 hours a day six days a week, so she embraces modern technology and, in addition to acting as her master's answering machine, she uses his cellular phone to talk to her friends while walking the dog.*
>
> —James and Firouzeh Attwood, "Hong Kong Notes"

"Good grief," I said, "the woman admitted she'd stolen and you're willing to have her work in your home?"

"She's destitute," Ann said. "She has six children back in the Philippines and she needs to feed them. If I were in her shoes, I'd pick pockets too—I'd probably rob a bank as well."

The kind man discovers it and calls it kind. The wise man discovers it and calls it wise. The people use it day by day and are not aware of it, for the way of the superior man is rare.

—I Ching: The Book of Changes, the Richard Wilhelm translation from Chinese into German, rendered into English by Cary F. Baynes

I saw her point. She went on, "Don't forget, Isabel, you should always tell yourself, when you think of thieves and prostitutes, 'There but for the grace of God go I.'"

During the next few days Ann attended the court hearing, saw Clara charged, spoke to her lawyer who put in a good word with the judge and sat in court next to the woman who had been robbed by Clara. Ann appealed to all these people for compassion; she asked them to see that Clara had been driven to desperate measures. The result was the judge passed a suspended sentence.

Ann described the scene that followed. "As soon as Clara and I heard the judge saying she was free to go, and he retired to his chambers, I started to walk up to her and she came towards me. A couple of police officers suddenly grabbed Clara and dragged her away. I screamed at them that she was free to go, but they told me they'd found she had a forged passport and was using a false name, Rita Velez. They were going to lock her up to try her again in a few weeks! I can't believe the inhumanity of those people. It's so maddening, I feel like resigning from the human race!"

When I related all this to some Filipino friends the next day, starting with my having witnessed the arrest, all agreed that Clara should be deported. "It's people like that who give us *Pinoys* a bad name," said Maria. "Why do they come here to steal, for God's sake?"

If Ann had been around, I could have guessed what she'd say to Maria—"Hungry people will steal. Where's your Christianity?"

When I said to Ann that the business of the forged passport was bad news, I asked if she'd still want to hire Clara to work for her. "My dear," she replied, "Mary Magdalene was a prostitute and yet Jesus forgave her. Who am I to judge Clara?"

I found out Ann is a Catholic after she sent me a note in which she mentioned purgatory. She is definitely one of those who practice their faith, not just mouth it.

So now, just before Clara-Rita is taken to court again in a few days, Ann has been visiting her and consulting with the lawyer. She suggested I visit Clara too, so that was how I got into Victoria Prison.

The jail occupies a whole block on the corner of Wyndham Street and Hollywood Road; it is neat and well-kept—but its keepers all seem to have hard-looking eyes. Perhaps one gets this way when dealing with criminals, but pickpockets and women with infants on their breast cannot possibly be hardened criminals. I found myself getting a bit like Ann—though I will never match her guts and determination. I haven't the stamina to be a do-gooder, I fear. I knew from books that English-women can be formidable in their strength, and I've been finding this out firsthand now.

Talking to Clara-Rita during those fifteen minutes allotted to us, I found her lapsing into Cebuano, so I made it easier for her by also speaking in that language. She told me she was from Davao, is thirty years old, had married at age fourteen and has six children. She said her mother, who looks after five of her children, is going blind. They all live in a hovel in a Davao slum (her father is dead). She said she left her husband because he was a *palikero* (playboy) who does not support her children.

> *Wisdom, benevolence, and fortitude—these three are the universal virtues. The means by which they are practiced is another thing. Some are born with a knowledge of these duties; some know them by study; some gain them as the result of painful experience. But the knowledge being possessed, it comes to one and the same thing. Some practice them with the ease of nature; some for the sake of their advantage; and some by dint of great effort. But when the work of them is done, it comes to one and the same thing.*
>
> —Confucius

Clara-Rita said that last year she was hired by a man to come to work in Hong Kong. When I asked what kind of man and what sort of work, she said he was a *bugaw* (pimp), like some other men she'd met before. She admitted she had worked as a prostitute and then was caught and deported some years ago.

Before she first came to Hong Kong, Clara-Rita said a friend of hers in Manila offered to look after one of her children. But when she got back to Manila after being deported from Hong Kong, the friend demanded P10,000 before giving the child back. At this point Clara-Rita began to weep quietly.

I asked her about the *bugaw*, what his name was, if she was one among many women he brought over, but she said she would rather not talk about him. She told me frankly that this time, when she arrived in the colony in February, she was installed at a hotel in Tsim Sha Tsui in Kowloon but she hated the work. "I didn't like being treated like a *baboy* (pig), with all those men mauling me, so I ran away." She said she had no money and wanted to find a job as a housemaid, so she began to look at advertisements in supermarkets. But after two days she was so hungry, she decided to pick pockets.

The police officer in the room began to tell everyone the time was up. All I could tell Clara-Rita was to have faith in Ann, that perhaps she'd be able to save her again. I quickly asked her if her cell was comfortable and she said she shared a dormitory cell with twenty other women, all Chinese, some with children. She said she couldn't eat well, often had headaches, and hardly slept.

What will become of this miserable Filipina, one among many who have fled the poverty of our country? As things stand now, there is a glimmer of hope. She may not get a suspended sentence again; she may be deported for the second time. But what will she be returning to—hungry children, a sick mother, a lost child, penury? Will she fall back into the clutches of her *bugaw?* Will she make another attempt to earn a living on her back in Hong Kong, much as she hates being treated like a pig?

I wish I had the answers. Perhaps people like the formidable Ann Smyth do.

*A long-time resident of Hong Kong, Isabel Escoda writes feature articles and stories, particularly about her compatriots, the Filipino migrant workers. A former broadcaster over Radio-Television Hong Kong, she has had two books of her collected radio essays published—*Letters from Hong Kong *and* Hong Kong Postscript. *Her articles appear regularly in the Philippines's largest-circulating Sunday publication, the* Sunday Inquirer Magazine. *She has also published three children's books.*

★

Minutes later, I was in a taxi winding along the narrow roads that snake through the hills of the "Mid-Levels." Below, in the distance, the city was a scintillant dream. Swerving up a steep incline, the car rolled into an underground garage complex and stopped by the side of three Mercedes, a Rolls, a Porsche, and a Ferrari. A noiseless elevator whisked me up to the eighteenth floor, and there, among the stars, stood Georges, a friend from Eton, tanned, barefoot, and shirtless after a day at the office. Only a few months earlier, when last we had met, Georges had exhausted all his savings on a squat studio apartment amid the clutter and clamor of Greenwich Village. Now, thanks to an overseas transfer, he was living in a three-bedroom luxury apartment, with exquisite framed Thai prints along the wall, glass cases for his books, a 21st-century stereo system alive with green and scarlet flashes. Through his picture window we saw the switchboard lights of the city below, a thousand fireworks arrested in midflight, and, beyond, the illuminated curves of the world's most breathtaking harbor. Far in the distance gleamed the hills of Kowloon.

"You know," said Georges, leading me out onto his terrace in the soft autumn evening, "this place is really something." Below us, the curving road was lit up by the moon. The night was polished to a sheen and the breeze was warm. "It's not easy to leave," he sighed. "Seventeen and a half percent taxes. A free flat. A Filipina *amah* who comes in once a week to clean the place. Expat Services, Ltd., to take care of all my maintenance. Free holidays. All this." He swept his hand across the multicolored night. "That's why *gweilo* never go home."

We stood outside and a breeze came up, as the nocturne soothed on. Below us, on the next block down, a roof was strung with colored lights. Bodies mingled and gyrated. The crystal tinkle of small talk drifted up to us, and, more faintly, the insistent bass of Tina Turner's "What's Love Got to Do with it?"

"You know," said Georges, talking slowly, "when you're 90 years old, and you're in your rocking chair, and you're talking to your grandchildren..." And, you know, he was right.

—Pico Iyer, *Video Night in Kathmandu*

EDWARD A. GARGAN

⋆ ⋆ ⋆

Wind and Water

A hunger for land displaces the bay.

WHEN SHE WAS SMALL, ROMY CHIU REMEMBERS, THE WATERS OF
Hong Kong harbor lapped against the sea wall at the end of Man
Yuen Street, a claustrophobic alley of noodle stalls, engine shops
and her family's Vietnamese restaurant.

"There was always the harbor there," she said, scrubbing a
plastic table top with a damp rag before clapping down a pair of
plastic bowls, chopsticks, and a sheaf of paper napkins. "We ran
down there as kids to watch the boats. It's long gone now."

Now, vast dunes and plains of sand and rock stretch from the
end of her street, far into Hong Kong's harbor. At the end of Man
Yuen Street, a solitary concrete bollard stands. It will never again
feel the tug of a ship's mooring line, for glass and cement towers
are planned for these fields of sand.

If there is one immutable legacy that British colonialism will
leave when China takes over Hong Kong in two years, it is the rad-
ical reshaping of its harbor, which separates Hong Kong island
from Kowloon. The reshaping is taking place with an accelerating
fervor in the Government's dying days.

"If this city is going to cope with pressures from over the
border, it has got to have more land," said Edward G. Pryor, the

principal Government planner who has overseen reshaping the harbor.

But there has been little public discussion of the plan, and now legislators, urban planners, and environmental groups are joining a rising storm of opposition.

"The Government is ramming things down people's throats," said Winston K. S. Chu, a prominent lawyer and dissenting member of the Town Planning Board, a secretive body with absolute authority on many facets of Hong Kong's development. "Hong Kong people will lose their natural heritage for all time. The damage can never be undone."

It is difficult to underestimate the importance of the harbor to Hong Kong historically.

Toward the end of last century, the intellectual Wang Tao fled China to Hong Kong to escape rebel fighting.

"The sea stretches out before you all the way to the endless horizon," he wrote of his new home. "Vast networks of mountains appear like little mounds. Ships and boats of every description lie at anchor in neat rows in the harbor. Such sights are a delight to the eye as well as the mind."

David Lung is one of Hong Kong's most noted practitioners of the traditional Chinese art of geomancy, which assigns beneficial or malevolent qualities to the shape and positioning of buildings, land, mountains and water. He is deeply worried about the vanishing harbor.

"It restricts the water flow and changes Hong Kong's natural shape," said Mr. Lung, who regularly advises the Hong Kong Shanghai Bank, the largest in the colony. "Traditionally, we think of water as bringing fortune to Hong Kong. And while

> *The highest goodness is like water, for water is excellent in benefiting all things, and it does not strive. It occupies the lowest place, which men abhor. And therefore it is near akin to Tao.*
>
> —Lao Tzu

I cannot give an accurate assessment yet since not all the reclamation is done, we can see this as restricting fortune from flowing into Hong Kong."

The harbor, which in places is more than a mile wide, is to be shrunk to a narrow channel. The serrated, twisting shoreline is to be smoothed and straightened, its islands absorbed like errant globules of mercury.

"The issue is very psychological," said Iris S. Y. Tam, the new president of the Hong Kong Institute of Planners, a professional association. "The water, the harbor itself, is part of our heritage."

But Mr. Pryor and other members of the tiny elite that governs this colony say they know what is best.

"At the end of the day, you're going to have a far better city than we have now," said Mr. Pryor. "When you know you're right, you have to stick to your guns."

Increasingly, though, many people in Hong Kong not only believe that the Government is wrong, but they are determined to do something about it.

"We have an executive-led Government and paternalistic Government," said Christine Loh, a member of the Legislative Council, which passes laws for the territory but has no oversight over planning.

"It's come to a physical stage where people can see the sea disappearing and are now saying, 'What's going on?' They have a plan that changes the face of Hong Kong. There was never any debate or discussion for the whole plan, only bits and pieces."

Over the last hundred years, nearly twenty-one square miles of land has been reclaimed from the sea around Hong Kong, including some along the harbor front. But the current plans to reclaim five square miles from the harbor for broad new highways, towering office buildings, housing, and some park land have drawn public attention as never before. Many people charge that the details are tucked in huge planning documents that have not yet been made public.

"Winston Chu recently showed me a map with the latest reclamation proposals in their entirety," said Peter Hills, who heads the Center for Urban Planning and Environmental Management at Hong Kong University. "It's staggering what's on the cards.

"There is a growing concern among some groups that the harbor is disappearing. There is a feeling that Hong Kong without the harbor is not Hong Kong."

Foreign urban planners are also concerned. "It's a fortress Hong Kong mentality," said Aprodicio Laquian, a professor of urban planning at the University of British Columbia in Canada and a frequent consultant to the United Nations and World Bank. "What the Government doesn't want to admit is that they don't want to expand toward the Chinese border.

"They really need to rethink what they are doing here."

Robert D. Pope, the director of lands for the Government, dismissed such criticism. "It's absolute rubbish," he said. "For Hong Kong to maintain its position as a financial center, it has to provide facilities," he said. "We shouldn't wash our hands and say it all goes to southern China."

Although nothing can be done about the two and a half square miles filled in already under current plans, there are increasingly strong signals of disapproval from China as well.

It had been many years since my last visit to Hong Kong, and of course, things had changed. I was confused, which I attributed to jet lag, but as the days passed and my confusion lingered, I began to realize that something was amiss. I couldn't square my perception that Kowloon had moved closer to Hong Kong, that the famous Hong Kong skyline had crept nearer to Kowloon. Was my memory faulty? Had my image of Victoria Harbor from many years ago been made grander with the passage of time? Then suddenly it hit me. Landfill. Of course, It wasn't faulty perception: Victoria Harbor had shrunk.

—Larry Habegger,
"New Days in Hong Kong"

"This is stupid," said David Chu, a member of the Beijing-appointed Preliminary Working Committee that is advising China on the turn-over of sovereignty. "This is because of one hundred and fifty years of British colonialism. We're doing everything possible to stop it."

But the opposition has come principally from Hong Kong's own civic leaders. "We would like the Government to review the reclamation to leave more of the water," said Ms. Tam, the planning institute president. "The Government says we don't need the water for Hong Kong's economy. We are saying that we are not talking only about economic activity."

For Mr. Chu, of the Town Planning Board, who can see dredgers and land fillers from his office window, time is running short.

"This time I have to stand up," he said. "The most important things in life are the things you cannot put your hands on. This is what Hong Kong lacks. It lacks a spirit, if I may say so, a soul. Filling in this harbor would be like filling in the Hudson River."

Edward A. Gargan also contributed "Shadow of the Manuchus" in Part 1.

★

Fortunate are the travelers who happen to be aboard ferry boats sailing into Hong Kong harbor at its most magical hour: dusk. I stepped outside in the gathering dark for a wider view. The hot wet wind blew across my face. We swept along the waterfront. The sea faded from copper to bronze. Across its surface moved all manner of craft: cruise ships, tugboats, ferries large and small, dredges, barges, container shuttles, hovercraft, freighters, and fishing junks. The glass skyscrapers mirrored the plum-colored sunset, as if they were burning within. Above, the lights were going on in thousands of apartments at Mid-Levels. Soaring far over everything, the benighted mountains were silhouetted against the stars.

> —Lynn Ferrin, "What to do in Hong Kong After You
> Buy the Camcorder and Cloisonné," *Motorland*

WILLIAM MCGURN

✦ ✦ ✦

Mad Dogs and Chinamen

The author reflects on racism and economic servitude.

AMONG OLD CHINA HANDS, FEW MORE CONTENTIOUS ISSUES EXIST than that of the "No Dogs or Chinese" sign said to have hung outside the Public Gardens atop the Bund of old Shanghai.

Never mind that the heirs of Chairman Mao run shops, restaurants, and hotels full of goodies reserved for foreigners and Party functionaries (membership has its privileges?). Never mind too that the sign never existed—not, at least, the way legend has it. Countless Chinese schoolboys still grow up with it drummed into their heads, and references continue to pop up in the press, Western as well as Eastern, inevitably to illustrate the wickedness of European colonialism. I have cited it to nice effect myself, once even after I was pretty sure it had never been there.

The last laugh, however, almost always belongs to history. Nowhere is this more true than in China. European colonialism may not have been the most congenial of systems, but a half-century of experience with its Asiatic competitors (not least of which has been Chinese Communism) makes Kipling look downright tender. And

> *It was, of course, Kipling who wrote "Here lives a fool who tried to hustle the East."*
>
> —JO'R, LH, and SO'R

events finally came full circle in Hong Kong when it turned out that a luxury apartment building had posted signs banning both maids and dogs from the main elevator. The prohibition on maids appeared in Chinese and Tagalog (the most common of the Philippines' many languages) and was posted under another sign forbidding dogs. Apparently the signs had been there for some time but had not been enforced until a recent change in management.

What lends the notice a racial cast in Hong Kong is the more or less exclusive identification of "maid" with "Filipina." Years ago, many families here had a Chinese maid, or *amah*, whose primary charge was the children. Today affluence has made the Chinese *amahs* largely a thing of the past, replaced by Filipinas forced by a succession of idiotic governments at home into seeking work as domestics abroad. Many of these Filipinas have college degrees. Even more have other family members here as well—mothers, sisters, daughters—working in other homes raising Chinese and European children so that their own might eat. And where five years ago there were just 25,000 Filipina maids here, today there are over 100,000.

Now, one of the most striking things for Americans living abroad is how little attention the rest of the world pays to our racial conventions. The Cantonese expression for foreigner, *gweilo*, translates roughly as "foreign devil," and though the expatriate community here takes it as a joke, the word is in its origins as rude as "nigger" is in English—and it can still have the same connotation. Of course, the Chinese are no more or less prejudiced than other Asians. On the whole, they do not much harbor illusions about a yellow man's burden.

In particular they dislike the thousands of Filipina *amahs* descending upon the city square on their one day off each week. A couple of months back, Hong Kong Land, which owns much of the commercial space around the area and is in turn owned by the powerful conglomerate Jardine Matheson (the real-life Noble House), became an instant press villain when it launched a push to sweep the Filipinas from the square. Although the charges of "ethnic cleansing" were absurd, so was the proposed alternative gathering place: a parking garage. More embarrassment followed when the *amah* for Jardine taipan Nigel Rich was quoted as saying that her boss's attempt to move the Filipinas to an underground garage "was not a nice idea."

This was the background to the brouhaha set off when a Filipina maid named Linda faxed off a note to the *South China Morning Post* about "No Dogs or Filipinas" signs posted in Tregunter Towers, where apartments rent for $7,500 per month. Although the signs were hastily removed, the spirit behind them lingers on. Just a few days after the story broke, the following note was slipped under the doors of Filipinas living in the building:

We were riding the tram back to our hotel in Wanchai when we heard a soft twittering, like birdsong, light, airy, rolling on the wind. We had no idea what it was until we spotted the Sunday gathering of Filipinas at Statues Square. The entire plaza and side streets near the Hong Kong and Shanghai Bank building were filled with Filipinas. The sound was their conversation, the musical hum of women far from home catching up with friends on their weekly day off work. We immediately got off the tram and wandered among them.

"That sound," Don murmured later. "I'll never forget that sound. Like a forest full of birds."

—Larry Habegger,
"New Days in Hong Kong"

> YOU SHOULD TAKE THE SERVICE LIFT WHERE YOU BELONG! IF YOU DON'T LIKE IT, PLEASE GO BACK TO YOUR COUNTRY. DON'T FORGET THAT YOU ARE EMPLOYED HERE AS SERVANTS! DON'T RUIN THE REPUTATION OF YOUR OWN KIND WHO DIS-AGREE WITH YOUR ATTITUDES AND ACTIONS. OBVIOUSLY THIS APPLIES TO THE USE OF THE SHUTTLE BUSES ALSO.

Not much subtlety here. It was signed "a group of very angry tenants."

Reaction was swift and ludicrous. The Philippine consul general lodged a protest and drew parallels with the Ku Klux Klan and neo-Nazi movement. The United Migrant Workers, United Filipinos in Hong Kong, and the Mission for Filipino Migrant Workers all issued denunciations. The incident was particularly embarrassing for some British Hong Kong civil servants (including Governor Chris Patten's press secretary) who live in Tregunter Towers and hurriedly denounced a sign they had given no thought to before.

But mostly the war was carried out on the letters page of the _Post_, where hostilities raged between those urging sympathy for the long-suffering Filipinas and those saying the Filipinas need to learn their place. "Yes, we are domestic helpers, but that doesn't make us less human," wrote Marrz Saludez Balaoro.

"Experienced colonials, unlike the nouveau expatriates, knew how to employ staff and treat them well, without going overboard," allowed Mina Kaye. "Although some of them allege that they are college graduates in the Philippines and therefore seem to have a corresponding sense of superiority, they come here to work as domestic helpers, and they should not expect to be treated more favorably than others in their position," said J. Ong.

But the most priceless letter came from a man who signed his name Robert Thio and was fool enough to append the letters "Ph.D." after it. "The signs," he declared, "were not put up without a valid reason." He then gave that reason. "I have observed," said Dr. Thio, "that many Filipino maids speak loudly among themselves in the lifts of the building and on public business (particularly in mini-buses). This is a nuisance and generates resentment among other people."

Well, the dam burst after this one. Anyone who has heard Cantonese speaking among themselves will concede that they are not exactly Trappist monks, a fact pointed out by the next round of correspondents.

Up at Tregunter Towers soon after, I ran into two Filipina _amahs_ who work in the complex but say they have decent employers. They tell me that the publicity has angered some Chinese in the building. "I don't know why they treat us like we're not human," says one. "We are the ones who are raising their children."

Can Cantonese be spoken quietly?
No.
—Dr. George Adams, _Hong Kong Watching: The Essential Guide to Hong Kong People's Behaviour_

And the infamous sign from atop the Bund? Again, the news is not comforting for those who associate all villainy with the West. In 1973 Richard Hughes returned to Shanghai after many years of absence and devoted his subsequent column in the *Far Eastern Economic Review* to puncturing the legend. "The sign," he said, "was not a sign at all but a paragraph in a great list of municipal proscriptions—in Chinese, never in English—which was exhibited outside the park from 1868 until 1925. Following the May 30 demonstrations in that year, the British quietly removed it." That may explain the origins. But no one has yet explained how so many people came to believe otherwise.

Until now, that is. Lynn Pan, author of several books on Shanghai, says the source of the myth was revealed to her during a visit to the basement of the Shanghai Museum. In the course of her research for a just-released photo essay on old Shanghai, she stumbled across not one but an entire cache of "No Dogs or Chinese" signs that had been manufactured by Party authorities to parade before visiting foreign delegations as evidence that Noel Coward really had it right when he linked mad dogs with Englishmen. "People swear until they are blue in the face that they saw it on the Gardens," says Miss Pan, who fled the city with her family in the 1950s. "But it was never there." Perhaps it was the noonday sun.

William McGurn is senior editor of the Far Eastern Economic Review.

*

Of the factors of government, Confucius had this to say:

Tsekung asked about government, and Confucius replied, "People must have sufficient to eat; there must be a sufficient army; and there must be faith in the nation."

"If you were forced to give up one of these three factors, what would you go without?" asked Tsekung. Confucius said, "I would go without the army first." And if you were forced to go without one of the two remaining factors, which would you rather go without?" asked Tsekung again. "I would go with out sufficient food. There have always been deaths in every generation, but a nation without faith cannot stand."

—Lin Yutang, *Between Tears and Laughter*

A. LIN NEUMANN

✦ ✦ ✦

Shopping with the Pirates

Information wants to be free—but this is going too far.

BARGAIN HUNTER OR INTERNATIONAL CRIMINAL? THIS IS THE situation I am mulling over as I stand here, feeling a little shabby, clutching my purchases to my side, knowing that I have been spoiled forever, that I will never want to set foot inside Egghead or any other full-price software emporium again. It's not something to be proud of, but I am prepared to admit this to the world: I am a partner in software piracy.

These thoughts occur to me as I prowl the aisles of the software piracy mother lode, the Golden Shopping Arcade in Hong Kong's Sham Shui Po district. All around me in the basement of this dingy, block-long urban warehouse, eager shoppers paw through the tables of the densely packed stalls. From an interactive Japanese porn CD-ROM starring the intriguingly named Conchita Matsumoto to AutoCad Release 13, the eager consumers at the Golden Arcade are snapping up wares with a Filene's basement kind of eagerness. It's like *Supermarket Sweep* in here—without a time limit.

This is what I have come to Asia to see: a dizzying variety of software at a price so low that air seems more expensive. Inside a stall called the Everything CD shop, a group of muscular young American men with close-cropped hair wearing shorts and Teva sandals—Sailors on leave? A band? A rugby team?—are consulting shopping lists and piling stacks of CD-ROMs into their bags. As one of them wonders aloud over the splendid possibilities of a piece called *Fuckman Interactive,* another guy counts out the CD in his hand and tells the clerk "Two more, I need two more of these." He then ticks off the names on his list: "Let's see: Office and WordPerfect for Brad. AutoCad for Marty. Installers for the guys at the house…." I try to engage the group in conversation. "You shop here often? Neat, huh?" They eye me suspiciously and move on without a word. We are pirates, after all, here to shop, not to chat.

Before leaving Everything CD, I buy the first of my Installer discs, Volume 2. This tribute to pirate technology costs the same as all the other CD-ROMs at Golden Arcade, about nine bucks or three for US$25. Incredibly, this disc has 86 programs on it, each compressed with a self-extracting installation utility. Volume 2 has a beta copy of Windows 95 as well as OS/2 Warp, CorelDraw! 5, Quicken 4.0, Atari Action Pack for Windows, Norton Commander, KeyCad, Adobe Premier, Microsoft Office, and dozens of other applications, including a handful written in Chinese. Connoisseurs of the genre compare the different versions of the installer discs like fine wines. Someone from Microsoft later tells me that the retail value of the disc is between $20,000 and $35,000. Not a bad deal for less than what it costs to fill the tank with unleaded at the corner gas station.

My trip to the legendary Golden Arcade comes in the midst of a four-country shopping tour of Southeast Asia. I have come to explore the consumer end of the software piracy business. To put it bluntly, I want to know what's in it for the shopper. By now I am pretty well acquainted with the Microsoft-driven Business Software Alliance, the group arguing aggressively that global software piracy is a crime against humanity and that it robbed software companies of $15.2 billion in revenue worldwide in 1994 ($4.3 billion of those losses happened in Asia). Stephanie Mitchell, a Hong Kong-based lawyer for Autodesk, one of the alliance's partners in the drive against piracy, tells me over lunch in a finely burnished restaurant at the Grand Hyatt Hotel in Hong Kong that "software piracy is a substantial regional criminal enterprise" with "octopus-like tentacles" reaching into all aspects of computer use.

*T*hose who do not know
the Plan of other leaders
*Are not able to prepare
for negotiations.*

*Those who do not know
the positions
Of the mountains, forests, passes,
and marshes
Are not able to move the Force.*

*Those who do not employ
local guides
Are not able to affect the
Situation to advantage.*

*Imitation is basic to Strategy.
Move to follow the advantages.
Divide or unite to follow the
Variations in action.*

*Hence, during swiftness, be
like the wind.
During stillness, be like the forest.
During aggression, be like fire.
During immobility, be
like a mountain.
Be as unknowable as the dark.
Move like a thunderbolt....*

*Those who triumph
Know beforehand how to calculate
the Direct and Indirect.
Such is Engaging the Force.*

—Sun Tzu, "Flexibility
and Imitation," *The Art of
War,* translated by R. L. Wing
as *The Art of Strategy*

That may be true, but the sentiment among consumers, sellers, visitors, and just about everybody else I meet here is substantially different. "You know, you're in Asia for a while and you start to think, Well fuck Bill Gates," said a friend who is an executive with a large telecommunications firm in Hong Kong. In Bangkok, Jamie Zellerbach, an American computer entrepreneur, said, "It's just a matter of necessity. We want the software and we want it now. We need it. But we can't get it any other way: the real stuff is overpriced, and there's zero support."

One thing is certain: despite international protocols on intellectual property rights, despite the millions being spent by large American companies to combat piracy, and despite the halting efforts of Asian governments to join in the battle against the techno-bluebeards, there is plenty of software to choose from, and the prices are impossibly great—if you know where to look.

So many titles, so little time. Before plunging into the Golden Arcade, I check 298 Hennessy Road, a relatively new computer mall located in the center of the Wan Chai district of Hong Kong island. Made famous by generations of sailors on leave and the legend of Suzie Wong, the girlie-bar trade is barely important to Wan Chai anymore. There is real money to be made in prosperous, modern Hong Kong, and you're unlikely to meet many Chinese ladies drawn to the oldest profession. In the new Wan Chai, 298 Hennessy Road is more like it: a shady enterprise with lots of money on the table, operating in the open. There are three floors of computer stalls here; most of them are selling pirated wares quickly and at a budget price even a bit lower, on average, than Golden Arcade.

The alliance folks had told me about 298, and I had no trouble finding it. But the place has been taking a little heat lately from the authorities, so I'm not surprised the clerks don't want to talk to me. But talk isn't important. I pick and choose, enjoying the air conditioning and the dizzying variety. I find a copy of AutoCad Release 13 for about $6. For the same price, I pick up *Weekend Home Projects*, *Encarta 95*, *3D Animation Bank Vol. 1*, and *A Hard Day's Night*. The retail on these things in the U.S. runs from about $4,000 for AutoCad to $29 for *Weekend Home Projects*. In Hong Kong, it doesn't seem to make any difference what's on the disc: a copy is a copy.

Mike Morrow, a Hong Kong–based publisher who has recently launched his own legitimate multimedia company, explains the system to me over a drink. The factories that produce these shadowy CD-ROM are almost all located in southern China, in the "special economic zone" of Shenzhen in the province of Guangdong. Costing several million dollars and using sophisticated Philips replicating equipment, the enterprises are usually joint ventures with Hong Kong businessmen, says Morrow. And even though some of his own titles have been ripped off by Chinese freebooters, he says that Microsoft does "too much huffing and puffing" about the problem. Piracy will eventually wither away, Morrow says, when American producers charge more realistic fees for their products.

For now, the market is wide open, and I'm off to the Golden Arcade, which, it turns out, is a splendid way to compare the old and the new in Hong Kong. To get there, take the gleaming, super-efficient MTR subway to Sham Shui Po. The MTR is the kind of mass-transit system an American city can only dream of: it's fast, cheap, and safe—a tribute to British administration and Chinese efficiency in the colony. And no problem finding your way: the arcade is so well known by now that there are even signs for it in the MTR, a fact that really irritates the alliance enforcers.

While the area may be known for the Golden Arcade and its illicit high-tech wares, the neighborhood is old China, a world away from the whirring frenzy of downtown Hong Kong's towering corporate center. Down Fuk Wa Street is an open market where canvas-sided booths peddle kitchenware, cheap plastic luggage, and wooden trinkets. The side streets are lined with noodle shops and medicine parlors that offer potions made from herbs, exotic snakes, and forbidden powdered rhino horn. The off-tract betting stand of the Royal Hong Kong Jockey Club is doing a brisk business, and the only reminder that we are in the computer age is the ever-present shops selling pagers and cellular phones—must-haves for everyone, it seems, in Hong Kong.

The unprepossessing mall, at the corner of Fuk Wa Street and Kwei-Lin, is notable only for the steady stream of traffic in and out of its doors. Inside, I get

Proto-China is a conception of China often confused with the present day People's Republic which, however, has no significant relationship with the PRC in an understanding of its function in cultural scripting. Proto-China is a largely abstract concept, equivalent perhaps to Britannia or Uncle Sam, in which certain cultural assumptions regarding identity and ultimate destiny are contained, albeit largely implicitly and unconsciously.... It manifests itself in deep-rooted behavioural patterns such as group identity, familial consciousness, harmony maintenance. It is the key factor in the conception of many even third generation Hong Kong people of their own cultural uniqueness.

—Dr. George Adams, *Games Hong Kong People Play: A Social Psychology of the Hong Kong Chinese*

busy. In addition to the installer disc I already mentioned, I follow the lead of an Australian woman I meet in one of the shops who recommends Myst. "It's a lot of fun," she says. What the heck, for $9, how can I lose? I ask if she's a regular here. Does the stuff work? How is it?

"Oh sure, everything here works," she says. "We have CorelDraw!, Office, Microsoft Publisher, and lots of games, and we haven't had any problems." That's enough recommendation for me. I pick up a few more things: another installer and a sexy-looking interactive Japanese CD before I go prowling upstairs. There, away from the pirate frenzy, I find a legitimate dealer, Software Collection. The store is stacked to the ceiling with boxed versions of much of the software for sale down below. Draw! 5 costs $255; Microsoft Office is $350; licensed versions of FoxPro, Delrina WinFax, and Lotus SmartSuite carry similarly lofty price tags. Predictably, the store is empty. "Who buys this stuff?" I ask the clerk. "It seems too expensive."

"We are legal," he says with irritation. "Have license. Technical support. No problems!" But how much do you sell? I ask, thinking that hardly anybody would want to spend $300 for something they can buy downstairs for $10. "We sell plenty," he spits back. The conversation is over.

Outside, as I head for the subway with my purchases, I encounter an American couple taking a break from their own shopping. How do they feel about buying illegal software? "I don't mind paying for software if it's worth something," said the man, an engineer from Oklahoma who has been working in Shanghai for the past six months. "But the prices now in the States are a little crazy. Here at least the prices are good."

The next day, I take the train to China—on a day trip to Shenzhen, as close to the source of this piracy as I am likely to get. Shenzhen is China's Tijuana, a border boomtown just beyond Hong Kong. If you want it, chances are you can find it in Shenzhen at a bargain price. Outside the train station, it is clear that we are no longer in Hong Kong. The place is dusty, chaotic, and bustling. In contrast to the British colony, which is orderly and maintained by a splendid civil service, Shenzhen looks out of control. Beggars jostle us on the sidewalk, one small child wrapping himself around my leg and howling for money; it takes several minutes to shake the young boy loose. In a central plaza, a gigantic Astrovision-style video screen is blaring soft drink commercials and Cantonese pop music into the glare of the sizzling afternoon, lending a *Blade Runner* feel to the place.

Undeterred by the weirdness, I head for the west side of town, following directions supplied by an investigator I had spoken with from Microsoft who urged me to check out the nefarious ways of Shenzhen's pirate marketplace. I cannot say I am disappointed when I finally discover the Shenzhen Science Market at the corner of Shennan Road Central and Huafa Road South. It's in the heart of a new financial district, on the second floor above a huge McDonald's outlet. Perfect. Pirate software and real Big Macs. The new Asia.

Upstairs, the place is open for business, if at a somewhat reduced scale, apparently as a result of a recent semi-crackdown urged by the United States government. Business Software Alliance investigators, as part of the global battle against intellectual piracy, had come to Shenzhen and worked closely with the Chinese authorities who raided the market earlier in the year. While this massive, shady superstore once boasted 100 or more stalls flogging their wares, there are fewer than 50 open on the day we visit. Still, business is brisk, and prices are roughly half the going rate across the border in Hong Kong. That famous installer disc can be had here for about $3. I picked up volume 4—this one contains Adobe Photoshop, a *Jurassic Park* screen saver, Paradox 4.5, Lotus Organizer, Turbo Pascal, the Holy Bible, and 47 other programs. Salespeople offer catalogs of titles in English and Chinese, and many customers appear to be negotiating for volume sales. There are video CDs of the latest movies being sold alongside the software, and a dozen TVs are competing for attention with kung-fu movies, as well as *The Godfather*, *Speed*, and *Total Recall*. "What a crazy place," says a smiling Italian woman, who is busy picking through a cardboard box of CD-ROM titles. I have to agree.

Before leaving Shenzhen, I stop for a late lunch at the Shangri-La Hotel's revolving restaurant, 31 stories above the jumble. This chain has become the *nouveau riche* hotel of choice throughout Asia, and it seems only fitting that I sample the sushi, Heineken, and French pastries here, away from the crowds, amid the splendid pretense of this ornate palace. During the slow turn, I count some 70 high-rise construction cranes. Below me, I can see the anachronistic barbed wire fence that still separates British-held Hong Kong from Red China. That will all change in 1997, of course, when Hong Kong becomes, once and forever, a part of the People's Republic. A day spent in Shenzhen is enough to make anyone wonder at the wisdom of that move....

Getting ready to leave Asia for the U.S., I realize I have collected quite a little bundle of counterfeit software: fourteen CD-ROMs containing several thousand dollars' worth of titles. I have spent a total of $187 in four countries [the Philippines, Hong Kong, China, and Thailand], on everything from AutoCad to a *Beavis and Butt-head* screen saver.

Now, don't forget—I know I didn't—this is *illegal*. As I'm packing to leave, I shuffle the CDs around. I hide some in layers of dirty clothes, others I stuff in my hand-carried luggage. I wedge a couple into the side pocket of a suitcase. Instead of carrying them, maybe I should send them in the mail. No, that's illegal, also. I'll take my chances with customs.

I remember what the Business Software Alliance people told me: this is a global criminal enterprise. I am certainly committing a crime. Specifically, I am violating Title 18 of the United States Code, which prohibits the unauthorized reproduction of software. The alliance also told me that the United States Customs Service has been trained in the apprehension of software pirates at ports of entry. The implied warning: Bill Gates is watching.

I keep my letter of assignment from *Wired* handy, figuring that if I am stopped at the airport, I can explain all of this. I'm a journalist, I'm on assignment, I'll tell them. I imagine the bright lights, dogs, stern faces in crisp uniforms. "Perhaps you can explain this disc with the Chinese lettering? Why does it contain the latest version of Turbo Tax?"

Arriving at LAX, the drama doesn't materialize. I'm waved through, following the blessed green line painted on the carpet that leads to the street. Nobody asks; nobody checks. The customs and immigration officers are busy inspecting the visas of foreigners. The only dog I see is a plant-sniffing beagle looking for medflies.

Once at home, I call the alliance office in Washington and tell them what I have done. "We're not going to bust you," Diane Smiroldo, the director of public affairs, assures me. She reckons I haven't committed a felony, although she's not sure; it depends on the value of what I am carrying. How much of this stuff is getting into the United States in the bags of travelers like me? I ask her. "We're not sure," she says. "It's hard to keep track."

A. Lin Neumann, a former foreign correspondent in Asia, is a firm believer in law and order, within reason.

★

The opium pipe is under glass in Hong Kong's Police Museum at 44 Coombe Road: an elegant old thing, ivory-bowled and sepia-tarred from frequent use.

The Royal Hong Kong Police confiscated it in a raid years ago on an opium den in Kowloon. It is an antique, dating from 1868, in the reign of the Dao Guang emperor of China. There's a couplet carved on its stem: "The crisp air refreshes the mind. The fragrant wind drifts through the nose...."

Succumb to the smoke of imagination. "Bite the clouds," as the Chinese say, and in a pretend-puff, think of Asia, vast and strange. Let Eastern phantasmagoria run riot in your mind, the rich plumage of this place, its moments of un-likeness to anything you have ever known or seen before.

—Michael Browning, "A Visual Feast," Fort Worth Star-Telegram

✶ ✶ ✶

Last Gasp in Guangzhou

Confucius said: "From the Emperor down to the masses of the people, all must consider the cultivation of the person the root of everything else."

I PREPARED TO EXPLORE GUANGZHOU ALONE. MY HANGOVER WAS killing me, so I fumbled through my survival gear for Tylenol. Dressing in local garb by the mirror, I groaned at a comparatively over-nourished, over-grown Cantonese anachronism with dental fillings, contact lenses, and a plastic Casio watch. Would I fool anyone this time? At 6 a.m., I left the luxury hotel to join an awakening city.

Near the Pearl River is Yang-Jiang Road. This is the people's open-air central market for fresh cultivated produce and stock. It is a long narrow street lined with sun-shaded foodstands. Vendors were already transporting their goods from the country on their back, by hand cart, or powered vehicle. Without buying, I closely studied each display. A few vendors would get annoyed with my wild-eyed wonder and suspicious scrutiny. Then I'd explain that I was from Los Angeles and that we didn't have such "delicious delicacies" over there.

I carefully chose my breakfast from a dizzying assortment of roots, melons, vegetables, and fruits as well as fowl, pork, snakes, turtles, frogs, toads, eels, pond snails, freshwater crustaceans, and (yummy, munchy, crunchy) arthropods. Everything was fresh-picked or alive-and-kicking, except pork, while some foods were served cooked and ready-to-eat. It was delicious and very cheap, although the most costly item was a gorgeous red apple; it had been imported from Washington State through Hong Kong. All-in-all, it's an adventure to feed yourself in China. Of course, that's assuming you're hungry.

Towards noon, the insufferable heat and humidity were torturous, but the people kept at their work. The narrow streets were choked with people, bikes, carts, and cars when a thin, wiry man, hunched beneath a heavy crate, scurried by me, slowed, and then collapsed while trying to set it down. Gasping face down between the pavement and the load, he was blocking traffic. Would anyone help? I stood watching. Soon cars were honking and cart-pushers were shouting while others maneuvered around. The gawking crowd did nothing. Could I help him? Should I try? I stepped forward and dropped by his side. Cutting the ropes binding the crate to his back, I toppled the load off him. The horns and shouts continued as I took his vitals; I hardly knew what I was doing. Barely conscious through his pain, he thanked me and called me doctor in Cantonese. I learned what I could until he lost consciousness, stopped breathing, and went into cardiac arrest.

First detached denial: "This isn't happening. Oh God! But this man is dying. They're going to arrest you and blow your head off. Run you fool, run, you're a hated U.S. citizen!! You're so dumb for telling those vendors you're from Los Angeles. This isn't happening!!"

Then resignation: "Get it together Jew, you're made of tougher stuff than this! Do what you can, you can't live with yourself otherwise. It's showtime, NOW!!"

Position, lift, hold mouth open, ventilate…ventilate, drop, target over heart, left-hand over right, compress…compress…compress…compress, reposition, lift (using my shoes to raise his neck), hold mouth open, ventilate…(crap, is that the taste of a cigarette?) ventilate, drop, target over heart, left-hand over right, compress…(HONK!! HONK!!") Damn drivers. Okay, I'll try to move him) compress…compress…compress, lift and drag two feet (good-bye footwear), continue CPR and dragging…

Check vitals. Any spontaneous pulse? Fingers to sides of throat, none. Press ear to chest, no sound. Check pupil reaction to light, still functioning. My Casio shows 11:54. Continue CPR…hold mouth open (notice his abdominal convulsions). Ventilate… (taste hint of gastric fluid), I gag and spit, ventilate (he vomits directly into me), drop, I vomit on him, target over heart (while retching), left-hand over right, compress (slip on vomit)… gag, turn, and vomit again behind me (spectator jumps clear), rip his shirt away, wipe hands between my thighs and calves, target over heart, left-hand over right, compress…compress…compress…lift him on his side, open-hand slam between shoulders, clear his throat with fingers, pull him on his back, take off my t-shirt, wipe out his mouth with t-shirt, reposition, lift, he gurgles (hope?), hold mouth open, I retch again (dread and nausea), ventilate…(he belches something foul; passage is still blocked; I'm breathing into his stomach), lift and tilt further, I gag then ventilate (he belches/vomits into me again), I vomit while attempting to clear his passage again, etc…

There are Good Samaritans in Chinese legend, but as a family man the Good Samaritan is suspect; how much might he have endangered himself and his kin by irresponsibly helping an unknown man who had been mixed up with brutal thieves? The Chinese, therefore, has no civic sense. His conscience may urge him to call a doctor or telephone for a fire engine if he sees a fire, but he has no real conception of the public weal. If he knocks someone down with his car and is sure he has either badly injured him or killed him, he will usually keep going. He cannot do more for the victim than the bystanders can, but if he stopped and were identified, his whole family would indirectly suffer.…

A Chinese shuns contact with authority, never wishes to report anybody, for fear of blame or reprisals. As for reprisals, the wary Chinese, for millennia deprived of equality before the law, warn their children: "Before you beat the dog, be sure to learn the master's name."

—Dennis Bloodworth,
The Chinese Looking Glass

Later at 12:45, my body is nearly paralyzed from exertion and pain plus being hoarse from gastric juices (his and mine) and shouting for help. The stench of vomit drew flies from everywhere. Earlier, I gave a male bystander 20 Yuan (US$5.40) to fetch a bottle of rice liquor. He doesn't return. I buy it from a passing cart. Not trusting the water from a nearby hose, I drink and gargle, wash him and myself, and splash the liquor around us. The flies vanish, and my pain begins to hide. Checking his vitals, I know I will lose him, if not already. We were both failing, but I continue CPR for my own conscience.

By 1:15, I finally accept his death (he was incontinent and defecating). Holding life so dear, it was torture to quit, yet torture to continue. Unbelievably, no one would help us, my shoes were stolen, and I began hating those around me. By then, the flies were everywhere again. I stood and stared at him, then finished the bottle to keep from breaking down. There was something ungodly about just leaving him dead in the street, but there was no other choice.

When Heaven is about to confer a great office on any man, it first disciplines his mind with suffering, and his bones and sinews with toil. It exposes him to want and subjects him to extreme poverty. It confounds his undertakings. By all these methods it stimulates his mind, hardens him, and supplies his incompetencies.

—Mencius

Without faith, I conjured a prayer and left my soiled t-shirt over his face. My hatred boiled as I walked away; it was an emotional reaction, a defense mechanism. Without shirt or shoes, and reeking of vomit and liquor, I wanted to kill. I began a torturous walk "home."

Later, the doorman at the White Swan Hotel refused to let me enter. I guess I was less than presentable. Or maybe I didn't look like their typical luxury hotel guest. They let me in a back way, but only after a few intensely confrontational moments and then identifying myself.

After the CPR ordeal and bruising/bribing the hotel doorman, I washed everything and slept until evening. Guangzhou had overwhelmed me. Wanting to hide from reality, I fought the two faces of fear trying to paralyze my being: debilitating anxiety and prudent caution—they are almost twins. That evening, I prepared to walk through a retiring city after forcing rationale against foreboding premonitions; my new-born fears must receive their first death blows.

I immediately bought a stringer of fresh litchi-nut fruits from a street vendor. This was my simple supper, and I ate as I toured the dark and cooling streets of Guangzhou. Most restaurants and some businesses stayed open into the night. They typically face streets that handle automotive traffic. In contrast, residential areas support only foot-traffic and pushcarts along a maze of narrow yet lengthy cobblestone alleys. Small, cramped homes open onto these alleys with no-glass caged windows and featureless doors. Observing family activities is a matter of strolling by and peering in. I studied their lives surreptitiously.

Most homes housed at least three persons, if not three generations. They had minuscule amounts of electricity, warm but suspicious tap water, and a porcelain enamel squat-over-a-hole-in-the-floor affair for a privy (at least they flush). Household life centers around the dining table, and close-by you would find their most treasured extravagance, the television. Not one home enjoyed air conditioning, but some did have a small refrigerator. And the bed would be a couch or a stow-away floor mattress. Stoves were fueled with wood or propane. Yes, they have the necessities of life, but little else.

Guangzhou is of a time long past. In fact, everything everywhere showed its age, dilapidation, and decades-old know-how. I saw no evidence of pride of ownership, individual or artistic expression, cultural appreciation, or conspicuous inconformity. They have lives like a goldfish in its bowl—no privacy, no intimacy, no sense of oneself, no outlet for creativity, no control of destiny. It's difficult to study what isn't seen; it's even more difficult to notice what doesn't exist, but should. These people have vast holes in experiencing life.

But how does a whole society cognitively come to know and accept their own comparative ignorance and naïveté? I don't know. Oddly enough though, they ask the same about our Western culture.

That night while traipsing through Guangzhou, I chanced upon a very peculiar encounter. In a local jewelry shop, I was attended to by its matronly proprietor. Using Cantonese, she presented jade carvings while I examined them. But this elderly woman had ulterior motives; as she did her Sherlock Holmes routine on me, I tried to ignore her scrutiny. Suddenly amused, she boldly asked in English, if I was available for marriage.

I was shocked to hear her spoken English, and jokingly answered that I was yet unmarried and could appreciate the experience, wealth, and wisdom of one such as herself. With a leering grin, I confessed "I'm flattered that you should have such interest in me." Squealing aloud with surprise, she apologized for being married already. Then she called for someone using the Cantonese words for granddaughter. I thought "Oh oh! It's a set-up."

Mei Qing (*mai-ching*) entered with a familiar air and then froze in horror at my smile. Covering her face, she ran off with a reprimand to her grandmother. I felt like a leper and tried to sneak out during their shouting. But they returned and called me back—I was mistaken for her blind-date suitor (due to arrive tomorrow) and she felt unpresentable. She looked wonderful.

While Mei Qing attended me as a customer, her grandmother deftly left the shop. Soon, I couldn't help but admire this young woman's innocent youthful beauty and embarrassed graciousness. Nodding to her Cantonese how-about-this-jade-piece-or-this, she coyly grinned at my focused attention and smile; evidently, her suitors are rarely so bold. Under my breath, I muttered "if only I could marry you myself, I would show you the world beyond your dreams." In shock, she stiffly drew in a quick breath, and I braced myself as I saw the comprehension in her eyes. Mei Qing was on a family visit from Beijing University, and her major is English.

After I bought several pairs of jade chopsticks, the old lady waived Mei Qing's workload and permitted me to dine with her, (much to the old gal's delight). Mei Qing donned a dress and we took a taxi to the luxurious White Swan Hotel.

My evening with Mei Qing confirmed many of my derived beliefs and suspicions about today's Chinese society. She also clarified and corrected a few misconceptions. But most of all, we shared a moment of discovery in each other's lives.

"If only I could marry you myself, I would show you the world beyond your dreams"—I doubt if Mei Qing would ever forget those words. I know I won't because she kept requoting them in jest. She had never met an American-born Asian and didn't expect someone so different. And though I understood both Cantonese and English, and even looked Cantonese, my inability to speak Cantonese was paradoxical, if not disgraceful. To say the least, I was not like her male counterparts. It didn't matter though, she wanted to practice English with a native speaker who didn't look like a foreigner. And I fit this perfectly.

So our conversations were an odd mix of two tongues (so to speak) and laughter amidst comments and questions. I was struck by her innocent naïveté, adherence to traditional rituals, and drive for success; she was amused with my American lifestyle, bold frankness, and outlandish pursuits: some drivel about sailing an old Norwegian junk (à la Chinese sailboat).

Over an exotic spread of gourmet entrees, she told me about herself, and explained how her grandmother learned English before World War II. Back then, foreigners invested in developing China's trade and she served as an interpreter. Mei Qing had been encouraged by her grandmother to learn English, so that she could become a highly-respected, university-level English teacher. This was her ambition.

Answering questions about my education and occupation raised her estimation of me with untold awe and respect. Computers are so rare in China that only the creme-de-la-creme students receive such education and employment. She did not accept that hordes of U.S. teenagers were more gifted with computers than myself. Then when she asked about my income, I said I made somewhat more than 37,000 Yuan/year (US$10,000). Thinking I'm wealthy too, she brushed-off my denials for modesty. For comparison, her sister is a registered nurse and makes 80 Yuan/month (US$260/year).

Later, Mei Qing would tell me about her fellow students at Beijing University, and how they were planning to bring democracy to China and eradicate government corruption. It was June 28, 1989 and somehow she hadn't learned of the Tiananmen massacre yet. Should I tell her what the government has evidently hidden so well?

Mei Qing was ecstatic and curious about our gourmet entrees; she had never experienced Western cuisine so I had to explain each dish. The White Swan Hotel typically caters to foreign guests so their menu is authentically international. I then asked about her people's standard fare.

About 80-90 percent of it is starch from mostly white unfortified rice and then wheat (noodles). Vegetables are used for variety, and tidbits of fatty pork are used for flavor. Boiled water and hot tea are important universal beverages; dairy products are considered unhealthful (salmonella?) and difficult to digest (adult Asians typically cannot tolerate milk products; I know I can't). Soybean milk has become a popular and nutritious substitute. In the cities, sweet pastries and other treats are sold by street vendors, but their diets are predominantly bland, restricted by finances and disinterest. This probably explains why I saw no obesity; everyone is trim without muscle tone or malnourished. I'm guessing this is typical of low-protein diets.

She enjoyed our meal immensely—it was special. But I could not convince her that I rarely ate this well. When the waitress, who recognized me from before, asked if my wife enjoyed the meal and would I sign the dinner charge to our room, I nearly died (I had earlier lied about staying at the Youth Hostel next door).

Expecting anger at my faux pas, she only used her English to say "It was delicious!!" perfectly assuming the role of my wife. I laughingly reminded myself that white lies and untruths are acceptable graces in Chinese society, and I signed the check to my room.

We relaxed outside in the courtyard by the swimming pool overlooking the Pearl River. The steady rapid thumping of old diesel-burning cargo boats could be heard ferrying up and down the dark waterway. And I solemnly dreamed of distant voyages aboard *Eventyr* (my wooden sailboat). As the monsoon breeze blew the scent of the river through my south Pacific fantasies, she quietly thanked me by taking my hand.

I was stunned seconds later when reality soon cleared my head. Culturally, it was unspeakably bold of her to touch me. Most mixed acquaintances enjoy time together with a chaperone in tow. So I carefully asked why her grandmother let her come with me unescorted. Mei Qing said I was the only "suitor" with enough guts to ask her grandmother for permission to dine with her, instead of asking her (Mei Qing) herself. This was supposedly proof of unabashedly good intentions, so I was her first unchaperoned date.

Reflecting upon the events of the day, I was glad to spend its closing hours sharing dreams. After breakfasting from strange outdoor vendors, trying to save a dying man, assaulting and then bribing the doorman, fighting new fears by venturing into the city again and then teasingly flirting with an old woman only to end up dining with her granddaughter, it's been quite a day!! I wanted to go home though—"there's no place like home."

The Chinese love to eat. This very physical relishing is captured by Dr. George Adams in his book, The Great Hong Kong Sex Novel:

I used to watch Vanessa eat. Her lips sucked at crab claws and her tongue dipped into the crevices of lobsters and clams. In her ecstasy, slime clung from her mouth and overflowed onto her lips. Her mouth slowly swallowed a branch of *choi sum* and lovingly caressed a penis-shaped mushroom. Her throat held the luscious oysters for a moment to feel their slightly pulsating tickle. Her teeth cracked through bones and gnawed the last fragment of meat from a chicken wing. She slurped, gurgled, munched, chomped, sipped, crunched, licked, oozed. She probed, prodded, turned, dug, snapped, stabbed, decapitated, eviscerated, deveined, skinned. She belched, sighed, laughed, giggled, choked, coughed, spat, regurgitated. She would pick her teeth and investigate her nose. All was noise, action, enjoyment.

—JO'R, LH, and SO'R

But then I remembered what I didn't want to tell Mei Qing earlier. Damn!! Gently turning and embracing her, my sudden forwardness mixed with anguish spooked her to a nervous giggle. When she at first refused to believe my story, I only stood wordlessly holding her. She soon realized the truth behind my words.

Probably many of her classmates were murdered in Beijing, and she felt guilty that her family visit had saved her; she was an activist too. I comforted her through growing sobs as she envisioned events and thought of the loved ones who were likely massacred. There were questions, of course, that I could not answer, and answers I should not have given. For the next hour, I felt like the father of a frightened six-year-old girl. Maybe I shouldn't have told her, but then, maybe it's better that I did. I don't know.

I sense as she drifted into resignation, she settled into just clinging to me. My red bandanna let her politely blow her nose (she wanted it as a memento, so I let her keep it). At a poignant moment, she quipped about not remembering ever being held in the arms of another: not mother or father, nor sibling or friend. Just me from across the sea, in a land of over a billion.

Earl Yin Jew is a writer with a presence on the Internet. We are unable to determine his corporeal location.

★

The only place the Chinese abandon their emphasis on the uniqueness of the individual is in their system of family relationships. A Chinese family shares the food and money of its members in a more embracing arrangement than the parientes system of the Philippines. Affections are focused within the family and Confucianism teaches the central goodness of filial respect for elders and parents. Children are necessary to your afterlife happiness, for only your own sons will make the sacrifices that will help your departed spirit. In contrast to the Japanese, the Chinese do not shore up their own superiority by admiring their ancestors, but they are always conscious of their ancestors being around them and sharing their lives.

—Dwight Cooke, *There Is No Asia*

NICHOLAS D. KRISTOF

⋆

The Rotting State

The flies and maggots are at work.

THE COMMUNIST PARTY WOKE UP TO THE POLITICAL RISKS OF corruption after the Tiananmen protests. A few anticorruption campaigns were announced, and the government shot a few people who had been convicted of corruption. Still, the crackdown has had no impact. The odds of being caught are not much worse than those of being struck by lightning. The potential profits are so huge, and so many people seem to be indulging, that very few officials are deterred. Of all our Chinese acquaintances, the one who probably understood most clearly the risks of corruption was a young Beijing judge who handled bribery cases. Every week he sentenced people to prison, or worse, for corruption.

We knew the judge simply because he was a member of the same health club we belonged to, in a five-star Western-managed hotel. I lifted weights with him and chatted in the locker room about recent events. The judge's salary was about $500 a year—yet he somehow managed to spend may times that much. The health club membership alone cost $500 a year, and he also owned his own motorcycle, which allowed him to zip around the city. He ate out in nice restaurants and owned an endless variety of fine Western clothes. I used to watch the judge peel off his expensive black leather motorcycle outfit and wonder if he ever worried that he would one day end up on the other side of the bench.

A particularly bad omen for Chinese development is that corruption tends to be worst in the most open, reformist areas, places that to outsiders represent the nation's best hope for the future. In Guangdong and Fujian provinces, for example, traditional Mafia organizations, known as triads, have reestablished themselves and formed close links with the triads in Hong Kong, Taiwan, and New York. Several triad leaders live in refuge in southern China and from their headquarters there oversee the bank robberies, prostitution rings, and gambling dens in Hong Kong. One Chinese "godfather," Paul K. F. Wong, lives in Fujian Province and from there directs the Green Dragon gang in New York City's Chinatown. Wong is wanted in connection with murder in New York, but naturally Fujian authorities can't seem to find him to extradite him.

The triads are criminal gangs, with blood oaths of secrecy and special handshakes. Punishment for betraying a triad is to hack off the traitor's arms and legs and leave him to bleed to death. The big difference between the triads and the American Mafia is that in New York the Mafia and the FBI are adversaries. In China, the triads and the police don't believe in confrontation; they often work together.

In 1993, the minister of public security held a press conference for the first time. I asked him about the links between the Chinese police and the triads, because I was curious to see how vehemently he would deny them. Instead, to everyone's surprise, he acknowledged that the authorities maintain ties to the triads, and he described them as patriotic organizations. He went on to say that the triads had helped provide protection for a Chinese leader traveling abroad; we later heard that he was talking about Deng Xiaoping's trip to the United States in 1979.

The best way to understand the cooperation between the triads and the Communist Party apparatus is to rent a Mercedes-Benz in Hong Kong and park it on the street overnight. In the morning it may be in China. Hong Kong thieves will have stolen it, driven it to a deserted dock, and loaded it onto an armored speedboat for the ride to Guangdong Province. The triads use a kind of boat called the *tai fei,* specially designed with a steel hull, bullet-proof cabin, and up to five 300-horsepower engines. The *tai fei* is based on a design for a Canadian racing boat but modified with a sharpened bow for ramming other vessels and bullet-proof plates to protect the crew. Banned in Hong Kong, the *tai fei* is typically kept in small coves along the southern Chinese coast and used each night to smuggle cigarettes, videos, and stolen cars. The scale is enormous. According to official estimates, more than one million video recorders are smuggled into China each year, accounting for 90 percent of all those sold. As for cars, the demand is for luxury models like the Mercedes-Benz; in 1992, one Mercedes-Benz was stolen in Hong Kong every five hours, and nearly all are suspected of having ended up in China. The latest car to win the compliment of being stolen in large numbers is the Mazda 929. It made an appearance at a car show in Guangzhou, and people were so impressed that they started placing orders—not with dealers but with the triads, for Mazdas stolen in Hong Kong and smuggled into China.

Naturally, Hong Kong car owners are concerned about theft, and dealers have come up with all kinds of alarms to keep cars from getting stolen. However, the only technique that has worked is the one pioneered by the Toyota distributor in Hong Kong to prevent its Lexus model from being stolen. Toyota's strategy is to make it useless for triads in China to steal its cars. Toyota does not market the Lexus in China, and it sells spare parts in Hong Kong only to people who can prove that they are legal owners of a Lexus. Toyota even took out advertisements in Guangdong newspapers, urging mainland Chinese not to buy its cars. The ads reminded people that the Lexus will break down after 20,000 miles unless it has unleaded fuel, which is unavailable in China.

The Hong Kong marine police used to think that they were battling just the triads, but then a few funny things started happening. Several times the police intercepted boats engaging in smuggling, only to discover Chinese troops on board. In 1991, the police were trying to board a smugglers' boat in Hong Kong waters when two uniformed Chinese police emerged from the cabin. The Chinese police pointed machine guns at the Hong Kong police and summoned two other Chinese police boats, which rescued the smugglers and escorted them to safety in Chinese waters.

> "*When a public officer is neglectful, what would you do with him?*"
> "*Cast him off,*" *replied the king.*
> "*When in the whole kingdom there is no good government, what then?*" *King Seuen looked to the right and left, and spoke of other matters.*
> —Mencius

For some time, we wondered who in China would dare to buy and use a stolen Hong Kong Mercedes-Benz. Such cars stand out, not only because they have no registration but also because they have the steering wheel on the right-hand side, in the British style, while cars sold in China have the steering wheel on the left. Who would dare to drive around in a car that was so obviously stolen and smuggled into the country? The police, of course! And Communist Party officials. And the army. And those with *guanxi* with the police. "It's hard to get a new car registered for the road if it has right-hand steering," a Guangzhou taxi driver told a friend. But he admitted that the problem could be solved by anyone with good *guanxi*. The driver knew what he was talking about: his own taxi was a right-hand-drive vehicle from Hong Kong. The *South China Morning Post* in Hong Kong collected independent evidence of where the stolen cars end up. A photographer for the newspaper shot pictures of a new black Lexus, with right-hand steering, in front of a five-star hotel in Guangzhou. The car was accompanied by another vehicle full of assistants and bodyguards, and its license plate showed that it belonged to a senior army general.

These days, Hong Kong isn't big enough to supply southern China with cars. So the triads are buying stolen cars in the United States and shipping them to China. Anyone can go to Guangdong Province and visit the lots where American cars are lined up, with their original license plates still attached. Some American reporters traced the cars' owners and called them up; the owners said that the cars had been stolen a couple of months earlier, and they were very surprised to hear that they had been found—in China.

The harder question is what all this corruption means. A skeptic can say that widespread graft clogs the wheels of commerce in most of the developing world, and certainly a number of other countries—South Korea, Taiwan, Indonesia, Mexico, and Thailand—have done very well for themselves despite mindboggling levels of bribery.

I'm not sure that China's graft is necessarily worse than that of other countries, but I do think it may be more threatening. China has none of the democratic mechanisms that normally help make a government legitimate in the eyes of its people. Italians and even Mexicans may regard their leaders as crooks, but they at least elected them, after a fashion. In China, by contrast, the leaders came into power without any legitimating mechanism, and their moral authority rests solely on their performance.

The rot has a tremendous corrosive effect on the Chinese political and social structure and on the Chinese people. It is particularly evident among young people, those who grew up in the moral vacuum of the Cultural Revolution and its aftermath. Some of them subscribe to only one value: the importance of getting rich. It has been disheartening to watch our reformist friends in the years after the Tiananmen crackdown. Journalists, who had championed the right of freedom of the press, now frequently are absorbed by only one thought: getting payoffs in exchange for writing nice stories about companies. Intellectuals, who used to quote Patrick Henry—"Give me liberty or give me death"—now adhere to a Wall Street credo: "Greed is good."

Private business owners may complain about officials who demand bribes, but their own moral standards are often primitive. Owners of food stands have taken to lacing their food with opium poppies in the hope that their dishes will become, literally, addictive. I don't know whether it works, but restaurateurs seem to swear by it. Restaurants and food stalls in six provinces have been caught adding poppies to their food, and in 1993 the Public

Security Ministry had to issue a formal circular pledging a crack-down on the practice.

Even peasants have been infected by the greed. A village called Haotou, in Guangdong Province, discovered a particularly lucra-tive way of entering the modern market economy. The peasants kidnapped women and girls from other areas and locked them up in their homes, forcing them to work as sex slaves. Many of Haotou's peasants ran brothels out of their homes as a sideline business. Officials took notice only after a Guangzhou newspaper dared to write about the village.

Corruption has not only corroded community values but also eaten away at the efficiency of China's autocracy. From outside its borders, China may seem a smoothly functioning dictatorship, but in fact the rot has clogged up the apparatus so that it often barely works. Li Peng may order somebody arrested, but that person may be able to make a ten-dollar payoff and slip free.

In China, in other words, the current social framework of Communism is already so weak, and the ideological underpinning of the state so flimsy, that the regime may not be able to take much more. The corruption risks creating a bog that impairs economic efficiency, and it also risks irritating people to the point that they take to the streets just as they did in Tiananmen. In 1989, with Deng Xiaoping and the other elders still alive, the party could withstand the challenge. Next time it may not be able to.

Nicholas Kristof grew up on a sheep farm in Oregon. He is a graduate of both Harvard College and Oxford University and he has worked for The New York Times *since 1984 holding positions as varied as economics reporter and Hong Kong bureau chief. He and his wife Sheryl WuDunn, a Harvard Business School graduate, are correspondents in Tokyo for* The New York Times. *They are the first couple to ever win a Pulitzer for journalism. This story was excerpted from their book* China Wakes: The Struggle for the Soul of a Rising Power.

★

The story of the Triad begins in a monastery, as do so many stories of violence in China, the traditional home of the fighting monks. The art of judo can be traced to these pious, yet pugnacious fellows, who traveled the bandit-infested roads without any weapons and therefore worked out their own system of unarmed combat. It is also said that the basic elements of "empty-handed" karate, including the spectacular trick of smashing a thick piece of timber with the edge of the palm, were evolved in the kitchens of Buddhist monasteries where the monks were forbidden by their faith to use a knife or ax and therefore chopped up the wood for their stoves with their bare hands. "We may not have knives, so make every finger a dagger; without spears, every arm must be a spear, and with every open hand a sword," the venerable brother who invented the art is recorded as saying.

—Dennis Bloodworth, *The Chinese Looking Glass*

PART FIVE

THE LAST WORD

LYDIA Y. MINATOYA

* * *

Victoria Peak

Change is inevitable and comes unbidden.

I STEPPED FROM THE AIRPLANE INTO A SEARING KOWLOON evening. Heat rose in sheets across the Hong Kong harbor, giving the city a tremulous image. High pungent notes of ginger and anise mingled with the vapors of melting asphalt and automobile exhaust, forming the city's dark and distinctive bouquet. Cool skyscrapers and twisted alleyways glittered with neon and consumer goods; jewels, furs, electronics, optics. Although it was nearly midnight, people and traffic still swarmed the narrow streets, like bees within a honeycomb. Horns blared, whistles shrilled, while throughout the city passengers in cream-colored Mercedes limousines slipped by in airconditioned quiet.

At four a.m., I awoke and dressed. From the chill of the hotel lobby, I entered an already steaming morning. A different Hong Kong greeted me than the one that had bid me good night. A silent sultry Hong Kong fanned only by the one low drone of cicadas. The boats at the Star Ferry terminal were docked. They bobbed on their lines as if responding to the memories and promise of clamorous passengers upon their decks. In front of the terminal, the pavement was strewn with dozens of huddled shapes.

I sensed life in the silhouettes before I knew it. I felt the rise and fall of warm breath in the still, early light—like a person who sees shadows in a distant pasture and somehow knows the sweet grassy scent of grazing creatures. As I approached, the shapes sharpened into workers, perhaps 50 of them: shrunken men in their 80s carefully clad in clean rags, skinny elementary school-age boys wearing nothing but tattered shorts. The workers were folding newspapers. They were quick and silent and full of the dignity that comes with attention to task. And with the rhythm of creasing came a faint swooshing sound, like the wings of a great bird attempting to rise in an airless morning.

At dawn, I took the tram to Victoria Peak. From the summit, Hong Kong and her famous harbor lay sleeping beneath quilts of mist. Old men and women, dressed in dark pajamas, moved through their *t'ai chi* exercises: slowly, deliberately, like a phalanx of ghost warriors.

The past reigned in stately supremacy. No future existed. Time flowed backward, unevenly stopping here and there like a branch in a stream catching on rocks and eddies. It carried me through generations. Insects whirred and chirped in primordial supremacy. "You may be right, Moe," I called to my memory of a friend as he spun past me in the rush of time. "Perhaps, somehow, I am changing."

Lydia Minatoya works as a counselor for a community college in Seattle where she lives with her husband and two children. This piece was excerpted from her book, Talking to High Monks in the Snow: An Asian American Odyssey.

Recommended Reading

We hope *Travelers' Tales Hong Kong* has inspired you to read on. A good place to start is the books from which we've made selections, and these are listed below along with other books that we have found to be valuable. Some of these may be out of print but are well worth hunting down. General guidebooks are also worth reading, and the best have annotated bibliographies or sections on recommended books and maps.

Adams, George. *Games Hong Kong People Play: A Social Psychology of the Hong Kong Chinese*. Hong Kong: Adams International Publishing, 1992.

Adams, George. *The Great Hong Kong Sex Novel*. Hong Kong: Adams International Publishing, 1993.

Adams, George. *Hong Kong Watching: The Essential Guide to Hong Kong People's Behaviour*. Hong Kong: Adams International Publishing, 1994.

Adams, George. *Wicked Hong Kong Stories*. Hong Kong: Adams International Publishing, 1992.

Baker, Dr. Hugh. *Ancestral Images: A Hong Kong Album*. Hong Kong: South China Morning Press, 1979.

Bloodworth, Dennis. *The Chinese Looking Glass*. New York: Dell Publishing Co. Inc., 1969.

Chatwin, Bruce. *What am I Doing Here*. New York: Viking Penguin, 1989.

Coates, Austin. *Myself a Mandarin*. New York: The John Day Company, Inc., 1969.

Cooke, Dwight. *There Is No Asia*. New York: Doubleday, 1964.

Escoda, Isabel Taylor. *Hong Kong Postscript: Radio, Press and Fictional Reflections on Life in Hong Kong*. Hong Kong: MediaMark, 1994.

Gershman, Suzy. *Born to Shop: Hong Kong.* New York: Bantam Books, 1991.

Gillingham, Paul. *At the Peak: Hong Kong Between the Wars.* Hong Kong: MacMillan Publishers Limited, 1983.

Gleason, Gene. *Tales of Hong Kong.* New York: Roy Publishers, 1969.

Goodwin, Jason. *A Time for Tea: Travels Through China and India in Search of Tea.* New York: Alfred A. Knopf, Inc., 1990; *The Gunpowder Gardens.* London: Chatto & Windus.

Greenwald, Jeff. *The Size of the World: A Global Odyssey—Around the World Without Leaving the Ground.* Old Saybrook, Connecticut: Globe Pequot Press, 1995.

Hinkelman, Edward G. *Hong Kong Business: The Portable Encyclopedia for Doing Business with Hong Kong.* San Rafael, California: World Trade Press, 1994.

Iyer, Pico. *Video Night in Kathmandu.* New York: Alfred A. Knopf, Inc., 1988.

Kristof, Nicholas D. and Sheryl WuDunn. *China Wakes: The Struggle for the Soul of a Rising Power.* New York: Times Books, a division of Random House, Inc., 1994.

Lord, Bette Bao. *Legacies: A Chinese Mosaic.* New York: Alfred A. Knopf, Inc., 1990

Minatoya, Lydia. *Talking to High Monks in the Snow: An Asian American Odyssey.* New York: HarperCollins Publishers, 1992.

Moores, Alan. *Another Hong Kong: An Explorer's Guide.* Hong Kong: Emphasis (Hong Kong) Limited, 1989.

Morris, Jan. *Hong Kong.* New York: Random House, 1988.

Newsham, Brad. *All the Right Places: Traveling Light Through China, Japan, and Russia.* New York: Vintage Books, a division of Random House, Inc. Toronto: Random House of Canada, 1989.

Packwood, Burley. *Bird Turd Peppers and other Delights.* Phoenix, Arizona: Quantum Press, 1993.

Pan, Lynn. *Sons of the Yellow Emperor: The Story of the Overseas Chinese.* London: Martin Secker & Warburg Limited, 1990.

Rafferty, Kevin. *City on the Rocks: Hong Kong's Uncertain Future.* New York: Viking Penguin, 1990.

Roberts, Elfed Vaughan. *Historical Dictionary of Hong Kong and Macau.* Metuchen, New Jersey: The Scarecrow Press, Inc., 1992

Rodwell, Sally. *Historic Hong Kong: A Visitor's Guide.* Hong Kong:

The Guidebook Company and The Hong Kong Tourist
Association, 1992.

Salisbury, Harrison E. *The New Emperors: China in the Era of Mao
and Deng.* Boston: Little, Brown and Company, 1992.

St. John, Robert. *Once Around Lightly: Travel Adventures in the Great
Cities of the Far East from Teheran to Tokyo.* New York:
Doubleday, 1969.

Storey, Robert. *Hong Kong, Macau & Canton - a travel survival kit.*
Hawthorn, Victoria, Australia: Lonely Planet Publications,
1992.

Tigay, Alan M. *The Jewish Traveler: Hadassah Magazine's Guide to the
World's Jewish Communities and Sights.* New York: Doubleday,
1987.

Tzu, Sun. *The Art of War*, translated by R. L. Wing as *The Art of
Strategy.* New York: Doubleday, 1988.

Viviano, Frank. *Dispatches from the Pacific Century.* Reading,
Massachusetts: Addison-Wesley Publishing Co., 1993.

Winchester, Simon. *Pacific Rising: The Emergence of a New World
Culture.* New York: Simon & Schuster, 1992.

Yeadon, David. *The Back of Beyond: Travels to the wild Places of the
Earth.* New York: HarperCollins Publishers, 1992.

Yutang, Lin. *Between Tears and Laughter.* New York: The John Day
Company, 1943.

*The Wisdom of China: The Sayings of Confucius, Mencius, Lao Tzu,
Chuang Tzu and Lieh Tzu.* Mount Vernon, New York: The
Peter Pauper Press, 1965.

Glossary

amah	maid; housekeeper
bugaw	pimp
bui	instrument used to predict the future
chih	life force
chim	numbered fortune
dai pai dong	market stands
dim sum	a selection of light Chinese refreshments that include small dumplings and rolls
fah wang	gardener
feng shui	literally "wind and water;" geomancy; divination by means of signs derived from the earth
fu kay	practitioner who receives medical prescriptions from the spirit world to have filled by an herbalist
geomancer	one who practices the art of *feng shui* or geomancy
go	a Japanese game of territorial possession played by two people with counters on a board that is ruled with nineteen vertical and nineteen horizontal lines
gweilo	literally "foreign devil;" Westerner
hai	magical force that flows through the environment
joss sticks	incense sticks which are burned as an offering before a Chinese idol or image
leppet	pickled tea
mah-jongg, mahjong	Chinese game usually played by four persons with 144 tiles that are drawn and discarded until one player secures a winning hand of

	four combinations of three tiles and a pair of matching tiles.
shih	the number four; Chinese homonym for death
sing pei	a method of predicting the future using two carved pieces of wood joined by a string or cord
tai chi, taijiquan	form of Chinese martial art
taipan	a European head of a business or firm
ting yat dai fook	big winner tomorrow
yang	active, male principle in Chinese philosophy
yin	passive, female principle in Chinese philosophy.

Index

Index of Contributors

Acknowledgements

Heartfelt thanks to Wenda Brewster O'Reilly, Andrea, Noelle, and Marielle O'Reilly, Paula Mc Cabe, Brenda O'Reilly, Clement, Seumas, and Liam O'Reilly, Michelle and Noel James, Bridget Davis, Jana Soriano, Ron and Joan Rochon, Timothy O'Reilly, Cindy Collins, Susan Brady, Raj Khadka, Judy Anderson, and Terry Lockman. Thanks also to Mary Bakht, Terry Fu, Diana Budiman, Stephen Wong, Iris Choi, and Pamela Kwok of the Hong Kong Tourist Association, Julia Wilkinson, David White, Debby Anker, Rick Helf, Linda Sirola, Edie Freedman, Hannah Dyer, Nancy Priest, Jennifer Niederst, Keith Granger, Cynthia Lamb, Elizabeth Oakley, Trisha Schwartz, Deborah Greco, Jennifer Leo, Kerri Bonasch, Dana Furby, Marguerita Castanera, Don George, Phil Siegle, Judith Babcock Wylie, Irene Jackson and Morris Simoncelli of Japan Airlines, and the staffs of the periodical department of the Phoenix Central Library and the Luke Air Force Base Library.

In Hong Kong special thanks to Eric Lockeyear of the Royal Hong Kong Police Force, Willi K. Kollman and Joanna McManus of the New World Harbor View, Johanna Hung, Sian Griffiths and Ivan Yeung of the Peninsula Group, Timothy Cumming and Amy Ho of the Regent, Eva Tsang and Camelia Lee of The Hong Kong Economic & Trade Office, Chung Wah-Pui of Chung & Ng Consulting Engineers, Anthony Lawrence, Beatrix Leung Hang-Lin, Nancy Nash, Liliana Ng of The Royal Hong Kong Jockey Club, and finally to the people of Hong Kong who by their determination and will power have created a city like no other in the world.

"Approaching Planet Hong Kong" by Kevin Rafferty excerpted from *City on the Rocks: Hong Kong's Uncertain Future* by Kevin Rafferty. Copyright © 1989 by Kevin Rafferty. Used by permission of Viking Penguin, a division of Penguin Books USA, Inc.

"A Perfect Pig" by Simon Winchester reprinted from the January 1987 issue of *Connoisseur.* Reprinted by permission of the author. Copyright © 1987 by Simon Winchester.

"City of the Main Chance" and "The Bones of Saint Francis" by Frank Viviano excerpted from *Dispatches from the Pacific Century* (pages 71-79; 103-113) by Frank Viviano, © 1993 by Frank Viviano. Reprinted by permission of Addison-Wesley Publishing Company, Inc.

"Towards Fragrant Harbor" by Jan Morris reprinted with permission from the author and *Travel & Leisure,* January 1988. Copyright © 1988. American Express Publishing Corporation. All rights reserved.

"My Hong Kong Neighborhood" by Angus Foster reprinted from the November 17, 1990 issue of *The Financial Times.* Reprinted by permission of The Financial Times Limited. Copyright © 1990 by The Financial Times Limited.

"A Leg up on Fate" by Yvonne Michie Horn reprinted from the March/April issue of *Islands.* Reprinted by permission of Islands Publishing Company. Copyright © 1993 by Islands Publishing Company.

"The Dragon-Lines" by Bruce Chatwin excerpted from *What Am I Doing Here* by Bruce Chatwin. Copyright © 1989 by the Estate of Charles Bruce Chatwin. Used by permission of Viking Penguin, a division of Penguin Books, USA and Jonathan Cape Ltd.

"Love Will Find a Way" by Austin Coates excerpted from *Myself a Mandarin* by Austin Coates. Reprinted by permission of Oxford University Press (China) Ltd. Copyright © 1968 by Austin Coates.

"The Food Doctor" by Charles Jennings reprinted from the May 30, 1993 issue of *The Sunday Telegraph.* Reprinted by permission of The Telegraph plc. Copyright © Charles Jennings/ The Telegraph plc, London, 1993.

"On the Offensive" by Alison Dakota Gee reprinted from the

Copyright © 1988 by American Express Publishing Corporation. All rights reserved.

"Hiking Hong Kong" by Garry Marchant reprinted from the May 1994 issue of *Discovery,* the inflight magazine of Cathay Pacific Airways. Reprinted by permission of the author. Copyright © 1994 by Garry Marchant.

"Tao of the Racetrack" by Larry Habegger reprinted by permission of the author. Copyright © 1996 by Larry Habegger.

"Hong Kong's Stanley" by Stanley Karnow reprinted from the November/December issue of *Islands*. Reprinted by permission of Islands Publishing Company. Copyright © 1993 by Islands Publishing Company.

"Archipelago" by Jan Morris reprinted from the October 5, 1986 issue of *The New York Times Magazine*. Reprinted by permission of the author. Copyright © 1986 by Jan Morris.

"Our Feathered Friends" by Michael Caruso reprinted with permission from *Travel & Leisure*, September 1993 and the author. Copyright © 1993 by American Express Publishing Corporation. All rights reserved.

"Heavenly Wardrobe" by Judith Babcock Wylie reprinted by permission of the author. Copyright © 1996 by Judith Babcock Wylie.

"A Return Home" by John William Fisher with Yvonne Michie Horn reprinted by permission of the authors. Copyright © 1996 by John William Fisher and Yvonne Michie Horn.

"Professor Tea" by Jason Goodwin excerpted from *A Time for Tea: Travels Through China and India in Search of Tea* by Jason Goodwin. Originally published as *The Gunpowder Gardens* by Chatto & Windus. Reprinted by permission of Alfred A. Knopf, Inc. Copyright © 1990 by Jason Goodwin.

"The Baghdad Connection" by Andrew Powell reprinted from the August 1993 issue of *Harper's Bazaar.* Reprinted by permission of the author. Copyright © 1993 by Andrew Powell.

"If You Knew Suzie" by John Hoskin reprinted by permission of the author. Copyright © 1982 by John Hoskin.

"Mr. Leung" by George Adams adapted from *Wicked Hong Kong Stories* by George Adams. Reprinted by permission of the author. Copyright © 1992 by George Adams.

"Man-Made Uppers" by Kelly Simon reprinted by permission of the author. Copyright © 1996 by Kelly Simon.

Wakes: The Struggle for the Soul of a Rising Power by Nicholas D.
Kristof and Sheryl WuDunn. Copyright © 1994 by Nicholas
D. Kristof and Sheryl WuDunn. Reprinted by permission of
Times Books, a division of Random House, Inc.

"Victoria Peak" by Lydia Minatoya excerpted from *Talking to
High Monks in the Snow: An Asian American Odyssey* by Lydia
Minatoya. Copyright © 1992 by Lydia Minatoya. Reprinted
by permission of HarperCollins Publishers, Inc.

Additional Credits (arranged alphabetically by title)

Selection from "Acting Globally" by Jamie James reprinted from
the September 1995 issue of *Hemispheres.* Reprint permission
Hemispheres, the inflight magazine for United Airlines, Pace
Communications, Greensboro, North Carolina. Copyright
© 1995 by *Hemispheres.*

Selection from *Ancestral Images: A Hong Kong Album* by Dr. Hugh
Baker reprinted by permission of South China Morning Post
Publishers Ltd. Copyright © 1979 by Dr. Hugh Baker.

Selections from *The Art of War* by Sun Tzu excerpted from *The Art of
Strategy* by R. L. Wing, a new translation of *The Art of War* by
Sun Tzu. Copyright © 1988 by Immedia. Used by permission
of Dolphin Doubleday, a division of Bantam Doubleday Dell
Publishing Group, Inc.

Selection adapted from "The Arts in Hong Kong: In the Limelight
at Last" by Julia Wilkinson which appeared in *Pacific Views.*
Reprinted by permission of the author. Copyright © 1996
by Julia Wilkinson.

Selection from "Asia: A Visual Feast" by Michael Browning reprinted
from the June 30, 1991 issue of the *Fort Worth Star-Telegram.*
Reprinted by permission of Knight-Ridder Newspapers.
Copyright © 1991 by Knight-Ridder Newspapers.

Selection from "Asiamerica" reprinted from the December 1, 1993
issue of *Asiaweek.* Reprinted by permission of Asiaweek, Ltd.
Copyright © 1993 by *Asiaweek.*

Selection from "Asian Organized Crime" by Linda L. Keene
reprinted from the October 1989 issue of the *FBI Law
Enforcement Bulletin.* Reprinted by permission of the Federal
Bureau of Investigation. Copyright © 1989 by Federal Bureau

Cathay Pacific Airways Ltd. Copyright © 1994 by Lulu Yu.

Selection from "For the Love of God" by Hilary Binks excerpted from *Another Hong Kong: An Explorer's Guide* edited by Emphasis (Hong Kong) Limited. Reprinted with permission from Emphasis (Hong Kong) Limited and the author. Copyright © 1989 by Hilary Binks.

Selection from "Fortress Hong Kong" by Harry Rolnick excerpted from *Another Hong Kong: An Explorer's Guide* edited by Emphasis (Hong Kong) Limited. Reprinted with permission from Emphasis (Hong Kong) Limited and the author. Copyright © 1989 by Harry Rolnick.

Selection from "Full of Eastern Menace" by Martin Vander Weyer reprinted from the March 4, 1995 issue of *The Spectator.* Reprinted by permission of *The Spectator.* Copyright © 1995 by Martin Vander Weyer.

Selections from *Games Hong Kong People Play: A Social Psychology of the Hong Kong Chinese* by George Adams reprinted by permission of the author. Copyright © 1992 by George Adams.

Selection from "Geography and Geometry" by Andrew Cowley reprinted from the November 16, 1991 issue of *The Economist.* Reprinted by permission of *The Economist.* Copyright © 1991 by *The Economist.*

Selection from "Get There Now—It's in its Prime: Hong Kong" by Alan Brown originally published in *Travel & Leisure*, March 1992. Reprinted by permission of the author. Copyright © 1992 American Express Publishing Corporation. All rights reserved.

Selection from *The Great Hong Kong Sex Novel* by George Adams reprinted by permission of the author. Copyright © 1993 by George Adams.

Selection from "Greater China, Greater Profits" by Andrew Tanzer reprinted from the August 3, 1992 issue of *Forbes Magazine.* Reprinted by permission of *Forbes Magazine.* Copyright © by Forbes Inc., 1992.

Selections from *Historic Hong Kong: A Visitor's Guide* by Sally Rodwell reprinted by permission from The Guidebook Company and The Hong Kong Tourist Association. Copyright © 1991 The Guidebook Company and The Hong Kong Tourist Association.

lished in *Travel & Leisure,* November 1981. Copyright © 1981 American Express Publishing Corporation. All rights reserved.

Selection from *Hong Kong Watching: The Essential Guide to Hong Kong People's Behaviour* by George Adams reprinted by permission of the author. Copyright © 1994 by George Adams.

Selection from "Hong Kong's *Feng Shui:* Popular Magic in a Modern Urban Setting" by Charles F. Emmons reprinted from the Summer 1992 issue of the *Journal of Popular Culture.* Reprinted by permission of Popular Press. Copyright © 1992 by Popular Press.

Selection from "Hong Kong's New Heights" by Jacqueline Duke reprinted from the January 8, 1994 issue of *The Blood-Horse.* Reprinted by permission of *The Blood-Horse.* Copyright © 1994, *The Blood-Horse.*

Selection from "Hong Kong's Pastoral Neighbor" by Cheryl Blackerby originally appeared in *The Palm Beach Post.* Reprinted by permission of *The Palm Beach Post* and the author. Copyright © 1990 by *The Palm Beach Post.*

Selection from *The I Ching [Book of Changes]* translated from Chinese to German by Richard Wilhelm and rendered into English by Cary F. Baynes. Reprinted by permission of Princeton University Press. Copyright © 1967 by Bollingen Foundation.

Selection from "The Invisible Man in Hong Kong" by Thomas Swick reprinted from the June 18, 1995 issue of the *Sun-Sentinel.* Reprinted with permission from the *Sun-Sentinel,* Fort Lauderdale, Florida. Copyright © 1995 by the *Sun-Sentinel.*

Selection from "Lamma Island" by Jonathan Maffay reprinted by permission of the author. Copyright © 1996 by Jonathan Maffay.

Selection from "The Land Beyond: Hong Kong's New Territories" by Joseph R. Yogerst reprinted by permission of the author. Copyright © 1996 by Joseph R. Yogerst.

Selection from *Legacies: A Chinese Mosaic* by Bette Bao Lord. Copyright © 1990 by Bette Bao Lord Enterprises, Inc. Reprinted by permission of Alfred A. Knopf, Inc.

Selection from "A Legend Lives On" by Joel Forrester reprinted from the Spring 1995 issue of *Mandarin Oriental.* Reprinted

Most Dynamic Capitalists" by Louis Kraar reprinted from the
October 31, 1994 issue of *Fortune*. Reprinted by permission
of Time, Inc. Copyright © 1994 Time, Inc. All rights reserved.

Selection from *Pacific Rising: The Emergence of a New World Culture* by
Simon Winchester reprinted by permission of Simon &
Schuster. Copyright © 1991 by Simon Winchester.

Selection from "Pouring Tea" by Iris Choi. Copyright © 1996 by
Iris Choi.

Selections from "Pot Luck" by Amanda Mayer Stinchecum reprinted
from *Departures*. Reprinted by permission of the author.
Copyright © 1994 by Amanda Mayer Stinchecum.

Selection from "Reflections on Victoria Harbour" by Morris Dye
reprinted from the June 19, 1988 issue of the *San Francisco
Examiner*. Reprinted with permission from the *San Francisco
Examiner*. Copyright © 1988 *San Francisco Examiner*.

Selection from "A Sense of Something Sacred" by Julia Wilkinson
reprinted by permission of the author. Copyright © 1989 by
Julia Wilkinson.

Selection from "The Snake that Lost its Bite" by Angela Palmer
reprinted from the February 16, 1994 issue of *The Daily
Telegraph*. Reprinted by permission of the author. Copyright
© 1994 by Angela Palmer.

Selection from *Sons of the Yellow Emperor: The Story of the Overseas
Chinese* by Lynn Pan reprinted by permission of Reed
Consumer Books Ltd. and Jennifer Kavanaugh. Copyright
© 1990 by Lynn Pan.

Selections from "South China Sea Journal" by Paula McDonald
reprinted by permission of the author. Copyright © 1994 by
Paula McDonald.

Selection from "Southeast Asia" by Mark R. Leeper reprinted by
permission of the author. Copyright © 1990 by Mark R.
Leeper.

Selection from "Spree Market" by Daniel Burstein reprinted from
the July 1990 issue of *Travel Holiday*. Reprinted by permission
of the author. Copyright © 1990 by Daniel Burstein.

Selections from *Tales of Hong Kong* by Gene Gleason reprinted by
permission of Ms. Patricia Gleason. Copyright © 1967 by
Gene Gleason.

Selection from "A Taxi Driver Tells About His Other Career" by

China and India in Search of Tea by Jason Goodwin. Originally published as *The Gunpowder Gardens* by Chatto & Windus. Reprinted by permission of Alfred A. Knopf, Inc. and Random House (UK) Ltd. Copyright © 1990 by Jason Goodwin.

About the Editors

James O'Reilly and Larry Habegger first worked together as late-night disc jockeys at Dartmouth College in New Hampshire. They wrote mystery serials for the *San Francisco Examiner* in the early 1980s before turning to travel writing. Since 1983, their travel features and self-syndicated column, "World Travel Watch," have appeared in magazines and newspapers in the United States and other countries. James was born in Oxford, England, raised in San Francisco, and lives with his family in Leavenworth, Washington and France; Larry was born in Minnesota and lives on Telegraph Hill in San Francisco.

Sean O'Reilly is a former seminarian, stockbroker, and bank slave who lives in Arizona with his wife Brenda and their four small boys. Widely traveled in Europe, he most recently spent time roaming East Africa and the Indian Ocean. He is also at work on a book called *Politics and the Soul: The River of Gold*, which he describes as a "re-examination of classic Greek, Roman, and Christian philosophies as tools for moral excellence in modern society."

TRAVELERS' TALES GUIDES

LOOK FOR THESE TITLES IN THE SERIES

Special Interest

THE GIFT OF TRAVEL
THE BEST OF TRAVELERS' TALES
Edited by Larry Habegger, James O'Reilly & Sean O'Reilly
ISBN 1-885211-25-2, 234 pages, $14.95

"The Travelers' Tales series is altogether remarkable."
—Jan Morris

We've selected some favorite stories from the books in our award-winning series, stories about simple but profound gifts travelers have received from people, places, and experiences around the world. *The Gift of Travel* will light a match in the firebox of your wanderlust. Join us on the quest.

THERE'S NO TOILET PAPER ON THE ROAD LESS TRAVELED
THE BEST OF TRAVEL HUMOR AND MISADVENTURE
Edited by Doug Lansky
ISBN 1-885211-27-9, 207 pages, $12.95

"Anyone who plans to travel should read this book. And then stay home."
—Dave Barry

LOVE & ROMANCE
TRUE STORIES OF PASSION ON THE ROAD
Edited by Judith Babcock Wylie
ISBN 1-885211-18-X, 294 pages, $17.95

"... a passion-filled tribute to the undeniable, inescapable romance of the road."
—Debra Birnbaum, Feature Editor, *New Woman*

A DOG'S WORLD
TRUE STORIES OF MAN'S BEST FRIEND ON THE ROAD
Edited by Christine Hunsicker
ISBN 1-885211-23-6, 232 pages, $12.95

"The stories are extraordinary, original, often surprising and sometimes haunting. A very good book."
—Elizabeth Marshall Thomas, author of *The Hidden Life of Dogs*

Check with your local bookstore for these titles
or call O'Reilly to order:
800-998-9938 (credit cards only-Weekdays 6 AM –5 PM PST)
707-829-0515, or email: order@oreilly.com

Women's Travel

WOMEN IN THE WILD
TRUE STORIES OF ADVENTURE AND CONNECTION
Edited by Lucy McCauley
ISBN 1-885211-21-X, 307 pages, $17.95

Meet women who foray into the wilderness, explore remote jungle rivers, climb Mt. Everest, and survive a shark attack. Their tales speak the soul's deepest language and show how travel into the wilderness can help you discover the wild woman within.

A MOTHER'S WORLD
JOURNEYS OF THE HEART
Edited by Marybeth Bond and Pamela Michael
ISBN 1-885211-26-0, 234 pages, $14.95

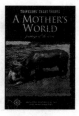

"Heartwarming and heartbreaking, these stories remind us that motherhood is one of the great unifying forces in the world."
—John Flinn, Travel Editor, *San Francisco Examiner*

A WOMAN'S WORLD
Edited by Marybeth Bond
ISBN 1-885211-06-6, 475 pages, $17.95

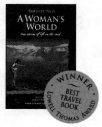

***Winner of the Lowell Thomas Award for Best Travel Book —
Society of American Travel Writers***

"I loved this book! From the very first story, I had the feeling that I'd been waiting to read these women's tales for years. I also had the sense that I'd met these women before. I hadn't, of course, but as a woman and a traveler I felt an instant connection with them. What a rare pleasure."
—Kimberly Brown, *Travel & Leisure*

GUTSY WOMEN
TRAVEL TIPS AND WISDOM FOR THE ROAD
By Marybeth Bond
ISBN 1-885211-15-5, 124 pages, $7.95

Packed with instructive and inspiring travel vignettes, *Gutsy Women: Travel Tips and Wisdom for the Road* is a must-have for novice as well as experienced travelers.

GUTSY MAMAS
TRAVEL TIPS AND WISDOM FOR MOTHERS ON THE ROAD
By Marybeth Bond
ISBN 1-885211-20-1, 150 pages, $7.95

A book of tips and wisdom for mothers traveling with their children. This book is for any mother, grandmother, son, or daughter who travels or would like to.

Body & Soul

THE ROAD WITHIN
TRUE STORIES OF TRANSFORMATION
Edited by Sean O'Reilly,
James O'Reilly & Tim O'Reilly
ISBN 1-885211-19-8, 443 pages, $17.95

"Travel is a siren song we are helpless to resist. Heedless of out-
comes, we are hooked on the glories of movement, passion and
inner growth, souvenirs in abundant supply in *The Road Within.*"
—Jeff Salz, *Escape Magazine*

FOOD
A TASTE OF THE ROAD
Edited by Richard Sterling
ISBN 1-885211-09-0, 444 pages, $17.95

"Sterling's themes are nothing less than
human universality, passion and necessity,
all told in stories straight from the gut."
—Maxine Hong Kingston, author of
The Woman Warrior and *China Men*

THE FEARLESS DINER
TRAVEL TIPS AND WISDOM FOR EATING AROUND THE WORLD
By Richard Sterling
ISBN 1-885211-22-8, 139 pages, $7.95

A pocket companion for those who like to see the world
through food. Bold epicures will find all the tips and wisdom
needed to feast with savages, break bread with kings, and get
invited home to dinner.

Country Guides

ITALY
Edited by Anne Calcagno
ISBN 1-885211-16-3, 463 pages, $17.95

These adventures into Italy take the reader far beyond a packaged
tour to encounter the land of magical extremes. Funny, heart-
wrenching, and smart, herein ancient Italy is revealed as always
new, while contemporary Italy speaks the old verities of the heart.

BRAZIL
Edited by Annette Haddad & Scott Doggett
ISBN 1-885211-11-2, 433 pages, $17.95
"Only the lowest wattage dimbulb would visit Brazil
without reading this book."
—Tim Cahill, author of *Jaguars Ripped My Flesh* and
Pecked to Death by Ducks

Country Guides

NEPAL

Edited by Rajendra S. Khadka
ISBN 1-885211-14-7, 423 pages, $17.95

"Always refreshingly honest, here is a collection that
explains why Western travelers fall in love
with Nepal and return again and again."
—Barbara Crossette, *New York Times* correspondent and author of
So Close to Heaven: The Vanishing Buddhist Kingdoms of the Himalayas

SPAIN

Edited by Lucy McCauley
ISBN 1-885211-07-4, 452 pages, $17.95

"A superb, eclectic collection that reeks wonderfully of
gazpacho and paella, and resonates with sounds of heel-
clicking and flamenco singing—and makes you feel that you
are actually in that amazing state of mind called Iberia."
—Barnaby Conrad, author of *Matador* and *Name Dropping*

FRANCE

Edited by James O'Reilly,
Larry Habegger & Sean O'Reilly
ISBN 1-885211-02-3, 432 pages, $17.95

"All you always wanted to know about the French but were
afraid to ask! Explore the country and its people in a unique
and personal way even before getting there. Travelers' Tales:
your best passport to France and the French!"
—Anne Sengés, *Journal Français d'Amérique*

INDIA

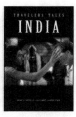

Edited by James O'Reilly & Larry Habegger
ISBN 1-885211-01-5, 477 pages, $17.95

"The essays are lyrical, magical and evocative:
some of the images make you want to rinse
your mouth out to clear the dust."
—Karen Troianello, *Yakima Herald-Republic*

THAILAND

Edited by James O'Reilly & Larry Habegger
ISBN 1-885211-05-8, 483 pages, $17.95

"This is the best background reading
I've ever seen on Thailand!"
—Carl Parkes, author of *Thailand Handbook,*
Southeast Asia Handbook by Moon Publications

Country Guides

MEXICO

Edited by James O'Reilly & Larry Habegger
ISBN 1-885211-00-7, 426 pages, $17.95

Opens a window on the beauties and mysteries of Mexico and the
Mexicans. It's entertaining, intriguing, baffling, instructive, insightful,
inspiring and hilarious—just like Mexico."
—Tom Brosnahan, coauthor of Lonely Planet's *Mexico – a travel survival kit*

City Guides

PARIS

Edited by James O'Reilly,
Larry Habegger, & Sean O'Reilly
ISBN 1-885211-10-4, 424 pages, $17.95

"If Paris is the main dish, here is a rich and fascinating
assortment of hors d'oeuvres. *Bon appetit et bon voyage!*"
—Peter Mayle

SAN FRANCISCO

Edited by James O'Reilly,
Larry Habegger & Sean O'Reilly
ISBN 1-885211-08-2, 432 pages, $17.95

"As glimpsed here through the eyes of beatniks, hippies,
surfers, 'lavender cowboys' and talented writers from all
walks, San Francisco comes to vivid, complex life."
—*Publishers Weekly*

SUBMIT YOUR OWN TRAVEL TALE

Do you have a tale of your own that you would like to submit to
Travelers' Tales? We highly recommend that you first read one or more of our
books to get a feel for the kind of story we're looking for. For submission
guidelines and a list of titles in the works, send a SASE to:

Travelers' Tales Submission Guidelines
P.O. Box 610160, Redwood City, CA 94061

or send email to ***ttguidelines@online.oreilly.com***
or visit our web site at **www.oreilly.com/ttales**

You can send your story to the address above or via email to
ttsubmit@oreilly.com. On the outside of the envelope, ***please indicate what
country/topic your story is about***. If your story is selected for one of our titles,
we will contact you about rights and payment.

We hope to hear from you. In the meantime, enjoy the stories!